LESSONS IN CONTEMPT

Jonathan Adams has a BA in Scandinavian Studies and an MA in Medieval Vernacular Languages and Literatures from the University of Hull, an MSt in the Study of Jewish-Christian Relations from the University of Cambridge, and a PhD in medieval Norwegian and Swedish Birgittine manuscripts from University College London. He is an elected fellow of the Society for Danish Language and Literature, and the Young Academy under the Royal Danish Academy of Sciences and Letters. He has published on medieval Scandinavian language and literature, modern Faroese, and early modern Hebraism. He is currently researching the portrayal of Muslims and Jews in medieval Scandinavian texts for the Royal Swedish Academy of Letters, History and Antiquities at Uppsala University, Sweden. Jonathan lives in Frederiksberg, Denmark.

LESSONS IN CONTEMPT

Poul Ræff's Translation and Publication in 1516 of
Johannes Pfefferkorn's *The Confession of the Jews*

Jonathan Adams

Universitets-Jubilæets danske Samfund, Copenhagen
University Press of Southern Denmark, Odense
2013

Jonathan Adams:
Lessons in Contempt: Poul Ræff's Translation and Publication in 1516 of Johannes Pfefferkorn's *The Confession of the Jews*

© Jonathan Adams and Universitets-Jubilæets danske Samfund 2013

Printed in Denmark by
Tarm Bogtryk A/S

ISBN: 978-87-7674-680-3

Issued as number 581 in the series of
Universitets-Jubilæets danske Samfund, ujds.dk
University Press of Southern Denmark, universitypress.dk

Supervisor: Marita Akhøj Nielsen

The book has been subject to anonymous peer review

Published with the support of The Knut and Alice Wallenberg Foundation, Niels Bohr Fondet, Den Hielmstierne-Rosencroneske Stiftelse and Svend Grundtvigs og Axel Olriks Legat.

The illustration on the front page is a detail from Poul Ræff's woodcut on fol. a1^v of *Iudeorum Secreta*. The picture is not a portrait of Pfefferkorn as such, but rather a recycled woodcut that he found among the printing equipment that he had purchased from Matthæus Brandis (see p. 190). The background is taken from fol. a3^r of the same book.

Contents

List of illustrations ix

Acknowledgements. xi

Abbreviations xiii

A note on quotations and transliterations xv

Introduction 1

1. *Enemies of God: The depiction of Jews
   in medieval vernacular writing in Denmark*. 5
      Baptismal font in Aakirkeby Church 10
      The Resurrection of Christ 11
      The Fifteen Places 14
      St Birgitta's *Revelations* 29
      Consolation of the Soul. 36
      Sermons and preaching. 41
          A sermon for the Fifth Sunday in Lent 42
          Christiern Pedersen, *Book of Miracle Sermons* 44
      Prayers. 50
      Christiern Pedersen's *Book of Hours* 61
      Mandeville's Travels. 69
      Guide for Pilgrims 78
      Reverend Michael, *On the Creation of Things* 80
      Summary. 84

2. *Exposing the Jews and their secrets: Johannes Pfefferkorn,*
   The Confession of the Jews, *Poul Ræff, and* Iudeorum Secreta 87

      Johannes Pfefferkorn (1469–1522/23) 88

Early life	88
Pfefferkorn's campaign against the Jews	99
The Reuchlin-Pfefferkorn controversy	105
The Confession of the Jews	110
Content	110
A new development in anti-Judaism?	115
Poul Ræff (died *c.* 1533)	122
Life and work	122
The publication of *Iudeorum Secreta*: Theological, social and psychological factors	124

3. *The language of* Iudeorum Secreta: *A linguistic description, Poul Ræff's translation, and the Hebrew words* 131

Ræff's orthography in *Iudeorum Secreta*	132
Vowels (in stressed position)	132
Summary	138
Vowels (in unstressed position)	140
Summary	142
Consonants	143
Summary	150
Style, translation and lexicon	150
Word pairs, doublets, tautologous constructions etc.	150
Word pairs and verbs of utterance	156
Omissions and simplifications	156
Additions	160
Native elements	163
Mistranslations and errors	164
Hapax legomena and unusual words	166
Conclusion	169
Hebrew words in *Secreta Iudeorum*	169
Misreadings	171
Phonology and orthography	172
Morphology and syntax	173
Pfefferkorn's translations	174
Conclusion	178

4. *The extant copies of* Iudeorum Secreta*: A physical description* 181

    Binding 182
    Damage and condition 186
    Foliation, collation and layout 186
    Typeface and abbreviations 188
    Woodcut 190
    Marginalia 190

5. Iudeorum Secreta*: An edition of the text with a description of editorial principles, critical apparatus, English translation and Latin original* 197

    The Danish transcription 197
    The Danish critical apparatus 198
    The English translation 198
    The Latin original text 198
    Abbreviations used in the apparatuses 199
    Edition 201

6. *Commentary: Notes to the edition of* Iudeorum Secreta 265

Appendix I: *Pfefferkorn's publications* 297

Appendix II: *The broadsheet against Pfefferkorn* 303

Bibliography 311

Index 341

Illustrations

Figure 1   Aakirkeby Church baptismal font

Figure 2   Frontispiece of *The Fifteen Places*

Figure 3   Crucifixion scene, Jetsmark Church

Figure 4   Woodcut in *Streydtpuechlyn*

Figure 5   Woodcut in *Iudeorum Secreta* (Bielke Library, Skokloster Castle)

Figure 6   Title page of *Iudeorum Secreta* (Bielke Library, Skokloster Castle)

Figure 7   Fols b6^v–c1^r of *Iudeorum Secreta* (Royal Library, Copenhagen)

Figure 8   Fols c2^v–3^r of *Iudeorum Secreta* (Royal Library, Copenhagen)

Figure 9   Synagogue interior

Figure 10   *Tashlikh* ceremony

Figure 11   *Kapparot* ceremony and ritual bathing

Figure 12   *Malqot* ceremony and candle lighting

Figure 13   Broadsheet against Pfefferkorn

Acknowledgements

I should like to record my gratitude to Universitets-Jubilæets danske Samfund (UJDS) for agreeing to publish this work, and to the Society for Danish Language and Literature (DSL), and in particular its former director, Prof. Jørn Lund, for unfailing support of my projects during my years in Denmark. In the spring of 2012, I moved to a research post financed by the Knut and Alice Wallenberg Foundation at the Department of Scandinavian Studies at Uppsala University in Sweden. My colleagues here have been most welcoming and helpful, and I would particularly like to express my very great appreciation to Prof. Henrik Williams and Prof. Staffan Fridell for their support and guidance. My work has also been encouraged by the Woolf Institute in Cambridge. Thanks to a generous scholarship in 2010–12, I was able to follow their part-time research degree in the Study of Jewish-Christian Relations, which provided me with an array of skills, resources and knowledge that I was sorely lacking. I would like to offer my heartfelt thanks to Dr Edward Kessler MBE, Dr Lars Fischer, Dr Emma Harris, Dr Helen Spurling (University of Southampton), and to my dissertation supervisor Prof. Ora Limor (The Open University of Israel). The Institute is at the forefront of the academic study of interfaith relations, and its work and staff are truly an inspiration.

Research grants from The Politiken Fund and the Danish-Israeli Study Fund in Memory of Josef and Regine Nachemsohn afforded me precious time in spring/summer 2010 to take leave and complete necessary research for this book in Jerusalem at the Hebrew University (HUJI), the Jewish National Library, and Hebrew Union College; the Danish section of The Letterstedtska Society provided a grant for a research trip to Skokloster Library in Sweden, and The Knut and Alice Wallenberg Foundation, Niels Bohr Fondet, Den Hielmstierne-Rosencroneske Stiftelse and Svend Grundtvigs og Axel Olriks Legat all generously funded the publication of *Lessons in Contempt*.

Many people have helped me in the preparation of this book and a number of words of appreciation are in order. In particular, it is a pleasure to acknowledge my most sincere thanks to Dr Yaacov Deutsch (HUJI) for very valuable comments on the manuscript at an early stage that not only improved the text greatly but also deepened my understanding of the complexities of early modern Jewish-Christian relations; for his kindness during my stay in Jerusalem, and for encouragement and suggestions on how to develop my work; to Prof. Robert

Chazan (New York University) for finding the time for an inspiring and thought-provoking conversation on a spring day in Manhattan; to Elisabeth Westin Berg (Skokloster Castle) for her hospitality and sharing information and ideas about the Skokloster copy of Ræff's work; to Yotvat Rieder Aviram (Tel Aviv) for indispensable help with parts of the Hebrew, and to Dr Peter Zeeberg (DSL), who was extraordinarily generous with his time and expertise, and who skilfully guided me through various Latin abbreviations, translations and marginalia.

I am also very grateful to the following who have also offered assistance or advice on specific points: Dr Nirit Ben-Aryeh Debby (Ben-Gurion University of the Negev); Rabbi Tirzah Ben-David (Kfar Hanasi); Niels Krause Brix-Thomsen (Frederiksberg); Niels Clemmensen (Vrå); Rebecca Hyde Parker (University of East Anglia, Norwich); Dr Eva Maria Jansson (Royal Library, Copenhagen); Rabbi Dr Deborah Kahn-Harris (Leo Baeck College); Prof. Robin May Schott (Danish Institute of International Studies: Holocaust and Genocide); Dr Avner Shamir (Roskilde University); Dr Marc B. Shapiro (University of Scranton); Prof. Sacha Stern (University College London); Dr Vibeke Winge (DSL); Laurel Wolfson (Hebrew Union College — Jewish Institute of Religion, Cincinnati), and Prof. Israel Yuval (HUJI).

One of the many joys of working at DSL was the vibrant scholarly environment and the intellectual camaraderie of a number of talented colleagues. I should like to thank my former colleagues in *Diplomatarium Danicum* for their understanding and cooperation during my research leave, and also the Society's other 'medievalists' and 'early modernists', particularly at *Gammeldansk Ordbog*, for their support and sharing with me their valuable expertise. As always in these circumstances, it is the author who is responsible for any remaining inaccuracies or poor judgement.

Staff at the Royal Library in Copenhagen (especially at the Oriental and Judaica Collection and the Centre for Manuscripts and Rare Books); at The Jewish National Library in Jerusalem; at Hebrew Union College in Cincinnati and Jerusalem; at Universitäts- und Landesbibliothek Münster and Munich University Library, both in Germany, and at Skokloster Library in Sweden have all offered unstinting assistance throughout this project.

Finally, thanks also go to Dr Marita Akhøj Nielsen of UJDS for generously commissioning the book and, together with Dr Simon Skovgaard Boeck, for guiding it through to publication, to staff at University Press of Southern Denmark and Tarm Bogtryk for attentively seeing to the details of production, and to the anonymous reviewers and readers of UJDS who commented most helpfully on the text.

Abbreviations

ANF	*Ante-Nicene Fathers* = Roberts and Donaldson 1866–72.
ChrPed. *Skr.*	*Christiern Pedersens Skrifter* = Brandt and Fenger 1850–56.
CSEL	*Corpus Scriptorum Ecclesiasticorum Latinorum.*
Dan.	Danish.
EJ	*Encyclopaedia Judaica* = Skolnik *et al.* 2007.
GdO	*Gammeldansk Ordbog*, the name of the Old Danish Dictionary project at the Society for Danish Language and Literature.
GG	*Gammeldansk Grammatik* = Brøndum-Nielsen 1928–74.
Heb.	Hebrew.
JE	*Jewish Encyclopedia* = Singer, Adler *et al.* 1901–06.
JPS	Jewish Publication Society = *JPS Hebrew-English Tanakh*. 2nd edn. Philadelphia: The Jewish Publication Society, 1999.
KLNM	*Kulturhistorisk leksikon for nordisk middelalder* = Karker *et al.* 1956–78.
Lib. I	Book I of St Birgitta of Sweden's *Revelations* in Latin = Undhagen 1978.
Lib. II	Book II of St Birgitta of Sweden's *Revelations* in Latin = Undhagen and Bergh 2001.
Lib. IV	Book IV of St Birgitta of Sweden's *Revelations* in Latin = Aili 1992.
Lib. VI	Book VI of St Birgitta of Sweden's *Revelations* in Latin = Bergh 1991.
Lib. VII	Book VII of St Birgitta of Sweden's *Revelations* in Latin = Bergh 1967.
LN	Lauritz Nielsen's *Dansk Bibliografi* = Nielsen 1996.
MLG	Middle Low German.
PL	*Patrologia Latina* = Migne *et al.* 1844–1905.
prep.	preposition.
pron.	pronoun.
Quat. Or. Δ	St Birgitta of Sweden's *Quattuor Oraciones* = Eklund 1991 (Delta manuscript).
Rev. Ex.	*Revelationes Extravagantes* = Hollman 1956.
vb.	verb.
WA	*Weimarer Ausgabe* = Luther 1883–2009.

A Note on Quotations and Transliterations

Biblical Quotations

Quotations from the Hebrew Bible are taken from the second edition of the *JPS Hebrew-English Tanakh* (Philadelphia: The Jewish Publication Society, 1999), which bases its Hebrew text on the *Biblia Hebraica Stuttgartensia*. New Testament quotations are from the *King James Version*, as are those from the Old Testament if used in a specifically Christian context. Talmudic references are to the Babylonian Talmud (Soncino edition) unless otherwise stated.

The transliteration of Hebrew

For well-known or established words, the common English spelling is used; for example, Rosh Hashanah, kosher, Yom Kippur and so on. However, for transliterating Hebrew text in book titles, biblical quotations and lexical items where a greater precision is deemed necessary, the following system has been used:

א	ʾ	ל	l
ב	b, v	מ	m
ג	g	נ	n
ד	d	ס	s
ה	h	ע	ʿ
ו	w	פ	p, f
ז	z	צ	ẓ
ח	ḥ	ק	q
ט	ṭ	ר	r
י	y	ש	š, ś
כ	k, ch	ת	t

xv

Transliterations of Hebrew are printed in italics. For example:

יִשָּׂא יְהוָה פָּנָיו אֵלֶיךָ, וְיָשֵׂם לְךָ שָׁלוֹם

Yiśa' YHWH [/'Adonai] panaw 'eleicha, weyaśem lecha šalom
'The LORD lift up His countenance upon you and grant you peace!'

Vowels are written *a*, *e*, *i*, *o* and *u* according to their pronunciation in Modern Hebrew; thus, for example, *qamez*, *pataḥ* and *ḥatef pataḥ* are all written *a* (and *qamez heh* as *ah*). The *ševa na* is indicated by *e* (*qedošim*), and the final combination *yud* + consonantal *waw* as *aw* where appropriate (*panaw*).

Yud is represented by *i* when it occurs as a vowel (*qedešim*), *y* when it occurs as a consonant (*Yešu*), and *yi* when it occurs as both (*yimaḥ*). *Waw* is indicated by *w* when consonantal (*kawanah*), and either *o* or *u* when a vowel (*yom*, *'aleinu*).

Dageš remains unmarked in the transliteration unless it affects pronunciation; for example, *sidur* (not *siddur*), but *šabat*. Personal names and place names are transliterated with a capital initial letter.

Quotations from Medieval Texts

In some of the quotations from medieval Danish works, it has been necessary to amend the text. This is shown in the following way:

dome[t>r]   t in the original should be read as **r**.

The lineation of the original has only been preserved in quotations from poetry, otherwise it is unmarked. The symbol ‖ marks a page break. Abbreviations are italicised in transcriptions of vernacular texts, but not Latin, and rubrics are in bold.

English translations of these quotations are in italics with explanatory comments contained in square brackets.

For the editorial principles applied in the edition of *Iudeorum Secreta*, see chapter 5.

Alphabetisation

In the biography and index, words are listed in the order of the English — not the Danish — alphabet. The letters 'æ', 'å' and 'ä' are treated as 'a', and 'ø' and 'ö' as 'o'. Furthermore, 'aa' comes at the beginning, not the end, of the alphabetised lists.

Introduction

Befindis nogen Iøde her i Danmarck/ uden Geleits-Breff/ hand hafver der med forbrut et tusinde Rix daler.

Frider. 3. Dat. Hafn. 6. Febr. Anno 1651[1]

When I was twenty, and travelled to Europe, the first country I visited was Denmark. As a Jew who had read extensively about the Holocaust since my teenage years, it was the only country in Europe toward which I felt unambivalent affection. Many other Jews I know have expressed the same sentiment.

Rabbi Joseph Telushkin (2001)[2]

The story of how countless Danish men and women, at great risk both to themselves and their families, saved their Jewish neighbours from being arrested and deported to the camps of central and eastern Europe during World War II is well known, and rightly so. The so-called rescue action of 1943 saved nearly the entire Danish Jewish population by evacuating them across the Øresund strait to neutral Sweden. Along with Bulgaria who also succeeded in saving a substantial portion of her own Jewish population from deportation, Denmark and the Danish people constitute one of the very few lights of humanity and hope from the dark years of the Holocaust. The rescue of the Danish Jews is described in numerous books (fiction and non-fiction), re-enacted in films and television programmes, included in exhibits at the Danish Resistance Museum and the Danish Jewish Museum (both in Copenhagen), commemorated by the sandstone monument at Israels Plads (Copenhagen) presented by Israel to Denmark in

---

1. Weylle 1652: 49: 'If a Jew is found here in Denmark without an entry permit, he is to be fined 1000 rigsdaler'. This was, incidentally, the maximum fine that could be paid for any crime under King Frederik III's national law of Denmark from 1651.
2. Telushkin 2001: 415.

1975, as well as in the Garden of the Righteous among the Nations at Yad Vashem in Jerusalem.[3]

However, the relationship between the Christian Danes and the Jews has not always been so cordial, and in recent years, there has been a growing scholarly interest concerning the perception of Jews in Denmark, in both the medieval and the modern eras.[4] This edition of the Danish translation of Johannes Pfefferkorn's *Nouiter in lucem data: iudeorum secreta* ['Recently brought out into the light: The secrets of the Jews'; hereafter *Iudeorum Secreta*] from 1516 presents not only one of the first books to be printed on a Danish press, but also what has been referred to as the first antisemitic work in the Danish language.[5] Published over a century before Jews were officially permitted to settle in Danish lands, the appearance of this libellous tract, translated, printed and distributed by the canon and university rector Poul Ræff, raises a number of questions: Why was the work translated from Latin into Danish at all? Who was the intended readership? What interest did Poul Ræff have in propagating its hateful contents? In what ways did he rework the text during translation to address his audience?

In this edition, the background to *Iudeorum Secreta* is presented and discussed. The book is put into its literary historical context by means of an investigation of the depiction of Jews in earlier Danish works in the vernacular from runic inscrip-

---

3. For popular accounts in English of the story of Bulgaria's Jewish population during World War II, see Bar-Zohar 1998, and on the rescue of the Danish Jews, see Pundik 1999. The story of the 1943 Danish rescue appears, for example, in the film *Miracle at Midnight* (Walt Disney, 1998), the popular Danish television series *Matador* (Danmarks Radio, 1978–81) as well as in the novels *Night of Watching* by Elliot Arnold (1967) and *Number the Stars* by Lois Lowry (1989). The Danish Resistance movement as a collective — rather than as individuals — is honoured at Yad Vashem.

4. See, for example, Martin Schwarz Lausten's comprehensive history of the relationship between Jews and the Church in Denmark (1992, 2000, 2002, 2005, 2007a, 2007b and 2012; cf. also reviews in Weinholt 2003 and 2008). Studies focusing on the modern age include the collection of articles edited by Michael Mogensen (2002), Vilhjálmur Örn Vilhjálmsson's work from 2005 on the Danes' attitude towards and treatment of Jewish refugees in the 1930–40s, the short book to accompany the exhibition on antisemitism in the media at the Museum of Media in Odense (Stræde 2009), and Sofie Lene Bak's publications on the experiences of the Danish Jews during the Second World War (2010 and 2012).

5. Rafael Edelmann (1948: 10) describes *Iudeorum Secreta* as 'det første antisemitiske Skrift, der er trykt paa Dansk [*the first antisemitic publication printed in Danish*]', and in Birkelund *et al.* (1949: 7), we read that *Iudeorum Secreta* 'nyder den tvivlsomme Ære at være det ældste danske antisemitiske Skrift, der kendes [*enjoys the dubious honour of being the oldest Danish antisemitic publication of which we know*]'. More recently Henrik Horstbøll (1999: 368) wrote that this work is an early example of 'et antisemitisk gejstligt progandaskrift [*an antisemitic clerical piece of propaganda*]'.

tions and religious poetry to pilgrimage guides and visionary literature. The lives and careers of Johannes Pfefferkorn and Poul Ræff are described, and their works, *The Confession of the Jews* and *Iudeorum Secreta*, are examined as ethnographic accounts of religious traditions during the Days of Awe (Rosh Hashanah and Yom Kippur) couched in virulent anti-Jewish polemic. The language of Ræff's translation is also described, whilst the text itself appears with a critical apparatus and commentary. The Latin text of the 1508 edition (the Cologne version with the Nuremberg text used for variants), from which Ræff made his translations, is also provided in the edition for comparison. Furthermore, there is an English translation of the Danish text for those readers not familiar with Old Danish, and foreign (particularly Hebrew) and technical words are explained throughout. I am aware that I am addressing several audiences with this book: one interested in Jewish history, another in the Christian past, and yet another in the history of Danish language and literature. I beg readers for forgiveness and understanding if I supply what is to them self-evident or superfluous information — I am merely trying to provide explanations of technical or religious terms and phenomena for whomever might need them. For those interested in following up some of the themes in this book, a comprehensive bibliography has been provided.

It is the author's intention that in addition to making this unique Danish source from the dawn of the modern period accessible to an international readership for the first time, *Lessons in Contempt* will provide its readers with useful insights into the Jewish, Christian and human conditions. With its account of how Jews are represented in medieval Danish writing, this work will be of use to both students and researchers of Danish language history, social history, the history of antisemitism, and Jewish-Christian relations.

CHAPTER 1

Enemies of God

The depiction of Jews in medieval vernacular writing in Denmark

Ingen Medynk var at finde,   *Han utrøstet maatte gaae,*
Ja mit gandske Huus-Gesinde   *Raabte: Hen til Golgotha,*
Pakke dig kun i en Fart,   *At vi der paa Jødisk Art*
Dig paa Korset kand vanære,   *Som du paa din Ryg mon bære.*

Anon. (early eighteenth century)[1]

Si le juif n'existait pas, l'antisémite l'inventerait.

Jean-Paul Sartre (1946)[2]

Af alle Nationer, *som ere fundne paa Jorden, er den Jødiske den allerforunderligste; Dens Historie begynder fra Verdens Skabelse, og gaaer lige til vor Tiid, da 100 andre store* Nationer *imidlertiid ere adspredede, og igien uddøed. Deres* Fata *ere selsomme, og saadanne, som ikke findes hos noget andet Folk; Thi man seer derudi intet, som er middelmaadigt, men lutter* Extremiteter. *Nu seer man dem at være en* Favorit-Nation, *og, (om det er tilladt saaledes at tale,) GUds Kiæledegge, saa at deres Historie er ikke andet end en Kiæde af Mirakler, og Verden synes at være skabt for deres Skyld aleene; Nu igien seer man dem nedsiunkne udi saadan Elendighed, saa at intet Folk paa Jorden kand lignes med*

---

1. *En sandfærdig Beretning om Jerusalems Skoemager, Hasverus...* (Dal and Edelmann 1965: 34): '[5.] There was no sympathy to be found, He had to walk without consolation. Indeed, my entire household shouted, "Up to Golgotha! Get a move on, so that we — in Jewish manner — can disgrace you there on the cross that you have to carry on your back!"'
2. Jean-Paul Sartre (*Réflexions sur la question juive*, 1946: 13): 'If the Jew did not exist, the antisemite would invent him.'

dem, saa at de, som tilforn var misundede af alle Folk, blive forvandlede til Verdens Skumpelskud, forhadte, forfuldte og forhaanede af alle Mennesker, og dog, dette u-anseet, ere ikke alleene endnu bleven ved lige, men opfylde alle Jordens Ekker og Hiørner.

Ludvig Holberg (1742)[3]

Jews were admitted into Denmark for the first time by royal decree in 1622. The first Jew we know of who is registered in the kingdom is, however, from a little earlier, *viz.* Jochim the Jew in 1592 in Helsingør, Sjælland.[4] Yet the lack of a permanent Jewish presence in Denmark did not mean that Jews were also absent from Danish artistic and literary works; indeed, Jews were very much part of cultural, literary and theological life in Denmark, albeit as fantastical, fabricated beings. Depictions and descriptions of Jews were everywhere, especially within the religious sphere, and they give the impression that hatred of

---

3. Ludvig Holberg (*Den Jødiske Histories Femtende Bog, cap. 17*, 1742; Holberg 1933: 532–33): 'Of all the nations that are found on Earth, the Jewish people is the most singular; their history begins with the creation of the world and continues to our time, while in the meantime a hundred other great nations have been scattered and died out. Their fates are mysterious, and of a kind that cannot be found among any other people, because one cannot see anything mediocre in them, just sheer extremities. They are seen as being a favourite nation, and (if it is permissible to speak in such a way) as God's little darlings, so that their history has been nothing but a series of miracles, and the world appears to have been created for them alone; then they are seen as being sunk in such misery that no other people on Earth can be compared to them, so that those who once were the envy of all people, have turned into the world's outcasts, hated, persecuted and mocked by all people. And yet, in spite of this, they have not only continued to maintain their numbers, rather they fill every corner and cranny of the Earth.'

4. On Jochim the Jew, see Christensen 1987 (cf. also Heimann 1982). There are also a number of people with the byname 'Jew' in medieval Danish records, although they may well not actually be Jews: 'Hr. Johannis Jødis' (Voer hundred, 1248); 'Jacobus Jøthæ' (Copenhagen, n.d.); 'Jacob Jothe' (1425, Lund), 'Anders Iøe' (Tranekær, 1500–02); 'Matz Iøæ' (Tranekær, 1500–02); 'Morthen Iude Kellæreswen' (1495, Sjælland); 'Iacop Yode' (between end of fourteenth and the Reformation, bell-founder in Landskrona). See Knudsen, Kristensen and Hornby 1949–64: 524.

The first official Jewish congregation was established in Copenhagen in 1684 by Israel David and Meyer Goldschmidt. The first synagogue was opened in Fredericia in 1719, and the first synagogue in the capital city was founded in Læderstræde in 1763, although it burnt down soon after in the city fire of 1795, and was replaced a number of years later by the great synagogue in Krystalgade. Despite there being under seven thousand Jews in Denmark today, there are no fewer than three Jewish congregations in Copenhagen: *Machsike Hadas* (orthodox), *Det Mosaiske Troessamfund* (orthodox) and *Shir Hatzafon* (reform/liberal).

Jews, and what they were believed to represent, was rife. This is hardly surprising given the anti-Jewish climate elsewhere in Europe and the very international nature of the Church and of literary and cultural trends generally during the Middle Ages. In Scandinavia, the figure of the Jew was largely a stereotype imported from abroad, where Christian representations of Jews — with the exception of some figures from the Old Testament — tended on the whole to be negative. In the twelfth and thirteenth centuries, these representations became even more sinister: Jews were no longer just blind and obstinate, but they were more actively menacing and dangerous. This is the legacy inherited by Denmark, where 'imaginary' Jews were depicted in devotional and didactic works as examples to Christian audiences of evil, ignorance, and obstinacy, whilst little mention was made of actual 'real' Jews living elsewhere in the contemporary world.

This chapter presents some of the most important medieval works in Danish that contain portrayals of Jews and that illustrate the principal 'Jewish types' found in medieval Danish literature.[5] There is no claim to comprehensive coverage here; the aim is merely to survey the important trends in the depiction of Jews in Danish works before the publication of Pfefferkorn's *Secreta Iudeorum* by Poul Ræff in 1516. I am not in any way attributing the creation of these images to the authors of the works presented, nor am I suggesting these texts represent the first occurrence of the image. It is also important to remember that the extant materials are all products of the learned Christian classes, although my hypothesis is that this limitation does not distort the popular views that they claim to reflect.

The examples are taken from vernacular literature; such works were usually aimed at a broader audience than just those able to read and understand Latin, and therefore better demonstrate the widespread attitudes, beliefs and assumptions that cut across all social groups in the majority population than do the authoritative writings in Latin of the religious establishment. Vernacular literature was the principal source of entertainment and instruction, and as such, the conception of the Jew that emerged from it became one of the basic convictions of the Danes in medieval and early modern periods.[6]

---

5. The reader is also referred to Lausten (1992: 46–108), whose overview includes Danish works in Latin. Another important source for the portrayal of Jews in medieval Denmark, church wall-paintings and religious art, has been dealt with elsewhere, *viz*. in Ulla Haastrup 1999 and 2003. See also Lausten 1992: 132–56.

6. Trachtenberg 1993: 12–14. For an overview of the perception of Jews in medieval Denmark, see also Adams 2012.

Figure 1 Aakirkeby Church baptismal font. Photograph by Lene Rybner.

Relief 11

Relief 10

9

Baptismal Font in Aakirkeby Church

Before the arrival of the Latin alphabet, Scandinavians, like several other Germanic peoples, wrote using runes, and today there are more than eight hundred extant runic inscriptions in Denmark alone. They vary greatly in length and are found carved on small items such as brooches, combs and decorations as well as the better known and substantially larger rune-stones and monuments. During the first few centuries after the introduction of Christianity (and with it the Latin alphabet) to Scandinavia, runes continued to be used, not just to write in the vernacular but also Latin.

In Aakirkeby Church on the Danish Baltic island of Bornholm, there stands a decorated baptismal font with twelve runic inscriptions.[7] Dating from *c.* 1200, the font is carved in a Romanesque style in Gotland sandstone by the rune-carver Master Sigreifr, and it is one of a group of similar baptismal fonts found in Skåne and on Gotland carved by the same man. On the outside of the font are eleven reliefs illustrating scenes from the life of Jesus. Carved in the arches above each relief are explanations in runes which form one of the earliest religious narratives in Denmark and date from just a few centuries after the country's Christianisation. Strictly speaking, the text is in fact written in Gotlandic (also known as Gutnish), the language of Gotland, not Danish, but it would have been comprehensible to anyone who was lettered as the differences between the East Norse languages at this time were minimal (and further reduced by the use of the Younger Futhark alphabet, here in its Gotlandic variety, in which distinct sounds and minimal pairs were not distinguished in writing).[8] The font's inscriptions with translations are:[9]

Relief	Inscription
1.	þita : iR : saNti gabrel : ok : sehþi : saNta mari(a) : at han sku Ldi : barn : (f)yþa : þita : iR : elicabeþ : ok : maria : ok : hailsas
2.	
3.	: hiar : huilis : maria sum han : barn : fydi : skapera : himic : ok : iorþaR : sum os : le ysti þita : iRu : þaiR : þriR : kunuGaR : (s)um : (f)y(r)sti : giarþu : ofr : u
4.	

---

[7]. On these runic inscriptions, see Wimmer 1887; Zetterholm 1947, and Snædal 2002: 112–17.

[8]. On the use of runes in medieval Scandinavia (as opposed to Viking-Age Scandinavia) and runic literacy, see Spurkland 2004.

[9]. The transcriptions are taken from the Danish National Museum's runic database at http://runer.ku.dk. The monument and inscription are registered in the database as DK Bh 30.

5.	arum : drotNi : hiar : tok : (h)aN (uiþ)r : (kunuG)a : o(f)ri : uar drotiN
6.	hiar : riþu : þaiR : burt : þriR : kunuGaR :
7.	siþan þaiR : ofra(t) : ---a : (o)rum : drotNi
8.	þaiR : þet : hi(a)- : fram : s--(u) : (io)þaR : toku
9.	uarn : drotin : ok --Nd- : --N : uiþ- -re : ok : (g)etu
10.	siþan : ladu : (þa)iR : haN : burt : þiaþa(n) : buNdiN
11.	ok : (n)ehldu : hiar : ioþaR : iesus : a krus : si : fram : a þita
column	sihraf(R) : (m)e--e-(i) :

This is Saint Gabriel and [he] said to Saint Mary that she would give birth to a child. This is Elizabeth and Mary and they are greeting each other. Here Mary is resting, having given birth to the child, the creator of Heaven and Earth who redeemed us. These are the three kings who first made offerings to our Lord. Here he accepted the kings' offerings, our Lord. Here they, the three kings, rode away after they had made offerings to our Lord. Then it is this far in the story [?]. The Jews took our Lord and bound him to a tree and placed him under guard. Then they led him away from there, bound. And here the Jews nailed Jesus to the cross. Witness that which is right before you! Master Sigreifr (made this)

As we can see from the inscriptions on reliefs 9–11, the Jews' responsibility for and involvement in the capture and crucifixion of Jesus have been literally carved into the cultural and religious history of Denmark. The Romans make no appearance in this account of Jesus' life and death at all. The image of the Jew as Christ killer is the source from which all other Christian anti-Jewish representations flow. The potent theme of deicide, based on the conception of Jesus as both a human and a divine being and who was killed by the Jews, is a recurring one and by far the most frequent in the presentation of the Jews in medieval Danish literature.[10]

The Resurrection of Christ

In the manuscript fragment, Stockholm, Royal Library, *A 115, from *c.* 1325, we find part of a poem about the resurrection of Christ based on the Passion

---

10. The notion of Jewish guilt for the death of Jesus was in fact not repudiated by the Catholic Church until the *Nostra Aetate* of the Second Vatican Council in 1965 over twenty years after the Holocaust (see Cohen 2007: 167–82).

Gospel of Nicodemus.[11] This apocryphal gospel deals with the behaviour of the Jews at the trial of Jesus as well as after his execution and resurrection, and it firmly places the blame for his death and crucifixion on them.[12] The Danish manuscript contains only a fragment of the story usually referred to as *Kristi opstandelse* ['The Resurrection of Christ'], and it comprises approximately one seventh of the entire gospel (in all just 2 folios). The work is a free rendering of the Latin prose gospel in a verse form known as *knittel* (the usual verse form in East Norse epic literature).[13] The refusal on the part of the Jews to believe in the divinity of Jesus and in his subsequent resurrection is one of the major themes of the extant parts of the poem. In the Danish text, the Jews, having heard reports of sightings of Jesus, are told by the high priests Annas and Caiaphas not to believe a word of what the eyewitnesses have said (fol. 1ʳ):[14]

> Tha sauthe annas oc cayphas. hui lata i sua.
> Ih*esu*s ithær nu ængte hialpa ma.
> I sculu thæt ikki tro for thætt ær æi satt.
> Att ih*esu*s stoth op af døth. sum i haua fratt.

> *Then Annas and Caiaphas said, 'Why do you wail like that?*
> *Jesus cannot help you now.*
> *You shouldn't believe — because it's not true! —*
> *that Jesus rose from the dead, as you have heard told.'*

---

11. The poem fragment has been published in Collijn 1913: 278–81, and Brøndum-Nielsen 1955. Note that Collijn believed that *The Resurrection of Christ* was written in a southern Småland dialect with Danish features. Brøndum-Nielsen disproved this and showed that the text is in fact entirely Danish. An English introduction to the text that builds largely on the work of Brøndum-Nielsen can be found in Wolf 1997: 280–83.

12. For an overview of the death of Jesus according to the gospels, see Crossan 1996. On the history and development of the image of the Jew as Christ killer, see Cohen 2007. Another early text (*c.* 1325) that blames the Jews for murdering Jesus is *Mary's Lament* in the runic manuscript Stockholm, Royal Library, A 120 (Brøndum-Nielsen and Rohmann 1929: 22):

> O uih uslæ iuþha, O uih umiłde iuþha, sparer mik æi. Mæþan i kryzæn min ening sun, kryzær ok mik hans usla moþær, ællar mæþ annan besk døþ dræpær mik, at iak þo dør mæþ hanum

> *O woe wretched Jews! O woe cruel Jews! Do not spare me. As you are crucifying my only son, crucify also his wretched mother, or kill me with a bitter death, that I thus die with him.*

13. For an explanation of this meter in English, see Pulsiano *et al.* 1993: 357, *s.v.* 'Knittel(vers)'.

14. Brøndum-Nielsen 1955: 71, ll. 9–14.

The Jews are thus portrayed as a single, lamenting crowd under the influence of their priests who criticise them for being gullible. Annas and Caiaphas appear several places in the gospels (Matthew 26: 3, 57; Luke 3: 2; John 18: 13–14, 24, 28, 49) as well as Acts of the Apostles (Acts 4: 6) where they act as judges for the Jewish authorities. The power of Jewish leaders to mislead and corrupt their followers is, incidentally, a belief later presented in a contemporary context by Pfefferkorn who believed that the Jews' rabbinical leaders kept their congregants in their power by lying and by distorting the truth of the Bible.

Later in the text, the Jews are shown to be cowardly and fearful of the 'truth' of Christ's divinity. Joseph of Arimathea, who had been imprisoned by the Jews for anointing the body of Jesus and placing it in the tomb that he had built for himself, is found to have been miraculously freed from prison. He is sent for by the Jews who, upon hearing how the risen Jesus had freed him from his cell and returned him to Arimathea, throw themselves to the ground in astonishment and terror (fol. 2ʳ):[15]

>Thaghan iutha hørtho all thæsse orth.
>the fiollo af fasa døthe nither a iorth.
>Oc undratho sua storleca a thætta maal.
>oc thætt hiarta ryghe sua hart sum ett staal
>
>*As soon as the Jews heard all these words,*
>*they fell to the ground in terror as if dead.*
>*And they were greatly astonished by this speech*
>*and remorse, [that was] as hard as steel.*

The impression one gets of the Jews from the Gospel of Nicodemus in its entirety is somewhat more sinister;[16] they are an angry, malicious group — a picture which we no doubt would have obtained from the entire Danish poem had it been extant. Upon witnessing or hearing of the resurrection, they still refuse to accept that Jesus was the messiah. So despite having been present at the Crucifixion and being fully aware of the miracle of the incarnation and resurrection, the Jews insincerely persist in rejecting Christ; they are thus not just unwitting unbelievers, but deliberate unbelievers. This stubborn failure to believe in the divinity of

---

15. Brøndum-Nielsen 1955: 72, ll. 61–65.
16. For an English translation of the entire gospel, also known as the Acts of Pilate, see James 1924: 94–146.

Jesus has been identified as the root cause of Christian anti-Jewish hostility. As Marcel Simon writes, 'Christian anti-Semitism is in the first instance an expression of the resentment aroused by Israel's resistance to the gospel.'[17] In *The Resurrection of Christ*, we have a medieval literary expression of this resentment from Denmark. The Jews may have been commanded and deceived by their leaders, but they still share in the collective guilt for killing God as they have yet to repent or convert to Christianity. This is all put very succinctly by St Augustine, who wrote of the Jews in *Tractatus adversus Iudaeos* VIII: 'Occidistis Christum in parentibus vestris [*In your ancestors, you killed Christ*]'.[18] The medievals tended to operate with a notion of the unchanging human character; so for medieval Christians, contemporary Jews shared the same proclivities as the Jews in the New Testament who had called for Christ to be crucified over a thousand years earlier.[19] The perception that all Jews at all times share in the collective responsibility for the Crucifixion has plagued Jewry the world over with catastrophic consequences.

The Fifteen Places

Hær begynnes the fæmthen stæder som wor herre tolde syn pyne paa ['Here begin the fifteen places where our Lord suffered his pain'; hereafter *The Fifteen Places*] is a printed devotional work describing the Passion of Christ. We know of three versions of the book in Danish. One was printed in Copenhagen by Gotfred of Ghemen in 1509. It comprises 28 folios and survives today in just two copies, both in the collections of the Royal Library in Copenhagen. The 1509 edition was republished in a facsimile edition in 1915, which has been used for the quotations in the following. The second version is undated and was printed together with a guide to confession, called *Modus confitendi*. It is now lost and survives only in a handwritten copy made by Jón Mortensen (Copenhagen, Royal Library, NkS 129, 4°) and later published by Christian Bruun in 1866. Jón Mortensen's manuscript was bought from the Luxdorph library (Bibliotheca Luxdorphiana, libri manuscripti, S. 16, Nr. 174) at auction for two *skilling*, and it has the following note written on the flysheet by Bolle Willum Luxdorph:

---

17. Simon 1986: 207.
18. *PL* XLII: 60.
19. See Chazan 1997: 15.

¶ Har begynnes the femthen stæder som wor herre tolde syn pyne paa' oc hoo som the betencker hwer daw i sith hierthe thñ forthiener stor afflaðh

Figure 2
Frontispiece of *The Fifteen Places*. Photograph by author.

> Findes i Geheime-Raad Grev Thotts Bibliothek, trÿkt in quarto, med Munkebogstaver, uden Capitæler, med Signatur A, bestaaende af 8 Blade, uden Stædets, eller Bogtrykkers Navn, eller Aarstall.

> *Can be found in Royal Councillor Baron Thott's library, printed in quarto with monk letters, without capitals, with signature A, comprising eight folios without the name of the place of publication or of the printer or the year.*

The librarian Rasmus Nyerup has added: 'Fandtes ikke i Bibliotheket efter Thotts Död [*NB was not found in the library after Thott's death*]'. Luxdorph's description of the letter type as 'monk letters' points to the book's originating from the press of Gotfred of Ghemen whose typeface was often described as 'monk letters'.[20] The final version is extant as a medieval copy dating 1475–1500, and found in Copenhagen, The Arnamagnæan Collection, AM 21, 4°, fols 184^v–92^r. There are small variations between the texts of the Danish versions which were most probably translated from a now lost Latin original. The Crucifixion scene in particular demonstrates a number of interesting points of comparison; for example, in the Ghemen print, where Mary faints at the cross and is 'near death', whereas in NkS 129, 4° and AM 21, 4° she faints and is nearly trampled to death by the Jews.[21] On the whole, however, the active involvement of the Jews in the Crucifixion is much more apparent in Ghemen 1509.[22] Although Poul Ræff's translation in 1516 of Pfefferkorn's *Iudeorum Secreta* has been called the first antisemitic book printed in Danish,[23] Gotfred of Ghemen's small, popular work could just as well be awarded this dubious 'honour'. Unlike *Iudeorum Secreta*, however, *The Fifteen Places* does not signal a new development in anti-Jewish polemic, but rather follows in the long tradition of Christian writing that depicts

---

20. See Bruun 1866: [i].
21. Ghemen 1509: fol. e1^v; Copenhagen, Royal Library, NkS 129, 4°, fol. 14^v (= Bruun 1866: 22), and AM 21, 4°, fol. 190^r.
22. There is also a Swedish version preserved in two manuscripts:
    - Stockholm, Royal Library, Codex Schürer von Waldheim 104, 12° (1530–40); edited by George Stephens and published in 1865 as 'Om Christi pina' in Stephens 1847–74, III: 69–107;
    - Stockholm, Royal Library, Nådendal Manuscript, A 49 (1442), fols 221–35; edited and published in Andersson 2003: 107–35 (cf. Klemming 1860: xxxi–xxxiii).

    The Danish and Swedish versions are rather dissimilar. The sites where Christ is tormented are different, and the Swedish version is more elaborate with longer passages for contemplation (taken from the Pseudo-Bonaventure's *Meditationes vitae Christi*).
23. Cf. comments by Rafael Edelmann (1948: 10) and Palle Birkelund (Birkelund *et al.* 1949: 7) quoted in the Introduction above.

Figure 3
Crucifixion scene, Jetsmark Church, northern Jutland (1474). Photograph by Niels Clemmensen.

the Jews of the New Testament as abusing, mocking and ultimately murdering Jesus.

The Fifteen Places is one in a long line of devotional texts that owe inspiration to *Meditationes Vitae Christi* (*c.*1300), written by Pseudo-Bonaventure (probably the Tuscan Franciscan John of Caulibus)[24] and offering readers graphic descriptions of Christ's sufferings and his tormentors' cruelty and providing cues for empathy.[25] Mary's visiting the sites of Jesus' life and death is found in other works too, such as the anonymous fourteenth-century *Speculum humanae salvationis* (chapters 35–36)[26] and in the *Legenda aurea*, the oldest extant Swedish translation of which reads:[27]

> sua scriuas aff siþan apostoli | skildos ok skiptos vm væruldena at prædica : boþe maria ii iher*usa*lem viþ montem sÿon : ok gik opta vm kring landet : at vitia þe staþa gesus fødes ok døptes fastaþe oc predicaþe . iærtigne giorþe ok døþ þolde : hans graf ok þær han tel himna stægh

> *Then it is written that after the apostles dispersed and sailed throughout the world to preach, Mary lived in Jerusalem at Mount Zion, and she often walked about the country to visit the places Jesus was born and baptised, fasted and preached, performed miracles and suffered death, his grave and there whence he ascended to heaven.*

The Fifteen Places describes the fifteen locations (or Stations of the Cross) where Jesus was abused during the Passion and which were regularly visited by his mother after his Ascension.[28] The number of years Mary lived after Jesus ranges from two (in the *Transitus Mariae* tradition) to twenty-four (in the *Legenda Aurea*). The fifteen-year period here probably derives from three of Bir-

---

24. See McNamer 2009.
25. Rubin 2010: 246–47; Bestul 1996: 43–56.
26. Buckl and Egbers 1994.
27. Stockholm, Royal Library, A 34, fol. 5[ra–b]; published in Stephens 1847–74, I: 12.
28. They are the sites of 1) the washing of feet; 2) the garden of Gethsemane; 3) Judas' treachery; 4) the trial by Annas; 5) the trial by Caiaphas; 6) the trial by Pilate; 7) the trial by Herod and Pilate; 8) the scourging of Jesus; 9) the crowning with the crown of thorns; 10) the walking with the cross; 11) the mocking at Golgotha/Calvary; 12) the crucifixion of the thieves and casting of lots for Jesus' clothes; 13) the crucifixion of Jesus; 14) Longinus' spearing Jesus' side, and 15) the burial of Jesus, and Mary's grief. On Mary as the first pilgrim, see Limor (*forthcoming*).

gitta of Sweden's revelations (*Lib.* VII 26, VI 61 and 62).²⁹ The number of stations is also due to Birgittine influence. The stations tradition was established in Europe in the Late Middle Ages by the Franciscans who, to duplicate those of the Via Dolorosa in Jerusalem, set up series of shrines usually numbering just seven.³⁰ Birgitta, however, identified fifteen stations for devotions commemorating the Passion.³¹

The Fifteen Places focuses on Jesus' sufferings and his mother's sorrow, and the story of the Passion is seen through the eyes of Mary, *mater dolorosa*. It is her steps the reader retraces. The Jews, held solely responsible for the misery, judgement and crucifixion of Jesus, play a central role in this core narrative of Christianity. Indeed, the book is one long tirade against the Jews who are presented as a singular group of cruel and barbaric Christ killers. With the exception of Pontius Pilate, the Romans do not appear in the story at all. Pilate serves only to find Jesus innocent and hand him back to the Jews, which emphasises their guilt by showing that it was not he, but the Jews, who condemned Jesus to death. In Christian tradition, the Jews' rejection and murder of Christ fulfilled the prophecy in Nehemiah 9: 26: 'Then, defying You, they rebelled; they cast Your Teaching behind their back. They killed Your prophets who admonished them to turn back to You; they committed great impieties.'

It was the cruel Jews ('the wmildhe iøde[t>r]', fol. a4ʳ, l. 2), who captured Jesus in Gethsemane and took him to the city 'meth alsom største daare oc spot [*with the greatest ridicule and mockery*] '. From this point on in the text, he is repeatedly beaten, kicked, whipped and mocked by the Jews who furthermore push down the crown of thorns so hard onto his head that his face becomes covered with his own blood and brain matter. Here, for example, is a description of his treatment in the house of the priest Caiaphas (fols b1ᵛ, l. 13 – b2ʳ, l. 4):

> tha sloo the wor herre ihesum cristum welsignedhe ligome met træ och meth knøpele oc spitthe hannum op wndher hans øgen. the drucke wijn tijl samen blandet mit watn alth thet the leffnedhe i skalen thet || slowe the op wor herre ihesum *cristi* øghen intil een andhen fra then langhe nath gaffue the hannum hwerken hwijlæ eller roo Amen

> *Then they beat our Lord Jesus Christ's blessed body with wood and with truncheons and they spat up into his eyes. They drank wine mixed with water. What they [did not*

---

29. See also Marx and Drennan 1987: 137.
30. Schiller 1971–72, II: 82.
31. On the number of the Stations of the Cross, see Gad 1964: 374.

drink and] left in the bowl they threw into our Lord Jesus Christ's eyes until another [text corrupt³²]. *During that long night they gave him neither rest nor peace. Amen.*

Jews spitting (fol. b1ᵛ, l. 16) is a common motif in anti-Jewish and later antisemitic literature, and the Jews spit at Jesus a number of times in *The Fifteen Places*; for example, when Mary looks at her crucified son lying in her lap after he has been taken down from the cross, she says 'Nw esthv giort dome[t>r] aff thin egen hierne oc blodh oc thet lede iødhe spoth som ær spyt paa teg [*You have now been blinded with your own brain and blood and the disgusting Jew spittle that has been spat at you*]' (fol. g1ʳ, ll. 6–9).³³ The spitting in the gospels supposedly fulfils the prophecy in Isaiah 50: 6: 'I offered my back to the floggers, And my cheeks to those who tore out my hair. I did not hide my face from insult and spittle.' However, unlike in *The Fifteen Places*, it is both the Roman soldiers (Matthew 27: 29)

---

32. The other Danish version of this scene (Copenhagen, Royal Library, NkS 129, 4°, fol. 10ᵛ; Bruun 1866: 15) reads:

> Tha slowe the vor Herræ jhesum christum paa sith velsignede legommæ meth træ, oc vendher, oc spytthæ hannum op vnderi sith hellige andledhæ. Then lange nat gaffwe the hannum hwercken hwilæ eller roo eller noghen liisæ.
>
> *Then they beat our Lord Jesus Christ on his blessed body with wood, and branches, and spat up into his holy face. During that long night they gave him neither rest nor peace nor respite.*

33. Another occurrence of this motif is found, for example, in the text on the Passion in Stockholm, Royal Library, A 31, fol. 42ʳᵃ (*c.* 1500):

> Iosephus sigher at iøderne haffde swa gantze saare forwend herr[en] Ihesum meth theræ spyt at the ekke kwnne see hans øghen eller mwn eller nogher skapnet wnder hans helgæ æntlite Ok hans hals og helgæ mwn ware fulle aff thet ylle luctendhe spyt
>
> *Josephus says that the Jews had so completely transformed Lord Jesus with their spittle that they were unable to see his eyes or mouth or any shape under his holy face. And his throat and holy mouth were full of the foul-smelling spittle.*

The Jews' foul smell was, according to the same manuscript (fol. 33ʳᵃ), not innate, but rather due to their eating 'rødh løg, ok hwidløg ok swamp og paddhe hatte Ok sligh owan kost [*red onions and garlic and mushrooms and toadstools and such unusual food*]'. For a discussion of Jews' fondness of garlic and its anti-Christian implications, see Diemling 2005. Sermons and the Danish prayer books (see below) also use the imagery of 'disgusting Jew spittle', a fluid that was thought to be both disgusting, and in the early modern period also the fluid vessel of evil. For example, in John Webster's *The Duchess of Malfi* (1614), Jews' spittle along with 'their young children's ordure' are listed among the ingredients one would expect to find in a shop of witchcraft (Webster 1964: 41), and on p. 55 of Robert Tofte's translation of Ludovico Ariosto's *Fourth Satire* (1611), we read that 'the spettle of a Iew' has a 'loathsome smell' and is an ingredient in 'plague-salues'. The folkloristic powers of spittle, to both bless and curse, are discussed in Bergen 1890.

and the Jews (Matthew 26: 67; Mark 14: 65) who spit at Christ in the Passion scenes of the New Testament.[34] Furthermore, this spitting is another graphic aspect of the inverted hierarchical relationship between the Jews and Christians that illustrates the horror of Christian defilement through contact with the Jews when social boundaries are transgressed.[35] Another related image found in *The Fifteen Places* is that of the mocking Jew with outstretched tongue (fol. c3^v, ll. 6–11):

> tha faldhe iøderne paa eth knæ oc gabedhe meth mwnd oc glode m*eth* øghen och wtracthe twnge*n* oc ropte och sagde Hælseth wære thu iøde koning Amen
>
> *Then the Jews dropped onto one knee and gaped with their mouths and stared with their eyes and poked out their tongues and shouted 'Hail! King of the Jews!' Amen.*

A poking tongue is an image of mockery, and as such was much used in the portrayal of Jews in Passion scenes in both art and writing. A good example is the altarpiece carved by Claus Berg in Bregninge Church on the island of Ærø.[36] The gaping mouth is also commonly found in descriptions of Jews and builds on Psalms 115: 5: 'They have mouths, but cannot speak.'[37]

The Jews are presented as barbaric and wild; indeed, Jesus is described as standing among them like a sheep among a pack of ferocious wolves: 'Wor herre ihesus cristus stodh saa toligh blandh them som eth faar ther stonder i blant alsom grommeste wlffue [*Our Lord, Jesus Christ, stood so patiently among them like a sheep who stands among the most ferocious wolves*]' (fol. b2^v, ll. 3–7).[38] But the Jews' cruelty is not only directed towards Jesus but also towards his

---

34. See Crossan 1996: 118–32 for a thought-provoking interpretation of the Romans' and Jews' abuse of and spitting at Jesus.
35. Bestul 1996: 87; cf. Douglas 2002: 121. There may also be a link between this spitting and contemporary Christians' anxieties about poisoning by Jews; see Bestul 1996: 106–10.
36. See Bolvig 2003: 258.
37. Cf. also Psalms 135: 6.
38. The Jews are also described as wolves in two works by Christiern Pedersen (discussed below), viz. in the Good Friday sermon from his *Book of Miracle Sermons* (1515): 'Der de saage ihesum da bleffue de glade som en wlff der fanger i lom [*When they saw Jesus they became happy like a wolf that catches a lamb*]' (ChrPed. *Skr.* I: 351), and in his *Book of Hours* (1514): 'Thii ath naar mine vuenner gribe migh da handtere de mig saa vmildelighe som grumme løffuer eller vlffue ther slyde eth vskyldigth lom [*So when my enemies seize me, they treat me like cruel lions or wolves that tear apart an innocent lamb*]' (ChrPed. *Skr.* II: 361). The portrayal of a lamb-like Jesus surrounded by wolves plays of course on the image of Christ as *Agnus Dei*, the Lamb of God.

mother, whom they repeatedly shove and prevent from tending to her suffering son. After being treated in this manner, a distraught Mary turns to John the Evangelist and blames the Jews for her son's slow and painful death (fols c4^v, l. 4 – d1^r, l. 5):

> tha kom wor herre ihesu cristhi moder iomfrw maria och wille husswale sijn kære søn och bære korsset met hannum Hun motthe icke komme til hanum for iøderne Alle iøderne støtte henne och skode henne bort Vden sanctus iohannes ewangelista han tog i mod henne oc husswalede henne hun talede til hannum oc sagde Iohannes iohannes Aldri wiste ieg at engelin kunne siæ wsand han talede til meg oc sagde Heel maria thu æst met naade herre ær met teg Sennelige siær ieg teg iohannes At iegh ær opfult meth alsom mesth an-||ger och drøwelse och herren ær lucht fraa megh han ær i dagh i the wmijlde iøderne hender och the pyne oc plawe hannum tijl døde

> *Then our Lord Jesus Christ's mother, the Virgin Mary, arrived and wanted to comfort her dear son and carry the cross with him. She was not allowed by the Jews to reach him. All the Jews shoved her and pushed her away, except Saint John the Evangelist, he took her in and gave her solace. She spoke to him saying 'John, John! I never knew that the angel could tell me an untruth. He spoke to me saying, "Hail Mary! You are with grace. The Lord is with you." Truly, I say to you John, that I am filled with the greatest remorse and sadness, and the Lord [Jesus] is barred from me. Today he is in the hands of the cruel Jews and they are abusing and tormenting him to death.'*

Even after crucifying Jesus, the fanatical and monstrous Jews continue to abuse him in a particularly macabre scene (fols e2^v, l. 14 – e3^r, l. 1):

> icke wore the vmilde iødher øffreth treth aff hans pyne the løbe om kringh korsset oc samen sanckede the døde mens been som til foren wor wndliuedhe paa then stadh och kaste oppa korsset tijl || wor herre iesum

> *The cruel Jews were not sufficiently tired of tormenting him. They ran around the cross and collected the bones of dead men who had previously been executed at that place, and they threw them up at the cross at our Lord Jesus.*

Parts of corpses and bones can be seen at the foot of the cross in the woodcut on the frontispiece of *The Fifteen Places* (see fig. 2). Scenes of Jews' rejoicing and of mockery at the foot of the cross also form the climax of a number of

European medieval mystery plays and appear to be a common image in representations of the Crucifixion.[39] This fanatical abuse of the dead physical body of Christ alludes to the alleged mistreatment of the metaphysical body of Christ by medieval Jews, *viz.* the desecration of the host. It also serves to demonstrate how the Jews are no longer God's chosen people but have become Gentiles, since in the prophecies that the Crucifixion is believed to fulfil, it is the Gentiles who 'hiss and wag their head at the daughter of Jerusalem' (Lamentations 2: 15).[40] *The Fifteen Places* stresses that all Jews — with the sole exception of the disciples and Mary — took part in this cruel treatment of Jesus, for example (fol. d1ᵛ, ll. 2–5):[41]

> alt thet folck ther wor i staden the kaste at hannu*m* drek oc dyn som man pleyer at steene wdedes menniske met

> *All the people who were in the town [i.e. Jerusalem] threw at him [the sort of] filth and mud that they usually stoned condemned people with.*

---

39. See Strumpf 1920: 9; Trachtenberg 1993: 22–23. Interestingly, in the Jewish anti-Christian polemical work, *Toledot Yešu HaNoẓri*, the Jews bind cords to the feet of Jesus' corpse (or in a variant text, bind him to the tail of a donkey), and drag him round the streets of Jerusalem (Schonfield 1937: 53). There is no connection between these two texts, but they graphically demonstrate the universality of the potent and emphatic symbol of the absolute death and the utter demise of one's enemy: the defiling of his corpse. In many Christian anti-Muslim polemical texts from the Middle Ages, for example, Muḥammad's corpse is devoured by dogs and pigs; see Cutler 1965.

40. Cf. also Jeremiah 48: 27.

41. At this point in the text, *en route* to the site of crucifixion, the Jews pull Christ up from the ground and say 'Hey hey thu karl hwij wilthu ey bære korsset (fol. d2ᵛ, ll. 7–8) / Heÿ Heÿ tw karl Hwÿ will tw eÿ bære korsith (Copenhagen, Royal Library, NkS 129, 4°, fol. 13ᵛ; Bruun 1866: 20) [*Hey! Hey! You fellow! Why don't you want to carry the cross?*]'. This mocking phrase has been read and discussed at some length by Lausten (1992: 78–79), who reads it as 'Hep hep! You fellow! *etc.*', providing us with the earliest recorded example in Danish of the word 'hep', an interjection used by antisemites and Jew-baiters to goad Jews. However, his interpretation is based on a misreading of the letter-type *y* as *p*. Unfortunately, the mistake has been left unchecked and copied in Dahlerup 2010: 337. The interjection 'hep' simply does not appear in Old Danish. According to the Dictionary of the Danish Language (*Ordbog over det danske Sprog*), the word is first recorded in Danish in 1819 and is loaned from German. The earliest quotation given in Grimm's dictionary of the German language is from W. Hauff (1802–27). See further Rohrbacher 2005 (with references), and *JE*, *s.v.* 'Hep! Hep!' (cols 350ᵇ–51ᵃ), where Joseph Jacobs argues that it is unlikely that 'hep' was used by the Crusaders, as is sometimes claimed, but that the word was first used in 1819 by antisemitic students in Würzburg, who themselves explained the word was from the phrase 'Hierosolyma est perdita [*Jerusalem is lost*]'.

It was the Jewish people *en masse* who called for his crucifixion (fols d3ᵛ, l. 13 – d4ʳ, l. 9):

> Ther iøderne soo ath han war saa ynkelijge och saa ledher giort aff sith eghet blod the mente ath han kunne icke løbe Tha toghe the hannum nøghen i theris hender oc dantze met hannum oc sprunge meth hannu*m* aff spot och spee. tha rophte all iøderne oc sagde seer oc skuder the*n*ne loynere och swijgere som segh kaller at være iødes konijng gijffwer dom offuer hannum tha ropthe the anne*n* syn alle samen oc sagde Crucifige Crucifige th*et* ær sa meget Korsfester Korsfester hannu*m* oc døder hannu*m* tijl døde

> *When the Jews saw that he had been made so pitiful and so vile by his own blood, they thought that he could not run away. Then they took him naked into their hands and danced with him and leapt about with him in ridicule and mockery. Then all the Jews shouted saying, 'Look and see this liar and deceiver, who calls himself the King of the Jews! Pass judgement on him!' Then they shouted a second time all together saying, 'Crucifige! Crucifige!' This means, 'Crucify! Crucify him! And kill him!'*

The collective guilt of the Jews is furthermore expressed through the infamous blood curse (fol. b4ᵛ, l. 10 – b5ʳ, l. 12):

> Tha togh pilatus hannu*m* nøgen i syne hender oc fuldhe hannu*m* wdh tijl al folketh oc sadde Jeg kan inge*n* sag fijnne m*et* thenne mand ther ‖ hanu*m* bør vndliffues fore men tage i hannu*m* oc hudstruger hannu*m* oc gører aff hannu*m* huad i wille tha tog pilat*us* watn i en mwlwe oc todhe syne hender oc sagde saa Vskyldigh wil ieg være i the*n*ne ma*n*tz døt och blodh som thette watn rensser mijne he*n*der tha ropte alle iøderne meth een hyw røsth oc sagde ha*n*s blod th*et* scal gaa offuer oss oc ofuer wore børn Amen

> *Then Pilate took him naked in his hands and accompanied him out to all the people and said, 'I can find no case concerning this man for which he should be executed, but take him and whip him and do with him as you wish!' Then Pilate poured water into a bowl and washed his hands and then said, 'I will be innocent in this man's death and blood as this water is cleansing my hands.' Then all the Jews shouted with one loud voice and said, 'His blood shall be upon us and upon our children!' Amen.*

Taking Matthew 27: 25, Jewish guilt for the Crucifixion can be considered heritable. Indeed, the (mis-)use of verbs to express the future in the phrase (for example, 'hans blod th*et* <u>scal</u> gaa offuer oss [*his blood <u>shall</u> be upon us*]') makes it sound like a prophecy to be fulfilled rather than an acceptance of the responsibility that otherwise would have been Pilate's. The phrase in the Greek New Testament reads 'Το αἷμα αυτοῦ ἐφ' ἡμᾶς και ἐπί τα τέκνα ἡμῶν' which contains no verb (literally: 'the blood his on us and on the children ours'). Through the blood curse, contemporary Jews, linked by a genealogical chain to the Jews of the New Testament, are thus also guilty of murdering God. In fact, the heritability of this guilt removes the sinfulness of the Jews from the religious sphere and turns it into a hereditary character trait, an incorrigible evil Jewish essence, an incapacity to be moral, the very concept that would form the basis of antisemitic race rhetoric in the modern era. That *all* Jews are guilty of killing Jesus and tormenting his mother is repeatedly emphasised in *The Fifteen Places* too. We read, for example, that 'Tha ropte och iøderne alth sammen [*all the Jews also shouted together*]' (fol. a4^v, ll. 5–6); 'tha ropte alle iøderne meth een hyw røsth [*all the Jews shouted with one loud voice*]' (fol. b4^v, ll. 9–10), and that 'Alle iøderne støtte henne oc skode henne bort [*all the Jews shoved her (i.e. Mary) and pushed her away*]' (fol. c4^v, ll. 9–10).

Several of the episodes, usually assigned to Roman soldiers in Christian lore, are acted out by the Jews in *The Fifteen Places*. As we have seen, it is only the Jews who spit at Jesus, and it is also they who cast lots for his clothes: 'tha saa ha*n* huor the dobblede om ha*ns* kled*er* hwelke som the*m* sculle beholde [*Then he saw how they (the Jews) cast lots for his clothes that they would keep*]' (fol. d4^v, 9–11; cf. John 19: 23–25).[42] Furthermore, they are the ones who set Jesus on the cross and hammer the nails through his hands and feet (fol. e2^r, l. 5 – e2^v, l. 3; cf. Matthew 27: 30):

> tha igenem slo iøderne wor herre ih*esu* høgre hand m*et* een stompt iern naule saa ynkelighe och saa hordelige at naufflen indgick oc blodet wdspranck ‖ the[t>r] the haffde korssfest then alsom megtigeste gudh tha opreysde the korset op i een sten
>
> *Then the Jews hammered through our Lord Jesus' right hand with a blunt nail so mercilessly and so hard that the nail went in and his blood spurted out. When they had crucified the almighty God, they raised the cross in a stone.*

The Jews had dulled the points of the nails used for the crucifixion in order to increase Jesus' suffering. According to Christian lore, the descendants of the tribe responsible for hammering Jesus to the cross were thereafter punished by God

---

42. Cf. also the medieval Danish prayer books below.

with the affliction of having live worms appear in their mouths when sleeping.[43] In spite of other Birgittine influence on this work, the method of crucifixion — fastening Jesus to the cross and then raising it — contradicts the method in Birgitta's vision (recorded in *Lib.* VII 15) where the cross is raised first and only then is Jesus attached with the help of ladders. The Swedish version of *The Fifteen Places* describes the crucifixion in the Birgittine manner.[44] The raising of the cross followed by the affixing of Jesus to it is also related by Bonaventure, and is furthermore discussed by the Danish canon and humanist scholar, Christiern Pedersen, in his *Book of Miracle Sermons* of 1515.[45] Similarly, in *Lib.* I 10 Birgitta mentions precisely how Jesus' feet were placed (the left foot over the right one) and fastened to the cross with two nails. Mereth Lindgren has noted that this is in fact rather unusual with less than five percent of medieval crucifixes showing Jesus with his left foot over his right foot.[46] As we can see from the frontispiece and text, this Birgittine element has not been incorporated into *The Fifteen Places* either.

It is also the Jews, in the role of Stephaton, who give the concoction of vinegar mixed with gall to the crucified Christ (fol. e3ᵛ, ll. 1–7; cf. Matthew 27: 34; Psalms 69: 21). The offering of gall and vinegar in response to Jesus' agony and thirst was considered the cruellest of all his torments as it was his last.[47] The blind Roman soldier, Longinus, who pierced the side of Jesus with a spear, appears here too, but no mention is made of his being a Roman. He does indeed cry out in Latin upon regaining his sight, but in fact, all the Jews — rather unsurprisingly taking the author and audience into consideration — seem to prefer speaking Latin rather than Aramaic or another local language in *The Fifteen Places* (cf. the call of 'Cru-

---

43. See Trachtenberg 1993: 52.
44. See Stephens 1847–74, III: 89, ll. 6–12.
45. For a medieval Swedish version of Bonaventure's description of the Crucifixion, see Klemming 1860: 199–200. For Christiern Pedersen's discussion, see ChrPed. *Skr.* I: 359, ll. 14–15.
46. Lindgren 1993: 246.
47. On Jews as sponge-bearers, see Jordan 1987; Mellinkoff 1993, I: 132–33. Cf. *Toledot Yešu HaNoẓri*, where Jesus is given vinegar to drink while being mistreated in a prison in Tiberias (Schlichting 1982: 124):

     והי' עומד קשור שלושה ימים לילה ויום לא אכל ולא שתה וביום הרביעי התחנן לפני שר בית הסוהר ליתן לו מים לשתות לצמאו ויצו וישת ויבך וצעק ואמר עלי אמר דוד ולצמאי ישקוני חומץ ויבך בכי גדול

    And he was tied up for three days, night and day, with nothing to eat or drink. On the fourth day, he pleaded with the prison governor to give him some water to drink. But [the governor] commanded that he be given vinegar. He drank, wept, cried and said, 'David has said about me: "For my thirst, they gave me vinegar to drink" [Psalms 69. 21]', and wept bitterly.

cifige!' on fol. d4ʳ). Whether Roman or Jew, Longinus is led (or tricked?) by the Jews in *The Fifteen Places* into stabbing Jesus (fol. f3ᵛ, ll. 4–13):

> tha fremledhe iøderne een blijn*d*er man som hedh longinus oc wor een riddere och fick hannum een hwast spiuth i ha*n*s hender at han sette thet paa vor herre ihesu cristi welsignede sijde oc tijl stack saa hordelige at spiudet ingick i gemen sidhen oc i hierte*t* tha flodh want oc blodh vth for menniskens synder tha fick longinus sijne øgen igeen tha ropte han och sagde O fili dei miserere mei

> *Then the Jews led a blind man forth who was called Longinus and was a knight, and they placed a sharp spear in his hands. He held it against the blessed side of Jesus Christ and stabbed so forcefully that the spear pierced his side and his heart. Then water and blood poured out for the sake of men's sins. At that moment, Longinus regained his sight. Then he shouted saying, 'O fili Dei! Miserere mei* [O Son of God, have mercy on me!]*'*

The portrayal of Longinus as a Jew was not uncommon, as can be seen from several wall paintings from before 1500 in Denmark.[48] See, for example, the wall painting in fig. 3 from Jetsmark Church, northern Jutland (1474), in which Longinus is painted as a Jew in oriental fashion with a beard and dressed in a long kaftan.[49] In the wall paintings in Keldby Church (from 1325) and Skibby Church (1350), both on Sjælland, he is portrayed wearing a 'Jew hat'.

By placing Mary centre stage, *The Fifteen Places* allows us to see events as they evolve from her perspective, and the story of the Passion becomes more immediate and compelling. The moving and graphic descriptions show Mary's suffering as only a mother can suffer over her son, and they give rise to pity, compassion and collective pain. The readers of this devotional work, who respect and love Mary, approach the Passion through her eyes and share her emotions with her. However, this 'sharedness' or inclusiveness goes hand-in-hand with exclusiveness, and the Jews stand in stark contrast to the readers and Mary: they are not just the guilty cause of all this pain, but they choose to remain outside of this shared 'emotional community'. The readers react with compassion to the story of

---

48. See www.kalkmalerier.dk. On the representation of Jews in medieval Danish art, see Haastrup 1999 and 2003. The role of Longinus is also taken by a Jew in a couple of medieval Danish prayer books — see below.
49. See also Mentgen 2001: 387. It is, however, a Roman in the two-coloured costume of an executioner who is giving him vinegar and gall to drink in this particular wall painting.

Jesus and Mary's suffering, whereas the Jews are portrayed as revelling in its macabre gore and torture. They are, at best, 'flawed human beings without a heart'.[50] In this way, *The Fifteen Places* establishes a very powerful dichotomy: Mary is the utmost symbol of purity, nurture, comfort and motherhood; the Jews are pollutants, depraved tormentors and bringers of death. A similar contrast is established between Christ's beauty and the ugliness of the torments inflicted by the Jews; for example, Mary's words to Jesus (fol. g1^r, ll. 2–9):

> O thu alsom benediede antlede thu wast klare en noger sool och alle the engle i he*m*-merige ære the attraade ath see tegh Nw esthv giort dome[t>r] aff thin egen hierne oc blodh oc thet lede iødhe spoth som ær spyt paa teg

---

50. Rubin 2009: 104. Miri Rubin's book, *Emotion and Devotion*, unravels the meaning of Mary in medieval religious cultures, and includes an examination of the polemical situations around Mary and the location of the Jews within them.

There is, incidentally, an interesting passage in Old Danish concerning the Jews' view of Mary's virginity. It stems from a Christmas Day sermon in Uppsala, University Library, C 56 (*c*. 1450; Klemming 1893: 456):

> Kære wænær j scwllæ ey wnd*re* wppa. hwi wor he*rræ* wilde fødes aff a*n*nærs ma*n*s fæstæ møø Th*et* giorde ha*n* for thy ath jøde logh war saa. ath hwilkæn q*winn*æ so*m* barn fingæ. och wistæ ey fadhæræn. he*n*ne scwlde the stene j heel Och for thy wilde wor he*rræ*. ath thee wtro jwdene scwlde jeffwe wm ath ha*n* føddes aff skær møø. Æn wor frwæ fødde hanu*m* skær møø. aff the*n* hælgæ ande. och saa so*m* ha*n* siælw*er* wilde. ath hwn ey scwlde stenes j hiel Wor frwge war festh een ma*n* so*m* heth josep. och ha*n* war smydh Och jødh-*er*ne wilde ey troo. ath war he*rræ* war fødd*er* aff reen jomfrwdo*m* Wdhen kallede hanu*m* smidsins søn tha scwlle wy rættæ c*r*istne mænniskæ wndherstandæ ath war he*rræ* jhesus christus ær also*m*megthastæ gwdz søn j himærighæ. ær th*en* smidz søn. som smidhæ bodhe hymærighæ och joderichæ: och alth th*et* so*m* skappeth ær aff inkthæ. och scwllæ wy troo sanneligh och stadhelighæ. ath wor frwge war och ær skær møø. bode før æn hwn føde si*n* søn jhesum christum Och saa och sydhen ha*n* war fødd*er*. och bliffw*er* ewin-nælighe

> *Dear friends, you must not be surprised by our Lord wanting to be born of another man's betrothed. He did so because the law of the Jews was such that they would stone to death any woman, who had a child and did not know who the father was, and so our Lord wanted the unfaithful Jews to doubt whether he had been born of a pure virgin. And our Lady gave birth to him as a pure virgin by means of the Holy Ghost and so as he himself wanted, so she would not be stoned to death. Our Lady was betrothed to a man who was called Joseph and he was a smith. And the Jews did not want to believe that our Lord was born of pure virginity, but called him 'the smith's son' [cf. Matthew 13: 55]. So we right Christian people should understand that our Lord, Jesus Christ, is the son of God Almighty in Heaven; he is the son of the smith who forged both Heaven and Earth and everything that is created from nothing. And we should truly and continually believe that our Lady was and is a pure virgin, both before she gave birth to her son, Jesus Christ, and then also after he was born, and she shall remain so eternally.*

> *O most blessed face! You were brighter than the any sun, and all the angels that are in heaven longed to see you. You have now been blinded with your own brain and blood and the disgusting Jew spittle that has been spat at you.*

Marian texts, perhaps more than any other, portray Jews in opposition to Christianity on an intensely human and emotional scale.[51]

St Birgitta's *Revelations*

St Birgitta of Sweden (1303–73) was an influential religious figure throughout Christian Europe and her *Revelations* and monastic movement had a huge impact, particularly in Scandinavia, on religious writing. Two monasteries were established in Denmark, one at Maribo on the island of Lolland in 1418 and the other at Mariager in Jutland in 1446. Despite the existence of these two houses, there remain today just a few fragments of the main body of her work, the *Revelations*, translated from Latin into Danish.[52] There is, however, no reason to think that the entire corpus did not exist in Danish as translating the revelations into the vernacular was standard practice in the Birgittine monasteries, and we can certainly see

---

51. Heil and Kampling 2001.
52. The extant fragments are:

Fragment		Revelation
B.I.a	Copenhagen, AM 1056, 4°. xxvi–vii. 1^{ra-vb}	*Lib.* II 17: C–G
B.I.b	Copenhagen, AM 1056, 4°. xxvi–vii. 2^{ra-vb}	*Lib.* II 19: F–K
B.II.a	Copenhagen, AM 1056, 4°. xxv. 1^{ra-vb}	*Lib.* IV 23: 20–34
B.II.b	Copenhagen, AM 1056, 4°. xxv. 2^{ra-vb}	*Lib.* IV 34 – *Lib.* IV 35: 4
B.III.a	Copenhagen, AM 1056, 4°. xvi. 1^{ra-vb}	*Lib.* VI 23: 25 – *Lib.* VI 24: 2
B.III.b	Copenhagen, AM 1056, 4°. xvi. 2^{ra-vb}	*Lib.* VI 39: 66 – *Lib.* VI 39: 77
B.IV.a	Copenhagen, AM 79, 8°. I γ 1^{ra-vb}	*Lib.* VI 33: 10 – *Lib.* VI 34: 5
B.V.a	Oslo, National Archives, No. 84. 1^{ra-vb}	*Lib.* VII 26: 1–6; *Lib.* VII 27: 0, 2–4, 6–8
B.V.b	Copenhagen, AM 79, 8°. I γ 2–3. 2^{ra-vb}	*Lib.* IV 133: 7–8, 10–11, 13–14, 15–16
B.V.c	Copenhagen, AM 79, 8°. I γ 2–3. 3^{ra-vb}	*Lib.* IV 143: 7, 10–12; *Lib.* IV 144: 1, 3–4
B.VI	Copenhagen, National Archives, E338, 4°. 2^{ra-vb}	*Lib.* II 19: G–I

Editions and discussions of the Danish translations of St Birgitta's *Revelations* can be found in Brandt 1857: 103–04; Diderichsen 1931–37: 77–121, 293–334; Diderichsen 1935–36; Johansen 1959, and Adams 2000. The entire corpus exists in Old Swedish and a selection of the revelations exists in an Old Swedish-Norwegian mixture. On these and other various European vernacular versions of Birgitta's *Revelations*, see Morris and O'Mara 2000.

the influence of Birgitta's thinking and writing in other Danish works and iconography. Furthermore, we also know that the *Revelations* formed an important element in Birgittine sermons, and that preaching *ad populum* (to the people) was done in the vernacular. For example, in her *Rev. Ex.* 23, Birgitta calls for a clear, plain style of preaching that is easily understandable to the common people [*populus simplex*].[53] Many elements of Birgitta's *Revelations* and thinking would thus have been familiar to large numbers of common folk. The absence of an extant full translation of all the *Revelations* into Danish does, however, mean that the quotations in this section are necessarily in Latin.

We have already noted how Birgittine thought and spirituality influenced *The Fifteen Places* with regard to Mary spending the final fifteen years of her life visiting the fifteen sites where her son suffered. Another noticeable point of influence is the similarity between the *Fifteen Oes* (or *Quindecim Oraciones*) and *The Fifteen Places*.[54] Arranged around the *septem verba* (the seven sayings of Christ on the Cross that were often used in Christian devotional and contemplative works), the *Fifteen Oes* are Passion prayers to Christ that retell the story of the Passion and focus on Christ's suffering body. There has long been discussion about the authorship of these prayers and there now seems to be little doubt that they were not in fact composed by Birgitta.[55] However, in the fifteenth and sixteenth centuries (and even up until the modern day in some circles), Birgitta was viewed as the author (she was thought to have received the prayers from Christ in a revelation), and the prayers formed an important part of Birgittine spirituality.

In addition to the numerical parallel between the *Fifteen Oes* and *The Fifteen Places*, the descriptions of the many sufferings endured by Jesus are also similar. This is perhaps hardly remarkable as they both are describing the Passion for devotional purposes using highly stylised standard iconography, but some of the detail in the imagery is strikingly alike. For example:

The Fifteen Oes, Prayer 2 (Stockholm, National Archives, E 9061):[56]

> Recordare amarissimi doloris, quem sustinebas, dum perfidissimi Iudei sanctissimas manus et delicatissimos pedes tuos ad crucem obtusis clauibus afflixerunt et cum

---

53. A modern edition of this revelation can be found in Hollman 1956: 133.
54. *The Fifteen Oes* have been translated more recently into Danish by Sebastian Olden-Jørgensen 1994.
55. See Gejrot 2000.
56. Quoted from Gejrot 2000: 221–22. There are several different versions of the *Fifteen Oes* both in prose and verse, so the quotations here should be seen as sample texts rather than definitive representations of the prayers. Gejrot's article contains several examples from the diverging textual tradition.

non esses conveniens uoluntati eorum, in longitudem et latitudem corporis tui ad foramina per ipsos in cruce perforata ad perforandum delicatissimos pedes tuos dolorem super dolorem addiderunt sanctissimis vulneribus tuis et ita crudeliter funibus et cordis te distraxerunt et extenderunt in longum et latum crucis tue, vt dissolverentur omnes compagines membrorum tuorum.

Remember the very bitter pain that you suffered when the most perfidious Jews nailed your most sacred hands and most delicate feet to the cross with blunt nails, and not finding you in a pitiable enough state to satisfy their rage, they enlarged your most holy wounds the length and breadth of your body, and perforated your most delicate feet, and added pain to pain, and with ropes and cords cruelly stretched your body on the cross, pulled you out vertically and horizontally, thus dislocating all your limbs.

The Fifteen Places, fol. e2^{r-v}:

tha igenem slo iøderne wor herre ihesu høgre hand m*et* een stompt iern naule saa ynkelighe och saa hordelige at naufflen indgick oc blodet wdspranck saa bunne the reff oc lijner om kring wor herre ihesu welsinede wenster handh oc vdrecthe he*nn*e wedh korsseth førsth twert oc saa endelangt ath alle hwor herre ihesus ryghbeen sloues aff lede tha igemen slowe the wor herre ihesu høgre handh m*et* stompet iern naule saa ynkelige at naufflen ingick oc blodhet vdspranck Saa toghe the reebe ‖ oc liner och bunne om wor herre ihesu føder oc neder tryckte them til korsset saa hordhelighe ath alle wors herre ihesus ledemot the at skyltes saa at inth*et* bleff i sin rætte sted. tha lode the then ene fodh offuer gaa then anne*n* oc igemen slowe hans werduge fødder m*et* then stompede iern naule saa hordelige at naulen indgick oc blod*et* vdspra*n*ck

Then the Jews hammered through our Lord Jesus' right hand with a blunt nail so mercilessly and so hard that the nail entered and his blood spurted out. Then they tied ropes and leashes around our Lord Jesus' blessed left hand and stretched it on the cross, first horizontally and then vertically, so that every one of our Lord Jesus' backbones was struck out of joint. Then they struck a blunt iron nail through our Lord Jesus' right hand so mercilessly, that the nail entered and his blood spurted out. Then they took ropes and leashes and tied our Lord Jesus' feet and pushed them so hard into the cross that all of our Lord Jesus' limbs were dislocated so that nothing remained in its correct place. Then they placed the one foot over the other and perforated his delicate feet with the blunt iron nail so hard that the nail entered and his blood spurted out.

Not only is it the Jews who are performing the crucifixion in both works, but blunt nails, smashed ankles and hands, body stretching and a dislocated spine all feature graphically in the two texts. Although these similarities do not show that there was any sort of direct connection between the texts, they show that they were part of a common pool that shared imagery, motifs and narrative details. Another set of Birgittine prayers, the *Quattuor Oraciones*, was composed by Birgitta herself and forms part of the official *Revelations* corpus. These prayers also contain descriptions of the Jews crucifying Jesus. For example (*Quat. Or.* Δ 51) :

> Gloria immensa sit tibi, Domine mi Ihesu Christe, quia sustinuisti pro nobis humiliter, vt Iudei tuas venerabiles manus et pedes cum fune extenderent et ligno crucis crudeliter ferreis clauis affigerent, te quoque proditorem vocarent et super te scripto confusionis titulo suis verbis nefandis te multipliciter deriderent.
>
> *Unmeasured glory be to you, O my Lord, Jesus Christ, because you humbly endured for us that the Jews stretched out your venerable hands and feet with rope, that they cruelly fixed them to the wood of the cross with iron nails, that they called you a traitor, that they derided you in many ways with unspeakable words while above you was inscribed that title of confusion.*[57]

Elsewhere in these prayers (for example, *Quat. Or.* Δ 46–50), we read about the mocking, scorning, spitting, beating and scourging that took place during the trials of Jesus, and also about the frenzied atmosphere of the crucifixion itself. Jews appear in about twenty of Birgitta's other *Revelations*, largely in bloody depictions of the Passion. In *Lib.* I 59, we read Jesus' words to Birgitta:

> Ego non erubui illam contemptibilem mortem pro eis. Ego, sicut natus fui, nudus stabam ante oculos inimicorum meorum. Ego fui percussus cum pugno in dentes, ego tractus in crinibus cum digitis eorum, ego flagellatus flagellis eorum, ego affixus ligno cum instrumentis eorum et pendebam cum furibus et latronibus in cruce
>
> *I did not blush to die a contemptible death for them [i.e. the Jews], but stood there just as I had been born, naked before the eyes of my enemies. I was struck in the teeth with their fists; I was dragged by the hair with their fingers; I was scourged by their*

---

57. The 'title of confusion' refers to the inscription '(Jesus of Nazareth) King of the Jews' on Jesus' cross. See Matthew 27: 37; Mark 15: 26; Luke 23: 38, and John 19: 19–20.

> scourges; I was fastened to the wood with their tools, and hung on the cross together with thieves and robbers.⁵⁸

Pontius Pilate is, as in *The Fifteen Places*, fully exonerated of executing Jesus and the blame is placed on the Jews (*Lib.* I 37):

> Pilatus quippe sciuit bene filium meum non peccasse nec dignum aliqua morte. Tamen, quia timuit amissionem temporalis potestatis et sedicionem Iudeorum, iudicauit quasi inuitus filium meum ad mortem [...] Pilatus iudicauit eum propter peticionem et voluntatem aliorum cum timore quodam.

> *Pilate knew well indeed that my Son had not sinned and did not deserve death. However, because he feared the loss of temporal power and the sedition of the Jews, he reluctantly sentenced my Son to death [...] Pilate sentenced him due to fear, in accordance with the petition and intention of others [i.e. the Jews].*⁵⁹

The blood-thirsty tendencies of the Jews are further underlined by Jesus' story of the Temple incident (*Lib.* I 57):⁶⁰

> Ipsi eiecerunt me de templo et habebant perfectam voluntatem interficiendi me, sed quia nondum venerat hora mea, exiui de manibus eorum.

> *They [i.e. the Jews] threw me out of the temple and were entirely intent on murdering me, but, because my hour had not yet come, I escaped from their hands.*⁶¹

The Jews' murderous aspect is also reflected in their attempted killing of Lazarus,⁶² and the comparison of the Jews who sought to kill Jesus with Absalom who sought to kill his own father, King David.⁶³

Often Birgitta's aim in describing the Jews as evil and presenting them as figures of vice is to provide a gauge for measuring the behaviour of bad contempo-

---

58. Translation from Searby and Morris 2006: 162.
59. Translation from Searby and Morris 2006: 115.
60. Cf. Matthew 21: 12–17, 21: 23–27; Mark 11: 15–19, 11: 27–33; Luke 19: 45–48, 20: 1–8; John 2: 12–25. Cf. also the stoning of Jesus in Marine Issdatter's prayer book, Copenhagen, Royal Library, GkS 1614, 4°, fol. 15ʳ⁻ᵛ (Nielsen 1945–82, IV: 159 [no. 925e]).
61. Cf. Luke 4: 28–30. Translation from Searby and Morris 2006: 157.
62. *Lib.* IV 72; Searby and Morris 2008: 131–32.
63. *Lib.* II 5; Searby and Morris 2006: 185–88.

rary Christians.[64] By conjuring up a Jewish people comprising evil tormentors and killers of Christ, Christians could measure their 'godliness' against the Jews' 'ungodliness'. In the *Revelations*, Christians who act disgracefully are described as being more sinful than the Jews who abused and killed Christ. The Jews, after all, only acted out of envy and did not, according to Birgitta, know he was God,[65] and they 'only' killed his body[66] and crucified his humanity.[67] Christians, who should know better but choose to reject God, are much worse as they kill Christ's spirit.

Birgitta travelled widely, from Sweden to Norway and Spain, and later to Italy, and from there to the Holy Land via Cyprus.[68] Unlike many of her fourteenth-century contemporaries from Scandinavia, Birgitta could therefore actually have come into contact with Jews. In a small number of revelations, Jews living at the time of Birgitta are indeed mentioned. Fourteenth-century Jews, just like those of the New Testament, are described as obstinate,[69] and as being blind and hidden behind a veil.[70] This veil will drop at the second judgement and the blind Jews will see the truth, *viz*. that Jesus Christ is the messiah.[71] The Jews will ultimately be saved, but until then Satan has blinded them, hardened their hearts and uses them as tools for shamelessness and evil.[72] The current misery in which the obstinate Jews live is entirely justifiable and fair,[73] in other words they deserve their suffering as a just punishment for deicide. Indeed, the degraded state of the Jews was seen by the Church and its theologians as empirical evidence in support of the Christian faith and God's judgement. In *Epistula* 149, Augustine wrote that the Jews were allowed to survive after the Crucifixion in order to act as reminders of faith to Christians.[74] The Jews, scattered across the Earth as punishment for abusing and murdering Jesus, exist only for the benefit of Christians who are not to kill them, but keep them in a position of servitude:

---

64. For example, *Lib*. I 57 and *Lib*. IV 99; Searby and Morris 2006: 157–58 and Searby and Morris 2008: 178 respectively.
65. *Lib*. I 37; Searby and Morris 2006: 114–16.
66. *Lib*. I 41; Searby and Morris 2006: 120–24.
67. *Lib*. I 53; Searby and Morris 2006: 146–49.
68. On the life of Birgitta, see Morris 1999 (includes a comprehensive bibliography).
69. *Lib*. I 41 and *Lib*. II 3; Searby and Morris 2006: 120–24 and 180–84 respectively.
70. *Lib*. I 59; Searby and Morris 2006: 160–62; cf. II Corinthians 3: 13–16.
71. *Lib*. I 41; Searby and Morris 2006: 120–24.
72. *Lib*. IV 61; Searby and Morris 2008: 114. The alleged connection between the Jews and Devil is discussed further under Christiern Pedersen's *Book of Hours* below.
73. *Lib*. II 5; Searby and Morris 2006: 185–88.
74. *CSEL* XLIV: 356.

Therefore it was made to happen that they [the Jews] would not be eradicated so as to have their sect completely cease to exist. But it was dispersed throughout the world, so that, carrying the prophecies of grace bestowed upon us in order to convince the infidels more effectively, it would benefit us everywhere. And this very point which I am stating — accept it — inasmuch as it had been prophesied: 'Slay them not,' he said, 'lest at any time they forget your law; scatter them in your might.' Therefore they have not been killed in this sense, namely, that they have not forgotten those things which used to be read and heard among them. For if they were to forget the holy scriptures entirely (even though they do not now understand them), they would be undone in the Jewish rite itself, because, if they would know nothing of the law and the prophets, the Jews could be of no benefit.[75]

In a revelation about Mary and Martha, Birgitta ominously warns about the corrupting power of Jews on true believers.[76] However, Jews who are secretly Christian (and it is unclear who she has in mind here) are mentioned a couple of times and described as friends of Christ.[77]

The appearance of Jews in Birgitta's *Revelations* is thus most usually within the context of the biblical world, with just few references to her contemporary world. They are never presented as the stereotypes that we sometimes meet in other fourteenth-century European works (for example, as moneylenders, Host desecrators, child-killers, well-poisoners and so on), but are principally used in their biblical setting to draw parallels between their alleged wicked behaviour and that of Birgitta's coreligionists who abuse Jesus by neglecting their faith. Birgitta's writings adopt the *topos* of the Christ-killing Jew, and although perhaps not setting out to demonise contemporary Jews further (she has other fish to fry), she does use Jews in their Christian mythological role as Christ killers to illustrate aspects of contemporary Christians' behaviour and to call them to a religious life. However, a Christian writer's use of the image of the Jew solely as a tool to castigate fellow Christians, as opposed to attacking the Jews *per se*, does not of course in any way mean this writer hated Jews any less than those writers who did attack Jews directly; Birgitta did, after all, link the Jews with the Devil. For Birgitta's audience, being placed in the same category as the Jews, or being described as worse than a Jew, would presumably have been enough to shame any self-respecting Christian into a life of proper devotion and piety. 'The

---

75. Quoted from the (rather free) translation in Cohen 1999: 39.
76. *Lib.* IV 72; Searby and Morris 2008: 132.
77. *Lib.* I 41 and *Lib.* II 3; Searby and Morris 2006: 120–24 and 180–84 respectively.

Jew' as metaphor was apparently an established symbol of evil for Birgitta's audience. Her influential descriptions of the Passion were developed further in other works which, as we have seen in *The Fifteen Places*, did demonise the Jews.

Consolation of the Soul

Siæla trøst ['Consolation of the soul'] is a collection of (im)moral tales that illustrate the Ten Commandments. There are just two extant fragments (Uppsala, University Library, C 529, and Stockholm, Royal Library, A 109) in Danish, the remains of what was once a single impressive parchment manuscript dating from *c.* 1425. These fragments are very similar to the Swedish version of the text (found in Stockholm, Royal Library, A 108 ['Ängsö Codex']). The relationship between all the manuscripts has been investigated by Johannes Brøndum-Nielsen (1934) and Ivar Thorén (1942), and the Danish version has been edited and published by Niels Nielsen (1937–52). Unfortunately, some two thirds of the original Danish manuscript are now lost.

References to Jews are largely confined to biblical characters such as King Solomon,[78] Abraham and Sarah,[79] and Isaac and Rebecca.[80] There is, for example, the story of how the Jews in Jerusalem greeted Alexander the Great (332 BCE),[81] and of how Jerome (*c.* 347–420) spent fifty-five years living in the Holy Land to learn Hebrew so he could translate the Bible into Latin.[82] In *Consolation of the Soul*, the Jews together with Pilate are held responsible for torturing and crucifying Jesus (A 109, fol. 15^r):[83]

---

78. Mentioned in passing Nielsen 1937–52: 6–7 (cf. Birgitta, *Lib.* II 4; Searby and Morris 2006: 184–85).
79. Nielsen 1937–52: 110–11.
80. Nielsen 1937–52: 111.
81. Nielsen 1937–52: 118.
82. '**Sidhan** fik han swa storan kiærlikhet til the hælghe skrift, at ha*n* for in i iudha landit **oc** bleef thær j fæm aar oc half thridhiasins tiwo aar, oc lærdhe thera maal, oc vænde oc skreef the hælghe skrift af ebraisko, oc grezsco maal, oc j latine [*Afterwards, he grew to love the Holy Scripture so much, that he went to the land of the Jews and stayed there for fifty-five years, and learnt their language, and translated and wrote the Holy Scriptures from Hebrew and Greek into Latin*]' (Nielsen 1937–52: 8, ll. 10–14). Here, at least, there seems an acknowledgement of the Jews as bearers of the language of scripture, and perhaps also, a recognition of their special relationship to and status regarding the written text.
83. Nielsen 1937: 29, ll. 7–9.

> Tha sakkathe the ærliga quinnan migit storliga oc saghdhe: Ha*n* ær min gudh oc min hæ*r*ra oc min trøst. pylatus oc judhane the hafva honu*m* pint oc corsfæst.
>
> *Then the honourable woman sighed greatly and said, 'He [i.e. Jesus] is my god and my lord and my succour. Pilate and the Jews have abused and crucified him.'*

In addition to the usual charges of deicide, we find what in the first instance appears to be a short ethnographical description of traditional Jewish prayer in one of these tales. This story, about Nebuchadnezzar, is taken from the Septuagint (the Greek translation of the Bible), where there is an interpolation between verses 23 and 24 in chapter 3 of the Book of Daniel. Totalling 68 verses, the interpolation includes some connecting narrative and two poems (the words sung by the three young men in Nebuchadnezzar's furnace). The text is not found in the Hebrew Bible, is considered deuterocanonical by Catholics and apocryphal by Protestants. In *Consolation of the Soul*, we read about these two songs that purport to have been sung by the three young men in Nebuchadnezzar's furnace (C 529, fol. 5ʳ):[84]

> Thæn ene songin børghas swa **B**en*e*dictus es do*m*ine deus patrum nostrorum. thæ*n* songin plægha ma*n* sivnga vm lioghir daghana, **q**uatuor temporu*m*. Thæ*n* andre laafsongin børghas swa, **B**enedicte o*m*nia opera do*m*ini domino etc. thæn plægha man læsa j oftosongin alla helgha dagha, **I** honu*m* manas al creatur oc skabath thing at lofva oc vælsighna gudh.
>
> *The one song begins 'Blessed art thou Lord God, our Father'. This song is usually sung on Saturdays, four times. The other song of praise begins 'Blessed are all the works of the Lord, O Lord'. It is usually read at dawn (services) on all holy days. In it, all creatures and created beings are called upon to praise and bless God.*

Both of these songs are in the form of prayers, the basic element of which in Jewish liturgical tradition is the blessing (*brachah*; plural *brachot*). Most *brachot* begin with the words 'Blessed are You, Lord, Our God, king of the universe' (*Baruch 'atah* YHWH *[/'Adonai] 'Eloheinu melech ha'olam*). In the *Septuagint*, the first prayer referred to in the excerpt quoted above ('The Prayer of Azariah', Daniel 3: 25–45) takes the form of a penitential lament, that describes the destruction of the Temple as a fitting punishment for the sins of Israel. In *Consolation of the Soul*, all that is quoted is the opening of the *brachah*, which, being the opening

---

84. Nielsen 1937: 11, ll. 23–28.

phrase to the majority of Jewish prayers, does not tell us a great deal by itself. This is followed by some ethnographical and liturgical information — when and how often the prayer is recited, *viz.* four times on Saturdays. Could it be that the author of *Consolation of the Soul* had an actual Jewish prayer in mind? The quoted words are, after all, very similar to the *'Amidah* (or the 'Standing prayer'), which is indeed recited four times during Shabbat (Friday evening to Saturday evening).[85] Similarly, the author tells us that the second prayer ('The Song of the Three Young Men', Daniel 3: 52–90), is recited at dawn on all holy days. The short text quoted by the author is again similar to a Jewish prayer, in this case the *Hakol yoducha* ('everything will thank you'), one of the special *brachot* used at the beginning of the *Shema* (*šema'*, 'hear') prayer at Shabbat morning services.[86] However, the author is, of course, not referring to Jewish prayers at all, but to Christian practice, in which 'The Prayer of Azariah' is used as a canticle (or hymn), and 'The Song of the Three Young Men' (known as the 'Benedicte Dominum' in the Catholic rite) is recited at Lauds, the early morning service on Sundays and feast days. So what at first glance appears to be a description of contemporary Jewish liturgy in a non-judgmental manner is, in fact, an example of the 'christianisation' of exemplary figures from the Hebrew Bible.

Under the discussion of the ninth commandment, there is an interesting section about whether or not it is acceptable for a Christian to accept interest on a loan from a Jew. Between 'brothers', usury — the lending of money at interest — is forbidden in the Bible.[87] That usury was a sin is stated explicitly in a number of medieval works in Danish. Here, for example, in *Modus confitendi*:[88]

> Auaricia. Ffemthæ sÿnd See om tw haffuer syndhet i gÿrighet eller Vidzskaff, Om tw haffuer meth meghen attraa sammenlagth verdens godz, Om tw haffuer giort aagær, [...] Om tw haffuer noghet køpth paa thet at tw skulle seliæ thet dÿræræ

---

85. The *'Amidah* begins '*Baruch 'atah* YHWH [/*'Adonai*], *'Eloheinu, we'Eilohei 'avoteinu* [Blessed are You, Lord, Our God, God of our fathers]'. It is a daily prayer, recited three times on weekdays, four times on Shabbat and five times on Yom Kippur. The prayer is usually prefixed nowadays with the biblical verse '*YHWH [/'Adonai] śefatai tiftaḥ ufi yagid tehilatecha* [Lord, open my lips, my mouth shall speak Your praises]' from Psalms 15: 17. During the Middle Ages other verses were sometimes used to head the *'Amidah*, for example Deuteronomy 32: 3 or Psalms 65: 3. See Elbogen 1993: 38 for details.

86. '*Hakol yoducha, wehakol yešabḥucha, wehakol yomru 'ein kadoš ka*YHWH [/*'Adonai*]. *Hakol yeromemucha selah Yoẓer hakol* [All shall thank You, and all shall praise You, and all shall say, 'There is none as holy as the Lord!' All shall exalt You, Selah, You Who creates everything]'.

87. Exodus 22: 24; Leviticus 25: 35–37; Deuteronomy 23: 20–21.

88. Copenhagen, Royal Library, NkS 129, 4°, fol. 5ᵛ; Bruun 1866: 6.

> *Greed: The fifth sin. See whether you have sinned through greed or on purpose, whether you have with much craving collected worldly goods, whether you have practised usury, [...] whether you have bought something with the intention of selling in on at a higher price*

The punishment in hell for the sin of usury is described in the text concerning Paul's descent into hell found in the late fifteenth-century work *The Women Saints* (Stockholm, Royal Library, K 4, fol. 39ᵛ):[89]

> Syden soa han en annen stath, ful bothe af karlæ oc quinne, oc atæ alle theræ eghn tungæ. Tha sagdæ engellen til hannum: thet ær okærkarle oc alle met okær faræ ok engen miskund hafdhæ yuer hin fatuk, forti tha haue the teligh pinæ
>
> *Then he saw another place, full of both men and women, and they were all eating their own tongues. Then the angel said to him, 'These are usurers and those people who practised usury and had no mercy towards the poor, for this reason they are now being punished in this way.'*

However, as Jews and Christians were estranged from one another, and the Jews were not the Christians' 'brothers', they were permitted to make them loans to one another. Indeed for Jews, moneylending became one of the few occupations permitted them by the authorities. However, the section in *Consolation of the Soul* about taking interest on loans does not concern Jews who lend money to Christians, but rather Christians who lend money to Jews, and whether they can receive interest payments on these loans. It reads (Stockholm, Royal Library, A 109, fol. 66ᵛ):[90]

> **vm ogir**
> **Ma iac taga ogir af en jødha. ælla hedhninga. M**in kiære son thw skal inkte ogir taga af nogrom man. **H**afvir thw tagit ogir af en jødha. oc vestu nogra cristna mænnisko som the hafva thæt gozit orætteliga af swgit. [hæn]ne ma thw thæt gifva. æn thæt ma thw ey sælfvir behalda
>
> *On usury*
> *[Question:] 'May I take interest from a Jew or a heathen?'*

---

89. Brandt 1859: 25.
90. Nielsen 1937: 102, ll. 12–17.

> *[Reply:] 'My dear son, you may not take interest from anyone. If you have taken interest from a Jew, and you know of some Christian whose goods they [the Jews] have deceitfully tricked from him, then you may give it [i.e. the interest] to him, but you may not keep it yourself.'*[91]

It is difficult to imagine the circumstances under which a Dane could make a loan to a Jew, but nonetheless, readers are here being advised that they may not charge interest on loans to anyone. In accordance with Deuteronomy 23: 20–21, moneylending was technically permitted between Jews and Christians, so the idea that it was forbidden for Christians to practise moneylending at interest to everyone, not just Christians, would have strengthened the idea that usury was a 'Jewish activity' as they continued to lend at interest. Doubtlessly, this provoked hatred as it was an activity described as a grave sin by the Church.[92] However, the need to be able to raise capital quickly as the basis of a society capable of expanding its economy, waging war and developing its urban centres was sorely noted particularly by the secular authorities and ruling classes. The agreement suited both these Christians, who were able to acquire credit, and Jews, who had to make a living in the few occupations allowed them (*viz.* currency dealing and loans).[93] One of the consequences, however, was the Jews' growing dependency on the goodwill of the secular leaders whom they provided with capital.

After mentioning the Jews' greed in the Old Testament, Christiern Pedersen described Jewish and Christian moneylending in the contemporary world in his *Book of Miracle Sermons* (fol. 78ʳ, ll. 11–16):[94]

---

91. Cf. the sermon by Christiern Pedersen in his *Book of Miracle Sermons*, fol. 156ʳ, ll. 20–23 (ChrPed. *Skr.* II: 110):

> I Anden maade om han fonger noget gotz aff nogen som før haffuer fonget det vretferdige Det skeer naar nogen tager gaffuer aff iøder eller obenbare aager karle Saadanne gaffuer bør huer at giffue fattige folk Item de som anamme gaffuer aff tyffue røffuere eller doblere Eller aff nogre andre som de vide at saadant gotz fonget haffue vretferdige Det skwlle de fonge dem igen eller giffue det fattige folk

> *Secondly, if he receives goods from someone who has in turn obtained them unfairly (this occurs when someone takes gifts from Jews or obvious usurers), then each person should give such gifts to the poor. Thus, those who receive gifts from thieves, robbers or gamblers or from some other person who they know has obtained the goods unfairly, they should return them or give them to the poor.*

92. See Chazan 1997: 36–37 on this aspect of Jewish moneylending.
93. On usury and the Jews, see Parkes 1938: 269–382; Hsia 1995.
94. ChrPed. *Skr.* I: 243.

Her met merckiss besynderlige iøderne som waare offuer maade gerige i det gamble testamente oc ære en nw saa paa denne tiid Thii brwge dhe obenbarlige oger De haffue och mange stalbrødre i blant cristne menniske nw diss vær som bruge oger. gøre de det icke saa obenbarlige som de da gøre De det alligeuel hiemmelige oc forkaste deriss sielæ der meth thi det er i stor dødelig synd

This means in particular the Jews, who were extremely greedy in the Old Testament and who still are now at the current time, since they publicly practise usury. Unfortunately, they nowadays also have many companions among Christians who engage in usury. Even if they do not do so as blatantly as they [i.e. the Jews], they nevertheless do so secretly and thus condemn their souls as it is a great mortal sin.

As in Birgitta's *Revelations*, it shows again that the fact that Jews did not live in Scandinavia, does not mean that they were not mentioned in a contemporary context in the literature of the time (here, for example, the translator of *Consolation of the Soul* could simply have expunged them from his text), nor that their purported greedy and deceitful characteristics were thought to be unfamiliar to, and therefore didactically ineffectual for, a Danish public.

Sermons and Preaching

Although sermons were preached at least once a week in every parish church in the land, we do not find a wealth of extant sermon texts from medieval Denmark. There may be a number of reasons for this. Firstly, the often rather *ad hoc* nature of preaching means that there is frequently no written record. Secondly, the destruction of monastic libraries in the post-Reformation era as well as the fires that destroyed important manuscript collections, in particular in Copenhagen, in the eighteenth century mean that many sources may have been lost to us. A third complicating factor is that although preaching to the people — *ad populum* — would have been in the vernacular, the written records are often in Latin. Of the few extant sermon manuscripts in Danish,[95] only three (*viz.* Uppsala, University

---

95. We have just the following extant sermon manuscripts in Danish:
- Vienna, Austrian National Library, Codex Vindobonensis 13013 (fifteenth century);
- Copenhagen, The Royal Library, GkS 1390, 4° (*c.* 1450);
- Uppsala, University Library, C 56 (*c.* 1450);
- Copenhagen, The Arnamagnæan Collection, AM 783, 4°, fols 263^r–68^v (*c.* 1500);
- Christiern Pedersen's *Book of Miracle Sermons* (1515).

Library, C 56; Copenhagen, Royal Library, GkS 1390, 4°, and Christiern Pedersen's *Book of Miracle Sermons*) contain references to Jews. In this section, we will investigate two sermons, one from the manuscript C 56 and one from Christiern Pedersen's *Book of Miracle Sermons*, to demonstrate how the image of the Jew was used in vernacular preaching in Denmark.

A Sermon for the Fifth Sunday in Lent, Uppsala C 56 (*c.* 1450)

The manuscript Uppsala C 56 dates from *c.* 1450 and is now housed in the collections of the University Library in Uppsala, Sweden. Written in a north-eastern Skåne dialect, it contains nearly a hundred sermons in 369 folios.[96]

The sermon for the Fifth Sunday in Lent (also called Passion Sunday) begins with a thema in Latin 'Quis ex vobis arguet me de peccato? [*Which of you convinceth me of sin?*; John 8: 46]', and the pericope is then given in full in the vernacular (John 8: 46–59).[97] The reading is the story of a confrontation in the Temple grounds between the Jews (described as the children of the Devil in John 8: 44)[98] and Jesus, in which Jesus makes a number of claims about himself (concerning his eternality and divinity) and in which he instructs the Jews to believe in him and calls those worshipping at the Temple liars. In turn, the Jews accuse him of being a demon-possessed fraudster. The scene is highly charged and ends with Jesus slipping away before being stoned by the enraged Jews.[99]

In the exposition, the preacher talks at some length about Jewish evilness. He compares this evilness to that of his fellow Christians, and uses the figure of the deicide Jew as a scare tactic to cajole Christians towards a better way of living (Uppsala C 56, fols 83ᵛ–84ᵛ):[100]

> Framdelis j læstinne skulom wj mærkia wars herra jhesu christi tholomot oc judhane jldzsko oc dyeffwlsleka wredhe som sigx aff ytarst j læstinne at the toko stena oc wildo stena honum j hææl Wi læsom at judhanne waro folhoxe twem sinnom at

---

96. It is edited and published by Klemming 1893.
97. The sermon is published in Klemming 1893: 121–29.
98. The 'synagogue of Satan' also appears in Revelation 2: 9 and 3: 9. In Christian lore, Christ had two enemies, *viz.* the Devil and the Jews. The relationship between the two is investigated in detail in Trachtenberg 1993; Dahan 1990, and Lazar 1991.
99. Cf. Birgitta's revelation in *Lib.* ɪ 57 quoted above.
100. Klemming 1893: 123–24.

dræpa war herra jhesum christum før æn the honum korsfæsto Som først war tha the leddo honum oppa een ganzskan høghan bærgx klint oc wildo honum ther skiuta wt fore oc honum dræpa/ tha war han osynleken fore them oc gik ater til ryggia mit gønum theras hopp Swa at the j thy sinneno kundo honum enkte skadha Medh thesse forbannadha judhana maa forstandas syndogha menniskior the som ekke haffua stadugha troo til gudz eller hedhra honum medh sina godhgerninga Som propheten salemon sigher aff/ Troon ær dødh fore gudh wtan godhgerningana følgha trona Mædh thenna bergh klinten maa forstandas høghfærdogha menniskio hierta som hælder skiuta war herra fran sik medh hoghmod oc forbolinhet æn the wilia honum nær sik behalda medh ødhmiukt oc tholamot/ oc for thy liknas the widher høgh bærgh Som propheten dauid sigher Høgh bergh æro hiortomin tilflyningh/ oc bærghhællor jghelkattana/ Medh hiortenom som ær eet høghfærdoght diwr oc dierfft aff sik wndirstas dyeffwlin som sina wijst oc wmgængilsse haffuer altidh j høgfærdogx manz hierta/ oc widher jghelkattin som hwas ær aff sik oc stingx liknas dyeffwlssins stingande jnskiutilsser som menniskionne samwit rørir til wærldhinna bælde oc framhop til nya osidher j osidhoghan oc olofflikan klædhabonadh oc smælekhet widher sin jeffncristin Medh them som swa gøra haffuer war herra enga samwaru wtan hælder flyr bort fran them jo længer tha the bidhia til honum j thøleke akt

Furthermore in the reading, we should note the patience of our Lord Jesus Christ and the evil and devilish anger of the Jews, about which it says in the end of the reading that they picked up stones and wanted to stone him to death. We read that the Jews fully intended to kill our Lord Jesus Christ two times before they crucified him. The first time was when they led him onto an extremely high cliff top and wanted to push him off and kill him. Then he vanished in front of them and walked back straight through the middle of the gathered crowd. So that time they were unable to do him any harm. What is meant by these cursed Jews is sinful people, those who do not firmly believe in God and praise him with good deeds. As the prophet Solomon says about this, 'Faith is dead to God unless good deeds accompany faith.' [cf. James 2: 14–25] What is meant by this mountain cliff is the hearts of arrogant people who would rather push our Lord away with arrogance and haughtiness than keep him close with humility and patience; for this reason, they are also like the high mountain. As the prophet David says, 'High mountains are the place to which deer flee, and flat rocks are the fleeing-place for hedgehogs.' [Psalms 104: 18] What is meant by these deer, which are arrogant and reckless animals, is the Devil who always has his abode and company in the hearts of arrogant men. And what is meant by the hedgehogs, which are sharp animals that prick, is the Devil's pricking impulses that nudge people's conscience towards worldly arrogance and the hope of success in new abuses comprising immoral and unlawful clothing and insults towards their fellow Christians. Our Lord is not with people who behave like this, but he prefers to flee from them so much further when they pray to him with such purpose.

Of utmost importance in this exposition is the Jews' wickedness, but as we have already seen with some of St Birgitta of Sweden's revelations and as we shall see further in Christiern Pedersen's *Book of Miracle Sermons*, the Jews and their wicked behaviour are used as metaphors to represent unacceptable negative qualities found among some of the members of the Christian community. They are portrayed as the very essence of evil and therefore used as a gauge of godliness and as a means of comparison. Here the cursed Jews represent sinful Christians, and the high cliff, where the Jews intended to murder Jesus, represents the hearts of arrogant men and women in which the Devil is at work. The cruelty of the Jews is not explained by the sermon writer, presumably he took it for granted that the audience would be all too familiar with Jewish perniciousness, but he does provide examples of their evil doings in the exposition, in which, following in the tradition of John 8: 46, he goes as far as to touch upon a collaboration between the Jews and the Devil.[101]

Christiern Pedersen, *Book of Miracle Sermons* (1515)

Christiern Pedersen (*c.* 1480–1554) was born in Helsingør and studied in Roskilde as well as at universities in Greifswald and Paris. He became a canon and was the chancellor to the archbishop and chaplain of King Christian II whom he followed into exile after a series of revolts. Later, after being pardoned by King Frederik I, Pedersen settled in Malmö, Skåne, where he worked as an author and printer. He converted to Protestantism and played a central role in the Reformation in Denmark, not least as one of the translators of Bible into Danish.[102]

The Danish medieval sermon studies scholar, Anne Riising, wrote that there is no hatred directed towards the Jews in Christiern Pedersen's sermons,[103] but

---

101. See also the sections on Christiern Pedersen's *Book of Hours* and prayers below.
102. On the life of Pedersen, see Brandt 1882 and Jørgensen 2007.
103. 'I øvrigt forekommer der ikke i prædikerne noget egentligt jødehad, heller ikke i passionsprædikerne [*Generally there are no occurrences of actual hatred towards Jews in the sermons, nor in the Passion sermons*]', Riising 1969: 333. Yet the descriptions of Jews in Christiern Pedersen's Passion scenes are in fact full of spite, loathing and hatred.

this statement is in need of immediate qualification, if not outright dismissal. The Jews are all consistently presented in entirely negative terms and there is certainly no sense of rapprochement or warmth directed towards them. Pedersen rehashes the standard contemporary interpretation of the events defining the relationship between the Jews and the Church: the Jews were once God's chosen people,[104] who were sent Jesus,[105] whom they subsequently rejected.[106] However, the Jews did not just reject Jesus, they despised, mocked and hated him; their cruelty is especially highlighted in the sermon for Good Friday (discussed below). Contemporary Jews do not entirely escape Pedersen's attention either, and they are described as being punished for their obstinacy,[107] and as being greedy, criminal usurers.[108] They do, however, retain the possibility of salvation through Christ, a conversion that Pedersen in keeping with the theological thinking of the time seems to expect will happen one day in the future.[109] Apart from warning against Jewish moneylenders, Pedersen's sermons make no further mention of contemporary Jews. He largely uses the Jews and their lost relationship with God as a means of encouraging 'bad Christians' to a life of piety and devotion and to remind his audience of the reality of God's anger and punishment.[110] It should also be noted, that in his *Den danske Krønike* ['The Danish Chronicle', begun 1515, but never finished],

---

104. ChrPed. *Skr.* I: 233–34. There is more on supersessionism or replacement theology in the section on Christiern Pedersen's *Book of Hours*.
105. ChrPed. *Skr.* I: 144 ('iøde konge [*king of the Jews*]'), and 193 ('Men Iøderne som kaldiss gudz eget folk for vor herre serdeliss vdsent aff gud fader at frelse dem De skulle kastiss i helueidiss mørk [*But the Jews, who are called God's own people, because our Lord was sent especially by God the Father to save them, they should be thrown into the darkness of hell*]'). The Jews, rather than the heathens, were chosen by God because the heathens were initially incapable of comprehending Christian learning and the means of salvation, as they 'tiene aff guder oc bede til stock oc stene och dywr som døde ere [*worship idols and pray to sticks and stones and animals that are dead*]', ChrPed. *Skr.* I: 285.
106. ChrPed. *Skr.* I: 234, 284.
107. ChrPed. *Skr.* I: 150.
108. ChrPed. *Skr.* I: 243; II: 110 ('[…] om han fonger noget gotz aff nogen som før haffuer fonget det vretferdelige Det skeer naar nogen tager gaffuer aff iøder eller obenbare aager karle Saadanne gaffuer bør huer at giffue fattige folk [(…) *if he receives some goods from someone who has obtained them by unjust means. This happens when someone takes gifts from Jews or public usurers. Each man should give such gifts to the poor*]'), and 186 (builds on Matthew 21: 13).
109. ChrPed. *Skr.* I: 62. The salvation of the Jews is also mentioned in Pedersen's *Vor froe Tider* ['Hours of our Lady'] from 1514. The idea rests on the prophecy in Romans 11: 26. See also below.
110. Cf. ChrPed. *Skr.* II: 172–75, and see also Lausten 1992: 105.

Pedersen, in praising the crusading efforts of Christian I (reigned 1448–81), mentions contemporary Jews in Europe and the Holy Land and describes them as enemies of Christendom (Copenhagen, Royal Library, GkS 828, 2°, fols 79ᵛ–80ʳ):[111]

> thi hand kom hiid ath hand will ophöge den hellige kircke, hand radde och alle christne konger herrer förster, ath the skulle alle mandeligh striide med then hellige christeligh troens fiender, som er Törker och Jödher Hedninge och Ketter
>
> *because he [i.e. Christian I] came here [i.e. to Rome] wanting to exalt the Holy Church, he also advised all Christian kings, lords [and] princes to fight manfully against the Holy Christian faith's enemies, they are the Turks and Jews, heathens and heretics.*

The Good Friday sermon takes its pericope from John 18–19. Rather than being a translation, it is a vernacular paraphrase that adds a number of details and interpretative interpolations not found in the gospel text. For example, when the Jews call for Jesus to be crucified in accordance with their law (John 19: 7–8), Pilate becomes afraid, not of the Jews, but of God. As Pedersen explains (*Book of Miracle Sermons*, fol. 110ᵛ, ll. 32–36):[112]

> Her offuer sige doctores at han icke reddiss for iøderness low thii han vor inthet plectig vnder hende Men han begynthe at frøcte effter iøderniss ord at han skulle vere gwdz søn Oc at han hagde saa ladet hustruget oc kroned hannem
>
> *On this subject scholars say that he was not afraid of the Jews' law, because he was not bound by it; but he began to fear the Jews' words, that he [i.e. Jesus] was in fact the son of God and that he had had him scourged and crowned.*

In Pedersen's paraphrase of John's account of the Passion and the Crucifixion, we learn that the Jews acted as a crowd; they shouted and yelled, often *en masse*; they performed their actions cruelly and harshly; they are powerful and danger-

---

111. ChrPed. *Skr.* v: 515.
112. ChrPed. *Skr.* ɪ: 345.

ous, but held under the control of their religious leaders, and obedient to their written law.[113]

The exposition subsequently develops the theme of Jewish cruelty from John adding many examples not found in the gospel text. For example, after the arrest of Jesus in Gethsemane, the Jews took him to the city (*Book of Miracle Sermons*, fol. 112^v, ll. 25–30):[114]

> Her scriffue somme doctores ath den tiid de komme till den aa som løber mellem staden oc oliueti bierg offuer huilken der laa en spong oc bro som de pleyde at gonge offuer paa naar det vor høyt vande Der slebede de vor herre vden faare i vandet paa de hwasse stene meth rebene som de hagde om hanss halss oc liff Oc røcthe hannem om kwld i vandet en dog det vor icke swarlige dybt Der slebede de hannem bort oc igen till han vor saa gaat som halff død

> *Some scholars write about this that when they came to the river [Qidron] that flows between the town and the Mount of Olives, over which there was a wooden gangway and bridge that they used to cross when the water level was high, they dragged our Lord alongside in the water on the sharp stones with ropes around his neck and waist, and they pushed him over in the water although it was not very deep. They dragged him back and forth until he was as good as half dead.*

---

113. Examples:
    - A great crowd: 'en stor hob [*a great mass*]', ChrPed. *Skr.* I: 341; 'denne store skare [*this great crowd*]', ChrPed. *Skr.* I: 342.
    - Shouting: 'Da robede de alle [*then they all shouted together*]', ChrPed. *Skr.* I: 345.
    - Cruelty: 'vmildelige [*cruelly*]', ChrPed. *Skr.* I: 342; 'haardelige [*harshly*]', ChrPed. *Skr.* I: 342, 343.
    - Violence and power: 'iøderness wold oc mact [*the Jews' violence and power*]', ChrPed. *Skr.* I: 344; 'Josep aff arimathia som vor ihesu lønlige discipell for den fare han hagde for iøderne [*Joseph of Arimathea was Jesus' disciple in secret because he was afraid of the Jews*]', ChrPed. *Skr.* I: 347; 'kom til vor herre om naten for iøderness fare skyld [*he came to our Lord during the night as he was afraid of the Jews*]', ChrPed. *Skr.* I: 347.
    - Power of leaders: 'Chaiphas han gaff iøderne det raad at de skulde i hiel slaa ihesum [*Caiaphas advised the Jews to kill Jesus*]', ChrPed. *Skr.* I: 342.
    - Obedience to the written law: 'han skal dø effter lowen [*he is to die in accordance with the law*]', ChrPed. *Skr.* I: 345.

114. ChrPed. *Skr.* I: 350–51. There are similar descriptions in Danish literature of Jesus' journey after his arrest (see, for example, the prayer in Else Holgersdatter's *Book of Hours*, Copenhagen, Royal Library, GkS 1613, 4°, fol. 117^{r-v}; Nielsen 1945–82, IV: 51 [no. 857k] quoted later in this chapter under 'Prayers').

The identities of the servants who tied Jesus to a stone pillar and tortured him are to remain secret until Doomsday (*Book of Miracle Sermons*, fol. 112ᵛ, ll. 37–41):[115]

> Da ginge de ypperste iøder bort oc lode hannem sette i eth fengzell som vor i en keldere oc lode binde hannem der til en sten pillere oc befole nogre obenbare bewebnede skalke at bliffue hoss hannem oc tage hannem vell vare ath han engelediss vndkomme skulde Hwilke skalke som giorde hannem der hemmelig pine som han icke obenbare will før paa den strenge domme dag
>
> *Then the highly ranked Jews left and had him put in a prison that was in a cellar and had him tied to a stone pillar and ordered some armed blatant thugs to stay with him and guard him well so that he should not escape. He will not say who these thugs were that subjected him to secret torture until the harsh day of judgement.*

The torture of Jesus at the hands of the Jews is returned to again and again in the exposition.[116] The actual crucifiers, however, are referred to as 'bødlene [*the executioners*]', and not as being specifically Jewish, or indeed Roman for that sake, although it is clearly stated that the Jews lead Jesus to Golgotha.[117] Even during the raising of the cross everything possible is done to make the act as cruel and inhuman an event as possible (*Book of Miracle Sermons*, fol. 115ᵛ, ll. 4–8):[118]

> Der de hagde saa fest hannem till korsset da opregsde de deth met hanss verdige legeme Och lode det saa falde ned till iorden igen met reth foract at de der met hanss pine for øge skulde Siden reyssde de korsset op igen oc støde det saa haardelige ned i hwlen som det skulde stonde med hanss suare legeme
>
> *When they had fixed him to the cross, they raised it together with his honourable body, and they then let it fall down to the ground with real spite so that they would thus increase his pain. Then they lifted the cross up again and thrust it very violently down into the hole in which it was to stand with his heavy body.*

---

115. ChrPed. *Skr.* I: 351.
116. See ChrPed. *Skr.* I: 354, 355, 356.
117. The Jews accompany Jesus to the site of the crucifixion in ChrPed. *Skr.* I: 357. Whether the cross was raised before or after Jesus was fixed to it is also discussed at length in this sermon (ChrPed. *Skr.* I: 359–60).
118. ChrPed. *Skr.* I: 359.

The Jews never seem to miss an opportunity to humiliate, torment, injure, punish and mutilate Jesus and his body. Throughout the exposition, the Jews are constantly referred to as cruel, wolf-like, unclean, and reckless.[119] As in other works we have been looking at here, their malevolence is also directed towards Mary.[120] The sermon contains common elements of a Good Friday sermon, such as the blood curse,[121] details of the pain during the crucifixion,[122] and the piercing of Jesus' side by Longinus.[123] We also find the motif of 'Jew spittle' covering Jesus' face no less than three times.[124] Furthermore, it is claimed that the Jews' power to corrupt lies in their money which is why Pilate did not want to upset them.[125]

In spite of this appalling picture of the Jews painted by Pedersen, he twice quotes Jesus' call to forgive his murderers,[126] and he makes no actual call for revenge against the Jews. As has already been noted, Pedersen sees an eschatological necessity in the presence of the Jews as their ultimate conversion to Christianity plays a pivotal role in salvation history and the final cataclysm of destruction and redemption. Following their becoming Christians, the events of the End will take place. His sermons thus clearly demonstrate the contradicting Christian attitude towards the Jews: on the one hand, Judaism was the path to damnation, and on the other, the conversion and salvation of the Jews in the final days was anticipated.[127]

---

119. For example, 'vmildelige [*cruelly*]', ChrPed. *Skr.* I: 350, 351, 365; 'som en wlff der fanger i lom [*like a wolf that catches a lamb*]', ChrPed. *Skr.* I: 351; 'fule [*vile*]', ChrPed. *Skr.* I: 353, 356; 'fortwilede [*reckless*]', ChrPed. *Skr.* I: 354, 365.
120. For example, ChrPed. *Skr.* I: 364.
121. See ChrPed. *Skr.* I: 355.
122. See ChrPed. *Skr.* I: 354, 358.
123. See ChrPed. *Skr.* I: 364.
124. See ChrPed. *Skr.* I: 351, 352, 357.
125. Fol. 114ʳ, ll. 39–40 (ChrPed. *Skr.* I: 355):

> Han vilde oc haffue venskaff met iøderne oc mente at de skulde giffue hannem store penninge
>
> *He also wanted to have the friendship of the Jews and thought they would give him much money.*

126. See ChrPed. *Skr.* I: 360, 361.
127. The Jews can be saved if they allow themselves to be baptised; fol. 109ʳ, ll. 15–19 (ChrPed. *Skr.* I: 62):

> Men hwo som helst de waare Iøder eller hedninger Rig eller fattig Fribaaren eller træl Ung eller gammel Mand eller qwinde Som hannem kerlighe anammede meth en stadig tro Dem gaff han alle mact med dob oc cristendom ath bliffue alle samme gudz børn til den ewighe salighed

Prayers

There are over a dozen extant medieval prayer books and in all nearly thirty manuscripts containing prayers in Danish (largely vernacular translations from Latin, German or Swedish).[128] They all date from the period *c.* 1470 to *c.* 1520, in other words from the very last years of Catholic primacy in Denmark, and have only recently appeared in printed editions.[129] These prayer books were owned by noble women and were commissioned by them or written specifically for them. They were intended for private worship either at home or, in the case of those noblewomen who had become nuns (for example, at the Birgittine house in Maribo), in a convent. The prayers in each book are grouped by category; for example, prayers to the Holy Trinity, to the suffering Christ, to the Virgin Mary, to the saints; prayers of praise, thanks or petition; prayers for particular days of the calendar, and so on. These prayer books were very important for the religious life of the individual, and although each book was personalised for its owner's use, it is noteworthy that many of the same prayers appear in the different collections. It is clear that these prayers had a broader audience and impact than might otherwise be assumed when looking at each book individually. For a start, the extant prayer books represent just a fraction of what must have existed in the Middle Ages. Prayer was (and, of course, still is) a central part of Christian life and the influence of these prayers must have been enormous. However, as in the review of preaching above, a single representation of the Jews is difficult to distil as we are looking at different books with different writers and owners. Nevertheless, they do share a number of important features: they are all the same type of text from around the same period and they represent a similar popular religious view in which standard tenets of faith are mixed with legends and Christian folklore. In this section, we shall look at some examples of how Jews from biblical, early Christian and modern times are represented.

But whoever they might be, Jews or heathens, rich or poor, freeman or slave, young or old, man or woman, that receive him lovingly with a constant faith, he will give all of them through baptism and Christianity the power to all become God's children for eternal salvation'.

On Christian attitudes towards the fate of the Jews, see Lipton 1999: 112–35.

128. The manuscripts containing prayers in medieval Danish are listed and described in Nielsen 1945–82, v: 1–26.
129. They have been edited by Karl Martin Nielsen (1945–82) and published as five volumes by DSL. Research into these prayer books has thus only recently got under way and is still in early stages. The prayers' religious content and sources, for example, remain largely unresearched. See Lausten 1992: 82–92, and Hansen 2004. Medieval Swedish prayers have been published by Robert Geete (1907–09), and most recently investigated by Ingela Hedström (2009).

The Jews of the New Testament are described in unflattering terms. They are charged with rejecting Jesus, being in league with the Devil and acting violently towards Jesus, Mary and the disciples.[130] Prayers focusing on the Passion and Crucifixion in particular are awash with anti-Jewish imagery. The descriptions are full of violence and gory details and include popular elements that even contradict the events of the gospels. For example, the Jews alone, without Roman involvement, are responsible for the suffering and killing of Jesus (Copenhagen, The Arnamagnæan Collection, AM 75, 8°, fols 134^v–35^v):[131]

> velsignet være tiidh kerlige hierthe oc hælighe kors, po hweket tu ledst thin bittere dødh, velsignet være thin torne krune oc thit hælige spywdh, velsignet være kære herre thin modhers ouerwettis hierthe sorgh, velsignet være the naglæ, meth hwicke tu vast hordelige fest til thet hælige kors oc then beske drick som tu drackt for mik oc alle synduge menniske, velsignet være thin forfærelse tu hadde then tidh tu saat atu vost omgiuen meth the grume iødher vdy || thin horde oc beske pine, velsignet være tu fore then spot oc spe tu lest, ther the husstroge thit werdige legeme, velsignet være tu fore the horde bandh som tu wast bwndhen til stodhen medh, velsignet være thu fore thine helige fem wndher oc tit werdege legommes mange saar, velsignet være then ydherste daw, i hwicken som tu wilt haue thin retferdige dom och døme alle menniske hwer || æfther sine gerningher.

> *Blessed be your beloved heart and holy cross, on which you suffered your bitter death. Blessed be your crown of thorns and your holy spear. Dear Lord, blessed be your mother's deep-felt grief. Blessed be the nails with which you were fastened firmly to the holy cross and the bitter drink that you drank for my sake and the sake of all sinful people. Blessed be the consternation that you suffered, when, in your harsh and bitter pain, you saw that you were surrounded by the cruel Jews. Blessed be you for the ridicule and mockery you suffered when they scourged your precious body. Blessed be you for the harsh fetters with which you were tied to the pillar. Blessed be you for the five wounds and your holy body's many sores. Blessed be the final day on which you will have your just judgement and judge all people according to their deeds.*

---

130. See Lausten 1992: 84.
131. Nielsen 1945–82, III: 106 (no. 463). In these prayers, it is also the Jews without Roman involvement who trap and capture Jesus: Nielsen 1945–82, I: 88 (no. 18a), 124 (no. 30c); II: 41 (no. 177c), 61 (no. 193), 102 (no. 223a); III: 88 (no. 443a), 299 (no. 667), 306 (no. 673), 311 (no. 676); IV: 51 (no. 857k), 186 (no. 943), and 374 (1111a).

Several prayers note that it was not just a small group of Jews, but all the Jews together without exception, who captured Jesus (Copenhagen, Royal Library, GkS 1613, 4°, fol. 117ʳ⁻ᵛ):[132]

> och tha so han iødærnæ ko*mm*æ som hanom skullæ gribæ Tha kam iudas oc kiøsthæ he*r*ren for sin mwndh Ite*m* thieræs tal som hano*m* fongedæ waræ iiii hu*n*dræt ridindæ væbnæræ oc tho hu*n*dræt fodgongæræ It*em* xxx skyttær oc sex tii The som baræ bluss oc fæm tii som baræ lyktærnæ och th*e*r owær bødh kayphas allæ iødærnæ i ihersualem at the skullæ bodæ til hæst och til fodh beliggæ oliueti biergh til ath vedhæ hano*m* som ieth a*n*næt dywr It*em* mærk at tha he*r*ræn vor greben i yrtægarde*n* och bwndæn m*eth* stærkæ har rebæ so bittærligh at blodæt sprak aff allæ ha*n*s neylæ røddær oc døtzsæns farghæ var owær all hans anlæt oc tha vorthæ han so iamerligh draghen oc slæppter in i stadæn oc alt th*et* ther waræ i veyæn thornæ stienæ oc stokkæ tha droghæ the hanom vt owær oc so neder støttæ the hano*m* th*e*r vti m*eth* thieræs føddher och m*eth* knippælæ och op droghæ hano*m* igien vedh haræt och skieggæth

> *[...] and then he saw the Jews coming who intended to seize him. Then Judas came and kissed him on the mouth. The number of those who captured him was four hundred mounted squires and two hundred foot-soldiers. Also thirty archers, sixty who carried torches and fifty who carried lanterns and in addition to these, Caiaphas ordered all the Jews in Jerusalem to go on horseback or on foot and besiege the Mount of Olives to hunt him [Jesus] as if he were just another animal. Likewise, note that when the Lord was captured in the herb garden and bound with strong hair ropes so bitterly that his blood spurted from the roots of his nails and the colour of*

---

132. Nielsen 1945–82, IV: 51 (no. 857k). There is a parallel prayer in Copenhagen, AM 782, 4°, fol. 127ʳ (Nielsen 1945–82, III: 311 [no. 676]):

> Tha saa han iøderne ko*m*me til yrtegarden och ville gribe ham, Tha kyste iudas ham for synd mwnd. Item t*et* tall th*e*r ham fangede, th*et* vor iiii hwndrede veffnde oc ii hwndret fodgangere oc xxx skÿtter oc sex tÿ som bare løckterne, oc th*e*r vdoffwer bath cayphas ath alle the iøder so*m* vor*e* y iherussalem ath the skwlle baade thil fod oc hest belægge calwarie biergeth thil ath vynde ham oc bynde ham oc gribe ham som th*et* hagde være*t*h eth vskyllickt dywr. Amen.

> *[...] and then he saw the Jews coming to the herb garden and wanting to seize him. Then Judas kissed him on the mouth. Likewise, the number of those who captured him was 400 armed soldiers and 200 foot-soldiers and 30 archers and 60 who carried lanterns and in addition to these, Caiaphas asked all the Jews who were in Jerusalem to go on foot and on horseback and besiege the Calvary Mount to vanquish him and tie him up and capture him as if he were a dumb animal. Amen.*

death [i.e. the red of his blood] covered his face, he was mercilessly dragged and pulled into the city, and they dragged him over everything that was in the way — thorns, stones and sticks — and then they knocked him down with their feet and with cudgels and pulled him up again by his hair and beard.

The scenes of torture during the Passion are grotesque, and in this prayer for Good Friday the various sufferings inflicted by the Jews on the body of Christ are described in graphic detail for its reader (in this case the noblewoman Else Holgersdatter) to contemplate and meditate upon. Indeed, the description forms a parallel to the other Passion scenes we have already met (for example, in *The Fifteen Places*, St Birgitta's *Revelations*, Christiern Pedersen's *Book of Miracle Sermons* and his *Book of Hours*), and the text is worth quoting at length here as an example of the kind of descriptions of the Crucifixion found in devotional literature (Else Holgersdatter's *Book of Hours*, Copenhagen, Royal Library, GkS 1613, 4°, fols 117^v–20^v):[133]

> Om longæ fredagh løss xv p*ater* n*oste*r/ oc xv aue maria/ oc bliffwæ trolighuoss herræn i hans pinæ/ och see m*eth* ‖ hiertæns drøffuilsæ/ huræ han vortæ bwnde*n*/ och draghen/ fra ien do*m*mer och til the*n* a*n*ne*n* han vort slaghen vidh sit kinbien for annas høffdingh/ och mangæ fold spyttæth/ han waræ draghen fra kaypha oc grim-mæligh til talæth bwnden for hans øghen ieth kledæ oc sattæ hanom i iærnhelder all then nat ow*er*/ han war falskæligh kiærdh for pilato/ han war sænd til herodem/ oc ther førdh i iet hwit kledæ/ han war draghen igien fra herode*m* oc til pylatu*m* oc hardæligh bwnde*n* til stødæn/ It*em* mærk at vor herræ vort hudstrøgæn so v mildæligh/ och hardæligh/ och ønkkæligh hudstøgæ the hano*m* hans helligæ li-gom*m*æ/ at allæ vors herræ rygbien siøntæs allæ blodugæ/ oc baræ/ At allæ/ vors/ herræ indwollæ/ varæ til at see/ som iet syndær reffwæt kledhæ/ th*er* heng*er* pa ien gardh/ oc røræs modh allæ handæ vedær/ aff ræt bittær suedæ oc wærk/ oc frost/ oc kwldh/ tha neder seynædæ vor herræ ih*es*us hwos stødæn/ och hengdæ so m*eth* ar-men/ Tha fram løb ien aff iødærnæ/ och skar vor herræ løss fra stødæn/ och tha styr-tæ vor herræ ih*es*us neder vidh stødæn/ i sit verdugæ blodh/ hwilkæth th*er* waræ so dywpt/ som aff hans wærdugæ ligommæ randh/ at th*et* gik ow*er* ankælæn/ oc so støttæ the fulæ iøder ha*n*um ther nedær vti/ trækkæt/ so*m* blændh waræ m*eth* blodh/ och tradæ hano*m* m*eth* thieræs føddher/ och op ryttæ hano*m* m*eth* haræt och skieg-

---

133. Nielsen 1945–82, IV: 51–55 (no. 857l). These prayers also describe the Jews (not the Romans) as tormenting and crucifying Jesus: Nielsen 1945–82, I: 124 (no. 30d); II: 290 (no. 334i), 307 (no. 343f); III: 85 (no. 441j), 89 (no. 443b), 90 (no. 443d–e), 106 (no. 463), 320 (no. 686); IV: 160 (no. 925f), 162 (no. 925n), 394 (no. 1130c), and 436 (no. 1154c).

gæt/ So ath th*et* op gik m*eth* roodhæ/ oc so op droghæ the hanom blegh oc blodhughæ/ och th*er* han op‖kam/ tha letthæ han æff*ter* sinæ kleder/ Æn the gaffwæ hanom æy so longh hwillæ oc roo/ ath han mattæ foræ sægh vt i sinæ kledær/ Tha togæ iødærnæ reb oc linær/ och bwndæ om kringh vor h*err*æ i midiæ/ oc ryttæ hanom aff ien høgh stien trappæ/ so hardæligh och ønkkæligh at hans vælsignæth thænd*er*/ neesæ oc mwnd/ togæ i stien trappæn/ oc brustæ op at blødæ/ och ligo*m*met faldh longt vt i gadæn Siden giordæ iødernæ hano*m* ien thorn kronæ/ aff huassæsthæ thornæ/ och hardæ/ som iærn/ och satthæ pa hans vælsignæt hoffwæt/ oc nedhær tryktæ he*n*næ m*eth* storæ stænger/ oc huassæ spywdæ/ so hardæligh at kronen indgik at issæn/ so ath han sprak/ och hiernæn vt flødh/ so at the thornæ th*er* ind gingæ at hans anlædæ/ the møttæs m*eth* them so*m* indh gik at hans nakkæ/ och the thornæ th*er* ind gingæ at th*et* iænæ øræ/ the møttæs vid the thornæ th*er* ind gingæ ath th*et* annæt øræ/ So møttæs allæ thornæ*n* i hans wælsignædæ hoffw*et*/ so at inktæt siøntæs bart/ aff them so at hans haar/ neesæ oc mwndh/ ørnæ och skiegh/ waræ op fylthæ/ m*eth* alzo meestæ leffræth blodh/ oc til frossæt m*eth* alzo hordisthæ eggælæ oc fæk vor h*erræ* chris*t*us ih*es*us/ M sar i hans wælsignedæ hoffwæt aff then thornæ kronæ/ It*em* sidæn toghæ iødærnæ th*et* storæ kors/ oc thwngæ oc laghdhæ th*et* pa hans ømæ rygh oc saræ/ och so bar han th*et* ind til then stadh/ som ha*n* frælsæt os allæ appa/ och aff korssæns thynge oc ligo*m*mens vo*n*mektughiet/ Tha nedhær seynædæ vor h*err*æ ihe*s*us vnd*er* korss*et*/ oc korssæt fieldh pa hano*m*/ so ønkkæligh/ oc so hardæligh at allæ vors h*err*æ rygbien the skildæs aff laghæ/ och blodæt th*et* hanom so stridæligh nedh*er* randh/ at han haffdhæ inghen makt pa ligo*m*mens vegnæ/ Then iødæ som for hano*m* gik/ han støttæ oc sloo hanom i tændæren/ oc then iødæ so*m* bagh hano*m* gik/ han skiødh vor h*err*æ m*eth* korsseth/ so ønkkæligh/ oc so hardæligh/ at allæ vors h*err*æ fodspor stodh fullæ m*eth* blodh/ oc framdiels skiødæ iødærnæ vor h*err*æ oc so/ ønkkæligh/ oc so hardæligh m*eth* korssæt/ at vors h*err*æ vælsignædæ mwn/ oc neesæ/ togæ vt i stienhallen/ oc thændærnæ sloghes løsæ/ och thornkronen støttæs dybæræ/ nedær i hoffdæt/ æn hu*n* war førræ/ oc øgnen throdnæ meeræ vt aff hoffdæt/ It*em* mærk ydærmeeræ/ at tha ‖ the ka*m*e pa kaluarie locu*m*/ oc sættæ vor h*err*æ nage*n* pa stenen/ tha skalff h*er*ræn ih*es*us oc beffwærdæ/ och hans tændær samen sloghæs so hardæligh/ at the mattæ høræs longt/ It*em* mærk hwad h*er*ræn saffdæ th*er* korss*et* waræ redhæ/ Th*er* æffth*er* tha talæt h*er*ræn iet grædæligh ord och saffdæ/ O kors thu æst benedidæ o kors thu æst vey/ O kors/ i thik skal iæc tholæ værk/ oc slag/ so harde/ var th*et* mowelig/ at iæc ku*n*dæ tolæ død ydermeeræ/ gernæ vilde iæc th*et* lidæ/ før noge*n* bleffue for tabet O edælæ me*n*niskæ/ op ladh thinæ øghen/ och see til mægh/ och thenk i thit hiertæ/ huræ ønkæligh mit ligo*m*mæ th*et* swidær for thinæ skyld/ It*em* mærk the fæm thræn/ som h*er*ræn op gik til korss*et* Th*et* fyrstæ war kierligh*et*/ Th*et* a*n*net war thollighet/ Th*et* tridiæ ødmygh*et*/ Th*et* fierdhæ varafftigh*et*/ Th*et* fæmtæ war/ warafftighet ind til dødæn/ Th*er* æffter vt raktæ vor h*err*æ ihesus sielffwiliendis/ sinæ hellige armæ pa korssæth/ som han vildæ so seyæ/ til allæ syndugæ menniskæ/ mynæ kiæræ wænær/ kommær nw hidh til mægh/ Iæch star nw redæbon/ oc villæ giøræ gud fadher/ fult for edher/ Tha igiømen sloghæ the vors herræ ihesu christi høghræ handh/ meth ien stubbædhæ iærn naglæ sa hardæligh/ och so ønkkæligh at naglæn indgik/ och blodæt vt stank/ och sidæn lagdæ the reb oc linær/ om kringh vors herræ ihesu christi rygbien/ och sidæ bien/ the skildæs aff laffwæ/ och tha igiømmen sloghæ the hans vinstræ handh/ meth ien stubbædæ naglæ hardæligh vden allæ miscund/ Siden togæ the reb oc linær/ oc bwndæ om kringh vors herræ føddær/ oc droghæ them so hardæligh i korssæt/ at allæ hans ledmodh atskildæs/ oc allæ senær oc adræ synder sledæs/ oc brystbeenæt ræffnædæ/ oc hans hud brast/ oc inktæt aff hans ledmod waræ i rættæ skickilsæ/ oc so giømmen slowæ the hans føddær/ meth ien stumppædæ naglæ/ Item mærk tha vor herræ thyrstædæ/ Tha samæn blændæ the eddikæ oc gallæ/ och mirram/ som waræ alzom bieskistæ/ thet lodhæ the i ien swamp/ oc sættæ pa ieth longt glaffwen/ och op raktæ til hans mwndh/ at han skuldæ thet drikke/ Men ther han haffdæ smagæt thet/ Tha gadæ han ikki drukket thet/ tha opstøttæ the thet i hans mwndh/ oc i hans || øghen/ so at swamp-pæn brast/ oc then surhiet giøtz ower alt hans ligommæ/ som fuld war meth sar oc giordæ hanom bittærligh vee Ther æffter saffdæ han consumatum est/ Nw æræ allæ tingh fulkommæth/

On Good Friday read fifteen 'Our Fathers' and fifteen 'Hail Marys' and remain faithfully at our Lord's side during his torment and see with sorrow in your heart, how he was bound and dragged from the one judge to the other. He was struck on the cheek in front of Annas, the chieftain, and spat at many times.[134] *He was dragged from Caiaphas and addressed in a terrible manner, blindfolded with a cloth and placed in irons for the night. He was falsely accused before Pilate. He was sent to Herod, and there dressed in a white cloth. He was dragged from Herod back to*

---

134. Here we again have the motif of Jews spitting. Other examples from the prayer books include 'bedrøffues meth spyt och suøbe slagh [*was tormented with spittle and lashes of the whip*]' (Nielsen 1945–82, I: 87 [no. 16]); 'O menniske, tenck nw grangiffwelige y thit hiarte hwor ynckelig iøderne slowe ham vnder hanss anledhæ oc spitthædæ ham wndher hanss øgne [*O person! Contemplate now carefully in your heart how pitifully the Jews beat him in his face and spat up into his eyes*]' (Nielsen 1945–82, III: 314 [no. 679]); 'then tidh thu so thinæ søn ønkke-ligh trakteræs/ Aff the fulæ iøder/ then tidh han var spyttæt i sit || vælsignæth anlæt [*when you saw your son be treated so pitifully by the foul Jews. When he was spat at in his blessed face*]' (Nielsen 1945–82, IV: 5–6 [no. 838]); 'hans verdughe hoveth [...] var bespitthet aff iødherne Saa at hans verdughe anledhe var saa ynckerlicth till at see aff blodh och iødhe spøth som thet hadhe væreth eth spedalsth menniske [*his honourable head (...) had been covered in spit by the Jews, so that his honourable face was so pitiful to see on account of the blood and Jew spittle and looked as if it belonged to a leper*]' (Nielsen 1945–82, IV: 310 [no. 1045]).

Pilate and harshly tied to a pillar. Similarly, contemplate how our Lord's body was so unkindly whipped, and they scourged his holy body harshly and mercilessly, so that all of our Lord's spinal discs could be seen bloody and bare, and all our Lord's intestines could be seen, just like a torn piece of cloth hanging on a fence and blown in every direction by very bitter sweat and pain and frost and cold. Then our Lord Jesus collapsed by the pillar and hung fast by the arms, but one of the Jews ran forward and cut our Lord free from the pillar, and then our Lord fell down by the pillar into his honourable blood, and so much blood had flowed from his honourable body that it reached him above the ankles. And then the vile Jews pushed him into the filth that was mixed with blood and trod upon him with their feet and pulled him up by the hair and beard so that it was torn out at the root. And so they pulled him, pale and bloody, to his feet. And when he had got up onto his feet, he searched for his clothes, but they gave him neither peace nor respite long enough for him to put on his clothes. Then the Jews took ropes and cords and tied them around our Lord's waist and pulled him down a steep stone staircase so harshly and mercilessly that his blessed teeth, nose and mouth struck against the stone steps and blood burst forth, and his body fell the long way onto the street. Then the Jews made a crown of thorns for him from exceedingly sharp thorns, hard as iron, and placed it onto his blessed head. With long sticks and sharp spears they pushed down the sharp spikes and the crown of thorns so hard that the crown pierced the top of his head so that it split open and his brain flowed out, so that the thorns that were pushed into his face met the thorns that pushed through from his neck, and the thorns that entered through the one ear met the thorns that entered from the other ear. Then all the thorns met in his blessed head so that nothing bare could be seen of them: his hair, nose and mouth, ears and beard were filled with clotted blood and frozen solid with exceedingly hard icicles, and our Lord Jesus Christ received a thousand wounds in his blessed head because of that crown of thorns. Likewise, the Jews then took the great and heavy crucifix and pushed it down and lay it upon his sore back and wounds, and so he carried it into the town, [the cross] upon which he saved us all. And because of the weight of the cross and his body's feeble condition, our Lord Jesus collapsed under the cross, and the cross fell upon him so mercilessly and harshly that all of our Lord's spinal discs were dislocated, and so much blood poured from him, that he had no power left in his body. The Jew who was walking in front of him hit and struck his teeth, and the Jew who was walking behind him shoved our Lord so mercilessly and harshly with the crucifix that all of our Lord's footprints were filled with blood. Indeed, all the Jews shoved our Lord so mercilessly and harshly with the crucifix that our Lord's blessed mouth and nose hit the rocks and his teeth were struck loose and the crown of thorns was forced deeper down into his head than it was before and his eyes bulged further out of his head. Likewise contemplate further that when they arrived at the site of Calvary and sat our Lord naked on a rock, how the Lord Jesus shook and shivered and his teeth chattered so hard that they could be heard far away. Likewise contemplate what our Lord said when the cross was ready. Then the Lord spoke a tearful word and said, 'O cross! You are blessed! O cross! You are blessed! O cross! On you I shall suffer pain and blows so harsh, if it were possible, that I could suffer death even more, I would suffer it happily before anyone was lost. O noble person! Open your eyes and look at me and think in your heart how mercilessly my body is pained for your sake.' Likewise, contemplate the five steps that our Lord walked to the cross. The first was love. The second was patience. The third was humility. The fourth was perseverance. The fifth was perseverance until death. Then our Lord Jesus voluntarily stretched his holy arms out on the cross as if he wanted to say to all sinful people, 'My dear friends! Come now hither to me! I am ready now and want to placate God the Father on your behalf.' Then they pierced our Lord Jesus Christ's right hand with a blunt iron nail so harshly and so mercilessly that the nail went in and the blood spurted out. And then they lay ropes and cords around our Lord Jesus Christ's backbone and ribs. They were forced out of position. And then they pierced his left hand with a blunt nail harshly without any compassion. Then they took ropes and cords and bound our Lord's feet and pulled them so harshly against the cross that all of his limbs were dislocated, and his sinew and arteries were smashed to pieces, and his breastbone split open, and his skin burst, and none of his limbs was in its proper form. And then they pierced his feet with a blunt nail. Likewise, contemplate how our Lord was thirsty. They mixed vinegar and gall and myrrh which were extremely acrid. They soaked a sponge in it and placed it on a long spear and lifted it up to his mouth so that he would drink. But when he had tasted it, he was not able to drink it. So they forced it into his mouth and into his eyes so that the sponge burst and the sourness poured out over his body which was covered in sores and caused him bitter pain. After this he said, 'Consumatum est. Everything is now finished.' [After this follows a description of Mary's suffering and Jesus' death.]

Once again the Romans have been written out of the Passion story and it is the Jews who inflict horrible injuries on Jesus' body all of which are described in graphic detail. This is not the only prayer in which the Jews' role is contrary to that outlined in the New Testament version of events.[135]

---

135. For example, the Jews stab Jesus in the side with a spear: 'tha ko*m*me iø*de*rne igeen far*e*nde wth aff staden we*m*pte, oc een aff th*e*m stak ha*nu*m *m*eth eth spywdh i hans benedede sydhæ wth i gene*m* hierth*et* [*Then the Jews armed with weapons came from the city and one of them stabbed him with a spear in his blessed side through his heart*]' (Nielsen 1945–82, III:

The Jews' evilness is not confined to the life and death of Jesus however, but continues through history. In a prayer to St Stephen (the protomartyr of Christianity, stoned to death c. 34–35), we can read how the Jews hated him for his learning and life of virtue (Copenhagen, The Arnamagnæan Collection, AM 782, 4°, fol. 62[r–v]):[136]

> O sancte Staffen, dw vost stend i hiel th*et* aar som vor herr*e* tolde syn død oc pyne po th*et* hellige kors, aff iøde slæckt vostw født, oc en iomfrw haffw*er* tw dødh. Thw vost opfylt m*eth* then helliantz nade, oc tw lerde the*n* helye christelige thro, for dyn lerdom oc dyt dydelickt leffn*et* haffw*er* dw lydh stor had aff iøderne, then helliand haffw*er* talet aff deg m*eth* visæ ord mod theriss falske lerdom oc raad ville the haffe ow*er*wwndet deg oc sade at dw vosth en falskener oc en løyner mod guth oc y mod moyses law som vor i thet gamle e som the hylle før vor herre vor pint, oc thw haffw*er* saare straffet them th*er* for*e* oc sade them at the skwlle effterfylge the*n* helly prophete ih*esu*s, then herr*e* som tw selff saa staa y hemelen hoss syn faders høyre hand oc styrckit deg i all dÿn nød vden for ih*erusa*l*e*m the*n* tyd the stenede deg i hiel,

> *O Saint Stephen! You were stoned to death in the year our Lord suffered his death and torment on the holy cross. You were born of the Jewish people and died a virgin. You were filled with the Holy Spirit and you preached the holy Christian faith. You suffered much hatred from the Jews on account of your learning and your virtuous life. The Holy Spirit has spoken through you with wise words against their false learning and counsel. They wanted to defeat you and said that you were a fraud and a liar against God and against the Law of Moses which was what they worshipped in the old days before our Lord was tortured. And you have sorely punished them for this and told them that they should follow the holy prophet Jesus, the Lord, whom you yourself saw standing in heaven at his father's right hand and who*

---

90 [no. 443e]), and 'Iek hedhrer oc loffwer tek for the*n* drøwelse th*er* tw fek the*n* tiidh iøderne ko*m*me oc vildæ thin kæristæ søns been senderslaa/ oc th*er* the stw*n*gæ igømmen hans verduge sidhæ och wdhflødh vatn oc blodh [*I honour and praise you for the sorrow that you felt when the Jews came and wanted to smash your son's bones, and when they stabbed his honourable side, and water and blood flowed out*]' (Nielsen 1945–82, IV: 162 [no. 925n]). The Jews steal Jesus' clothes: 'O herre ih*esu christ*e the fwlæ iøder the røffuede thine clæder fra tek [*O Lord Jesus Christ! The filthy Jews robbed you of your clothes*]' (Nielsen 1945–82, II: 103 [no. 223d]); 'och thinæ kledær waræ kaste lodæ appa och skyfftæ iblant iødærnæ [*and the Jews cast lots for your clothes and shared them out*]' (Nielsen 1945–82, IV: 23 [no. 848]).

136. Nielsen 1945–82, III: 230 (no. 599).

> *strengthened you in your hour of need outside of Jerusalem when they stoned you to death.*[137]

Contemporary Jews are mentioned in passing and not particularly frequently. They appear, for example, together with heretics and bad Christians in a list of evil people and lost souls to be punished by God (Copenhagen, The Arnamagnæan Collection, AM 782, 4°, fol. 138ʳ):[138]

> ieg beder teg for then store sorg tw hadde then tÿd tw betenckte then store pÿne som mange onde menniske skwlle lÿde som vor hedninge och iøder oc kættere oc onde kristne som ecke ville nÿde tÿn død och pyness verskyld ath skwlle bliffwe fortabede.
>
> *I pray to you for the great sorrow you felt when you contemplated the great torment that many evil people would suffer, being heathens and Jews and heretics and bad*

---

137. The Jews' anger and stoning of St Stephen (Acts 7: 57–60) is described in a sermon in Uppsala, University Library, C 56 (Klemming 1893: 460): 'tha worde iødhær wredhæ meer æn før. och droge hanum aff stadhen [...] och stende hanum til døde [*then the Jews became even more angry than before and dragged him (Stephen) from that place (...) and stoned him to death*]'. A graphic account of the Jews' treatment of the Apostles is also found in the same manuscript (Klemming 1893: 163):

    Oc then timme apostoli predicathe gudz nadha Judei huthstrugho somma aff them, swasom, sanctus paulus sigher oc steende the j hiel somma, swasom sanctum stephanum, oc somma halshugo the, swasom sanctum jacobum, Oc somma medh eet oc somma annat, Thetta giorthe iøtha widher apostolos, For thy at the haffdhe ey ræt vndirstandilsse, oc gudhlek kænnedom, ther Moyses them kendhe, Moyses spadhe aff thy, at ihesus sculde føthas aff jwthom, ok manadhe them ther til at the sculde oppa jhesum troo, ok lydha hans kennedom,

    And when the apostles preached God's mercy, the Jews whipped some of them, as St Paul says, and stoned some of them, such as St Stephen, to death, and beheaded some of them, such as St James, and one way or the other with others of them. This is what the Jews did to the apostles, because they did not have the correct understanding and divine knowledge that Moses passed on to them. Moses foresaw that Jesus would be born of the Jews and commanded them that they believe in Jesus and obey his teaching.

    The same manuscript (Klemming 1893: 205) also mentions that 'judhane skulo wtkasta jdher aff sina kyrkior [*the Jews were to cast you (believers in Jesus) out of their synagogues*]'; cf. John 16: 2. Note also that in Marine Lauridsdatter's prayer book, God is thanked for saving the Christian reader from her enemies 'ßaa ßom thw frelste pedher apostell oc Sancte powell aff iøderniiss bande [*just as you saved Peter the Apostle and Saint Paul from the Jews' curses*]' (Nielsen 1945–82, ɪv: 250 [no. 996]).
138. Nielsen 1945–82, ɪɪɪ: 326 (no. 692).

> *Christians, who did not want to enjoy the reward of your death and torment so that they would be damned.*[139]

One book includes a prayer for the conversion of contemporary Jews to Christianity (Copenhagen, The Arnamagnæan Collection, AM 782, 4°, fol. 199^v):[140]

> oc beder iek teck ydmÿgelige at tw ville forlade oss alle vore synder oc styrcke oss alle i eth goth leffneth oc beskerme oss fran alle vore vwenner bode synlige och vsynlige oc omwenth alle syndige menniske hiarte effther thÿn ville, bode iøder oc hedninger oc alle the som ære gangne fran then hellige thro,
>
> *I pray humbly to you that you will forgive us all our sins and strengthen us all to live a good life and protect us from our foes, both visible and invisible, and convert all sinful people's hearts according to your will, both Jews and heathens and all those who have strayed from the holy faith.*

The image of the Jews in these prayer books does not differ from that we have seen in other religious works. The Jews are quite simply the enemies of God and Christianity, a claim often made by Jesus and Mary themselves in these prayers. The Jews are represented as a singular group of violent, demonic deicists who revel in torture and death.[141] It is difficult to know what sort of response these depictions were meant to elicit, but the graphic descriptions would have helped the reader form vivid mental images for meditation and devotion during prayer. They were to be used by the reader for contemplation and instruction and ultimately as part of a complex spiritual method of obtaining a state worthy of God's mercy and blessing.

---

139. Jews are also listed among heretics in the medieval Danish text 'Whom the Church Refuses Her Protection' (*c.* 1500 in the manuscript Copenhagen, The Arnamagnæan Collection, AM 683a, 4°), where they are placed first in a list of undesirables (Diderichsen 1931–37: 179):

    Tesse effter screffne forbywder then helghe kerke syn hegn oc beskermelse The førsthe ære jøder hetninghe oc kettere [...]

    The Church forbids the following people Her defence and protection: The first are Jews, heathens and heretics [...]

    The other excluded groups in this list include excommunicated men, usurers, robbers, suicides, blasphemers, monks with property, those who foster heathen children, traitors and children who die without being baptised.

140. Nielsen 1945–82, III: 403 (no. 782).

141. These four prayers refer to the Jews as Jesus' enemies, as violent and as a furious mob: Nielsen 1945–82, III: 295 (no. 662), 312 (no. 677); IV: 39 (no. 857c), and 159 (no. 925e).

Christiern Pedersen's *Book of Hours*

In 1514, Christiern Pedersen published a book for use in private devotion, *Vor froe Tider* ['Hours of Our Lady'], which was printed in Paris by Josse Badius Ascensius. The primer, or book of hours, has 200 or so folios and contains a number of depictions of, and references to, Jews.[142] As far as Jews are concerned, the theme that runs through the book is that although they were the first to receive the word of God, they were replaced in God's scheme by the pagans (i.e. the Romans and other Europeans), who converted to Christianity (for example, *Book of Hours*, fol. Bb4^v, ll. 15–18):[143]

> Du gaffst iøderne først dyne budord: och siden omwende hedningene til dig som dyrkede diefflene oc baade til aff guder
>
> *You first gave your commandments to the Jews, and then converted the pagans who worshipped devils and prayed to idols.*

Supersessionism or 'replacement theology' underlines the position towards Jews during the medieval and early modern periods. According to this view, God chose the Jewish people in order to prepare the world for the coming of Jesus. However, after his coming the special role of the Jewish people ended and their place was taken forever by the Church, the new Israel.[144] In Christian theology, we find examples of punitive or retributive supersessionism, which emphasises Israel's disobedience; having rejected the messiah, the Jews are rejected and punished by God for eternity and forfeit the promises they were due under the covenant.[145]

---

142. He gives his reasons for publishing the work in the preface (ChrPed. *Skr.* II: 274):

    Ere disse tider nw vdsatte paa ret danske ath hwer man dem forstonde skal [...] och icke saa grofflige som de førre vdsatte vaare i dhe andre tide bøgher

    These Hours are now translated into correct Danish, so that every man may understand them [...] and they are not [translated] as crudely as they have been translated earlier in the other Books of Hours

    In total, Pedersen's *Book of Hours* contains seven sections: 1) Hours of the Virgin; 2) Hours of the Holy Spirit; 3) Hours of the Holy Cross; 4) The Seven Penitentiary Psalms; 5) Litany; 6) Office of the Dead; 7) 'Many holy and godly prayers'.

143. ChrPed. *Skr.* II: 291.

144. On supersessionism, see Simon 1986; Wyschogrod 1989, and Soulen 1996.

145. This theology was espoused by Christian thinkers such as Origen (*c.* 185–254) in *Against Celsus* 4.22 (*ANF* IV: 506); Lactantius (*c.* 240–320) in *Divine Institutes* 4.11 (*ANF* VII: 109); and

There are also examples of economic or functional supersession whereby the role of Israel in God's plan is replaced by the Church. In other words, God transfers his plan for the people of God from a single group — the Jews — to a universal (catholic) church.[146] From a Jewish perspective, supersessionism is, at best, just plain nonsense as it runs contrary to the Hebrew Bible according to which the Torah is the eternal covenant between God and his people.[147] Supersessionist arguments, particularly those emphasising the Jews' punishment by God, were, and still are, often of an extremely sinister character and lie at the root of antisemitism in western culture.

Supersessionist theology is espoused a number of times in the prayers found in Pedersen's *Book of Hours*. The replacement of the Jews is stated explicitly (fol. Ee7^r, ll. 16–20):[148]

> Han fordreff oc vnder trychte hofferdighe iøder och phariseer aff deriss mact oc velde oc ophøgde ydmyghe hednynger i den hellighe kirke

---

later in 1544 by Martin Luther in *On the Jews and Their Lies On the Jews and Their Lies*, where, for example, he writes that (*WA* LIII: 418):

> Denn solcher grausamer zorn Gottes zeigt alzu gnug an, das sie gewislich muessen jrren und unrecht faren, solchs mag ein Kind wol greiffen. Denn so grewlich mus man nicht von Gott halten, das er solt sein eigen Volck so lange, so grewlich, so umbarmhertzig straffen, Und da zu stil zu schweigen, weder mit worten noch wercken troesten, kein zeit noch ende stimmen. Wer wolt an solchen Gott gleuben, hoffen oder jn Lieben? Darumb schleusst dis zornig Werck, das die Jueden, gewislich von Gott verworffen, nicht mehr sein Volck sind, Er auch nicht mehr jr Gott sey. Und gehet nach dem spruch Hosea .j.: 'Lo Ammj. Jr seid nicht mein volck, So bin ich nicht ewr Gott'. Ja es gehet jnen leider also, und alzu seer und schrecklich. Sie muegen deuten, wie sie wollen, So sehen wir das werck fur augen, das treugt uns nicht.

> *For such ruthless anger of God is enough evidence that they assuredly have erred and gone astray. Even a child can comprehend this. For one dare not regard God as so cruel that he would punish his own people so long, so cruelly, so mercilessly, and furthermore keep silent, comforting them neither with words nor with deeds, and setting no length of time and no end to it. Who would have belief, hope or love in such a God? Therefore this work of anger is proof that the Jews, surely rejected by God, are no longer his people, and nor is he any longer their God. This is in accordance with Hosea 1: [9], לא עמי [Not my people] You are not my people, so I am not your God.' Yes, unfortunately, this is how the situation is for them, truly a great and terrible one. They may interpret this as they will. We see the facts before our eyes, and these do not deceive us.*

146. See, for example, Augustine's *Epistula* 149 quoted above (*CSEL* XLIV: 356).
147. For example Exodus 12: 14–15; 31: 16–17; Deuteronomy 4: 2; 12: 32.
148. ChrPed. *Skr*. II: 313. Cf. also ChrPed. *Skr*. II: 329 and 357–58 with the same wording.

> He ousted and suppressed haughty Jews and Pharisees from their positions of power and authority and elevated the humble pagans to the Holy Church.[149]

We also find the following short text on replacement theology (fol. Gg6^r, ll. 15–24):[150]

> O du iherusalem som merker oc betegner den hellige kirke All cristne menniskes samfund Den alsommectiste gudh haffuer taledh erefulde ord om digh sigendiss) Ieg skall omuende till den hellige tro hedninge som lenge dyrket haffue diefflene och bedet til affgude at de skulle anamme cristendom oc elske mig deriss rette gud oc skabere

> *O you, Jerusalem, who stands for and represents the Holy Church, the community of all Christian people! God Almighty has spoken honourable words about you saying, 'I shall convert pagans, who have long worshipped devils and prayed to idols, to the holy faith, so that they accept Christianity and love me their true God and creator.'*

There are a couple of important points to note here. In addition to the Jews evidently being dropped from God's divine plan and the pagans now being converted and becoming the true followers of God (the 'new Israelites'), we see also how Jerusalem has been appropriated and turned from a terrestrial entity with a Jewish history into a 'heavenly Jerusalem', representing the Mother Church, that is the Christian community.[151]

The Jews' disobedience has not gone unnoticed according to Pedersen, and they are being punished for refusing to believe that Jesus was the messiah. Indeed, they are described as nothing less than the enemies of God (*Book of Hours*, fol. Aa4^r, ll. 11–15):[152]

> Thet giorde dw iøderne dyne vuenner til blysel oc skendsel fordy at de icke ville tro at han vor sander gud oc dyn eneste søn aff hiemelen

---

149. Cf. also *Book of Hours*, fol. Ff2^v, ll. 6–10 (ChrPed. *Skr.* II: 316):

> Gudz naade som førre gaffs dem som leffde effter moisi low Hun giffuiss nu alle i den hellighe kirke som leffue effter gudz budord

> *God's mercy, which previously was given to those living according to the Law of Moses, is now given to all those in the Holy Church who live according to God's commandments.*

150. ChrPed. *Skr.* II: 327.
151. We will see another example of the de-Judaising of Jerusalem in *Mandeville's Travels*, discussed below.
152. ChrPed. *Skr.* II: 283.

You made it a shame and disgrace for the Jews, your enemies, because they did not believe that he was the true God and your heavenly son.[153]

As in much other Christian literature of the time, the Jews are held responsible for the Crucifixion, and they are charged with mocking and tormenting Jesus (for example, *Book of Hours*, fols Hh4^v, l. 12 – 5^r, l. 20):[154]

> Ihesus cristus euige gudz søn sand gud oc mand vor greben longe fredagiss nath aff de grumme iøder [...] Och han bleff haardelige bunden oc vmildelige slagen och dragen aff samme forbannede iøder oc hedninger [...] Om midnatiss tide vor ihesus ledt till pilatum oc kerd oc beklagen aff mange løgnere oc falske vidende Siden bunde de hanss hender oc skyulte hanss øgen Oc sloge hannum haardelige mellem hanss herder (sigendiss) gæd til huo dig slo men du est saa viss oc klogh saa bespøtte de hanss deglige ansict saa ath han neppenlige kendelig vor. [...] LOnge fredag at morgen ropte samme forbannede iøder til pilatum sigendis Korss feste korss feste den ihesum som siger sig at være gudz søn aff hiemmelen [...] Da ropte de igen (sigendiss led borten: led borten oc korss festen)

> *Jesus Christ, son of the eternal God, true God and man, was seized by the cruel Jews on the eve of Good Friday. [...] And he was harshly bound and cruelly beaten and dragged off by the very same cursed Jews and pagans [...] At midnight, Jesus was led to Pilate and accused and charged by many liars and false*

---

153. Cf. also *Book of Hours*, fol. Ee1^r, l. 18 – ^{v}, l. 6 (ChrPed. *Skr.* II: 308):

> ALsommectiste gud fader sagde til gudz søn sid hoss min høgre hond dw skalt haue mact at dømme alle dine vuenner som icke ville verkende dig at være deriss gud och skabere || ligemectig met mig i guddommen Dw skalt anamme mandom oc din guddommelige mact skall obenbariss i iherusalem aff dyn predicken oc iertegen Och der skalt du hedriss oc eriss for en veldig gud mit blant dyne vuenner

> *Almighty God said to his son, 'Sit on my right hand. You shall have the power to judge all your enemies who did not want to recognise you as being their god and creator, equal to me in godliness. You shall be given human form and your divinity shall be revealed in Jerusalem through your preaching and miracles. And there you shall be praised and honoured as a mighty god among your enemies.*

And *Book of Hours*, fol. Ff2^r, l. 7 – ^{v}, l. 10 (ChrPed. *Skr.* II: 315):

> Ieg skal giffue euigh dom pine och skendsell offuer hanss vuenner som er genuordige iøder oc andre onde menniske.

> *I shall give eternal judgement, pain and shame to his enemies, who are the troublesome Jews and other evil people.*

154. ChrPed. *Skr.* II: 332.

witnesses. Then they bound his hands and covered his eyes, and beat him harshly between the shoulders, saying, 'Guess who hit you! Since you are so wise and clever!' Then they spat on his delicate face, so that he was hardly recognisable. [...] On the morning of Good Friday, the same cursed Jews shouted to Pilate, saying, 'Crucify! Crucify that Jesus, who says he is the son of God in heaven!' Then they shouted again, saying, 'Take him away! Take him away! And crucify him!'

In the crucifixion scene that follows this paragraph, there is no call for forgiveness (cf. Luke 23: 34). The actual crucifixion is carried out by 'them', which could refer to either the Jews or the Romans,[155] although we do later read that none of Jesus' disciples stood alongside him because they were so afraid of the wicked Jews,[156] and that Mary was afraid the Jews were going to take her son's body away from her after it was taken down from the cross.[157] The cruelty of the Jews and the fear that they could invoke seem to have known no bounds. Jesus himself

---

155. However, the Jews are named explicitly as the perpetrators of the torture and murder of Jesus in other prayers. For example, in ChrPed. *Skr.* II: 398, we read: 'Hill være ihesu christi venstre hond som aff iøderness vmilde hender egennem slaghen wor [*Hail Jesus Christ's left hand, which was struck through at the cruel hands of the Jews!*]'. And in ChrPed. *Skr.* II: 400, we read 'Hill være vor herriss ihesu cristi alderclariste ansict i hwess beskwelse alle engle glædiss til huilket alle menniske haffue hob oc begeerelse som forsmædelige bespøtted och aff iøderness vmilde hender slaget wor [*Hail our Lord Jesus Christ's most pure face, in the sight of which angels are joyful, to which all humanity has hope and desire, which was ignominiously spat upon and beaten by the Jews' cruel hands*]', and 'Hill være ihesu cristi alder ydmygeligste halss som for wor skuld aff iøderne meth reff och liner hardeligen betwinget wor [*Hail Jesus Christ's most humble neck which for our sakes was harshly pulled at with ropes and cables by the Jews*]'. In a prayer to Mary (ChrPed. *Skr.* II: 407), we read: 'dw hagde alder swariste oc beskiste pine i dit hellige hierte for din kæriste søn den tiidh han tracterediss saa vmildelige aff de slemme iøder [*You experienced the heaviest and most bitter pain in your holy heart for the sake of your beloved son at that time when he was being treated so cruelly by the evil Jews*]'. In ChrPed. *Skr.* II: 361, it says: 'Oc ath de vmildhe grumme iøder mwe gribe mig sla mig træde migh vnder deriss føder hustruge mig Oc syden pine migh till døde och plath vdsløcke mit naffn oc ere blant mennisken [*And that the cruel mocking Jews can seize me, beat me, tread me underfoot, scourge me, and then torture me to death and crudely erase my name and honour from among people*]'.
156. 'Enghen torde bliffue hoss mig for de grwmme iøder [*No-one dared stay with me for fear of the wicked Jews*]', ChrPed. *Skr.* II: 379.
157. 'den tiid dyn benedide søn wor neder tagen aff deth hellighe korss och lagd i dit skød och dw sost iøderne komme igen aff iherusalem och mente at de vilde tag[et>e] hannwm fra digh [*When your blessed son was taken down from the holy cross and laid in your lap, and you saw the Jews coming back from Jerusalem, and you thought that they would take him away from you*]', ChrPed. *Skr.* II: 410.

asks the Jews why they are so cruel, although his question remains unanswered (*Book of Hours*, fols D8ᵛ, l. 18 – E1ʳ, l. 4):158

> O i iøder som ieg er fødder aff paa mandommenss vegne hauer ønck offuer mig Gud fader i hiemmelen haffuer tilladet ath ieg er kommen i ederss hender hwi ere i saa grwmme oc vmilde emod mig ‖ oc aldrig fornøgiss kwnde met min pine Myne ord oc disse slemme gerninger som i gøre emod mig de skulle icke forglemmiss aff alle
>
> *O you Jews, of whom I have been born as a man, pity me! God the Father in heaven has let me come into your hands. Why are you so cruel and mean towards me and never satisfied with tormenting me? My words and these evil deeds which you do to me shall never be forgotten by all.*

The Jewish leaders in particular are cursed for their role in the Crucifixion (*Book of Hours*, fol. Ee2ʳ, ll. 1–4):159

> Gud fader skall giffue ewigh forbandelse offuer de vmildhe høffdinghe som pinthe och dømde hanss søn til døde
>
> *God the Father shall send an eternal curse over the cruel leaders who tortured and judged his son to death.*

The most disturbing story about the Jews in *The Book of Hours* describes how the Jews and their leaders plotted against Jesus from the moment he appeared on Earth. They wanted nothing more than to do away with him and obliterate his name and memory. As Jesus explains (fols D4ᵛ, l. 13 – 5ᵛ, l. 13):160

> Iøde høffdingene oc mine vuenner dhe baare stor awend ved mig oc sagde Naar skulle wii fonge lempe till at tage liffuid aff hannwm oc aldeliss vdslycke hanss naffn her i verden Kom der nogen aff dem til mig ath høre mine ordh eller see mine vnderlige gerninger oc iertegen Da giorde de deth aff ret awind som deriss hierter vore opfulde met at de kunde ‖ noget hørth eller seeth aff huilked de kwnde fongh-ed aarsage till ath kære paa migh oc dræbed migh fore Den tiid de icke kwnde fonge aarsaghe till aff mine ord eller gerningher ath straffe migh obenbarlige Tha

---

158. ChrPed. *Skr.* II: 379.
159. ChrPed. *Skr.* II: 309.
160. ChrPed. *Skr.* II: 376.

ginghe de borth och hemelige fortalede migh De knwrrede och stedsse i deriss hierter och giorde lønlighe raad huorlediss de kwnde komme migh aff dage De hagde stedsse saadanne ord som dieffuelen skød dem i deriss bryst (sigendiss) kwnde wi men først fonge liffuit aff hannwm tha gør han oss ey mere vmage thi han stonder icke mer op igen aff døde En mand som ieg daglige fødde til krop oc siel oc hagde altiid kerligh omgengelse meth (Som vor iudas) han forraadde mig oc gaff samtycke till myn død oc pine O euige gud fader send mig din naade oc lad mig op staa igen aff døde Siden skall || iegh selffuer heffne mig offuer mine vuenner Ieg bekender din kerlige vilge mod mig i det at iøderne ey lenge glædiss skulle aff myn død Thii at min clare opstandelse kundgøriss skal vdi iherusalem oc offuer all verden Oc det bliffuer dem till ydermere sorg i deriss hierter oc blysell oc skendsell aff alle andre O hemelske fader dw anammede mig for myn vskyldighed oc sette mig hoss din høgre hond till euig tiid Loffued oc velsigned være dw fordi ewindelige.

The Jewish leaders and my enemies hated me greatly and said, 'When are we going to have a chance to take his life and completely erase his name from the world?' If one of them came to hear my words or see my marvellous deeds and miracles, then he did so from the pure hatred with which their hearts were filled, and to try and hear or see something which they could use as a reason to charge me and kill me. When they could find no reason from my words or deeds with which to punish me publicly, they went away and secretly slandered me. They constantly grumbled in their hearts and secretly plotted how to kill me. In their breast, they always had the words that the Devil shot into them, saying, 'If only we could take his life, then he would cause us no more displeasure, as he will not rise from the dead.' One man, whose body and soul I nourished daily and whom I loved (he was Judas), betrayed me and agreed to my death and suffering. O eternal God, Father, send me your mercy and let me rise again after death! Then I shall personally take revenge on my enemies. I acknowledge your loving will towards me, so that the Jews for a long time shall not feel pleasure from my death, as my clear resurrection shall be proclaimed in Jerusalem and across the world. And it shall furthermore cause the Jews sorrow in their hearts and shame and disgrace from all other peoples. O heavenly Father! You received me because of my innocence and placed me at your right hand for all eternity. Praised and blessed are you for that reason forever and ever.

This text, written as a first-person account by Jesus, states that the Jews collaborated with the Devil in their efforts to kill him. The demonic Jew and the union between the Jews and Satan, the two arch-opponents of Christ, were both standard *topoi* in the medieval world view, and they occur several times in medieval Danish works. We saw, for example, a parallel to this in the sermon for the Fifth Sunday in Lent (Uppsala, University Library, C 56) discussed above, and Satan is also described by St Birgitta as acting through the Jews in at least one of her *Revelations* (*Lib.* IV 61). It would seem that popular religious texts in medieval Denmark taught their audience that the Jews were the Devil's henchmen, who as the living breathing representatives of pure evil walked the Earth to destroy Christendom. They are imbued with quasi-metaphysical characteristics and turned from human beings into the Devil's lackeys. The passage also contains allusions to 'secrecy' and 'conspiracy', allegations that have been made against the Jews in order to marginalise them throughout the medieval and modern periods.[161]

Not all pre-Christians, that is Jews from the time of the Old Testament, were necessarily bad, however (*Book of Hours*, fol. Cc6^r, l. 19 – ^{v}, l. 4):[162]

> Gode menniske baade aff thet gamble och ny testamente som rettelighe leffde her paa iorden ere opfarne til hannwm ath loffue hanss benedide naffn ewindelige || deriss sæde ere skickede i hemmelen oc de skulle side dom meth hannwm paa den yderste dag offuer leffuendis oc døde
>
> *Good people from both the Old and the New Testament, who lived righteously here on Earth have ascended to him to praise his blessed name for all eternity. They have been given seats in heaven and alongside him they shall judge the living and the dead on the Last Day.*

---

161. Cf. this description of the secret desires of the Jews in a sermon in Uppsala, University Library, C 56 (Klemming 1893: 31–32): 'Ok tha opinbaradhis the jldzsko fulla thankane mot gudz son, som førra ware lønlike j iudhana hierta som honu*m* pinto oc forradho [*Then (at the crucifixion) were revealed the angry, ugly thoughts against the Son of God, that previously had been secret in the hearts of the Jews, who tormented and betrayed him*]'. In the Passion text, Stockholm, Royal Library, A 31 (*c.* 1500), the Jews are accused of plotting Jesus' death in a secret council: 'iøderne ware i eeth hemelikt radh at tracteræ aff Ihesu døt [*the Jews were in a secret council to bring about the death of Jesus*]'.

   The attribution of secrecy was an essential ingredient in the religio-psychological shaping of perceptions of Jewry in medieval and modern Europe. Among Christian writers there was an impulse to expose these secrets, even in the most day-to-day aspects of Jewish life, and show that nothing Jewish was as innocent as it appeared to be on the surface (see Carlebach 1996; Deutsch 2012). In the introduction to his work *Iudeorum Secreta*, 'The Secrets of the Jews' on fol. a1^r, Pfefferkorn promises to reveal the secret affairs of the Jews so that his Christian readers will understand why they should be punished.

162. ChrPed. *Skr.* II: 310.

The final conversion of the Jews is also foreseen in *The Book of Hours* (fol. Kk2^r, ll. 2–6):[163]

> Israels folk som ere iøderne oc alle andre baade konger oc herrer offuer all verden skulle komme omsiger til den hellige tro oc tiene den alsommectiste gud samdrectelige
>
> *The people of Israel, that is the Jews, and all others, both kings and lords across the entire world, will finally come to the holy faith and serve the almighty God in harmony.*

The Jews have been held responsible by God and Jesus for the Crucifixion, their unsurpassed cruelty has been mentioned repeatedly, and they have been cursed for all eternity by God. Their role in God's plan has been taken over by the Christians, the builders of the New Jerusalem. They act as tools on Earth through which Satan operates. However, presumably due to the ultimate and universal truth of Christianity, the Jews will, according to Pedersen, eventually convert and find grace with God.[164]

Mandeville's Travels

Mandeville's Travels is an entirely fictitious mid-fourteenth-century description of a journey to the East undertaken by the English knight, Sir John Mandeville, and it is one of the few medieval non-religious works in Danish that mentions the Jews. It was a medieval 'bestseller' and survives today in over 250 manuscripts and 130 printed editions in at least ten languages.[165] The Latin versions of *Travels* are shorter than many of the vernacular versions (for example, the German, English and French ones). In all, five independent Latin versions have been recorded, but only the principal one, known as the Latin vulgate, has been printed. The printed edition of this vulgate text appeared in 1484 in Strasbourg and it is this

---

163. ChrPed. *Skr.* II: 343.
164. The universal nature of the Christian God is stated in Christiern Pedersen's *Book of Hours*, fol. Ff4^r, ll. 11–14 (ChrPed. *Skr.* II: 317):
    > Han er eth liuss och skin met huilket alle iøder och hedninge skulle optendiss til den christelighe tro. Och siden ære och loffue hanns benedide naffn
    >
    > *He is a light and ray with which all Jews and heathens should be lit up to the Christian faith, and [should] then honour and praise his blessed name.*
165. See Braude 1996: 136.

common abridged version from which the Danish translation has been made. I have used the text of this Latin edition from 1484, a copy of which is housed in Copenhagen (Royal Library, Inc. Haun. 2616) for the quotations below.[166] The Danish translation dates from 1434 or 1444, and is extant in four manuscripts of a later date (one of which is, however, only fragmentary).[167] Marius Lorenzen published an edition of the Danish version in 1882, which has been used here for quotations.

---

166. During the abridging process several references to Jews have been expunged. For example, in the English versions, Mandeville claims to have first-hand knowledge of a plan among contemporary Jews to murder all Christendom with a poison derived from an exotic tree:

English version (Seymour 1967: 139–40):

> And other trees that beren venym ayenst whiche there is no medicyne but ‹on› [*one*], and that is to taken here propre leves [*their own leaves*; text corrupt here] and stampe hem and tempere him with water and than drynke it; and elles he schalle dye, for triacle wil not avaylle ne non other medicyne. Of this venym the Iewes had let seche [*search*] of on of here frendes [*one of their kind*] for to enpoysone alle Cristiantee, as I haue herd hem seye in here confessioun before here dyenge. But, thanked be allemyghty God, thei fayleden of hire purpos, but alleweys thei maken gret mortalitee of poeple.

But the Latin vulgate reads (fol. e7^{ra}, l. 27 – ^{b}, l. 2):

> Contra venenum quoque de quarto genere arborum stillans. solum est intoxicato remedi|um vt de proprio fimo per puram aquam distemperato bibat.
>
> *The only thing to be done against the poison that drops from the fourth type of tree is to drink a concoction of one's own excrement mixed with clean water.*

And subsequently the Danish translation has (Lorenzen 1882: 100, ll. 3–7):

> Jtem hoo so*m* vor for gifue*n* aff teth eder, som vd aff t*eth* fieræ træ fong*iss*, ta er ha*nn*um ikcæ ann*it* til hielpp: Ha*n* skal blandæ sith eygit møk m*eth* *r*ent vatn oc sigæ t*eth* j giøm*m*e*n* een *r*en cludh oc drikcæ t*eth*, ta fong*er* ha*n* bodh.
>
> *Futhermore, whoever is poisoned by the poison which can be obtained from the fourth tree, cannot be helped by any other means: He must mix his own excrement with clean water and sieve it through a clean cloth and drink it; then he will be healed.*

167. The extant manuscripts are:
  • Stockholm, Royal Library, M 307 (previously K 31; dated 1459);
  • Stockholm, Royal Library, M 306 (1584);
  • Odense, Karen Brahe Library, E III 6 (late sixteenth century);
  • Copenhagen, Royal Library, GkS 3559, 8° (1575).

The datings are taken from Helge Toldberg in *KLNM* xi, *s.v.* 'Mandevilles rejse', cols 309–11. For an overview of the four extant Danish manuscripts and their relationship to one another and the Latin archetype, see Seymour and Waldron 1963, and Bradley 1969, 1976, 1993 and 1999. As the Danish translations of *Travels* have been made from the Latin vulgate text they are shorter than many other vernacular versions.

Mandeville's Travels provides us with a mirror of medieval knowledge and fantasy about the East, and almost all scholars who have worked with the book agree that it represents a remarkably tolerant universalist view in its descriptions of 'the Other'.[168] The book describes a host of 'Others' (for example, Greek Orthodox; Jacobite, Syrian and Nestorian Christians; Muslims; Hindus; Tibetans, and Mongols), who are all presented in positive or neutral terms, and whose humanity is underlined throughout the work. However, there is one notable exception to this favourable presentation: the Jews.[169] The book includes a number of short descriptions of Jews, all of which are negative, and they are something of an aberration in the overall tone of the book. Indeed, whereas the other cultures and peoples described seem to be in a state of passive, naive (even primitive) otherness, the Jews are portrayed as being deliberately different and cultivating otherness.

There are some revealing comparisons between the beliefs and adherents of the different Abrahamic faiths. In their view of the Jews, Christians and Muslims can, it would seem according to Mandeville, find some common ground:[170]

> Merk, at Saraceni siæ Iødernæ ath varæ megit ondhæ, mest forty at tee ikcæ hollæ gutz logh, som thøm se*n*d er m*eth* gutz buth Moyse.

> *Note that the Saracens [i.e. Arabs or Muslims] say that the Jews are very evil, mainly because they do not keep to God's law which was sent to them by God's messenger Moses.*

Of all the Peoples of the Book, the Jews are the lowest, and they are also accursed by the Muslims. Not following but rather perverting God's law was a standard accusation against the Jews by Christian writers, and, as we shall see later, the charge forms the basis of Johannes Pfefferkorn's allegations and polemics against his former coreligionists. In a description of Muslim beliefs about the afterlife, a sort of Paradise of the senses, there is, however, the erroneous suggestion that Christian and Jewish scripture share the same view about the location of the afterworld:[171]

---

168. Relevant works with extensive bibliographies include: Waters Bennet 1954; Campbell 1988: 122–62; Deluz 1988; Ridder 1991; Seymour 1993; Braude 1996; Tzanaki 2003.
169. See Braude 1996; Greenblatt 1991: 50–51; Tzanaki 2003: 229–32.
170. Lorenzen 1882: 72, ll. 6–7.
171. Lorenzen 1882: 63, ll. 2–21.

J muæ oc vidæ, at the Saracen*er* ok hetn*i*ngæ oc allæ and*ræ*, som ikcæ æ*ræ* C*r*istnæ eller Iødh*er*, te thro, ath ikcæ er and*et* h*em*mæ*r*igæ, ter som godæ oc helgæ me*n*niskæ j blifuæ skullæ efth*er* t*et*tæ neruæ*r*endes liff, som vy her vdh y lefuæ, vdh*en* th*et* P*a*radiis, som paa iorden er, th*er* som vo*ræ* forældræ Adam oc Eua fo*ræ* therris vlidelssæ vo*ræ* vdh scutnnæ ov vth kastæ. Tee siæ och, ath th*er* ryndh*er* honikh, melk oc vin, oc at the faa th*er* costæligæ hus fo*ræ* th*ø*m bigdæ m*eth* gul oc sølf oc kostæligæ stenæ oc allæ ho*n*næ legemligæ løst oc glædæ til euig tyd, effter thi som h*er* huer fortiænt hafuer. Tessæ forscrefnæ fa*ræ* thi ver blindæ, effther ty at tee hafuæ ikcæ tee helly trefollichets thro, oc tro ikcæ po*n*næ Ih*esu*m C*h*r*istu*m, gutz enigæ søn. Jt*em* C*r*istnæ oc alle som døptæ æ*ræ*, oc Iøder, the troo oppa tet he*m*melskæ P*a*radiis, oc at allæ me*n*niskæ efter tø*r*res godge*r*ningh*er* skulæ ther hafuæ løn meth gudh oc nydæ oc see guts cla*ræ* enlydhæ oc n*er*uæ*r*elssæ met vbeg*r*ifuælich ewinnælig glædæ til euig tiidh.

You should also know that the Saracens and heathens and all those, who are not Christians or Jews, believe that there is no other Heaven (where good and holy people will be after this current life which we are living here) than that Paradise that is on Earth and from which our parents, Adam and Eve, were removed and cast out because of their sin. They also say that honey, milk and wine flow there, and that they will have exquisite houses built for them of gold and silver and precious stones, and [there will be] all sorts of sensual pleasure and joy for all eternity, according to what each person has earned in this life. These aforementioned people are unfortunately lost, as they do not believe in the Holy Trinity, and do not believe in Jesus Christ, the only son of God. Christians and all those who have been baptised, and Jews, believe in celestial Paradise, and that all people according to their good deeds shall receive their reward there with God and enjoy seeing God's bright face and presence with incomprehensible eternal joy for all eternity.

The intention here is to denigrate Muslims by mocking their belief in a paradise of carnal delights — Christian polemicists accused them of all sorts of lecherous behaviour — and comparing this belief to the pure, spiritual ideals of Christians (and, according to this writer, of the Jews).[172]

---

172. However, the facts here seem to be wrong. There is little common ground between the elaborate Christian imaginings of the afterlife and that of the Jews. Judaism concentrates on the Earthly realm, and although affirming the survival of the soul after death, the hereafter or world-to-come (עולם הבא, *'olam haba'*) is largely considered a mystery. An underworld called Sheol (שאול, *še'ol*), is however mentioned in the Hebrew Bible (for example, Proverbs 9: 18; Deuteronomy 32: 22; Amos 9: 2), and the concept is probably due to Hellenistic influence. With the exception of two apocryphal texts (the Book of Enoch and II Maccabees), descriptions of the

An interesting point to note, and one for which there unfortunately is not sufficient space for a full investigation here, is the fact that many of the descriptions of Jews in the Latin original are substantially longer and have been abridged in the translation into Danish. This shortening has, in fact, expunged some of the anti-Jewish material in the Danish version. For example, the Danish translation of the section above ends with the words 'til euig tiidh [*for all eternity*]', but the Latin original is longer and continues (fol. d3^{ra}, ll. 12–17):

> Attamen iudei quia contra scripturas suas sanctissime et indiuidue trinitati contradicunt et christo obloquuntur qui est vera via nesciunt quo vadant
>
> *Nevertheless, the Jews, who contrary to the teachings of their scriptures oppose the most holy and indivisible Trinity and abuse Christ (who is the true path), know not where they are heading [i.e. to damnation].*

As can be seen, the Jews' inability to understand scripture and their abuse of Jesus are not included in the Danish translation. The Muslim story of the Jews not torturing Jesus before his death is another example of abridgement in the Danish translation of the Latin original:

Latin version:[173]

> Item liber dicit || iudeos perfidos fuisse. quod Ihesu eis primum a deo missum et tanta ac talia facienti miracula ac prodigia credere noluerunt. quodque per ipsum tota gens iudeorum fuit digne decepta. ac merito illusa per hunc modum. Ihesus in hora dum proditor iudas eum pro signo traditionis osculabatur. posuit per methamorphosin figuram suam in ipsum Iudam. Sicque iudei in ambiguo lumine nocturni temporis pro Ihesu capientes Iudam ligantes. trahentes. deridentes. in fine crucifixerunt. putantes se omnia facere Ihesu. qui protinus capto et ligato Iuda. viuus ascendit in celum. descensurus iterum ad generale iudicium in die finali. Et addit iudeos falsissime vsque hodie nos christianos suo mendacio decipere quo dicunt se crucifixisse Ihesum. quem nec retingerunt.

---

world-to-come are very vague (see Johnston 2002: 69–124). The company of God in a celestial Paradise as a reward for good deeds is not a Jewish belief. In Christian theology, where 'otherworldliness' and the City of God are central, the afterlife in heaven is more clearly defined as a place of eternal life where those who are pure will find eternal joy in the vision and presence of God's essence.

173. Fols d3^{vb}, l. 30 – d4^{ra}, l. 28.

The book [i.e. the Qur'ān] speaks of the treacherous Jews, because they do not believe that Jesus was sent from God and performed many and great miracles and prophetic signs. Also all the Jewish people were worthily deceived by him and better deluded in this way: Jesus, just at the moment when Judas betrayed him with the sign of surrender by kissing him, put himself into the likeness of Judas by means of metamorphosis. And thus the Jews in the uncertainty of the night-time light captured Judas instead of Jesus, bound him, dragged him off, mocked him and finally crucified him, in the belief that they were doing all this to Jesus, who, as soon as Judas was captured and bound, ascended alive into heaven to descend a second time for the Final Judgement in the last days. And it adds that the Jews right up until today are deceiving us Christians most falsely when they say that they crucified Jesus, whom they did not capture.

Danish version:[174]

Jte*m* si*æ* S*a*race*ner*, at Iødernæ æræ vantro och gioræ illæ, at the ikcæ villæ thro Ihe*su*m, som thøm aff gud se*n*dh*er* wor. Te thro oc ikcæ, at han villæ ladæ sek pinæ af Iødernæ, men at Ihesus ford til he*m*mæ*r*ygiss, och Iødernæ pintæ een a*n*ne*n*.

The Saracens say that the Jews are infidels and are evil in not wanting to believe Jesus, who was sent to them by God. They also do not believe that he allowed himself to be abused by the Jews, but that Jesus went to heaven and the Jews abused someone else.

This story is based on Sūrah 4: 157–58 in the Qur'ān:[175]

157. And because of their [*the Jews'*] saying: We slew the Messiah Jesus son of Mary, Allah's messenger — They slew him not nor crucified, but it appeared so unto them; and lo! those who disagree concerning it are in doubt thereof; they have no knowledge thereof save pursuit of a conjecture; they slew him not for certain,
158. But Allah took him up unto Himself. Allah was ever Mighty, Wise.[176]

---

174. Lorenzen 1882: 65, l. 17 – 66, l. 2.
175. The Qur'ān (القرآن, *al-qur'ān*, 'the recitation') is the principal religious text of Islam, revealed to the prophet Muḥammad during the seventh century CE and considered the final revelation by God. A Sūrah (سورة, *sūrah*, 'chapter') is a chapter in the Qur'ān of which there are 114.
176. Translation from Pickthall 1992: 113.

Although not stated explicitly in the Qur'ān, the interpretation is that at the time of his capture Jesus was replaced by another man at the last minute, possibly whilst carrying the cross, and this man (usually Judas Iscariot, but Simon and a watchman have also been mentioned as likely candidates), rather than Jesus, was crucified. Again, however, we find common ground between Christians and Muslims: they both agree that Jews are infidels, evil and deceitful. The belief that the Jews did not capture and torture Jesus is described as 'vantro oc villelsæ [*heresy and error*]',[177] so including this Qur'ānic story and using it in *Travels* serves in fact only to affirm the Jews' guilt and deicide.

The legend of the Lost Ten Tribes locked up in the Caspian mountain range is also presented in a rather condensed fashion in the Latin vulgate and subsequently also in the Danish version.[178] In other continental versions, the Jews are awaiting their imminent release by the Antichrist, which explains why throughout the world they continue to learn to speak Hebrew: so that upon the arrival of the Antichrist, Jews throughout the world will recognise one another and be able to band together and destroy all Christendom.[179] This tale of an international Jewish conspiracy against Christians which uses Hebrew as its secret vehicle is, however, absent in the Danish version, which reads:[180]

---

177. Lorenzen 1882: 66, ll. 2–3.
178. The story of the Ten Tribes in the Caspian Mountains is discussed in detail in Anderson 1932.
179. In their teachings on the Book of Revelation, some later influential Danish churchmen and theologians claimed that the Antichrist will be of Jewish descent (for example, Blædel 1884: 821–24, and Kok 1878: 89; cf. Wolff 1878: 385–96). On Blædel, Kok and Wolff, see Lausten 2007a: 53–117.
180. Lorenzen 1882: 158, ll. 7–15. For the 'full' story see, for example, the English version of *Travels* (Seymour 1967: 192–94). The Latin vulgate has just the following (fol. g9^{vb}, ll. 11–27):

> Et inde in meridiem per aliquot dietas potest venire ad primas Caspie alpes. que descendendo descendunt in occidentem vsque ad amazoniam de qua tractatum est insula mulierum. Intra quas alpes retinetur maxima multitudo iudeorum decem tribuum israel. per dei voluntatem ita inclusa vt in copiosa numerositate non possint a nostra parte exire quamuis aliqui pauci nonnunquam sunt visi transisse. haberent autem competentem exitum circa insulam Amazonie. sed illum regina diligenter o[b]seruar.

> *And from that place in the south, it is a few days' journey to the first Caspian Mountains, which stretch down westwards as far as Amazonia, an island of women, about which has [already] been written. Held back in these mountains is a huge number of Jews belonging to the Ten Tribes of Israel, thus enclosed by the will of God, so that they cannot leave in abundant numbers for our part of the world. Should, however, a few at some time be seen crossing, they would nevertheless have to exit around the island of the Amazons, but their queen carefully keeps watch.*

Oc tæde*n* synder ud noger dags ferd ta ko*mmer* ma*n*d jntil the førstæ steenbiergæ aff Caspan, huilkæ steen biergæ strekcæs ne*ter* tel Amasonia*m* veste*r*ud, aff huilkit Amaso*n*ia til for*e*n er sc*r*efuit, oc udi te bierghæ boo ma*n*gæ Iødh*er* innæluctæ aff te thy slekt*er*, som thædh*e*n jkcæ ud kommæ ku*n*dæ ude*n* siælden, at nogher ko*mmer* thæth*e*n, hoo thædæn skal, ha*n* skal fre*m* at Amasonia*m*, oc drotni*n*gen stædær thøm jkcæ fre*m* at kommæ.

And from there a journey of several days southwards, then you come to the first Caspian Mountains, whose rocky mountains stretch westwards down to Amazonia, about which I wrote earlier. And in these mountains live many Jews, locked up, [descendants] of the Ten Tribes, who are unable to leave there except rarely. For someone to leave there, he must go towards Amazonia and the queen will not let them advance.

The short Danish version does, however, still manage to draw our attention to two significant 'facts' about the Jews. Firstly, they are so weak, unmanly and unwarlike, that the Amazon women — women, no less! — are capable of containing them.[181] And secondly, they are a landless people, displaced from the centre (Jerusalem) to the margins, prevented from returning, and presumably laying claim to Israel, which

---

The story of the Jews imprisoned in the Caspian Mountains can also be found elsewhere in East Norse, *viz.* in the Old Swedish tale *Aff konung Alexander* ['On King Alexander', from *c.* 1380]. Here we read how King Alexander locked the 'filthy, cannibalistic, red Jews' in the mountains (see Klemming 1862: 130–33 [ll. 3945–4044]). The story of these 'red Jews', widespread in the European Middle Ages, is dealt with in detail in Gow 1995.

181. The unmanly Jew also appears in one of Pedersen's sermons. He claims that ever since crying out for Jesus' blood (Matthew 27: 25), Jewish men have been cursed with menstruation (ChrPed. *Skr.* I: 355–56):

> Ieg er wskyldig aff denne retuise mandz blod Iøderne robede Hanss blod skal komme offuer oss oc vaare børn Det skede oc saa aff gudz heffn || Thii de finge oc haffue alle blodsot saa lenge de leffue men verden stonder Men de hagde icke trod at der skulde kommet saadan heffn der effter

> *[Pilate:] 'I am innocent in this righteous man's blood!' The Jews shouted, 'His blood shall come over us and our children!' This happened through God's revenge. That is why they all got and still have menstruation as long as they live and the world stands. But they had not thought such revenge would come from this.*

The bloodthirsty Jews who brought about the death of Jesus were forever more to bear the badge of their crime: menstruation. Jewish men were thus thought not to be like other men. Their character and sex were ambiguous: a male exterior but with female bleeding. The only way to replace the blood they lost was by ingesting new blood. And so the myth of the menstruating male Jew became one of the contributing factors to the belief that Jews commited ritual murders and drank their victims' blood.

spiritually, if not politically, now belonged to Christendom.[182] It seems that unlike the continental versions, the Danish *Travels*, while supporting its readers' sense of Jewish antipathy, views Jewish subjugation throughout the world and for all eternity as a fact. Although they may be inherently hostile, they are under the control of the Christians (or here the Amazons) and pose no serious or noteworthy threat.

There are also a number of descriptions of monstrous races in the book, and it is not impossible that some of them build on Jewish stereotypes, a sort of hidden allusion or depiction of Jews in disguise. For example, Mandeville writes about a dog-headed race, the 'Cynophaly' (*Cynocephali*), who worship the idol of an ox and are extremely devoted:[183]

> Tæden oc ofu*er* [t*eth* vestræ haff far man ind vdi eet rygæ, heth*er* Natu‖me*ra*m [...] T*eth* falk, so*m* ther fød*ess*, hafuæ hofuith som andræ hundæ; [tee hetæ in g*r*eco Cynophaly [...] Te bedæ oc allæ til een oxæ, oc ter for*æ* bær huer t*err*æ the*r* j sith ænlidæ een oxæ aff guld eller aff sølff.

> *From there and across the western sea one travels into the kingdom called Natumeran [...] The people who are born there have the head of a dog; they are called Cynophaly in Greek [...] They also all worship an ox, for which reason they each wear [the image of] a golden or silver ox on their face.*

We have here a clear parallel to the worshipping of the Golden Calf (Exodus 32: 1–6) and the use of the dog to represent Jews.[184] By providing the calf-worship-

---

182. The continental and English versions of *The Travels* also contain another story that has been interpreted by Benjamin Braude (1996) as an attempt to obscure the Jews' connection to the Holy Land, namely that Noah's son Japheth, who is traditionally believed to be the father of the Europeans (based on Genesis 10: 5), is in fact the father of the people of Israel.

> And of the generacoun of Iapheth is comen the peple of Israel and though that wee duellen in Europe.
>
> (Seymour 1967: 161)

By contradicting the events of Genesis 10–11, and writing the Jews out of the history of the Holy Land, *Mandeville's Travels* presents the Christian worldview of the post-Crusades era. This 'de-judaising' also provides a parallel to the appropriation of Jerusalem seen in Christiern Pedersen's *Book of Hours* earlier in this chapter. Christians were intent on lessening the strength of the Jews' historical and spiritual claims to the Holy Land and Jerusalem, which acted to strengthen their own claims to the land and provided additional justification for their creed. However, Rosemary Tzanaki (2003: 186) argues that the author's intentions may not have been so far-reaching.

183. Lorenzen 1882: 103 l. 23 – 104, l. 14.
184. See *Iudeorum Secreta* p. 26: 15, with note.

pers with dog-heads, they are deprived of their humanity-defining attribute and become non-human.¹⁸⁵

Why, then, does Mandeville describe so many different peoples in favourable terms, and yet at the same time never let an opportunity go by without castigating the Jews? The most likely answer is that these other peoples, distant from western Europe and little more than a traveller's tales or creations, required no real tolerance on the part of the author. The Jews, however, were different. The author shared his physical and spiritual world with them. As Jean-Paul Rubiés writes:¹⁸⁶

> [The] wide toleration of a writer who does not need to share his moral space with a different culture, because he is not a real traveller, and it is indeed very significant that it is precisely the Jews, who lived in parts of Europe and shared the same sacred space of Jerusalem, that he cannot tolerate in his writing.

The anti-Jewish passages that did find their way into the Latin vulgate were further thinned out by the translator of the Danish version. This may be significant. Of course, the translator is not doing this out of consideration for the Jews; indeed, whenever he does mention them in the text, he allows the Jews no redeeming qualities whatsoever. However, it may be the case that as the Danish translator, not having to share his physical space with the Jews, who for him would have been as distant as Orthodox Christians or Muslims, was simply not that interested in them and therefore deleted a number of references to them.¹⁸⁷

Guide for Pilgrims

The *Guide for Pilgrims* is a short text measuring nineteen pages in length and existing in just one rather worn copy from the end of the fifteenth century, now in Copenhagen, The Arnamagnæan Collection, AM 792, 4°. Its source is unknown, although it is possibly a translation of a German work.¹⁸⁸ Despite describing Jeru-

---

185. There was also a widespread association in the Middle Ages of Saracens and Cynocephali (Friedman 1981: 67; Strickland 2003: 204). See also Adams 2012: 87–88.
186. Rubiés 2000: 17.
187. It should be noted that it is not just passages about Jews that have been abridged in the Danish version of *Mandeville's Travels*.
188. Lorenzen 1882: LXXIII points to a few loanwords in the text (*viz. ærstæ* 'first', *æræstæ* 'first', *meister* 'master', *to* 'to') as evidence of a possible German origin.

salem and its surroundings, the *Guide* makes no mention of the Jewish community, known as the Old Yishuv (*hayišuv hayašan*), that lived in the Holy Land during the Middle Ages; only Muslims, referred to as *hedhninge* 'heathens', are mentioned.[189] When Jews appear in the *Guide* it is within the context of the Passion story according to both the New Testament and medieval Christian lore. Thus, building on the story in Matthew 26: 57, the house of Caiaphas is mentioned. The Jews had arrested Jesus but grown tired, so they imprisoned him in Caiaphas' house until morning, when they would be refreshed and able to restart their interrogation and mockery of him.[190] As we have already noted in other texts, the Jews are seen as taking a very active leading role in the Crucifixion and performing acts assigned in the New Testament to the Romans; for example, by taking the cross from Jesus at Golgotha to prepare it (and him) for crucifixion.[191] Fear of the Jews is also a motif and they are described as turning on the disciples who were forced into hiding after the Crucifixion (AM 792, 4°, fol. 192va, l. 28 – ^{b}, l. 4, 14–20):[192]

> nedher i omgongen ær een Capelle i then stedh som Ihesus kom || in til discipele ogh dørrene bleue luctæ thær the sade samen for iødhe resle [...] i then same capelle myt i alteret ær eet stykke af then stolpe som iesus war til bunden then time the hannum hwdstrughe

> *Down in the bend, there is a chapel at the site where Jesus entered to meet the disciples and the doors were closed when they sat together because they were afraid of the Jews [...] In the same chapel in the middle of the altar is a piece of the pillar to which Jesus was tied when he was scourged.*

---

189. After the last Jewish War against Hadrian (135 CE), the Jews were expelled from Jerusalem and forbidden to return. They were permitted a couple of hundred years later by Constantine I (c. 272–337) to live in the surrounding hills, including the Mount of Olives, and later still allowed once a year on *Tiš'ah Be'Av* into the city itself to mourn the destruction of the Temple by Titus in 70 CE. After the Muslims took control of Jerusalem in 638 CE, the Jews were allowed to return to the city for good. According to the Navarrese rabbi, Benjamin of Tudela, there were about two hundred Jews living in Jerusalem by the middle of the twelfth century (Adler 1907: 22; see also Kedar 1971, 1973; Moshe 1992: 65–74). The Old Yishuv dwelled principally in the four holy cities: Jerusalem, Tiberias, Safed (Ẓefat) and Hebron, but at various times there were also smaller communities in Jaffa, Haifa, Peki'in, Acre, Shechem, Shefar'am and Gaza. On immigration to the Land of Israel during the Middle Ages, see Yuval 2006: 267–74.
190. Fol. 192ra, ll. 6–12; Lorenzen 1882: 215, ll. 5–8.
191. Fol. 189rb, ll. 18–25; Lorenzen 1882: 210, ll. 3–6.
192. Lorenzen 1882: 216, ll. 14–24. Cf. John 20: 19, ChrPed. *Skr.* II: 410, and the sermons in Uppsala, University Library, C 56 (Klemming 1893: 142 [ll. 26–27], 143 [ll. 17–18] and 164 [ll. 21–22]).

Thus, the picture of the Jews presented in the *Guide* is the usual one peddled by the Church clergy, of blood-thirsty, evil Jews torturing and murdering the messiah and terrifying the disciples who were subsequently forced into hiding. However, 'real' Jews living at the time of the author and reader, and who would have been encountered on a pilgrimage, have been written out of the account of the Holy Land, and despite living at the heart of Christian sacred space, they are not mentioned.

Reverend Michael, *On the Creation of Things*

Finally, let us consider the interesting case of a poem by the priest Michael Nielsen (or possibly Clausen) from 1514. Michael (*c.* 1450–*c.* 1510) was from Odense, Fyn, and is the author of three religious works in verse: *De creatione rerum* ('On the creation of things'; 1514), *De vita hominis* ('On the life of man'; 1514), *Expositio pulcherrima super rosario beate marie virginis* ('A beautiful exposition on the rosary of the Blessed Virgin Mary'; 6 February 1515). All these works were published after the death of Michael by Poul Ræff, the same man responsible for the translation and publication of *Iudeorum Secreta*.[193] In a short afterword in *Expositio...*, Ræff describes Michael as a 'gammel dandhæ mandh som heed her Michael: och war sogneprest vti Othensæ til sancti Albani kirckæ [*an old honourable man who was called Reverend Michael and was the parish priest in Odense at St Alban's Church*]'. Little else is known about this man, who is one of just two known medieval poets in Denmark who composed original works in the vernacular. The sources for his poem on the Creation, *On the Creation of Things*, have been investigated; of interest to us are the three references to rabbinical commentaries concerning Genesis:[194]

Fol. a5ᵛ, l. 10:	Uælløst och glædhæ haffdhæ gud them giord	
	swo klaer war paradises iord	Rabbi zacha.
	som nogher cristal kan wæræ	in glo geñ .ij.
	The vrther ther stodhæ haffdhæ krafftig lwcht	
	aldrig saa nogher swo løstælig frwcht	
	som træenæ the mwnæ bæræ	

---

193. The poems have been edited and published again in Molbech 1836.
194. On the sources to Michael's work, see Toldberg 1961: 18–26. The three references to rabbinical commentaries are mentioned but not identified in Gad 1963: 76 and Lausten 1992: 107.

>   *God had created pleasure and happiness for them*
>   *(Adam and Eve)*
>   *The soil of Paradise was as clear*
>   *as crystal can be. (Rabbi Zachariah's gloss of Genesis 2)*
>   *The plants which were there had a strong scent*
>   *Never did anyone see such pleasant fruit*
>   *as the trees could bear.*

Fol. b2ᵛ, l. 12: Thi adam tænckthæ grandgiffuælig paa
huad ændhæ th*et* bid th*et* sculdhæ faa
stor rætzlæ bar ha*n* ther foræ   Rab. isaac. geñ
Dieffuele*n* sagdhæ: ada*m* æsthw ræd   iij in glo.
allæ ting ære wnder thinæ fødher træd
som the tilforen woræ

>   *For Adam thought about exactly*
>   *what consequence that bite would have,*
>   *So he was very afraid. (Rabbi Isaac's gloss of Genesis 3)*
>   *The Devil said, 'Adam, are you afraid?*
>   *All things are still trodden under your feet*
>   *as they were before.'*

Fol. c3ʳ, l. 24: for gang som adam och eua the gaa
gud ladhæ th*et* foræ theres synder staa ||
begynthæ tha baadhæ at raabæ
Allæ diwr som sckapthæ waaræ   Rab moy.
mello*m* ada*m* och gud the witnæ baaræ   geñ iij.
aff paradijs strax th[?>e] løbæ

>   *What a path Adam and Eve go!*
>   *May God let it be the punishment for their sins.*
>   *Both began then to shout*
>   *All the animals that had been created*
>   *They bore witness between Adam and God*
>   *(Rabbi Moses Genesis 3)*
>   *They immediately ran out of Paradise.*

These glosses do not appear in the most important classical or medieval rabbinical commentaries, and it has thus not been possible for me to identify them using

81

Jewish material.[195] This is most probably because they are in fact derived from a Christian source, such as Petrus Comestor's *Historia scholastica*, the biblical commentaries of Nicholas of Lyra, the *Speculum humanae salvationis*, or the apocryphal *Vita Adae et Evae*.[196] They may even be the inventions of Michael, Poul Ræff or someone else, attempts to mimic these great biblical commentaries. Perhaps references such as these were considered as artistic embellishments or even desirable elements that added a sense of greater truth, authority or wisdom, or an international flavour.[197] However, the commentaries are close to one another in the poem, and this could be because Michael had at hand a commentary about precisely this section of Genesis. Whatever their origin, these marginal references to rabbis are unique in a Danish text from the beginning of the sixteenth century, and they show us that, in learned circles at least, it was possible to make non-polemical references to rabbinical literature (real or otherwise). Cultural and religious channels from Europe did not just bring anti-Jewish sentiment, but possibly also an awareness of (and a respect for?) Jewish exegetical works, albeit on a rather superficial level.[198]

Jews appear elsewhere in a number of places in Michael's poems, not least in the Passion scenes of the *Expositio*. The 'action' starts with Judas' betrayal:

Fol. h6^v, l. 2:   Iudas gick bort fran gudz samfwnd,
                     til iødernæ mwnæ han ko*mm*æ:

---

195. There is certainly no 'rabbi Moses' known before the tenth century, which would date the third gloss, if indeed it is a genuine Jewish source, as medieval.

196. The first example may be from or inspired by chapter 22 of *Historia scholastica* (Genesis); it also has a parallel in Revelation 21:11 where the light of Jerusalem is described as 'like unto a stone most precious, even like a jasper stone, clear as crystal'. Elsewhere in Europe, the use of Hebrew sources in popular expansions of the Bible was not uncommon. See, for example, the book by Murdoch 2003. On Hebrew traditions in *Historia scholastica*, see Shereshevsky 1969.

197. There are other similar examples of authors attributing certain knowledge to Jews in order to make their work more prestigious and reliable; for example, the fourteenth-century *Epistle of Rabbi Samuel of Morocco*, supposedly translated from Arabic, but in fact composed, by the Spanish Dominican friar Alfonso Buenhombre (see Ora Limor 1996; cf. also Kessler 2010: 82). However, the use of a fictional reference in this way is highly unusual.

198. In Old Danish, the term 'rabbi' is only found here and in the story of Judas kissing Jesus (Matthew 26: 49). For example, Judas greets Jesus with 'ave rabbi' in two accounts of the Passion (Stockholm, Royal Library, A 31, fol. 29rb; Copenhagen, The Arnamagnæan Collection, AM 72, 8°, fol. 50^r) and in Pseudo-Bonaventure's *Meditationes vitae Christi* (Stockholm, Royal Library, A 31, fol. 73vb). In Old Swedish, it also appears twice as an epithet for Moses, 'raby moyses', in the *Pentateuch Paraphrase* (Klemming 1848–55: 474, l. 20, and 485, l. 3).

Bad them gribæ ha*n*nu*m* i mydnatz stwnd,
sig sielff til lidhen fro*m*mæ.

Judas left God's congregation,
he had to go to the Jews:
He asked them to capture him [Jesus] at midnight,
just to receive a small reward.

Jesus is arrested, interrogated by Annas and Caiaphas, struck by Malchus, and appears before Pilate, where the Jews present their cases against Jesus:

Fol. i1ʳ, l. 25:   The iøder kærdhæ paa ha*n*nu*m* mangfold
och kærdhæ mod allæ rætthæ:
Uort falck haffuer han locket bort m*et* wold,
mod oss yppedæ han stoer trættha.

Uij sculdhæ ey keyseren giffuæ sckat,
ha*n*nu*m* huercken tyænæ eller lydhæ,
Sagdæ han, som wij hær haffuæ fat:
ondt bør ha*n*nu*m* th*et* at nydhæ.

Gudz søn kaller han sig waræ sand,
swo ynckælighen kan han liwffuæ:
besckoder nw allæ thennæ fwlæ mand,
om th*et* ha*n*nu*m* nogh*et* kan dwæ.

Forbywder han ether giffuæ keyseren sckat,
th*et* maa ieg ickæ høræ.
Til domeræ aff ha*n*nu*m* er ieg hær sat,
ieg sigher huad i scullæ søræ.

Binder ha*n*nu*m* m*et* reeb och stærckæ band,
synæ ord scal han vndgældhæ:
Faar ha*n*nu*m* herodi vti syn hand,
tog han haffuer guddoms wældhæ.

The Jews accused him in many ways,
and accused him against all justice:

> 'Our people has been lured away by force,
> he has picked a quarrel with us.'
>
> 'This man, whom we have captured here, said
> that we should not pay tax to the emperor,
> nor serve or obey him.
> This man deserves retribution.'
>
> 'He calls himself the true son of God,
> so pathetically can he lie:
> Everyone behold this ugly man,
> and see whether it can help him.'
>
> [Pilate replies:] 'If he prohibits you from paying tax to the emperor,
> that I may not hear!
> I am seated here as his judge,
> I will tell you what you should do.'
>
> 'Bind him with rope and strong fetters!
> He shall pay for his words:
> Put him in Herod's hands,
> as he [Herod] has divine power.'

After Herod's judgement, the crucifixion is performed by 'them' (presumably the Jews), and so the Passion scenes are very much like those we have already reviewed from the period.

Summary

This overview of the depiction of Jews in medieval Danish writing shows that anti-Jewish texts and images in Denmark clearly originated from, and were further nurtured by, the Church. There was an established practice of using the *topos* of the 'imaginary Jew', a near mythological being, and it did not matter that very few Danes would ever have met a Jew in order for the stereotype to be effective: The Jew became an established figure in the collective Danish religious, literary and cultural imagination. The grotesque figure of the 'pernicious Jew' had long entered the realm of European folklore and imagination, and almost all the motifs that appear in German writing on Jews can also be found in these Danish texts as propagandistic elements to justify and glorify the beliefs and actions of Christians. There are, however, notable absences in the Danish material, including the *Judensau* ('Jews' sow' and other images of Jews in obscene contact with non-kosher animals),[199] stories of blood libel, Host desecration and plague contagion.[200] The principal difference is that Danish literature focuses on the Jews of the Old Testament and the gospels. This may be due to the lack of a Jewish presence in medieval Denmark, although in other countries with no resident Jewish population, for example England, the images, albeit very negative, are still more varied despite this lack of a Jewish community to lend them reality.[201]

The Jew motif appears to have been recognisable and understandable to Danish audiences as it was often used without being explained. It was most frequently employed as a metaphor for evil, an inverse Christian ideal, in order to castigate Christians and call them to a more religious and observant life. By describing Jews as the adversaries of the Church, the eternal enemies of Christendom and the allies of the Devil, the clerics aimed to enhance the image of the Church and unify its members. Below are listed (in no particular order) the often contradictory stereotyped depictions of the imaginary Jews we have met in the surveyed literature:

- the manipulating Jewish leaders (calqued on Annas and Caiaphas);
- the manipulated Jewish masses (resulting in the contemporary Talmud Jew who has deserted 'authentic Judaism');
- the witness of the Incarnation/Crucifixion/Resurrection (living testimony to the truth of Christianity);

---

199. In St Mary's Church, Helsingør, there is, however, a remarkable wall-painting of the Last Supper. Jesus and the disciples are depicted seated around a table, in the middle of which there is a pig's head on a serving platter, presumably as a sign of the replaced covenant and the 'un-Jewishness' of Jesus, the disciples and the Church.
200. It should also be borne in mind that certain motifs could be found in neighbouring Scandinavian countries; for example: a well-poisoning accusation in 1350 on Gotland (Trachtenberg 1993: 104; Harrison 2000: 405), and also the *Judensau* carving in Uppsala Cathedral (Nordström 1956: 51–58). Similarly, there are later occurrences of motifs not found in the Middle Ages; for example the insinuation of ritual murder by Jews in 1699 (Trachtenberg 1993: 125). These motifs may well have been widespread in Denmark during the medieval period, and even current in Danish oral and/or written literature, but they cannot be found in the extant written record.
201. For example, the story of Host desecration that became ever more popular in England and was included in miracle stories, art work and theatre (see Cohen 2007: 103). Consider also the Jewish characters in Shakespeare's *The Merchant of Venice* (Shylock) and Marlowe's *The Jew of Malta* (Barabas) — moneyed, cruel, lecherous, avaricious outsiders. On the image of the Jews in post-expulsion England, see Glassman 1975 and Bale 2006. For an account of the representation of Jews in West Norse literature, there is Berulfsen 1958.

- the deliberate non-believer in the truth of Christianity (the blind Jew becomes the stubborn Jew);
- the deicist (the Christ-killing Jew);
- the violent Jew (the wolf-like, cruel, blood-thirsty, violent, mocking Jew — taking the place of the Romans in the Passion story);
- the persecutor of Mary/the disciples;
- the enemy of God/Jesus/Christendom/good Christian folk;
- the supplanted servant of God (supersessionist theology) ;
- the dispossessed Jew (no longer in the centre with a homeland and the Temple in Jerusalem, but forced to the periphery);
- the usurer (avaricious, deceitful) ;
- the demonic Jew (collaborator with Satan) ;
- the weak, feminine, unwarlike Jew (imprisoned and guarded by the Amazonian queen; cursed with male menstruation);
- the Jew who stands outside the shared emotional experience of human beings.

In the works reviewed, there are also a couple of spurious references to Jewish religious practice (in *Consolation of the Soul*) and the rabbis (in Michael), but as we have seen they both build on Christian, not Jewish, sources.

The adjectives typically used to describe the Jews in these vernacular works are *forbannet* (cursed), *fortvivlet* (desperate), *ful* (bad; unclean, sordid), *genværthigh* (hostile), *grim* (vile), *hoffærthigh* (arrogant), *slim* (filthy; bad), *umild* (cruel), and *vil* (savage), with *ful* and *umild* being clear favourites among the writers. The Jews of the New Testament are compared to wolves, while contemporary Jews are said to be inspired by Satan. When speaking, the Jews rarely 'say' anything, preferring to *rope* (shout) and *skrike* (scream, yell), and often doing so *alle samen* (all together).[202] The Jews are inverted ideal Christians — they are morally corrupt, physically repulsive, untamed in their actions, violent, a danger to God's work and all humanity, and furthermore they are destined for damnation, and yet ultimately — at least according to some writers — for salvation. They are a constant reminder and warning to Christian society, a method of castigation, and a call to piety. It is against this background and array of anti-Jewish stereotypes, that we shall be examining the depiction of Jews in Pfefferkorn's *Iudeorum Secreta*.

---

202. For an outline of how specific Danish words were used to construct the image of the Jew, see Adams 2012: 90.

CHAPTER 2

Exposing the Jews and their secrets

Johannes Pfefferkorn, The Confession of the Jews, *Poul Ræff, and* Iudeorum Secreta

Raro Iudæus aliquis Christianus factus, fuit bonus, semper sunt nequam.
Joseph Scaliger (1669)[1]

Deinde vide, quaeso, quonam organo vtantur isti verae religionis haudquaquam veri professores: homine prorsus idiota, frontis perfrictae, et de quo peccando nullum omnino detrimentum fieri possit; cui non esset impingendum semiiudaei vocabulum, nisi factis sese declararet sesquiiudaeum. Quod aliud instrumentum optaret sibi diabolus, Christianae religionis aeternus hostis, quam istiusmodi angelum Satanae transfiguratum in angelum lucis, et falsissimo defendendae religionis praetextu id vbique turbantem quod nostrae religionis et caput est et optimum, nempe publicam orbis Christiani concordiam? Quid indignius quam viros immortali memoria dignos cum istiusmodi portento digladiari? cuius ego solo nomine chartas pollui puto.
Erasmus in a letter to Willibald Pirckheimer (1517)[2]

---

1. Joseph Justus Scaliger 1669 (see also Reinach 1929: 174). 'A Jew who has converted to Christianity is seldom a man of any good; the converts are generally bad people'.
2. Erasmus of Rotterdam in a letter to Willibald Pirckheimer (Allen 1906–58, III: 117 [Epist. 694]; translated into English in Rummel 2002: 143): 'Consider moreover, the tool these false professors of true religion are using: a man [*i.e. Johannes Pfefferkorn*], who is a layman, who has no shame, and who can hardly be called a half-Jew, for his actions show that he is a Jew and a half whom no kind of misdeed could make worse than he already is. Could the Devil, that eternal enemy of the Christian religion, have wished for a better tool than this angel of Satan transformed into an angel of light, who under the pretext of defending religion disturbs the peace and concord of the Christian commonwealth everywhere — peace which is the principal good of the Christian religion? What can be more unworthy for men who deserve to be immortalised than to fight with such a monster? His very name, I believe, would dirty the paper on which it is written.'

[E]in unwissender, grundgemeiner Mensch, der Abschaum der Juden, welcher nicht verdient hat, daß von ihm in Literatur und Geschichte die Rede sei.

Graetz 1866: 75[3]

There are many people in Germany and Denmark behind the writing, production and publication of *The Confession of the Jews* and its Danish version *Iudeorum Secreta*: a Jewish convert to Christianity, a judge of the Inquisition, the first-ever Danish book-printer and a bewildering backdrop of Dominicans, scholastics, reformers and humanists. There are thus a vast number of interests at play, and in order to shed light on the reason why the book was even translated and published in Denmark, a country with no resident Jewish population, we will focus on the two main individuals: the original author Johannes Pfefferkorn who put himself at the disposal of the Dominicans and acted as one of their most vociferous propagandists, and the translator and printer Poul Ræff, also a tireless fighter for the Catholic Church who was almost as reviled by reforming figures in Denmark as Pfefferkorn was by similar groups in Germany. This chapter looks at these two men's lives and their motivation for distributing this book. Furthermore, it discusses the nature of the content of the works and considers whether their publication marks a new development in the history of Judaeophobic writing and thought in northern Europe.

Johannes Pfefferkorn (1469–1522/23)

Early life

We know little about the life of Johannes Pfefferkorn, but various documents, not least those concerning the heated controversy between him and the humanist Johann Reuchlin, contain fragmentary comments that can be pieced together to form a picture of this fanatical Jewish apostate to Christianity.[4] Of course, the polemical context of remarks in these writings is somewhat problematic, and con-

---

3. Graetz on Pfefferkorn: '[A]n ignorant and invidious creature, the scum of the Jews, who does not deserve to be mentioned in literature and history.'
4. There is, rather confusingly, another converted Jew called Johannes Pfefferkorn, also known as Pfaff Rapp (Stokes 1909: 63 n. 51), from the beginning of the sixteenth century. He was slowly

temporary descriptions of Pfefferkorn and his background need to be treated with caution.⁵ This is particularly relevant in the books of Johannes Reuchlin, who portrayed him as ignorant and insincere, and in the humanist satirical work *Epistolae obscurorum virorum*.⁶

Pfefferkorn's precise date of birth is not known, but in his pamphlet *Zu lob vnd Ere* (1510), he writes that at the time of conversion he 'ob den xxxv jarn in dem jüdischen Irthum gewest [*had been living in Jewish delusion for 35 years*]' (fol. a3ᵛ). His year of conversion was 1504/05, which places his birth by his own reckoning in the year 1468 or 1469. He provides us with his Jewish name, *Yosef*, in the introduction to his first anti-Jewish pamphlet *Der Juden Spiegel* (fol. a1ᵛ):⁷

> ich, Johannes, der nach lawt vnde Inhaldt des alden testaments aus dem geslecht pefferkorn Joseph ghenant vnd eyn Jude was
>
> *I, Johannes, who in accordance with the word and content of the Old Testament, of the Pfefferkorn family called Joseph, was a Jew*

---

roasted to death for a number of crimes including murder, kidnap, blasphemy and sacrilege. Trachtenberg (1993: 82–83) writes the following about him:

> A strange case is that of the converted Jew, Johann Pfefferkorn (not identical with the convert of the same name whose debate with Reuchlin over the Talmud made history), executed in Halle 1514 or 1515. He is reported to have confessed stealing an 'imprisoned devil' from a priest (!) in Franconia, for five gulden. Nor was this the full measure of his crime. He had also gone in for poisoning on a large scale, stole several consecrated hosts, and kidnapped two children, one of whom he sold to the Jews that they might extract its blood, the other one he let go free 'because it had red hair'! Besides all this, he seems to have been a fairly common type of criminal — and a little demented in the bargain, to judge from the scanty information available.

See also Schudt (1714–18, I: 355–56, §§5–6), where the author, in order to avert any confusion, describes the lives of the two Pfefferkorns in detail to demonstrate that they were not one and the same person. These two notorious Pfefferkorns are found compared in Ioannes Vickephius' letter in *Epistolae obscurorum virorum* (Böcking 1864–69, I: 36):

> Iam combusserunt in Hallis unum baptizatum iudęum qui etiam vocatur Ioannes Pfefferkorn, et fecit multa mala. Ego timeo quod ille faciet semel talia, tunc vos male staretis.
>
> *In Halle, they have already burnt another baptised Jew who was also called Johannes Pfefferkorn and who did many evil deeds. I am afraid this man [i.e. Pfefferkorn, author of Confession of the Jews] will also do such things, and then you will be in trouble.*

5. For a summary of previous scholarship on Pfefferkorn, see Cape and Diemling 2011: 7–10.
6. See Rummel 2002: 3.
7. Kirn 1989: 205, ll. 6–8.

His place of birth is not entirely certain. The following lines from *Epistolae obscurorum virorum* (I, 36) describe Pfefferkorn as coming from Moravia:[8]

> Vester Ioannes Pfefferkorn in Colonia est unus pessimus trufator: nihil scit in hebręo; ipse factus est christianus ut suam nequitiam occultaret. Quando fuit adhuc Iudęus in Moravia, percussit unam mulierem in faciem quod non potuit videre in bancis, ubi mutantur floreni, et accepit plusquam .CC. florenos aufugiens

> *That Johannes Pfefferkorn of yours in Cologne is a terrible braggart: he knows no Hebrew, and he made himself a Christian to hide his own bad behaviour. When he was still a Jew in Moravia, he hit a woman at a money-changer's counter in the face so that she was blinded, and he seized more than 200 florins and ran off with them.*

The family name Pfefferkorn does indeed feature on a number of gravestones in the Old Jewish Cemetery in Prague, Moravia.[9] However, the historian Ludwig Geiger suggests that the Pfefferkorn family in fact came from Nuremberg, as the city's oldest extant tenancy book from 21 October 1384 makes mention of a resident called Minneman Pfefferkorn from Bamberg.[10] Another historian, Ellen Martin, also identifies Nuremberg as Pfefferkorn's birthplace.[11] However, the Pfefferkorns are never mentioned in the writings of the Nuremberg Jews themselves.[12]

He grew up in the house of his uncle, Rabbi Meir Pfefferkorn, who, Johannes Pfefferkorn writes in his *Handt Spiegel* (1511), could count himself among the most learned rabbis of the time (fol. e1^r):[13]

> Aber als jch daruon schreib / hab ich von jrem höchsten / groß geachtet ein fürst des Talmuds / vnnd ist mein angeborner vetter sein namen Rabi Mer pfefferkornn

---

8. Böcking 1864–69, I: 55, ll. 11–15.
9. Brod 1965: 182.
10. Geiger 1910: 33. The tenancy book reference is in Nuremberg, Staatsarchiv (Kgl. Kreisarchiv), S 14 R 1 (no. 301), fol. 27^v and is published in Stern 1894–96: 33.
11. Martin 1994: 11.
12. See, for example, the register of Jews present in the Nuremberg synagogue on Saturday 14 March 1489 recorded in Kgl. Kreisarchiv D no. 1837 and published in Stern 1894–96: 92–94; cf. also Kirn 1989: 11 n. 14.
13. On Meir Pfefferkorn, see Graetz 1866: 66.

> *But whatever I write about this [i.e. the Talmud], I have learnt from their [i.e. the Jews'] highest [authority/rabbi?], greatly esteemed, a prince of the Talmud and he is my uncle by birth, his name Rabbi Meir Pfefferkorn*

Boasting of one's learned background is a convention frequently used in the autobiographical literature of converts, and it does not always reflect the writer's true circumstances.[14] However, in the case of Pfefferkorn there is evidence that he is not exaggerating. In a Hebrew chronicle from Prague (*c.* 1615), Pfefferkorn's uncle is, in fact, described in terms of praise and lauded with the honorific title *ga'on*, 'genius':[15]

> רנ"ח לפ"ק הגיד הראש הגאון מהר"ר מאיר פפעפירקארין מסכת בבא קמא בעל פה גמרא, ופרש מידי
> יום ביומו הלכה, והתחיל אחרי חנוכה וסיים כ"ח ואדר בק"ק אובין, תנצב"ה.

> *In the year ‹5›258 AM [=1497/1498 CE], the wise head, our teacher the rabbi, Reb Meir Pfefferkorn, spoke the treatise Bava' Qama' in the oral Gemara', and he interpreted the* halachah[16] *every day, and he started after Ḥanukah and finished on the twenty-eighth of 'Adar II in the sacred community 'Ofen [=Buda in Budapest]. May his soul be bound up in the bundle of life [1 Samuel 25: 29].*[17]

According to his contemporaries, Johannes Pfefferkorn worked as a butcher (or *kaẓav*, an occupation that ranked below *šoḥeṭ* or ritual slaughterer). For example, in 1509 the Jews of Regensburg wrote concerning the confiscation of books from their community that:[18]

> Jusef jud metzgir, Pfeferkor ginent, so sich in neulichen zieten zu Cöln taufen losen hat, izunt Johanis Pfefferkorn ginant wert, etwan hinter mir zu Tabau weselich giwont

> *Josef, Jew, butcher, called Pfefferkorn, recently had himself baptised in Cologne, thereupon called Johannes Pfefferkorn, thereafter mainly lived in Dachau.*

---

14. See Carlebach 2001: 95–100.
15. David 1984: 5.
16. The *halachah* (הלכה, Heb. 'path') is Jewish religious law that governs Jews' behaviour and beliefs, and includes the biblical commandments (*miẓwot*), Talmudic and rabbinical law, as well as customs and tradition (*minhag*).
17. It is thus certainly not correct when Hans-Martin Kirn (1989: 11) writes that Johannes Pfefferkorn has 'aufgewachsen [...] bei seinem Onkel, einem ansonsten unbekannten Rabbi Meir Pfefferkorn [*grown up (...) in the home of his uncle, an otherwise unknown Rabbi Meir Pfefferkorn*]'.
18. Kirn 1989: 12.

That same year, the Jews in Frankfurt wrote:[19]

ביום ו בערב סוכת ע"ר לפ"ק בא טריפה קצב י"ש ואתו ג גלחים וב עירוני העיצה יר"ה פה ק"ק ורנק־
בורט דמיין ולקחו בעו"ה הספרים בבי כנישת' תפילות ומחזורים וסליחו' את כל אשר מצאו וציוה עלינו
בציווי הקיסר יר"ה שלא להתפלל עוד בבית הכנסת

> *On Friday, 'Erev Sukot [28 September 1509], the treyf butcher [i.e. a butcher who sells non-kosher meat] — may his name be obliterated! — and with him three priests [or monks; lit. 'shaven ones'] and two townsmen from the city council — may its glory be elevated! — came to us here in Frankfurt am Main, and among their many offences they seized the books in the synagogue (the Tefilot, Maḥzorim and Seliḥot),[20] everything that they found, and forbade us in the name of the emperor — may his glory be elevated! — to pray anymore in the synagogue.*

However, in *Der Juden Spiegel* (1507), Pfefferkorn writes about himself saying that he had, in fact, been a money lender (fol. c3ʳ):[21]

> Ich byn jm judschen glawben geboren vnd nun aus der gnad gotz Cristen, wan ich mit den iuden tzohielte vnd woicher neme [...]

> *I was born into the Jewish faith and now, due to the grace of God, am a Christian, when I belonged to the Jews and practised usury [...]*

And in *Handt Spiegel* (1511; fol. c3ʳ):

> Ist wol war/ do jch ein jud was/ do tatt ich wie andere/ dann wer in der wüst wondt/ der muß auch wüstlich leben [...]

> *It is entirely true that when I was a Jew, then I did as others, for he who lives in the desolate wasteland must also live desolately [...]*

Around 1500, he moved together with his wife and children to the city of Cologne, whose Jews had been permanently expelled in 1426, and it was there

---

19. Kracauer 1900a: 119.
20. *Tefilot* are general prayer books; *maḥzorim* are prayer books containing rituals prescribed for holidays, and *seliḥot* are prayer books containing petitions for forgiveness for the ten days preceding Yom Kippur (*'Aseret Yemei Tešuvah*).
21. Kirn 1989: 221.

he was imprisoned by Baron Heinrich von Gutenstein after being found guilty of theft.[22] This may not have been his only crime: an extant anonymous broadsheet from 1515 enumerates the many crimes that Pfefferkorn is alleged to have been guilty of before his baptism secured him absolution.[23] These crimes include theft, failure to repay loans, pick-pocketing and fraud. After his release in 1504, Pfefferkorn came into contact with the Dominicans and in that same year, at the age of 35, he converted to Christianity together with his wife (who was baptised Anna) and at least one of his children (who was baptised Laurentius).[24] Pfefferkorn changed his name from Josef to Johannes. He explains his motivation for conversion in twelve articles in his *Beschyrmung* (1516; fol. 14ᵛ ff). However, they are rendered in such theological terms that they amount to little more than propaganda rather than a genuine insight into his reasons for conversion.[25] Maybe it was indeed a personal, spiritual decision that marked a profound change in his relationship to God. His enemies, however, wrote that he converted to Christianity as he feared the Jews would kill him for his crimes. So, for example, in *Epistolae obscurorum virorum* I, 23:[26]

> Sed dicitur hic quod Ioannes Pfefferkorn, quem etiam defenditis vos, est malus nequam, et non est factus christianus amore fidei, sed propterea quod Iudęi voluerunt eum suspendere propter suas nequitias, quia dicunt quod est fur et proditor, et sic fuit baptizatus;

> *But it is said that Johannes Pfefferkorn, whom you defend, is a bad man, and did not become a Christian for love of the Faith, but rather, because the Jews wanted to hang him for his wrong doings, for they say he is a thief and a traitor, and this is why he was baptised.*

---

22. See Graetz 1875: 340–41.
23. The broadsheet was unknown to researchers until it was acquired by the Hebrew Union College Library (Cincinnati) in the first half of the twentieth century. It is reproduced and translated in Appendix II (see also Zafren 1961: 142; Kirn 1989: 179–81). One contemporary author accounts for Johannes Pfefferkorn's criminal malevolence by describing him as 'quod Iudas de testiculis scalpsit [*sprung from the seed of Judas*]', Böcking 1864–69, I: 299, l. 32.
24. After converting, his son, Laurentius, devoted himself to the study of the liberal disciplines and the poets (Böcking 1864–69, I: 145, ll. 31–35).
25. See Martin 1994: 12–18; Cape and Diemling 2011: 12–16.
26. Böcking 1864–69, I: 36, ll. 11–15.

And in *Epistolae obscurorum virorum* II, 3:[27]

> Respondit doctor Murner [...]: 'de honestate Iohannis Pfefferkorn non multum audivi, sed quod de eo audivi, bene possum dicere, quod nisi Iudęi voluissent eum mortificare propter maleficia sua, Ipse nunquam fuisset factus Christianus'.
>
> *Doctor Murner replied [...], 'I have not heard much of Johannes Pfefferkorn's honour, but from what I have heard of him, I can well say that unless the Jews had intended to put him to death on account of his crimes, he would never have become a Christian.'*

Thus, a reason for Pfefferkorn's conversion might be due to his criminal behaviour and the possible consequences of this under Jewish law. If he faced punishment or sanctions in his community, he could avoid them by conversion. One of Pfefferkorn's alleged crimes, according to the broadsheet of 1521 (see Appendix II), was the selling of *treyf* or non-kosher meat which would have been grounds for a temporary excommunication (known as *niduy*). The fear of alienation and vulnerability, that a *niduy* ban would have caused, could have made conversion an attractive option for Pfefferkorn. Other modern scholars have taken a similarly cynical view of his actions. The scholar Sander Gilman has suggested Jewish self-hatred,[28] while Max Brod has written that there might be a connection between Pfefferkorn's conversion and the (need to avoid the) expulsions of the Jews from various cities in Germany around 1500.[29] Indeed, taking their place in the Christian mind into consideration, conversion offered Jews a potential escape from a life of scorn and hatred at the hands of the majority population. The Jews viewed apostates who converted to Christianity rather poorly, and Jewish medieval sources cite the material rewards to be had as the principal cause. For example, in the polemical work *Sefer Niẓaḥon Yašan*, we read:[30]

> [...] one should not be surprised at the bad deeds of an evil Jew who becomes an apostate, because his motives are to enable himself to eat all that his heart desires, to give pleasure to his flesh with wine and fornication, to remove from himself the yoke of the kingdom of heaven so that he should fear nothing, to free himself from all the commandments, cleave to sin, and concern himself with worldly pleasures.

---

27. Böcking 1864–69, I: 190, ll. 12–15.
28. Gilman 1986: 53–56.
29. Brod 1965: 178–79.
30. Berger 1979: 206.

Indeed, Pfefferkorn himself warns his readers in chapter 6 of *Confession of the Jews* against Jews who convert to Christianity for economic gain alone. After his conversion, Pfefferkorn worked hard to coerce his former coreligionists into embracing Christianity, which led him to act for some years as a wandering preacher, among other places in Dachau and Nuremberg, and in 1516 he declared that he had converted fourteen Jews. During this time he came into contact with the Franciscans who since the end of the fifteenth century had been preaching hatred towards the Jews.[31] It seems probable that Pfefferkorn's anti-Jewish ideas and arguments began to take form at this time.

The Dominicans of Cologne were under the leadership of Prior Jacob van Hoogstraten (1465–1527), who was employed at the city's university and who also acted as a judge of the Inquisition. He wanted the Dominicans to gain the same level of influence and power in Germany as they had in Spain, from where the Jews had been expelled under terrible circumstances in 1492, and Hoogstraten aimed to use the case against the Jews — the most conspicuous non-Christian minority in Europe — to help him achieve this goal. Pfefferkorn proved himself to be a most willing tool for Hoogstraten and the Dominicans to exploit, and it was he who took up the fight against his former coreligionists and later against the humanists led by the scholar Johann Reuchlin of Pforzheim. Having received sanctuary among the powerful Dominicans and under the guidance of Hoogstraten, he published a series of pamphlets which aimed to show that Jewish religious texts were anti-Christian and that the Jews themselves were a danger to Christianity.[32] The controversy between him and Reuchlin (described below) ensured notoriety for Pfefferkorn and a wide circulation for his works at the time, but his pamphlets do not seem to have enjoyed a long-lived popularity as opposed to those of other converts such as Anthonius Margaritha. Pfefferkorn's career as an author is relatively short, and his works were only reprinted once or twice and never again after 1521. Furthermore, he is not mentioned in the works of other Christian ethnographers such as Johannes Buxtorf or Ernst Friedrich Hess.[33]

---

31. On his years as a wandering preacher, see Kracauer 1887; Hsia 1988: 122–23; Kirn 1989: 10; Martin 1994: 11, and Rummel 2002: 3–4. Pfefferkorn writes in *Streydtpuechlyn* (1516; fol. e4ʳ), that he had 'durch die gnad gotz xv selen dem Teuffel abgrissen [*by the grace of God torn fifteen souls from the clutches of the Devil*]'. On the role of the Franciscans in anti-Jewish agitation, see *JE*, III: 554, *s.v.* 'Capistrano, John of'; *JE*, V: 510–11, *s.v.* 'Friars'; Cohen 1982; McMichael and Myers 2004.

32. See Peterse 1995: 22–30.

33. I have, however, found a single reference to him on fol. K6ʳ of *Jüden Feind* (1570) by Georgius Nigrinus (Georg Schwartz): 'man list in Johan Pfefferkorns Schrifften wider die Juden [*One reads in the Johannes Pfefferkorn's writings against the Jews*]'.

One famous humanist who does mention Pfefferkorn is Erasmus of Rotterdam. In a letter dated 15 November 1517 he writes the following to his friend Reuchlin:[34]

> Si vales, Germaniae nostrae decus, est vnde plurimum gaudeam. Recutitus ille ex nocentissimo verpo scelerator non Christianus sed Christianistes, edito libello, eoque vulgari lingua, ne non intelligant ipsius sodales, lenones ac nautae, doctos omnes, vt audio, nominatim lacerat. Sed meo iudicio monstrum omnibus modis indignum est cuius mentio fiat in literis hominum eruditorum. Proh Deum immortalem, quali organo vtuntur personati illi religionis euersores! Plus vnus ille semiiudaeus Christianus nocuit rei Christianae quam vniuersa Iudaeorum sentina; planeque, ni fallor, id suae genti praebet quod Dario Zopyrus, quanquam hic multo scelerator. Nos, mi Reuchline, neglectis portentis in Christo nos oblectemus et honestissimis fruamur studiis.

> *If you are well, O glory of our modern Germany, I have good reason to be glad. That product of the circumcision [i.e. Johannes Pfefferkorn], who started as a criminal in the ghetto and is now a greater felon since he became, I will not say a Christian, but a Christian ape, is said to have published a book [i.e.* Streydtpuechlyn, *1516] — and that too in his native tongue, for fear his cronies the pimps and the bargemen might not understand him — in which, they tell me, he attacks all the learned world by name. In my opinion the monster does not in the least deserve to be mentioned in the writings of the learned. In heaven's name, what a tool they have chosen, those who behind their masks would overthrow religion! This half-Jew Christian by himself has done more harm to Christendom than the whole cesspool of Jewry, and clearly, unless I am mistaken, is playing the game for his nation that Zopyrus played for Darius, though this man is much more treacherous. Let us, my dear Reuchlin, forget these monsters, let us take joy in Christ, and pursue honourable studies.*[35]

Although his new career as a polemic pamphleteer might suggest otherwise, Pfefferkorn appears to have been a man of little learning, and indeed according to Reuchlin, who deplored the former Jew's lack of education and described him as an ignoramus, he could hardly read Hebrew.[36] This may indeed have been the

---

34. Allen 1906–58, III: 143 (no. 743).
35. Translation from Erasmus 1974–93, V: 203–04 (no. 713).
36. See, for example, Edelmann 1948: 10. In his *Ain clare Verstentnus* (n.d. [1511/1512]; fols 39ᵛ and 40ᵛ), Reuchlin wrote, that Pfefferkorn was unable to read *Sefer HaMordechai*, a rabbinical law collection from the second half of the thirteenth century composed by the rabbi and *poseq* Mor-

case, but we should also bear in mind that Reuchlin was a learned Hebraicist, who had been a pupil of Elias Levita (1469–1549), the famous Hebrew grammarian and poet, and one of the first authors to write in Yiddish, who taught Hebrew in Venice. Reuchlin was the first Christian to write a dependable elementary grammar of Hebrew, his *De rudimentis hebraicis* (1506), which, largely derived from the work of Rabbi Dawid Qimḥi (1160–1235), was one of the first books printed in Germany to contain Hebrew letters. Reuchlin thus had an entirely different approach to and an analytical understanding of what Hebrew and Judaism were than had Pfefferkorn, a man who would have grown up chanting Hebrew prayers, singing Hebrew songs and hearing *parašah* and *hafṭarah* readings, although probably understanding very little.[37] Indeed, there is no reason to think that Pfefferkorn read Hebrew any better or any worse than other Jews of mediocre learning at the time.[38] Pfefferkorn is also credited with having translated three short key Christian texts — the *Pater Noster*, *Ave Maria* and *Credo* — into Hebrew (1508). It seems likely, however, that it was the Dominican theologians at the University of Cologne rather than he who produced the Hebrew versions of these texts, just as it was they, and principally Ortwin Gratius, who produced the Latin translations of his works. Nonetheless, if Pfefferkorn had worked as a butcher, it would have required of him some understanding of certain elements of *halachah* ('religious law').[39] Yet, in reading any of Pfefferkorn's vicious and libellous pamphlets, one can see that his understanding of Jewish practices and religion is at times limited and that his translations from Hebrew are, either intentionally or unintentionally, somewhat contorted (more on this in the discussion on Hebrew words in *Iudeorum Secreta* in chapter 3). However, the true level of his understanding of Judaism would most probably have been of no relevance to his Christian public, many of whom would have believed whatever he wrote simply because of his 'credentials' as a born Jew; it seems to be the case that anti-Jewish comments

---

dechai ben Hillel (see Guggenheim 1995: 129 n. 12). Similarly Reuchlin called Pfefferkorn's presentation of Hebrew in his pamphlet *Der Juden veindt* of 1509 'foolish nonsense and childish prattle' (Reuchlin 2000: 45). In *Defensio* (1513; fols a4[v] and b2[r]), he alleged that Pfefferkorn could only write his pamphlets with substantial assistance from the Cologne Dominicans.

37. The *parašah* (פרשה, 'portion') is the section of the Torah read aloud each week at synagogue services on Shabbat and on holidays. The entire Torah is read from start to finish during the course of a year. The *hafṭarah* (הפטרה, 'parting', 'taking-leave') is the accompanying section comprising one or more chapters from the Prophets (*Nevi'im*) that is also read aloud to the congregation.

38. See Martin 1994: 24.

39. Pfefferkorn does, for example, describe how a *šoḥeṭ* should inspect an animal's innards in *In lob und eer*, fol. c[v]; see Kirn 1989: 10 n. 21.

uttered by Jews possess a special authority.⁴⁰ Another consequence of Pfefferkorn's poor linguistic abilities is that we do not know to what extent he had control over the Latin translations of his pamphlets that he composed in German. In addition to being derisive of Pfefferkorn's Hebrew, Reuchlin also doubted his ability to understand Latin. Pfefferkorn maintained, however, that he translated his works into Latin himself. In a protest composed in German against the 'dark men' called *Beschyrmung* (1516), Pfefferkorn insists that he has full control over the translations and that his Latin is good enough for him to be able to check every single word:⁴¹

> Dyß buchlyn hab ich gedachter Ioannes Pfefferkorn. zo retung meyner eren yn vergangen tagen yn dem dutschen lassen vßgan Daweyl mich aber dy obscurorum virorum epistolen. als weyt die welt so vnkristenlichen geschmecht vnd beleydiget haben. damit ich aber vur eynen solchen leichtfertigen man nyt gehalten wurde So hain ich das genant dutsch buchlyn mit weiteren mereren ab vnd zo gethanen worten nach mynem eygen willen vnd wolbefallen. in das lateyn vbersetzen lassen. von wort zo wort vorgeben mennichmol verhort. vnd also trucken lassen. vnnd eynen yeden da von. vur aller welt. red vnnd antwert alleyn zo geben bereit byn. des ich mich protesteirt hab vur notarius vnd getzuge .et c.

> *I, the aforementioned Johannes Pfefferkorn, have had this book published in German to rescue my honour these last days. 'The Letters of the Dark Men' have slandered and insulted me before the whole world in such an unchristian manner. Since*

---

40. 'More specifically, anti-Jewish thinkers have cited the antisemitic works of self-haters in order to bolster their own attacks on Jews, their presupposition being that antisemitism uttered by Jews possesses a special authority. Hence, for example, the popularity among latter-day anti-semites of Johannes Pfefferkorn (1469–1522), a converted Jew who vilified Judaism' (Reiter 2005: 648). Note also, how the title of the Danish translation makes the book sound as if it is written by a former insider, a man of authority, imparting secrets and informing his audience of plots and beliefs concealed by the Jews. Particular attention is drawn to Pfefferkorn's credentials on p. 3, ll. 6–10 of the *Secreta Iudeorum*:

> Forbeneffndhæ Iohannes Pfefferkorn / han er en iødhæ føddher oc om kring skaaren. Men nw haffwer han ladt sig døbæ / oc er en godh Cristhen lærdt man / thi wed han bæsth theris hemæligh leglighet hwilcken han obenbarlighen sckriffwer vti thennæ lildhe bog

> *The aforementioned Johannes Pfefferkorn was born a Jew and circumcised, but has now had himself baptised and is a good Christian learned man; therefore he knows best their secret affairs which he makes public in this little book.*

41. Böcking 1864–69, I: 175, ll. 29–38. However, in *Hostis Iudeorum* (1509), he writes that he engaged the help of some people to translate his booklet from German into Latin. See Rummel 2002: 67 n. 40.

> *I am not to be considered such a reckless man, I have had the said German pamphlet translated into Latin with further additions here and there according to my wish and liking; I decided on every single word and examined the translation many times, then allowed it to be printed. I am ready to talk and answer questions by myself in front of the whole world to every person who has protested against me, in front of a notary and witnesses etc.*

Of more recent scholars, Max Brod has a very dim view of both Pfefferkorn's Latin and his German, which he describes as 'Kauderwelsch [*gibberish*]',[42] and Francis Stokes describes him as 'almost illiterate'.[43] It is of course very unlikely that Pfefferkorn would have known much Latin. Regarded as the language of the Church by Jews and as such as *treyf*, he would not have had the opportunity to be exposed to Latin before his conversion. The role of the Dominicans as ghost writers in the writings of Pfefferkorn and other converts came to be an important subject in the Reuchlin-Pfefferkorn controversy and also in the satirical work, *Epistolae obscurorum virorum*, especially the role of Ortwin Gratius (d. 1542), who seems to have been particularly involved in the production of polemical works by former Jews. Indeed, Gratius was much ridiculed by the humanists for his role as translator and accused of intellectual poverty and moral wantonness.

In 1513, Pfefferkorn was given the sinecure of superintendent at the Dominican hospital of St Ursula (Revilien) in Cologne where he worked until his death.[44]

Pfefferkorn's campaign against the Jews

We cannot know what is was that caused Pfefferkorn to turn his back on his fellow Jews and then attack them so forcefully, but he was not alone. A number

---

42. Brod 1965: 185.
43. Stokes 1909: xxii. For a study of Pfefferkorn's (German) language and style, see Spanier 1936. In should be noted that not all might agree with the picture of Pfefferkorn presented above. For example, Friedrich Lauchert, writes in *The Catholic Encyclopedia* (Herbermann *et al.* 1913–14, XI: 786, *s.v.* 'Pfefferkorn, Johannes'):

    > Pfefferkorn was a fanatic and his public and literary life had little sympathy or grace, but he was certainly an honourable character and the caricature which his opponents have drawn of him is far from true.

44. In his final pamphlet, *Ain mitleydliche Claeg vber alle claeg* (1521; fol. i2ᵛ), he has the title 'hospice warden': 'Pefferkorn wont a dem Rhein. Zů Cöllen meyster im Spital [*Pfefferkorn lives in the Rhineland, a warden in the hospice in Cologne*]'.

of converts from the period published works on Jewish customs, the best known being Anthonius Margaritha, who converted in Wasserburg in 1522.[45] These works, extremely critical of Judaism, can be considered as an attempt by former 'insiders' to attack Judaism from within. Christian readers were provided with works describing carefully selected Jewish practices that aimed to uncover Judaism's alleged inanity and superstitious beliefs so that Christians would understand why the Jews were blind to the 'truth' of the gospels and why they were so dangerous.[46] It is thus in the tradition and guise of whistle-blower that Pfefferkorn's attacks on his former coreligionists finds expression in his attempts to prove that Jewish literature and practices were pernicious and hostile towards Christians. His pamphlets, numbering 13 in total, had four main aims:[47]

1) to ridicule every aspect of Jewish life;
2) to present Jews as a sinister threat to Christendom;
3) to suggest measures to deal with the Jews and their evil writings;
4) to evangelise among and convert the Jews.

His measures to deal with the Jews included prohibiting them from engaging in money lending (usury), forcing them to listen to Christian sermons, confiscating their religious books, and — if all else failed and they refused to convert to Christianity — expelling them from the land.

Pfefferkorn believed that Jewish leaders and the 'Talmudic religion' they had created prevented Jews from seeing the truth, *viz.* that Judaism had been fulfilled

---

45. A comprehensive list of Margaritha's publications can be found in Shachar 1981: 112 (no. 307). See also Diemling 2006. Other well-known sixteenth-century converts, together with the place and year of conversion, are Victor von Carben, priest (Cologne?, 1507); Paul Ricius, kabbalistic scholar, professor of philosophy in Pavia and Maximilian I's physician (Augsburg?, 1505); Paul Staffelstein of Nuremberg (Bamberg, 1530s); Paul Emil (Rome, 1549); Philipp Wolff (Danzig/Gdańsk, 1554); Paul of Prague (Nuremberg, 1556); Paul Weidner (Vienna, 1558); Philip Auerbacher of Nikolsborg (Carinthia, 1597); Johann Adrian of Emden (Frankfurt, 1607). See Blumenkranz 1966 and Hsia 1997: 40 for further details.

46. The idea of the Jews' blindness is based on Paul (Romans 11: 25). Because of the Jews' alleged harmful influence on Christian society, they began to be confined to ghettos from the beginning of the sixteenth century in some of the cities in which they permitted to reside. The first ghetto was instituted in Venice in 1516 with others soon following to enforce the separation of the Jews and keep Christians safe from their contagion. However, 'ghettoisation' did not take place in German lands during the sixteenth century. See Ravid 2008.

47. Cf. Yerushalmi 1975: plate 6. A list of all Pfefferkorn's publications can be found in Appendix I.

and replaced by the coming of Jesus.[48] Convinced that if deprived of rabbinical leadership and literature, the Jews would convert *en masse* to Christianity, he managed to gain support from a number of Dominican institutions to recommend him to the emperor's widowed sister Abbess Kunigunde, and through her he won the favour of the Holy Roman emperor Maximilian I (d. 1519). Maximilian had already exiled the Jews from his territories of Styria, Carinthia and Carniola, and now he was convinced by Pfefferkorn to order the confiscation and destruction of all books written in Hebrew with the exception of the Bible. On 19 August 1509 and again on 1 November 1509, two imperial decrees were issued ordering the destruction of these Hebrew books.

Pfefferkorn wasted little time and instigated the confiscation at the Judengasse synagogue in Frankfurt am Main (with 168 manuscripts being removed on Friday 28 September, *'Erev Sukot* [the Eve of the Feast of Tabernacles]). He subsequently moved on to confiscate hundreds of books in Mainz, Bingen, Lorch, Lahnstein, Worms and Deutz.[49] At the same time, the old rumours concerning Jews' ritual murder of Christian children and their desecration of the Host began once again to circulate.[50] The confiscations and associated violence spread terror among the Jews of the Rhineland, but also alarm in some quarters of the Christian clergy who were concerned to see how much power a layman (and former Jew to boot!) had been given in questions of religion. The archbishop of Mainz, Uriel von Gemmingen (1468/69–1514; archbishop 1508–14), and the city council in Frankfurt managed to put a stop to Pfefferkorn's actions. In response, Pfefferkorn persuaded the emperor to establish a commission to investigate Jewish texts and advise whether or not Jewish books should be destroyed while at the same time restarting his confiscations. The commission was inaugurated on 10 November 1509 and Archbishop Uriel von Gemmingen was appointed its head.

---

48. After their discovery of rabbinic literature around the end of the twelfth century, Christian scholars concluded that Jews did not adhere to the Mosaic law of the Bible anymore but to what they described as the false Talmudic religion. The Talmud was viewed as a law set against divine law which meant that Jews no longer should be tolerated by Christians as they did not adhere to the Hebrew Bible (Old Testament) but rather followed a law that subverted it. See Cohen 1999: 317–63.

49. The cities are listed by Pfefferkorn himself in a letter of 1510 (see Spanier 1934: 584). On the confiscation of books in Frankfurt am Main in 1509, see Graetz 1875; Kracauer 1887, 1900a, 1900b; Stokes 1909: xxv–xxvi; Wenninger 1981: 195–96; Rummel 2002: 128–31, and Shamir 2011: 37–54, 108–11. For confiscations in Worms, see Freundenthal 1931; Stern 1932. All these towns are in the Rhineland. Frankfurt and Worms had sizeable Jewish communities, but the other towns had very small populations (see Shamir 2011: 38).

50. Aring 1998.

The commission was to collect the opinions of the universities in Mainz, Cologne, Erfurt and Heidelberg, of the inquisitor Jakob Hoogstraten in Cologne, of the priest (and former Jew) Victor von Carben (1442–1515), and of the scholar Johannes Reuchlin (1455–1522), who seems likely to have been the only man in the commission with a mastery of Hebrew (although not Aramaic, the language of the Talmud).[51] For his part, Pfefferkorn tried to secure the emperor's continued good favour with his publication *In Praise and Honour of the Most Glorious and Powerful Duke and Lord Maximilian*, printed in both German and Latin, in which he heaps compliments on the emperor. In April, Pfefferkorn was back in Frankfurt and undertook a new confiscation of about 1500 Jewish books, the vast majority of them prayer books.[52] In October 1510, both the University of Cologne and Hoogstraten presented their findings (*Gutachten*): Jewish literature was anti-Christian and heretical, and they advised the emperor to destroy all Jewish books (with the exception of the Bible). The University of Mainz agreed, but advised furthermore that the Hebrew Bible be censored according to the Vulgate, as the Jews had falsified their Bible in places to free it from original references to Jesus. The University of Heidelberg suggested another commission was necessary, while Erfurt advised the destruction of only those books which were explicitly anti-Christian.[53]

Reuchlin's answer (Stuttgart, 6 October 1510) was entirely different in both its content and its tone. He divided Jewish literature into seven groups, and defined them thus:[54]

1) Holy Scripture:
 The Hebrew Bible, the highest authority, called *'Eśrim we'arba'* (עשרים וארבע, 'twenty-four') as it contains twenty-four books divided into three sections:

---

51. On the role of universities as religious authorities in the later Middle Ages, see Lytle 1981a (especially p. 82).
52. The numbers are quoted from Elisheva Carlebach in Reuchlin 2000: 23. The city had not been successful in preventing Pfefferkorn's confiscation. A petition that was prepared on 28 March 1510 for submission to the emperor Maximilian I demonstrates the city council's determination to defend its Jewish community and the Jews' right to practise their religion under ecclesiastical and civil law (Frankfurt am Main, Institut für Stadtgeschichte, Juden Akten 779, fol. 36ʳ–38ᵛ). However, we do not know whether the petition was actually sent. Among the same collection of protocols of meetings between the Frankfurt city council and the Jewish community, there are six entries describing encounters between the Jewish community, the representative of the city council, the confiscation commission and Johannes Pfefferkorn; see fols 6ʳ–13ᵛ, 19ᵛ.
53. For more detailed information on the institutions' and commission's findings and recommendations, see Shamir 2011: 55–74.
54. Reuchlin 2000: 33–34; Rummel 2002: 88.

Torah (Pentateuch), *Nevi'im* (Prophets), *Ketuvim* (Writings), the first letters of which form the acronym *Tanach*, another term for the Hebrew Bible.

2) The Talmud:
A collection of teachings and explanations of the 613 precepts and prohibitions (*mizwot*) in the *Torah*, the five books of Moses (Reuchlin does not mention the *Mišnah* or the Oral Law);

3) Kabbalah:[55]
The secret speech and words of God which neither Pfefferkorn nor the Cologne theologians seem to be aware of, but which formed an important part of Reuchlin's work as a Hebraist;[56]

4) Glosses and commentaries:
Commentaries on every book of the Bible, called *peruš*;

5) Sermons, disputations and prayer books:
Called *midraš* or *derašot*; Reuchlin does not mention liturgy;

6) Philosophical and scholarly treatises:
Called *sefarim* ('books') and designated according to the scholar or discipline;

7) Folk literature:
Books that the Jews themselves regard as fiction and invention, such as poetry, fables, verse, tales, satires and collections of moral exempla.

He noted that the vast majority of Jewish literature paid no attention whatsoever to Christianity and references to non-Jews tended to be to pagans, not specifically to Christians. In his opinion, works that offended Christianity by using slanderous and blasphemous language to speak of Jesus Christ, the Virgin Mary, the apostles or the saints could only be found in the last group comprising folk literature. He himself knew of just two works that contained such scurrilous stories, *Sefer Nizahon Yašan* and *Toledot Yešu HaNozri*, and — referring to Paul of Burgos'

---

55. Kabbalah (קבלה, *qabalah*, 'receiving') is a school of mystical thought in Judaism based on a set of esoteric teachings and interpretations of Jewish sources that aims to reveal the hidden meanings in the Hebrew Bible and rabbinical literature, as well as to explain the significance behind religious observances and rituals.
56. For example, his kabbalistic works *De verbo mirifico* (1494), and *De arte cabbalistica* (1517).

assertion in chapter six of the second half of his *Scrutinium scripturarum*, that the Jews themselves considered the works apocryphal — Reuchlin remarked that these two works were also held in little regard by Jews.[57] Furthermore, he argued that works in this group only expressed the thoughts and opinions of their author and not of the Jewish people as a whole. In Reuchlin's view, such books should be destroyed and the Jewish owner punished:[58]

> By welchem juden wissentlich gefunden würd ain sollich buch, das mit ausgetruckten worten schlechts und stracks zu schmach, schand und uneere unßerm herrngott Jesu, syner werden mutter, den hailigen oder der christenlichen ordnung gemacht were, das möcht man durch kaißerlichen bevelch nemmen und verbrennen und denselben juden darumb straffen, das er es nit selbs zerrissen, verbrennt oder undergetruckt hett.

---

57. He writes in *Augenspiegel* (Reuchlin 1961: fol. b2ʳ):

> deren hab ich nit mer dann zway geleßen/ das ain wirt genant Nizahon das ander Tolduth Jeschu/ ha nozri/ das auch von de*n* iuden selbs für apocrypho gehalten wirt
>
> *Of these I have read no more than two. The one is called* Niẓaḥon; *the other* Toledot Yešu HaNoẓri. *They are also considered apocryphal by the Jews themselves.*

In 1494, Reuchlin was given a copy of the anonymous anti-Christian polemical work *Sefer Niẓaḥon Yašan* ['The Old Book of Victory']. It dates from the end of the thirteenth century or the beginning of the fourteenth century and is a Franco-German work that addresses Christian charges concerning Judaism and Jews. It contains much material that is critical of Christianity and the New Testament. See Berger 1979 for a critical edition with an introduction, translation into English and commentary, and Trautner-Kromann 1993: 102–16 for a description and discussion. On the *Toledot Yešu HaNoẓri* ['Generations of Jesus of Nazareth'; also known as *Ma'asey Taluy* 'Deeds of the Hanged One' and *Ma'asey Yešu* 'Deeds of Jesus'], a Jewish counter-history to the Christian gospels written in light-hearted mocking tones to render the gospels innocuous, see Schonfield 1937; Goldstein 1950: 147–66; Krauss 1977; Torm 1984: 44–47, and Biale 1999. On Jewish polemics against Christianity in the Middle Ages, see Berger 1975; Cohen 1992; Cohen 1993; Trautner-Kromann 1993; Limor and Stroumsa 1996; Berger 1998; Chazan 2004, and Lasker 2007 (includes an overview of Jewish anti-Christian polemical works on pp. 13–22).

Niẓaḥon and *Toledot Yešu HaNoẓri* are part of a broader literature that aimed to alert Jews to the claims being made around them by Christians and to guide them in their engagement with the Christian majority. How widely these two books were circulated and read and how many persons were influenced by them is, of course, open to speculation. There is no eminent Jewish scholar through the centuries who refers to them, although from the Middle Ages to today Christian anti-Jewish polemicists have dredged up these texts and exploited them to fan the flames of hatred.

Nonetheless, it is clear that Jews did have a highly developed discourse to mock Christianity, and we should take the claims of converts to Christianity seriously when they talk about Jews putting anti-Christian meaning into their rituals, while remembering that a clear intent of the converts was to imbue Jewish customs and observances with a malevolent intent towards contemporary Christians (see Carlebach 2001: 195).

58. Reuchlin 1965: 33.

> *If such a book is found among the holdings of a Jew who knowingly harbours it, a book that expressly and clearly heaps scorn, offence and dishonor upon our sacred Lord Jesus, his venerable mother, the saints or the Christian Order, then one would have the right by Imperial mandate to confiscate and burn it and duly punish said Jew for having himself failed to tear it up, burn it or otherwise dispose of it.*[59]

All the other works were to some degree necessary for Jewish worship and as such were licensed under both papal and imperial law, and should in Reuchlin's opinion therefore be left alone. Indeed, such books that violated the law could be condemned under existing statutes so there was no need whatsoever to confiscate all Jewish books or, in fact, to introduce new laws and restrictions concerning them. He took vigorous exception to the statements against Hebrew texts expressed by Pfefferkorn and the Dominicans of Cologne, saying that no confidence should be placed in the lies that they were circulating. He argued that the Jews should have their books returned to them and that Hebrew should be established as a subject with two chairs at all universities in the empire and that the Jews should furnish these institutions with books. Having heard the findings of the commission, the emperor annulled his edict of 1 November 1509, and the Jews' books were returned to them. Pfefferkorn and the Dominicans were furious.

The Reuchlin-Pfefferkorn controversy

Incensed by Reuchlin's victory, Pfefferkorn attacked him in the pamphlet *Handt Spiegel* (1511), in which he claimed the Jews had bribed the humanist scholar to find in their favour. Reuchlin complained to the emperor and also replied to Pfefferkorn's allegations in a book of his own, *Augenspiegel*, published later that same year. This book was criticised by Hoogstraten who sent it to the theological university in Cologne where a commission of two theologians recommended that the book be destroyed. Reuchlin's reply came in *Ain clare Verstentnus* (1512), to which Pfefferkorn responded in the pamphlet *Brantspiegell* (1512). As the controversy subsequently developed, the entire scholarly establishment was divided into two camps: pro-Reuchlinists, comprising champions of humanism and reformers, and anti-Reuchlinists, comprising scholastics, the Dominicans and their supporters as well as the reactionary forces who disapproved of the modernising forces that in their view were leading people away from orthodoxy and were thus weakening the power of the Church.

---

59. Translation from Erasmus 1974–93, v: 203–04 (no. 713).

Figure 4
Pfefferkorn toppling the two-tongued Reuchlin and the blind 'dark men'; *Streydtpuechlyn* (1516), fol. g4ᵛ. With the permission of Universitäts- und Landesbibliothek Münster.

The controversy became so bitter that the emperor was forced to send out a decree on 7 October 1512 ordering all sides to be silent. The following year, however, Pfefferkorn instigated public burnings of Reuchlin's books. In 1514, the Pope made known his recommendation concerning Jewish writings, and largely agreeing with Reuchlin's views, considered Jewish anti-Christian books as already forbidden under existing legislation. In spite of this, however, Pfefferkorn published a new pamphlet against Reuchlin and the Jews, *Sturm Glock* (Cologne, 1514). The controversy took a more literary turn when the humanists responded with a collection of satirical letters, the *Epistolae obscurorum virorum ad venerabilem virum Magistrum Ortvinum Gratium* ['Letters of Obscure Men to the Venerable Reverend Ortwin Gratius'], in which the authors (Ulrich von Hutten 1488–1523 and Johannes Jäger *c.*1480–*c.*1539 among others), known as the 'dark' or 'obscure men', mocked the doctrines and ways of living of the scholastics, and among other things, accused the addressee of the letters, Ortwin Gratius, of having been intimate with Pfefferkorn's wife Anna (Letter XIII).[60] The *Epistolae obscurorum virorum* view the controversy as concerning scholarship rather than orthodoxy, and the letters thus deal with academic matters rather than the relationship between the Jews and Christians *per se*. Indeed, the evolving conflict had very little to do with the relationship between Jews and Christians; that it no longer concerned Talmudic writings, which had been saved by Reuchlin in 1510, can further be seen by the fate of this book in Christian circles. In 1521, Pope Leo X (1513–21) permitted the printing of the Babylonian Talmud by the Christian Daniel Bomberg in Venice. The Palestinian Talmud was printed soon after.[61]

From 1517 onwards, it was Martin Luther's *Ninety-Five Theses* against the offering of indulgences that were attracting the attention of most people, and the controversy surrounding Pfefferkorn died down noticeably. When, in 1520, Pope Leo X condemned Reuchlin for his writings (particularly *Augenspiegel*) and ordered him to be forever silent, Pfefferkorn wrote his triumphant *Ain mitleydliche*

---

60. The text has been edited and published in Böcking 1864–69, I: 20–21. An English translation (and Latin text) can be found in Stokes 1909: 314–16. See Becker 1981 for an introduction to the work. The authors, readers and disseminators of *Epistolae obscurorum virorum* were all excommunicated by Pope Leo X in 1517.
61. On the printing of the Talmud in Venice, see Goldstein 1950: 215–16, and Heller 1992: 135–54. The situation soon changed, however, and the Jews in Venice (who had been confined to a ghetto since 1516) were themselves no longer allowed to print books from 1548, and the Talmud was banned in 1553 (see Heller 1992: 217–28). The Talmud and other Jewish books were publicly burnt in Rome in 1553, and two years later Pope Paul IV segregated the Jews of Rome in a ghetto. By the mid-sixteenth century, a period of largely fruitful Christian-Jewish coexistence in Italy had come to an end.

Claeg vber alle claeg (Cologne, 1521) and thereafter disappeared from history, probably dying in 1522 or 1523. Reuchlin, however, took up a post at the University of Tübingen where he taught Hebrew and Greek until his death in 1522. He remained in the Catholic Church and took no further part in the disputes over the interpretation of Scripture that characterised the beginning of the sixteenth century.

The Reuchlin-Pfefferkorn controversy was not so much about the Jews and their writings, but about the significance of the new humanism for Church theology, and it did a great deal to damage the Catholic Church.[62] By revealing some of the internal weaknesses in the Church, the affair became an important factor in the creation of the protestant Reformation. In reality, the humanists and scholastics had an equally poor view of the Jews. Reuchlin did not particularly like the Jews and he was not interested in them *per se*; he was interested in how their sacred Jewish writings could enrich the study of Christian texts.[63] Nevertheless, in subsequent Jewish historiography, Reuchlin is usually accorded a somewhat ambivalent place of honour as a man who, although steeped in the anti-Jewish prejudices of his day, defended the Jews, in sharp contrast to many of the other 'big

---

62. For a different opinion, see Overfield 1971, and 1984: 247–97. He argues that hatred of Jews and the question of Jewish books were not merely side issues to the greater conflict between humanism and scholasticism as earlier scholarship suggests. However, Overfield has been criticised for overstating the anti- vs. philo-semitic discussion of the conflict; see Oberman 1981: 30–39; 1983: 330–35, and 1993.

63. Marcus 1999: 179; Elisheva Carlebach in Reuchlin 2000: 21–22; Edwards 1988: 53: 'In 1504, in a *German Open Letter*, Reuchlin clearly stated that he regarded "the Jews" as collectively guilty of the death of Jesus, which they called upon themselves in the famous statement by the crowd in Matthew's gospel'. However, in 1513, he wrote in his *Defensio Joannis Reuchlin contra calumniatores suos Colonienses* (fol. H4ᵛ):

> Ita faveo judaeis ut injuriae non subjeceant & injuriam non faciunt, haec mihi visa est naturalis vitae societas & human consyderatio, qua hominem etiam peccatorem a jure non expulsum neque prohibitum tractare jubemur. Injusticia enim est immanitas omnem humanitatem repellens, cuius qui sunt appetentes vel turpi quaestu vel odiosa superbia moti, tanquam immanes beluae nihil absunt a natura ferarum.

> *I favour the Jews to the extent that they do no injustice and are also subjected to no injustice. I deem it the natural bond of life and human decency that we are required to treat a man, who is even a sinner, as not excluded from or denied the law. For injustice is beastliness, banishing all human feeling. Those who strive for it, driven by base greed or hateful arrogance, are such monstrous beasts that they differ not at all from the nature of wild animals.*

> (Translation from Overfield 1984: 257)

Reuchlin's relationship with the Jews is clearly ambivalent. James Overfield (1984: 256–60) argues that Reuchlin, a lawyer and a judge, viewed the attack on the Jews in purely legal terms and as an affront to his sense of justice and equity.

names' of the sixteenth century, not least Martin Luther, one of the founding fathers of modern German antisemitism.[64] The name Pfefferkorn, on the other hand, became synonymous with antisemitic propagandist. For example, in an article in the *Palestine Post* from 1940 about the demise of Julius Streicher, founder and publisher of *Der Stürmer* newspaper, we read:[65]

> For the German Jews Streicher was the incarnation of the greatest torment and deepest humiliation Jewry has experienced in her history. If Hitler was the new Haman, Streicher was the new Pfefferkorn. Week after week his paper, 'Der Stuermer,' published the vilest accusations against the Jews, from the 'ritual murder' libel[66] to the ridiculous charge that 'Jews taught Germans to smoke in order to poison the German nation.'

---

64. On the Reuchlin-Pfefferkorn controversy in nineteenth- and twentieth-century Jewish historiography, see Schuder and Hirsch 1989: 307–51; Manuel 1992: 46–48, and Schoeps 1993. On Luther and the Jews, see also Bienert 1982; Kremers 1985, and Kaufmann 2006; on Luther and Jewish converts, see Gilman 1986: 57–67.

65. *Palestine Post*, 8 August 1940, p. 6.

66. Pfefferkorn's stance on the blood libel and ritual murder accusations was somewhat ambiguous. Initially, he rejected these myths. For example, he writes in *Der Joeden spiegel* (1507; fol. g3^r; Kirn 1989: 51 n. 156):

> Vort verkundigen ich allen ind ycklichen mynschen na dem dat vnder vns cristen eyn gemeyn rede sprechende ist, dat die joeden genoedigt syn, Cristen bloitz gebruchende die jonge cristen kyndere deshaluen vmb zo brengen, vnd dair beneuen mit anderen vnnat[u]yrlichen krenckden beladen sullen syn. Myn allerlieffsten Cristen, wilt geynen gelouuen her vp hauen noch setzen, want idt widder die hillige schrijfft vnd dat gesetz der naturen vnd widder die redelicheit verfangen wird, vnnd dair vmb ich ehe die joeden yrre vnschoult disser sachen vntschuldigen moiß

> *Furthermore, I proclaim to each and every person, that there is among us Christians a commonly stated belief that the Jews, requiring Christian blood, kill young Christian children, and that they moreover are weighed down with other unnatural pestilences. My most dear Christians! Harbour and place no belief in this because it is harmful against the Holy Scriptures and the law of nature and against reason, and as far as this is concerned, I must declare the Jews' innocence in these matters.*

But later in *Ain mitleydliche Claeg* (1521; fol. d3^{r-v}), he claimed that:

> das vns Juden fur feinde maynen ist offenbar. das sie in menschlicher gedechtnuß. die jungen Christen kinder gemartyrisiert. peynget vnd getödt haben. auch das heylig sacrament an vielen || unden gelestert vnnd gemißmandelt

> *That the Jews consider us enemies is apparent to all, as they have in living memory martyred, tortured and killed young Christian children. [They have] also attacked and abused and mistreated the holy sacrament [i.e. the Eucharist].*

Cf. also his comments on the use of Christian blood by Jews in *Beschyrmung* (1516; fol. a4^v) and *Streydtpuechlein* (1516; fol. c2^v).

The Confession of the Jews

Content

Pfefferkorn's *The Confession of the Jews* first appeared in German as *Ich heyß eyn buchlijn der iuden beicht* in 1508, and in Latin as *Libellus de Judaica confessione* a little later that same year. It is a pamphlet that that describes Jewish rituals and customs concerning the Days of Awe in the month of *'Elul* (that is, the Jewish New Year, the Ten Days of Repentance and the Day of Atonement) in often mocking terms. Furthermore, it warns of the Jews' dangerous influence on Christians and blames their ignorance on the false teachings of their leaders and the Talmud. The book provides its readers, and the secular and religious authorities of the land in particular, with a series of solutions to the dangers of the Jews. There are six chapters in all:

Chapter	Content
1	The rituals and customs during the month of *'Elul* (August/September), focusing on: a) *Rosh Hashanah* (Jewish New Year) The presentation is largely polemical and includes allegations of prayers for the destruction of Christendom.
2	Further rituals and customs used during the month of *'Elul* (August/September), focusing on: a) *'Aśeret Yemei Tešuvah* (Ten Days of Repentance) b) *Yom Kippur* (the Day of Atonement) Again the presentation is polemical and describes rituals associated with repentance and confession.
3	Pfefferkorn's programme to convert the Jews to Christianity by: a) Revealing the Jews' secrets so that they may be ridiculed and shamed; b) Preaching the word of God; c) Confiscating the Talmud and other rabbinical writings.
4	The Jews are not only a danger to themselves but also to Christians, because they: a) Take away Christians' faith using intellectual methods;

b) Damage Christians' worldly belongings;
  c) Mock Jesus, the Virgin Mary and the Cross (in this 'they surpass even the Devil') .

5   What the authorities should do:
  a) Force them to do manual labour;
  b) Force them to attend Christian sermons;
  c) Expel the Jews from their lands.

6   The danger of baptising Jews who are only interested in the economic benefits that conversion offers. Therefore, caution should be exercised when baptising Jews:
  a) Foreign Jews should be sent back to their home country for baptism;
  b) Converts should not be rewarded but forced to work;
  c) Converts should practise their faith properly (attend Mass and sermons, fast, pray etc.).

The descriptions of rituals during the Days of Awe focus particularly on the blowing of the shofar, the ceremonies of tashlich, kaparot and malqot, and the lighting of the candles.[67] The actions and physical aspects of the rituals are largely portrayed accurately and in some cases in surprising detail (for example, the number of blasts of the shofar, the form of the Torah scroll, the number of penitential lashes, the need for a 'Sabbath gentile' to make sure the candles burn safely, and so on). Pfefferkorn describes dangerous anti-Christian motivation as lying behind these rituals, and more precisely what it is that Jews think and say during them; for example, that Jews hate Christians whom they consider to be very unclean and that they pray for the destruction of Christendom. Pfefferkorn does not fail to mention that it is only Christians — and no other people — who are singled out by the Jews in this way. Jews are also portrayed as greedy hypocrites who are prepared to break their own law lest they lose money by not doing so.

Pfefferkorn wishes to bring the Jews out into the light in his publications and he believes that by documenting their way of life, exposing their corrupt literature, and ridiculing their rituals, they can be cajoled into conversion: once Christians

---

67. For readers unfamiliar with these rituals, *The Oxford Dictionary of the Jewish Religion* edited by Werblowsky and Wigoder (1997) is a good introduction. See also the commentary in chapter 6 of this book for shofar (4: 7, 9: 2, 8–10, 10–18), tashlich (11: 1–4), kaparot (12: 8–9), malqot (13: 15–23), and candle lighting (17: 5–13).

are suitably enlightened about Jewish practices and start to bully the Jews and mock their way of life and customs, then the Jews will recognise the inanity of their own ways and beliefs, which are so evidently ludicrous, and rush to convert to Christianity. He identifies the source of their delusion and error as their rabbis and the Talmud. He writes that the rabbis meet on Yom Kippur and hold a secret council where they invent new beliefs and rituals and discuss ways to keep their congregation enthralled in their power. These 'secret' customs and traditions are invented by rabbis and written in 'their book' the Talmud, which at the time was considered by learned Christians to be the Jews' book of secrets. The Talmud is mentioned several times in *The Confession of the Jews*, and we know that it topped Pfefferkorn's list of books to be burnt. Ever since Innocent IV's *Apparatus* of 1254, the Church had jurisdiction over those Jews who went unpunished by Jewish authorities for committing 'hæreses circa suam legem [*heresies against their own laws*]', in other words transgressing the true divine Mosaic Law, by which was meant the moral code of the Old Testament as the Church understood it. The destruction of the Talmud, considered to be a collection of rabbinical fables, was thus justified in the eyes of Christians as it perverted this moral code and led Jews astray. The Talmud is described by Peter the Venerable in 'De ridiculis et stultissimis fabulis Iudeorum [*On the ridiculous and most foolish stories of the Jews*]', chapter 5 of *Tractatus adversus Iudaeorum inveteratam duritiem* ['Treatise against the longstanding insensibility of the Jews'] as their great secret and in his refutation of the book, he calls it the source of 'hidden secrets':[68]

> Sed miraris, cum Iudeus non sim, unde michi hoc nomen innotuit, unde auribus meis insonuit, quis michi secreta Iudaica prodidit, quis intima uestra et occultissima denudauit?
>
> *But, you will wonder, how did I who am not a Jew learn its name and how did its name reach my ears? Who revealed the secrets of Judaism to me? Who uncovered your most hidden secrets?*[69]

Victor von Carben, another Jew who converted to Christianity and published attacks on his former coreligionists shortly before Pfefferkorn, also railed against the Talmud, not least in his *Opus Aureum* from 1509.[70]

---

68. *PL* CLXXXIX: 602.
69. Translation from Friedman 1985: xiv.
70. On von Carben, see Diemling 1999.

Literally meaning 'learning', the Talmud is a record of rabbinical discussions on Jewish history, philosophy, folklore, theology and law. It has two main parts: the *Mišnah* (a compendium of the Oral Law completed *c.* 200 CE) and the *Gemara'* (a discussion of the *Mišnah* completed *c.* 500 CE).[71] With its two and a half million words, collected in more than twenty tractates, the Talmud has become an extremely important work in Judaism, second only to the Bible in significance. For modern readers its style and tone may seem strange and alien. The propositions and argumentation can seem rather convoluted and redundant, and it also contains some statements which many readers today — both Jewish and non-Jewish — would find repugnant. However, the vast majority of these comments are not meant as paragraphs of law but suggestions, ideas and thoughts of individual rabbis in their continuing discussions about a huge number of topics that were of interest to the Jews living in the first centuries of the Common Era.

There is a long Christian polemical tradition on the Talmud and its interpretation by Jews.[72] Christian theologians regarded these later 'human' additions to the shared biblical legacy as inauthentic and corruptive. By quoting certain paragraphs from the Talmud out of context, the polemicists demonstrated that Judaism fed hatred to non-Jews (especially Christians) and that the Talmud encouraged immoral behaviour among Jews and acted as an obstacle that prevented them from converting to Christianity.[73] In order to make the

---

71. Two clear and highly readable introductions to the history and meaning of the Talmud can be found in Steinsaltz 2006 and Stemberger 1996.
72. The Talmud appeared on the Church's first index of forbidden books in 1559 (Stemberger 1996: 223). On the Talmud as victim of Christian anti-Judaism, censorship and antisemitism, see Popper 1899 (especially pp. 22–26 on Pfefferkorn and Reuchlin); Kedar 1979, and Heller 1992: 201–15. For an introduction to Christian anti-Jewish polemic in the Middle Ages, see Funkenstein 1968 (and also abridged in 1971), and Schreckenberg 1994.
73. Although the Talmud is anything but anti-Christian, that does of course not mean that Jews have never been hostile towards aspects of the Church and Christianity. Judaism and Christianity have coexisted for nearly two thousand years, most of them marred by Christian anti-Jewish polemics, persecution and murder, so in some areas and at some times, rabbis have fulminated against the Church and a body of oral folk literature has come into being that demeans Christianity. This includes anti-Christian phrases and words; for example, the Yiddish phrase (still) used when saying something is a lie, similar to 'when pigs fly!' ('ništ geštoygn un ništ gefloygn [*not risen and not flown*]'), which builds on a disbelief in the divinity of Jesus (Wex 2006: 20–21). The gospels have been called *'awen gilayon* (עון גליון, 'page of wickedness/ emptiness'), and *Sefer Ṭe'iyot* (ספר טעיות, 'book of confusions'), since the genealogies at the beginning of the gospels by Mark and Luke seem worthy of scepticism. In *Iudeorum Secreta*, there are examples of Hebrew words and phrases that were used to demean Jesus, the Virgin Mary, the saints and Christian places of worship (these are discussed in the next chapter). There

passages serve their purposes, these Christian writers quoted sections out of context, or mistranslated and contorted the Talmud, and attempts by others (for example, Johannes Reuchlin) to correct these translations were seen as hair-splitting or, worse still, as being pro-Jewish. There was no attempt to explain the nuanced approaches in Jewish scriptural interpretation, and only the Talmud's most literal reading was given. This resulted in a monstrous fabrication of Judaism that was antithetical to Christianity, and it was this 'Frankenstein Judaism', a Christian, not a Jewish creation, which Pfefferkorn and other anti-Jewish writers presented their readers and attacked. In this respect, Pfefferkorn also continued the medieval tradition, whereby the only Jews whom Christians recognised were in fact inventions of their own imagination.[74]

Pfefferkorn also points the finger of blame at those who protect the Jews and who profit from their money-lending activities. He views the Jews as a social and economic threat to the provinces in which they live, and subsequently to the empire as a whole. He offers his readers a number of permanent solutions to the 'Jewish problem': book confiscations, forced attendance at Christian sermons and hard manual labour. He suggests that if the Jews do not convert to Christianity, learn to work with their hands and stop their alleged war against the Christian community, then they should be expelled. His readers are also warned about Jews who convert insincerely, and whose 'sin' is apparently not washed away by baptismal water but requires further efforts to be eliminated. Finally, the readers are warned that Jews who are learned from books are particularly dangerous to Christians as they seem so knowledgeable, yet their understanding of the Bible is in fact extremely limited as they have not understood how the Old Testament prophecies were fulfilled in the New Testament. The same methods for dealing with the Jews, including expulsion, were taken up and expanded upon by the religious reformer Martin Luther, whose writings on the Jews contributed significantly to the development of modern antisemitism.[75]

---

are also anti-Christian works, such as the *Sefer Niẓaḥon Yašan* ('The Old Book of Victory') and *Toledot Yešu HaNoẓri* ('Generations of Jesus of Nazareth'), which are both described above.

74. This is largely the theme of Cohen 1999. Cf. also Sartre's words: 'Le Juif est un homme que les autres hommes tiennent pour Juif: voilà la vérité simple d'où il faut partir [*The Jew is a man whom other men take for a Jew: that is the simple truth from which we must start*]' (1946: 88).

75. Wallmann 1987.

A new development in anti-Judaism?

Anti-Judaism is often distinguished from antisemitism on biological-racial grounds.[76] Anti-Judaism concerns opposition to Jewish beliefs and practices, and a Jew who converts to Christianity is thus no longer subject to such prejudice. Antisemitism, on the other hand, is a modern (post-Enlightenment) phenomenon, a hatred of Jews based on a combination of racial, ethnic or religious prejudices. Yet the evidence from the Middle Ages shows us that the distinction is not always so clear-cut. Long before explicitly racial doctrines appear, converted Jews were still considered inferior because of their background or inherent qualities.[77] Any religious or cultural changes that the Jews underwent were considered ineffectual, and their essential characteristics and evil essence remained unaltered.[78] Belief in the inadequacy of baptism to cleanse a Jew also lies at the root of Reuchlin's name-calling such as when he used the term 'dißer taufft iud [*this baptised Jew*]'[79] as a slur against Pfefferkorn, and he referred to much of what Pfefferkorn wrote as the 'vnwarhait des taufften iuden [*the untruth of the baptised Jew*]'.[80] Rather tellingly, even Pfefferkorn himself does not think that baptismal water is enough to cleanse a Jew of Jewishness.[81] This 'race theory' appears to have been widespread in sixteenth-century Germany, where Luther declared that it was impossible to convert the Devil and his creatures (i.e. the Jews),[82] and the Lutheran cleric Georg Schwartz, under the alias Georgius Nigrinus (1530–1602), wrote these lines in his *Jüden Feind* (1570; fols H5ᵛ–6ʳ):

Ich halte Jüden für Jüden /	*I consider Jews to be Jews,*
Sie seyen getaufft oder beschnitten. ‖	*Whether they are baptised or circumcised.*
Sind sie nicht all einer Ankunfft /	*If they are not all from one descent,*

---

76. See Nicholls 1993: 314. For a discussion about the problems with the terms used to describe anti-Jewish sentiment, imagery and behaviour, see Chazan 1997: 125–40.
77. On Christian discourses on Jewish conversions in the sixteenth and seventeenth centuries, see Hsia 2009.
78. As the Dane Peder Laale wrote in his proverb collection (1506: fol. g1ᵛ, no. 592): 'Kastæ hwnd i iordens flodh tha ær hwnd som føre war [*Throw a dog into the River Jordan and it stays a dog just as before*]' — i.e. even a baptised Jew remains in essence a Jew.
79. Brod 1965: 178.
80. For example, Reuchlin 1961: fol. 32ᵛ, where he also describes revenge as the traditional manner of Pfefferkorn's ancestors. On converted Jews being seen as 'taufjuden', interminable Jews baptised but not truly converted, see Carlebach 2001: 35–37.
81. See, for example, *Iudeorum Secreta*, chapter 6.
82. See Trachtenberg 1993: 218, especially n. 3.

gehören sie doch in ein Zunfft	*They still belong to one guild.*
Sie dienen all gleich einem Gott /	*They all serve the same one god,*
Den Christus Mammon genant hat.	*Whom Christ has called Mammon [cf. Matthew 6: 24],*
Welcher mit sein Dienern entlich gleich /	*Who together with his servants in the end,*
Wird faren in des Teuffels Reich.	*Will go to the Devil's realm.*

Theories concerning the inadequacy of baptism were not restricted to Germany, however, and elsewhere they led to actions of an extreme and serious nature. Fifteenth-century Spain and Portugal introduced Europe's first anti-Jewish blood laws, whereby the proto-racist theory of 'cleanliness of blood' (Spanish: *limpieza de sangre*; Portuguese: *limpeza de sangue*) kept *conversos* or new Christians — those descended from Jews or Moors — in inferior positions and under the constant and watchful eye of the Inquisition. This can be considered as a form of emergent antisemitism based on ethnic and racial prejudice. The last *converso* to be accused and tried by the Inquisition was Manuel Santiago Vivar in Córdoba 1818, and these blood laws were not abolished until by royal decree in 1834.

The history and development of Judaeophobia in Europe during the Middle Ages have been described and analyzed by a number of scholars.[83] As we have seen, its expression in the vernacular literature of Denmark was largely of the kind found in northern European Christian anti-Judaism, and the depictions of Jews, which include chimerical beliefs and irrational fantasies, are literary and theological *topoi* found in both translated and original works. The representation of Jews in medieval Danish writing is in full agreement with the supersessionist thinking of the Church, according to which Judaism and the Jews had been superseded by the new law (the New Testament) and the new Israel (Christendom), *Ecclesia* had triumphed over *Synagoga*. The memory, hope and identity of Israel had been appropriated by the Church in order that it might understand and define itself.

The Jews were nevertheless not entirely redundant in this scheme of things, as their survival in a degraded state provided the Christian faithful with providential witness to divine justice. The supposed crime for which the Jews were being punished was, of course, deicide and the rejection of Christ, and their immoral, cruel, evil, stupid and obstinate nature was a standard stereotype in Denmark as elsewhere in Europe. However, the Jew in Danish writing remains largely in the biblical or exotic realm, that is at a distance in time and geography. Without doubt, it is only due to the lack of a Jewish presence in Denmark that we find no contem-

---

83. See, for example, the bibliographies in Stow 1992; Foa 2000; Bale 2006, and Chazan 2006.

porary accusations of blood libel, Host desecration or well-poisoning.[84] Nonetheless, literature that contained references to Jews was widespread across the medieval world and, as can be seen from the Danish sources, the absence of Jews in a given country did not have much of an effect on attitudes towards them. Jews, imaginary and real, played an important role in the discourse of the Church across Europe, and Denmark was no exception.

The Church's treatment of the Jews can at times seem rather ambivalent: on the one hand holding a protecting hand over the Jews, and on the other punishing them for killing its God. During the Middle Ages, there were in effect two

---

84. Earliest recorded accusations, that resulted in persecution, in Europe and Scandinavia were:

Blood libel

Europe: William of Norwich, d. 1144 (see *JE*, *s.v.* 'William of Norwich; Thomas of Monmouth 1896; McCulloh 1997; Yuval 1993; Dundes 1991); Little Hugh of Lincoln, d. 1255 (see *JE*, *s.v.* 'Hugh of Lincoln'; Michel 1834; Dundes 1991); Simon of Trent, d. 1475 (see *JE*, *s.v.* 'Simon (Simedl, Simoncino) of Trent'; Hsia 1988; Hsia 1992; Dundes 1991).

Scandinavia: As late as 1699 (after the arrival of the Jews in Denmark), a poor woman, in order to make some money, offered to sell her baby to Meyer Goldschmidt, court jeweller to the king of Denmark, for the Jews to kill and extract its blood (Trachtenberg 1993: 125).

Host desecration

Europe: Berlitz in 1243; Paris 1290; Laa 1294; Röttingen and Korneuburg 1298; Regensburg 1299; St Pölten 1306; Cracow 1325; Güstrow 1330; Deggendorf 1337; Pulkau 1338; Brussels 1370; Prague 1388; Posen 1399; Glogau 1401; Segovia 1410; Ems 1420; Breslau/Wrocław 1453; Passau 1478; Sternberg 1492; Mittelberg 1514; Knoblauch 1510 (see *JE*, *s.v.* 'Host, desecration of'; Hsia 1988; Rubin 1995; Rubin 2004).

Scandinavia: None.

Well-poisoning

Europe: Franconia 1319; from 1348 (the outbreak of the Black Death) onwards there were literally hundreds of accusations and subsequent massacres, particularly in Germany and Switzerland (see *JE*, III: 233–36, *s.v.* 'Black Death'). The period of the Black Death in which Jews were massacred *en masse* in Europe is known as *'emeq habachah* [the vale of tears] in Jewish historiography.

Scandinavia: There is a recorded accusation of well-poisoning at the hands of Jews, from Gotland, Sweden, in *c.* 1350 (see Trachtenberg 1993: 104; Harrison 2000: 405).

Other common accusations against Jews were that they were trying to despoil Christianity with usury, they were allies of the Devil, they were trying to destroy society and that they were 'pollutants'. This hostility resulted in a series of often extremely violent and bloody expulsions across Europe: England (1290), France (the fourteenth century), Spain (1492), Portugal (1497), and the Netherlands (the end of the sixteenth century).

churches: the hierarchy that laid down and defined general principles, and the lesser clergy and laity who translated and put these principles into practice. These two churches were not always in agreement, so despite the hierarchy (and to some extent secular authorities) forbidding violence against Jews (albeit half-heartedly at times), the populace was incited by the preaching and teachings of the clergy to shun the Jews. As Joshua Trachtenberg puts it rather concisely, there was 'a Church-fostered contempt and hatred which had sunk so deeply into the public consciousness that not even the highest authorities of the Church and state were able to meliorate it'.[85] In other words, the Church was able to promulgate the theology that fed mob violence whilst at the same time condemning such attacks. This was the Church's ambiguous message of contemptuous toleration.[86]

By writing his anti-Jewish pamphlets describing religious rituals and customs and by lampooning the Jews, their religious leaders and the Talmud, Pfefferkorn was one of those who opened a new chapter in the history of anti-Jewish polemics.[87] Rather than functioning as moral devices in Christian devotional literature and acting as warnings against sin and impenitence, Jews and aspects of their religion were being represented by these writers for the first time as they supposedly 'really were' in order to inspire outright hatred and contempt. Jews were no longer just to be seen as Old Testament patriarchs or New Testament deicists, but as a very real contemporary, present evil in the world against which the reader is called upon to fight. Instead of arguing about certain biblical quotations or spreading the usual lies about ritual infanticide or well-poisoning, Pfefferkorn fought Judaism from within.[88] He used ethnographic descriptions that actually related to the practices of the Jews to attack their observance of the *miẓwot* ('commandments') and the use of the Talmud, as well as to demonstrate their animosity towards and dangerous influence on Christians. In his work, the Jews are not blind naïfs, but rather they behave in an outright malicious and hypocritical manner. It is not enough for him just to portray the Jews' ceremonies and practices as absurd and inane; he also uncovers their anti-Christian content and quotes actual Jewish curses against

---

85. Trachtenberg 1993: 166–67.
86. Cf. Epstein 2002: 332.
87. Victor von Carben (1442–1515) is the first convert who can be linked to this new ethnographic genre. Pfefferkorn and his fellow converts' works on Jewish ceremonial practice have a parallel in the literature of the Jews of northern Europe, an area in Medieval Hebrew called *'Aškenaz* and meaning 'Rhineland' (but also 'Germany' or even more broadly 'northern Europe'). The Ashkenazi Jews wrote extensively about their own ritual and practices (*minhag*). On *minhag* literature, see Carlebach 2001: 175–77.
88. He states for example, that Pilate (not the Jews) is responsible for the death of Jesus (*Iudeorum Secreta*, p. 28, ll. 9–11).

Christians, explains the true and hidden meaning of Jewish prayers, and describes their abuse of baptism for financial gain. In fact, because of Pfefferkorn's insistence on describing Jews as evil and a danger to Christendom, the German scholar Ellen Martin has credited him with contributing to the birth of modern antisemitism.[89]

Ronnie Po-Chia Hsia was the first to highlight an important and innovative aspect of Pfefferkorn's writings, which he places into a Christian ethnographical context.[90] He views them as texts that describe religious rituals, language and other cultural practices and symbols (in other words, ethnography's very field of activity), while at the same time also serving as an instrument that can be used to reject Judaism and define 'the Other'. The tradition of describing foreign peoples in this way goes back to Herodotus, and in the fifteenth century, there was a flowering in ethnographic writing which described foreign cultures.[91] There was an ethnographic impulse to define identities and affirm boundaries.

Yaacov Deutsch takes a similar but critically different view.[92] Although recognising that there are parallels between the subjects discussed in works about the Jews and those about other peoples and religions, he notes the unique character of descriptions of Jewish practices and customs, not least their theological and religious polemics which are largely absent in ethnographic descriptions of other cultures. He emphasises the polemical aspects of Pfefferkorn's works whose descriptions of Jewish practice are determined theologically (they underline superstitious beliefs and departure from Mosaic Law) and socially (they highlight anti-Christian elements in prayer and ceremonies). Pfefferkorn clearly had a polemical anti-Jewish agenda and his descriptions are therefore not biased due to his inability to understand a culture from the outside; indeed, he had been born and raised a Jew. Deutsch refers to these types of descriptions as 'polemical ethnography' — they are largely accurate descriptions of ceremonies but are couched in anti-Jewish polemic, because the authors only depict those rituals and ceremonies

---

89. Martin 2005: 543. Pfefferkorn's proposed measures for dealing with the Jews appear not to have been forgotten, and some 35 years later, Martin Luther makes the same demands to princes, prelates and market towns in his pamphlet *On the Jews and Their Lies*, 1543 (edited in *WA* LIII: 412–552). However, Luther was to go much further than Pfefferkorn, and called not only for the destruction of the Talmud and the Jews' prayer books, but also for the burning down of their synagogues and homes, the prohibiting of their rabbis from teaching and preaching, the banning of Jews from practising usury, the confiscation of their wealth, and eventually, like Pfefferkorn, the driving of the Jews out of 'our land' (see *WA* LIII: 523–29).
90. Hsia 1994 and 1997. On Christian ethnographies of the Jews, see also Burnett 1994.
91. Hodgen 1964: 20–29.
92. See Deutsch 2004, 2006 and 2012.

that support their agenda. The selection of the authors is key to understanding their intentions and methods. Through his work on the depictions of Yom Kippur in the writings of Christian Hebraists and Jewish converts to Christianity in early modern Europe, Deutsch has shown that the consequences of this polemical ethnography that aimed to expose secret Jewish practices and clandestine acts of opposition were not entirely negative for European Jewry. The genre which aimed to discredit Judaism fostered a certain disenchantment with the religion and 'shifted the Christian interest from dealing with Judaism to dealing with Jews — a shift that later paved the road to the naturalisation of the Jews.'[93]

Pfefferkorn's *The Confession of the Jews* is clearly something of an innovation within Christian anti-Jewish writing. Unlike the polemicists before him, he is not just writing about Judaism, but he is concentrating on the Jews, their customs, rituals and way of life. The critical focus has shifted from the religion to the people. Whilst building on the many motifs developed since the early Church (the Jews' rejection of Jesus, their misuse of the Old Testament, the power of their leaders, their greed and their hypocrisy), the author presents us with a work of polemical ethnography in which he exploits his status as a former insider to add authenticity to his account and weight to his message. *The Confession of the Jews* is a pioneering work as it is one of the first accounts for a Christian readership of the ceremonies and customs of contemporary Jews. His efforts both to ridicule Jewish beliefs and to expose the dangers of contact with them also mark a change in approach. In his work, there is no need for theological arguments or historical explanations to condemn the Jews or demand their conversion to Christianity; it is the Jews themselves together with their rituals and behaviour that, by being brought from under their mantle of secrecy and out into the light, invite condemnation and refutation. The Jews were to be vanquished on their own terms. Indeed, some of Pfefferkorn's observations are correct: there is evidence that medieval Jews cursed Christians, they had anti-Christian texts, they referred to Jesus as a bastard (*mamzer*), and they sometimes converted to win financial help.[94] Nonetheless, Pfefferkorn may have felt that the image of the Jews that readers would

---

93. Deutsch 2004: 224; see also Deutsch 2006: 356.
94. On anti-Christian semantics in everyday language, see Funkenstein 1993: 171 n. 5; Carlebach 2001: 99. On anti-Christian elements in prayer books, see Raz-Krakotzkin 2004 (especially pp. 140–42), and 2007: 141–42; Yuval 2006: 115–34. On curses on Yom Kippur, Passover and in *piyuṭim*, see Goldschmidt 1956; Merḥavia 1972; Kirn 1989: 42–46, and Yuval 2006: 93–109. Verbal acts, such as curses, prayers and blasphemy, were included in the charges against the Jews during the ritual murder trials in Trent in 1475 (see Hsia 1992: 88). All Jewish behaviour that directly or even obliquely criticised or expressed hostility towards the Christian faith was, of course, absolutely forbidden by the Christian authorities.

derive from his descriptions of ceremonies during Rosh Hashanah and Yom Kippur were too favourable, and that is why he added a section after these descriptions, in which he both highlights the social and economic dangers posed by the Jews and explains why he published the work and how his readers can save themselves from the Jews' wickedness. Pfefferkorn may have felt that he had to increase the level of his invective here in order to establish his own Christian orthodoxy and to show his readers that he had not again fallen into the Devil's trap and taken a step back towards being seduced by his former coreligionists' error.[95]

Towards the end of his *Confession of the Jews*, Pfefferkorn describes the Jews as more evil than the Devil and being like dogs. In making a link between the Jews and Satan, he follows in the long tradition of Jewish stereotypes. Elsewhere in the work, however, the Jews are on the whole described as people, albeit somewhat unpleasant people, going about their business. Indeed, they are described as sincere believers who are convinced that they are good and that they are following God. 'Jewishness' is essentially presented as a behaviour expressed through word and act rather than an innate condition, and as such it can be 'cured' by thorough teaching (through preaching), conversion and hard work. The Jews can, and should, be transformed. In addition to defending Pfefferkorn's own conversion, the *Confession* thus also insists that the core of man is pure (that is, in his view, Christian), and can be reached by peeling of the 'malignant layers of Jewishness'.[96] In several places, Pfefferkorn draws comparisons between Jewish and Christian ceremonies, presumably to help his readers imagine and relate to the Jewish ritual but thus also making the Jews seem like fellow human beings. For example, the rabbi and his recommendations during the Days of Awe are compared to the admonitions of Christian bishops, prelates, teachers and confessors during Lent; the use of a prayer shawl is compared to the vestments of a Christian priest at Mass, and the joyous singing at Rosh Hashanah is compared to Christian singing at New Year.[97]

There are two further important stereotypes used in Pfefferkorn's *Confession of the Jews*. The first is an economic threat to society: the usurious Jew. Their usury robs money from good Christian folk, deprives the Church of money that is theirs by right and provides the Jews with illegitimate wealth. The second stereotype and charge against the Jews is that they benefit from the authorities' special treatment and unwarranted protection. The kings, barons, lords and princes are using

---

95. See Deutsch 2006: 339–40.

96. Carlebach 2001: 173. Cf. *Iudeorum Secreta*, pp. 19: 25 – 20: 4, where Jews are described as being able to learn and use good sense just as well as anyone else.

97. See *Iudeorum Secreta*, p. 4: 7–14; p. 5: 16–19, and p. 15: 4–8 respectively.

the Jews as their henchman in their efforts to fill their coffers, and in so doing the Jews came to be perceived as 'lackeys of the ruling class'.[98] By focusing on descriptions of cultural and commercial practice, rather than using theological arguments, Pfefferkorn shows his Christian readership that their Jewish neighbours are human with the potential to be good, but that unless they are converted or shunned, they pose a serious threat to all Christendom. Indeed, every Jewish man and woman going about everyday activities is portrayed as engaging in anti-Christian acts, and Jewish knowledge — as displayed in books, prayers, verbal acts and rituals — is viewed as vehemently antisocial.

Although *Confession of the Jews* describes the Jews as humans, they are nonetheless both different and harmful. They are different culturally and religiously — these are the areas dealt with in the book's descriptions of ritual during the High Holy Days. They are harmful economically, because of their money-lending activities, and politically, because they are both the historic enemies of Christendom and the allies of the ruling secular authorities. These harmful aspects are the main topics in the final chapter and invite Pfefferkorn's most severe invective. It is also here at the end of *Confession of the Jews*, that he presents his readers with a series of solutions that will deprive the Jews of the source of their 'otherness' and will render them economically and politically harmless.

Poul Ræff (died *c.* 1533)

Life and work

The man who translated, printed and sold Pfefferkorn's pamphlet was none other than the first born-and-bred Danish book-printer to operate in Denmark, Poul Ræff, a man about whom we unfortunately know very little. He studied abroad, where he would have been exposed to the milieu of German humanists as well as Catholic and radical reform movements. He became a *magister* (Master of Arts) and later a canon in the Copenhagen college chapel. In 1508, he was elected rector of the University of Copenhagen. His brother, Hans Ræff, was the last Catholic bishop in Oslo, who during the Reformation converted to Lutheranism and subsequently became the city's first superintendent in 1541. Poul Ræff, however, was a staunch opponent of the Reformation and placed himself at the service of the Catholic Church, producing books for use by the Church and in schools. His

---

98. Chazan 1997: 34.

presses printed a broad range of Catholic writings and manuals, ranging from church texts to Poul Helgesen's fiery writings against the Reformers.

Ræff acquired his printing equipment from the German Matthæus Brandis who left Copenhagen in 1512 after a very short career there as printer. Ræff's first publication was *Manuale Curatorum secundum vsum ecclesie Rosckildensis* from 25 March 1513, and is one of twelve extant books from his presses (see the LN references for further details):

Date	Place	Title	LN
1513 (25/3)	Copenhagen	*Manuale Curatorum secundum vsum ecclesie Rosckildensis*	165
1514 (25/2)	Copenhagen	*[E]uangelium nicodemi*	191
1514	Copenhagen	[Michael:] *De creatione reru*m	175
1514	Copenhagen	[Michael:] *De vita homini*s	176
1515 (6/2)	Copenhagen	Michael: *Expositio pulcherrima super rosario beate marie virgini*s	177
1516	Copenhagen	Johannes Pfefferkorn: *Nouiter in lucem data: iudeorum secreta*	219
[c. 1517]	Copenhagen	*Statuta synodalia Reuerendi Patris Domini Laghonis Dei gratia Episcopi Roschildensis* [not extant]	258
1519 (25/5)	Copenhagen	*Missale pro vsu totius regni Noruegie secundum ritum sancte Metropolitane Nidrosiensis ecclesie*	182
1519	Copenhagen	*Index eorum que in hoc volumine continentur* [Johannes Murmellius: *De latina constructione xxv præcepta ad puerorum institutionem*; Johannes Bugenhagen: *Regulæ grammaticales*; Johannes Despauterius: *Rudimenta*. Ed. by Christian Therkelsen Morsing]	190
1522 (17/5)	Nyborg	*Canon secundum vsum ecclesie Roschildensis*	38
1530	Århus	Poul Helgesen: *Letter against the Marriage of Priests* [not extant; see Kristensen *et al.* 1932–48, III: 285, 300–01]	79a
1531 (21/4)	Århus	Poul Helgesen: *Een kort vnderwiisning paa then hellige Mess*e	84
1531 (28/6)	Århus	Poul Helgesen: *[E]en kortt oc Christelig vnderwiisning paa thet hemelige stocke ij messen som kaldis Cano*n	83
1533	Århus	Poul Helgesen, ed: *Menige Danmarkis Rigis Biscoppers och Prelaters christelige oc retsindige geenswar. till the Lwtherianscke artickl*e	72

His masterpiece in the art of printing is without doubt the *Missale Nidrosiense* from 1519, which he printed in honour of Erik Valkendorf, archbishop of Trondheim, Norway. It is a 608-page book in folio containing type and woodcuts in black and red ink. We do not know what happened to Ræff after this publication, until he appears three years later in 1522 as a printer in Nyborg, on the island of Fyn. We have just one extant book from his Nyborg press, *Canon Roschildensis*, produced for Bishop Lave Urne in Roskilde. It is the last book of Catholic ritual to be published in Denmark before the Reformation. Ræff disappears again from the record for another eight years, until reappearing in 1530 in Århus, Jutland, where he continues his printing career until 1533. His books from these final years demonstrate a marked deterioration in terms of technical production. In 1534, his printing equipment was being used by another printer, Hans Barth (active in Roskilde 1534–40), and it would seem that Ræff, and with him his printing career, had passed away.[99]

During his lifetime, Ræff had a poor reputation outside the Catholic Church and was despised by those promoting the Reformation in Denmark. In 1531, the reformer Frands Vormordsen (1491–1551) of Malmö in Skåne warned against putting too much trust in 'alt thet, paawel Ræff prenter emoot osz vnder scrifftens oc hellige apostlers falske titell oc nafn, eniste til at bedrage oc forlede enfoldige menniske met oc komme osz i menige mandz hadt oc affuind [*everything that Poul Ræff prints against us (i.e. the Reformers) under the false title and name of Scripture and Holy Apostles only to deceive and lead simple people astray and cause us to be hated and envied by the common man*]'.[100] On the subject of Ræff's printing of Poul Helgesen's *Letter against the Marriage of Priests* (1530), the reformer Peder Laurentsen (c.1485–1552), also of Malmö, wrote in 1532 about 'det vchristelige breff och løgnachtige falske vnderuisningis tilhobe skrabelse, som her Pouil Reff prentede [*the unchristian letter and untruthful, false heap of scraped together teachings, which Reverend Poul Ræff printed*]'.[101]

The publication of *Iudeorum Secreta*: Theological, social and psychological factors

There are probably a number of reasons why Ræff decided to translate and publish Pfefferkorn's book in Denmark eight years after its publication in Germany

---

99. Nielsen 1982.
100. Engelstoft 1848: 459, *n*, 1.
101. Kristensen *et al.* 1932–48, III: 300–01.

and two years after Pope Leo X gave his ruling on Jewish books. In the introduction to *Iudeorum Secreta*, Ræff provides us with three motives:

1. Those unable to read Latin can also learn about the secrets of the Jews and understand why they should be punished;[102]
2. Christians may protect themselves from Jews and Jewish matters, because if not they risk forsaking the salvation of their own souls;
3. Common Christian folk will understand that they should flee and avoid the unclean Jews who are constantly working to corrupt the lives and souls of Christians.

But do these reasons make sense by themselves? Do they explain why a book about the dangers of contact with the Jews and the inanity of Jewish ceremonies should be published in a country with no resident Jewish population?[103] Of course, Jews may have come in limited numbers as traders to the various market towns and cities in Denmark and in this way members of the Danish population may have come into contact with them. The passing of a law in 1536 that prohibited

---

102. This may mean that the Latin version of the book, *Libellus de Judaica Confessione*, printed in Germany, was available in Denmark, and that there was felt to be a demand for the work to reach a wider audience on the margins of literacy. Whether this need for a more widespread circulation was identified by Ræff, his target audience, the Church or some other group is not known. Pfefferkorn himself aimed at as wide an audience for his works as possible publishing them in (High) German, Ripuarian (a dialect of Low German spoken in and around Cologne) and Latin. See Schmitz 1990: 109–11.

It is also worth noting Ræff's comments concerning Danish and Latin at the beginning of Michael's *Expositio pulcherrima super rosario beate marie virginis* from 1515. By printing the text in Danish, Ræff writes on fol. a1^r, ll. 9–10, that it will be of use to '[s]wo wæl klærckæ som liggfalk til vnderwissning och salighet [*both clerics and laypeople for learning and salvation*]'. He clearly views the vernacular as *the* means of mass communication.

103. Although Jews may well have been resident in the Danish territories in Normandy as early as the twelfth century, we know of no Jews living in Denmark proper before the beginning of the seventeenth century. In 1622, King Christian IV (1588–1648) invited the Portuguese Jews in Hamburg and Amsterdam to settle in Glückstadt in the Danish province of Holsten-Slesvig (modern-day Schleswig-Holstein).

At the end of the German text of Pfefferkorn's *Confession of the Jews* (*Ich heyß eyn buchlijn der iuden beicht*; Cologne, 1508, fol. d1^r), 'Denmerck' is mentioned in a list of countries from which the Jews had been driven out prior to the book's publication. However, Denmark is missing in these same lists in the Latin and Danish translations. It reappears again, however, as a land from which Jews have been expelled in his tract *Beschyrmung* from 1516. The appearance of Denmark in these lists is either a mistake (which was subsequently corrected in the Latin versions of the texts), or it is an intentional falsification and expression of the anti-Jewish sentiment prevalent at the time. See Schuder and Hirsch 1989: 318, and Lausten 1992: 110–11.

Jews from entering Denmark could indicate significant numbers of Jews were travelling to the country which caused the authorities to act in order to protect their citizens from such a menace. However, on the basis of a lack of evidence for a Jewish presence in Denmark at the time, it seems more likely that this ruling was just a piece of stock post-Reformation legislation that did not have any basis in 'the facts on the ground', but whose roots rather lay in standard Lutheran anti-Jewish conviction. The fact is that very few Danes indeed would have come into contact with Jews at the beginning of the sixteenth century.

Nonetheless, we have already seen that Jews were a common motif used in Danish religious literature because, among other reasons, the continued existence of the Jewish people and their beliefs drew into question the self-understanding and self-definition of the Church as the new Israel. So even in countries with no Jewish population, the age-old problem of how the Church was to understand both itself and its relation to the Jews remained. It became important to show that although contemporary Jews were those who killed Jesus, they were also no longer the authentic Jews who had entered the covenant at Sinai; they had, in fact, left God and been corrupted by their rabbis and their writings (not least, the Talmud). In this way, the Jews were of universal rather than just local concern to all Christian readers including those in Denmark. Furthermore, the very subject of Pfefferkorn's book, atonement, lies at the core of Christian theology, and by laying Jewish customs concerning Yom Kippur open for view and ridicule, *Iudeorum Secreta* helps cement readers in their faith and belief in salvation through Christ. The supposed absurdity and futility of Jewish practice serve to highlight the certainties and efficacy of Christianity.

Theological factors thus also lay behind Ræff's motives to publish *Iudeorum Secreta*. The enormous and constant campaign of anti-Jewish propaganda being peddled by the Church to its members was so successful that it helped create a market for Ræff's book among a public who had never made the acquaintance of a single Jew. Although only a minority interest when compared to other books of the religious, polemical and ethnographic genre, literature revealing the secret life of Jews became increasingly popular in Germany during the sixteenth century, so it is not surprising if this embryonic and growing interest spilled over into Denmark. But with this increased awareness of diversity in early modern Europe came fear and defensiveness.

Denmark was very much in the German sphere of influence as regards culture, politics and religion during much of the medieval and modern period, and subsequently important theological matters and social affairs in Germany would presumably also have been of great interest to Danes. Ræff's translation and publication of *Iudeorum Secreta*, provided the Danish public with an opportunity to find out about one of the Church's great tasks — the fight against the Jews — as well as to read one of the very important texts that sparked the Reuchlin-Pfefferkorn affair and the subsequent formation of public opinion in two camps — a reforming movement and a reactionary one — a division that was soon to be felt in Denmark. In 1516, the year *Iudeorum Secreta* was published, the Reuchlin-Pfefferkorn controversy was still at its height and the *Epistolae obscurorum virorum* had just been published in Germany. If the Reuchlin affair is to be considered one of the galvanising forces behind the nascent humanist movement in northern Europe, then Ræff seems to want to present the great social, judicial and ecclesiastical challenges of Europe (or, more importantly perhaps, of Denmark's culturally dominant neighbour, Germany) to the Danes and show his readers that the anti-reformists (Pfefferkorn, the Dominicans *et al.*) were the real champions of true Christianity. More specifically, he wanted to prepare both the common man and the authorities in particular for the fight against Jewish and 'Judaising' elements — should that ever be necessary. One is left wondering whether Ræff also chose to publish a Danish translation of Pfefferkorn's *How the Blind Jews Keep Easter* (1509), which describes Jewish rituals during Passover and acts as a sort of sequel to *Confession of the Jews*. He may well have done so, but if he did, it has since been lost. It is noteworthy that in the Bielke Library copy, *Iudeorum Secreta* has been bound together in the sixteenth century with theological texts from the time of the Reformation that argue for and against Catholic and Lutheran teachings. This does not tell us much about Ræff's motives for publishing the book, but it does indicate at least one context in which *Iudeorum Secreta* was read.

Like much of Europe, Denmark at the beginning of the sixteenth century is characterised by instability of the political order. The country was in a state of social and political change as well as religious and economic upheaval. The reign of King Hans (1483–1513) was marred from 1500 onwards by bitter wars with rebels in Sweden (where he was renounced as king between 1501 and 1509), with the Ditmarshers (in northern Germany), and the Hanseatic towns (particularly Lübeck). Under his successor, Christian II, things got even worse. He also fought against the power of the Hanseatic League and invaded Sweden to bring the country under his control (an act which culminated in 1520 with the infamous Stockholm Bloodbath). He was increasingly unpopular with the Council of the Realm (*Rigsrådet*) and the nobility in general, although he did manage to remain popular with the internationally oriented citizens of the largest cities of his kingdom. In 1523, he was forced to flee to Holland and replaced by Frederik I as king. The beginning of the sixteenth century is also characterised by the first stirrings of discontent towards the Church. For example, during Christian II's reign (1513–23) there were attempts at legal reform. As part of this process, the failings of the bishops, prelates and 'men of the cloth' were investigated, and a series of problems — including abuses of the ecclesiastical courts, appropriation of land by the Church, the high rents demanded by the Church for use of its properties as well as other payments that lay folk were expected to pay to abbeys — were uncovered.[104] The humanism of the Renaissance was beginning to make itself felt, and concerns for academic freedom as well as a debate about corruption in the Church were being voiced. This rapid change and weakening of the foundations of society was disorientating and caused anxiety for many. The Jews — pushing at the borders to the south and known only to the Danes in the guise of the 'fantastical Jew' — were perceived as threatening the order and wellbeing of society. In this northern European disequilibrium, Pfefferkorn — and Ræff after him — are presenting the Church as the honourable defender of Christendom and guarantor of stability in the battle against the real social, economic and religious enemies — the Jews.

In addition to these social and political motives, there may be a broader, more universal, psychological explanation behind the publication of *Iudeorum Secreta*. Ræff printed the tract just as the Reformation was about to burst forth in northern Europe: one year before Martin Luther nailed his *95 Theses* to the Schlosskirche door in Wittenberg, and just nine years before the monk Hans Tausen began preaching the first Lutheran sermons in Denmark. The social, political and religious atmosphere of the early sixteenth century was tense across much of north-western Europe — and, as we have seen, Denmark was no exception. Anti-Jewish feeling generally has a tendency to rear its ugly head at such times; tensions within Christian society create a climate in which rhetorical, or frequently also physical, aggression towards the Jews can thrive. This type of violence — in word or deed — towards the minority population is at certain times of tension a compelling way for the majority population to make sense of a world in turmoil and to assert their identity and interests.[105] In this way, mythology becomes psychology, and challenges to the established order can be brought back under control by the creation of a 'mythical' threat. The need to redefine social values and reaffirm social unity is met by identifying and excluding an out-group; the denigration of the 'other' can thus be used to defend one's intellectual construction of the world. The British anthropologist, Mary Douglas, has shown the ways in which local consensus on how the world is organised is enforced and protected through the creation of taboos. Her book *Purity and Danger* (first published 1966)

---

104. See Wittendorff 2003: 83.
105. This use of violence against Jews is a theme returned to time and again by Miri Rubin in her book on allegations of Host desecration in the Middle Ages (from 1999; paperback edition from 2004). See also Davis 1973; Rubin 2009: 45–77.

with its notions of pollution and taboo helps us to understand the reasons why an imaginary — and what initially might be considered an irrational — threat to society was created and placed into the consciousness of the Danes. Because Jews existed socially at the periphery (outside of the established social structure of four classes — the clergy, nobility, merchants and craftsmen, and peasants — which was thought to mirror the cosmic structure of heaven), geographically at the outermost borders of the kingdom, and metaphysically in the dual role both of God's chosen people and of his killers, they were seen as being both powerful and dangerous. Such ambiguity causes cognitive discomfort, and ambiguous things and people can be seen as very threatening and dangerous. Wavering certainties as well as intellectual and social disorder can be reduced by shunning this ambiguity. The Jews were anomalies that did not fit neatly into early modern Danish society's classification of the world and thus they created disorder and ambiguity and were regarded as threatening and dangerous. These anomalous people had to be moved to a new status through a ritual act (in this case, baptism)[106] or else they had to be shunned and avoided as a taboo or contagion, or alternatively expelled and held back beyond the borders. Thus can the challenges to the established order be brought back under control. By the early 1500s, the pollutant Jews — *de fwlæ iøder* 'the unclean Jews' — and their inherent danger had become stock, and even necessary, elements in the Danes' worldview and fantasies of purity. In his *Iudeorum Secreta*, Ræff offered the Danish people a series of reasons why and instructions how to use the Jews to absorb their pent-up aggression, fears and anxiety and by doing so helped them to make sense of their own world, restore order to it and assert their interests and identity during a time of turmoil and change. By presenting these outsiders as objects for scorn, *Iudeorum Secreta* underlines the need for Christian unity in the face of the enemy — a potent message for Denmark at the beginning of the sixteenth century.

---

106. According to Pfefferkorn, only by drawing Christians to the pure faith and converting the Jews, could the world be brought 'wider in ir naturlich regyment [*back to its natural order*]' (*Der Juden Spiegel*, fol. f3^r).

CHAPTER 3

The language of Iudeorum Secreta

A linguistic description, Poul Ræff's translation, and the Hebrew words

> *Thenne bog er vtdraghen aff latinen oc vtsæth paa dansckæ/ til theris behoff som icke kwnne forstaa latinæ. Hwn tracterer oc indhæ holdher/ alle the hemelighæ stycker som the fwlæ iøder haffue mellom sig sielff*
>
> Poul Ræff (1516)[1]

> *l'Escriture des Iuifs Alemans, est fort mauvaise [...] Il faut estre accoustumé pour entendre les Juifs Alemans parler Hebreu, ils prononcent aleph, hé, hain tout de mesme, les Italiens le prononcent mieux, ie ne pourrois entendre R. Acher, il estoit Moravien, qui est une terrible langue; ils m'entendent fort bien, mais non pas moy eux, jentends bien les mots, mais non pas la prononciation.*
>
> Joseph Scaliger (1669)[2]

There is as yet no comprehensive study of the language used by Poul Ræff in his printed works. This chapter describes a number of aspects of the Danish found in one of his publications, *Iudeorum Secreta*, and includes characteristic features of the book's orthography, aspects of style and vocabulary,

---

1. Poul Ræff, *Iudeorum Secreta* (1516): 'This book is taken from Latin and translated into Danish to meet the needs of those who cannot understand Latin. It deals with and contains all the secret affairs that the bad Jews keep between themselves'.
2. Scaliger 1669: 176, 177–78: 'German Jews' writing is very poor [...] One needs to get used to hearing German Jews speak Hebrew in order to be able to understand it. They pronounce *'alef*, *heh* and *'ayin* the same way. The Italians pronounce it better. I was not able to understand Rabbi Ascher. He was Moravian, which is a terrible language: they understood me very well but I not them. I understand the words well enough, but not their pronunciation.'

the accuracy of the Danish translation, and an investigation of the Hebrew words that occur in the work. The language of the text is of course particularly interesting as it is a translation into Danish undertaken by Ræff himself (or by his workshop); Ræff's other publications were composed either in Latin or in the vernacular by someone else.

Ræff's orthography in *Iudeorum Secreta*

There follows a description of the orthography used in *Iudeorum Secreta* — put rather crudely, which letters Ræff uses for which sounds. As there was no standardised spelling norm at the time, I have chosen the normalisation developed by the *Gammeldansk Ordbog* project ('The Dictionary of Old Danish', hereafter GdO), which, although representing a rather earlier stage of the language, does at least provide us with a normalised (albeit artificial) standard with which we can compare and contrast aspects of Ræff's orthography. The description begins with vowels, diphthongs and finally consonants in Ræff's orthography.

Vowels (in stressed position)

/ă/ In the vast majority of cases, Old Danish /ă/ corresponds to ⟨a⟩: *acht; af; affgrwnd; affguder; al; aldrig; artz; belackæ; dansckæ; faræ; forladelsæ; fortabæ; framgang; Frankærighæ; haffdæ; halsen; handlingher; hanæ; kalffwe; langht; mangffoldug; psaltheren; samen, sammen; sandinghen; sandkorn; skal; taber; tribulatz; vndherstandilsæ.*

In those instances where Old Danish /ă/ has become lengthened in short open syllables, we also find spellings with ⟨a⟩ (never, for example, with ⟨aa⟩): *talæ; faræ; forladher.*

We find ⟨o⟩ in a few words: *holdendes, holder, holdhes, holdhæ; hondæ; hordhedher, hordæ; huorledis; mangffoldug; vppeholdhæ, vppæholdhæ; wold; wordhæ.* These forms demonstrate the lengthening and rounding of /ă/ before /ld, nd, r[ð]/: *hăld-* > *hāld-* > *hold-*, etc.[3] There are a few double forms in the text with ⟨a⟩ ~ ⟨o⟩, showing that Ræff was inconsistent in how he represented this sound in his orthography: *huar, huarledis, hwarledhes* as well as *huor(ledis)*, and *handhæ* as well as *hondæ*.

---

3. *GG* I: 370–74 (§189).

There are, however, a number of instances where we find ‹æ› where we expect ‹a›. Two occurrences appear to be mistakes: *bewæredhæ*, and *ældherdom* (note *bewaræ* occurs twice, and *alders* once elsewhere in the text). A parallel to these words, are the instances when Ræff uses ‹a› in unstressed positions where, considering his pattern of spelling, we would expect ‹æ› (see below under 'Vowels [in unstressed positions]'). This confusion between ‹a› and ‹æ› could just as much be due to the type-setter of *Iudeorum Secreta* as to Ræff's own orthography.[4] In addition to these apparent mistakes, we find the words *bedrægheræ* (cf. GdO *bedragere* 'charlatan') and *bedræghæ* (cf. GdO *bedrage* 'deceive'), which have no parallel forms with ‹a›, suggesting that ‹æ› is intended in these forms. The MLG forms *bedrêchster* 'charlatan' and *bedregen* 'to trick' could well have influenced these Danish forms.[5] We also find ‹æ› in *sæt(h)* (cf. GdO *sat* 'placed'); for example, *tilhobe sæt*; *vtsæth*; *sæt fran sig*; *sæth*. This form with /æ/ is typical of Sjælland dialects.[6]

/ā/ Old Danish long /ā/ most frequently corresponds to ‹aa› in both open and closed syllables: *baadæ*; *forraadhæ*; *forsmaa*; *faafenghæ*; *forhaaning*; *haarclædher*; *maa*; *maal*; *maaned*; *raabæ*; *raad*, *sckriffthemaall*; *saa*; *traad*, *traadæ*; *vndersaathæ*; *vpstaar*; *vpaa*; *aaben*; *aagher*; *aar*.

In a limited number of words, spellings with ‹o› occur: *suo, swo*; *suodan, suodane, suodant, suodanæ, swodan, swodane, swodant, swodanæ, swodænæ*; *sckrifftemol, sckrifftæmol*; *todhæ, toedt*; *two*; *Uor, Uort, Uoræ*; *vor, voræ, wor, wore, wort, woræ*. We also find ‹oo› in word final position: *afftoo*; *soo*; *too*. With regard to these spellings with ‹o› and ‹oo›, we can see that an Old Danish /ā/ in combination with /v/ has been labialised: *soo, suo* (cf. GdO *svā*, 'so'); *swodan* (cf. GdO *svādan*, 'such'); *too* (cf. GdO *thvā*, 'wash'); *two* (cf. GdO *tvā*, 'two'); *Uor* (cf. GdO *vār*, 'our').[7] Note that the /v/ has disappeared in *soo*; *too, todhæ, toedt*; *afftoo*. The words *sckrifftemol* and *sckrifftæmol* are also found spelt with ‹aa› (*sckriffthemaall, sckriffthæmaal, sckrifftæmaal*), showing that ‹aa› also represents this labialised pronunciation.

Less common are forms with ‹a›: *clart*; *forclaring*; *fran*; *han*; *naboer*; *nar*; *sla*; *tha*; *Uare*; *vdsla*. Although ‹a› is otherwise uncommon for the vowel /ā/, the short

---

4. On the fluctuation between ‹a› and ‹æ› in another of Poul Ræff's publications, see Skovgaard 2005: 66.
5. *GG* I: 126 (§81).
6. *GG* I: 52 (§15).
7. *GG* I: 270–71 (§155).

words *fran*,[8] *han*, *nar* and *tha* are characteristic as they are always written with ⟨a⟩, as also is *klar* and its derivatives (*klarlighe, forclaring, forklaris*). Finally, note ⟨ae⟩ in the word *suaer* (GdO *svār* 'heavy'). Marking a long vowel with a following ⟨e⟩ is also found in the word *stoer* (GdO *stōr* 'big').[9]

/ĕ/ See /ǣ/.

/ē/ Old Danish /ē/ corresponds most frequently to ⟨e⟩ (most often in open syllables, but occasionally even in closed syllables): *allenisthœ*; *breff*; *dreffnœ*; *eghen*, *egne*; *eth*; *ewig*; *formering*; *gedhæbwckœ*; *hedhen*; *her*; *hiem*; *merœ*; *reghel*; *reyser*; *sckedt*; *smegring*; *speghel*; *steghœ*; *teghen*; *the*; *tracterer*; *Ue*; *wredhœ*.

In short words with closed syllables, Old Danish /ē/ is often written ⟨ee⟩: *been*; *bereedt*; *deel*; *deeldt*; *eedh*; *eens*; *heest*; *meesth*; *reenth*; *seedt*; *sckeer*; *sweed*. But it can also be written so in open syllables: *bespeedœ*; *ee*; *eenœ*; *heelœ*; *meenighœ*; *meenœ* ('common'; cf. *myenœ* below); *spee*; *steenœ*; *tree*; *vreenœ*.

We find ⟨ye⟩ used for the long vowel in the verb *mēne* 'to think, be of the opinion' and the related word *mēning* 'opinion'; for example: *myen, myenœ*; *myening*. We also find *myenlig* (cf. GdO *mēnlig*, 'common') once in the text.[10] These spellings reflect the diphthongisation of /ē/ after /m/. The spelling *ild* (cf. GdO *ēld* 'fire') with is closed vowel is the only form used in the text,[11] and GdO *rēkenskap* (from Middle Low German *rekenschop*, 'account') is printed *rœghenscaff*.

/ĭ/ Old Danish /ĭ/ usually corresponds to ⟨i⟩; for example: *afftwinghœ*; *alminneligt*; *behindrer*; *besckickelighet*; *bindœ*; *bitherœ*; *Cristus*; *dricke*; *fisckenœ*; *gildhœ*; *himmelen*; *hwilcketh*; *ickœ*; *kirckis*; *lillœ*; *mig*; *mildheligen*; *plichtug*; *qwinder*; *sckrifft*; *silkœ*; *tig*; *til*; *twingher*; *vildfarelse*; *vilghœ*; *visseligen*; *wilghœ*; *winghernœ*.

Another spelling in a limited number of words is with ⟨y⟩: *paamyndher, paamyndhœ*; *paamyndilsœ, myddaghen*; *mydtnat*; *myndelsœ*; *myndhes, myndhœ*; *myndrœ*; *myt*. It will be noted here, that ⟨y⟩ is used after ⟨m⟩ and may have been intended to assist the reader in distinguishing between a series of minims that could have appeared confusing. In other words, it is easier to distinguish between

---

8. Possibly a dialect form from Sjælland; *GG* I: 52 (§15).
9. The phenomenon is also known in medieval West Germanic languages and dialects, for example in Low German and Dutch.
10. *GG* I: 364 (§186).
11. *GG* I: 243 (§145).

the different letters in **mynðhes** than in **minðhes**. Ræff could have adopted this practice from handwritten manuscripts.[12]

There are several cases, particularly before /ð/, where /ĭ/ has been opened to /e/ and is written ‹e›: *ether*; *leffnet, leffneth*; *leffuæ, leffendhæ, leffuendhæ*; *ned*; *nedtryckæ*; *sedwane, sedwaner, sedwanæ*; *slemme*; *smegring*; *trediæ*; *wenner*.[13] GdO *mikil* and *mikit* are written with ‹ø› as *møghel* and *møghet*, and GdO *dirve* as *dørghen*, although the pronouns with ‹i›, such as *mik, sik* and *thik*, appear as *mig, sig(h)* and *tig(h)*.

/ī/ Old Danish /ī/ usually corresponds to ‹i› in both open and closed syllables; for example: *bedriffuæ*; *betideligen*; *bliffue*; *firækant*; *hwith*; *krig*; *lidhæ*; *rigdom*; *sidhen*; *skinindæ*; *swigefuldæ*; *thi*; *tidhen*; *twiffuel*; *vbegribelighæ*; *wiseræ*.

However, in closed syllables we also find ‹ii›: *fliidh*; *høgtiid*; *liif*; *moltiid*; *siisth*; *tiid*; *wiis* (also *wiisæ*); or ‹ij›: *altijd*; *flijd, flijd*; *tijd*; or even ‹ig›: *frigbornæ*. Note also that ‹ij› is used in word-final position: *frij*; *ketterij, kettherij*; *Uij, wij*.

In a few words, it is also not uncommon that Old Danish /ī/ appears as ‹y›: *myn, myt*; *pynæ*; *syn, syt, synæ*; *thry*; *thyn, tyt, thynæ*; *tymelighe*; *vyn*. It is thus typically used before or after other letters consisting of two or more minims, perhaps with the intention of making the letters more dissimilar and easy to read (see also under /ĭ/ above).

Finally, note the forms *trøsser* and *trøssuer* with ‹ø› (cf. GdO *thrīsver*, 'thrice, three times').[14]

/ŏ/ Old Danish /ŏ/ corresponds to ‹o›: *afkommæ*; *behoff*; *bespottedæ*; *bord*; *clocken*; *folk*; *for*; *got*; *horn*; *konning*; *korses*; *lort*; *morghen*; *oc*; *offuer*; *ondt*; *ord*; *oss*; *sorg*; *tilfforn*. However, in those cases where /ŏ/ has been lengthened (typically in open syllables), it can be spelt ‹aa›: *forspraakeræ* (cf. GdO *forsprokkere* 'spokesman'); *skaaren* (cf. GdO *skorin* 'cut'); *aaben* (cf. GdO *opin* 'open'); *aagher* (cf. GdO *oker* 'interest [on a loan]').

/ō/ Old Danish /ō/ usually corresponds to ‹o› in both open and closed syllables: *bloth*; *bog*; *clogheræ*; *flodhen*; *fodspor*; *god*; *modher*; *stor*; *tro*. Although in closed syllables and word-final position, we also find ‹oo›: *boo*; *flood*; *hooss*; *koo*; *stoor*; *troo*.

---

12. On the use of ‹y› in distinguishing between minims in medieval manuscripts, see Haastrup 1974: 384.
13. *GG* I: 292 (§159).
14. *GG* I: 313 (§164).

Occasionally, it is spelt with ⟨aa⟩: *beraabæ* (cf. GdO *berope* 'call upon'); *forhaaning* (cf. GdO *forhoning* 'mockery'); *haaff* (cf. GdO *hop* 'hope'); *raabæ* (cf. GdO *rope* 'shout'); and on one occasion, we find ⟨oe⟩: *stoer* (cf. *suaer* above). Note also the form with ⟨ø⟩: *øllie* (cf. GdO *ōlie*, 'oil').[15]

/ŭ/   Old Danish /ŭ/ corresponds to either ⟨u⟩ or ⟨w⟩. The distribution is equal between the two graphemes. For example, with ⟨u⟩: *fuld*; *hugorm*; *institut*; *kunne*; *sculle*; *spunden*; *stund*; *vgunsth*. And with ⟨w⟩: *affgrwnd*; *bwckæ*; *fornwfftheræ*; *frwctsomeligt*; *fwnd*; *hwndhæ*; *hwngher*; *kwndhæ*; *paafwndhet*; *rwldhen*; *scwllæ*; *stwndwm*. There are thus a number of parallel forms (for example: *fuldkommelighen* ~ *fwldkommelighen*; *kunnæ* ~ *kwnnæ*). In word-initial position, however, ⟨v⟩ is always used: *vnder*; *vnderstandilsæ*; *vnderwisæ*; *vnghæ*; *vp*; *vphengt*; *vppeholdhæ*; *vpstaar*; *vpaa*.

In those short words where /ŭ/ has shifted to /ŏ/ before a nasal (usually /m/), it is written ⟨o⟩; for example: *gomp* (cf. GdO *gump* 'backside'); *hondæ* (cf. GdO *hund* 'dog'); *om* (cf. GdO *um* 'about'); *omgengelsæ*; *omgaass*; *omkring*; *omkringsckornæ*; *som* (cf. GdO *sum* 'which'). Note also ⟨o⟩ in *bort*,[16] and ⟨ø⟩ in *løstelig* (cf. GdO *lustelik*, 'joyous').

/ū/   Old Danish /ū/ usually corresponds to ⟨w⟩ except in word-initial position: *brwghæ*; *fwlæ*; *hws*; *iomfrw*; *nw*; *pwr*; *vblwffue*; *wti*.

In word-initial position, the grapheme ⟨v⟩ is nearly always used: *vd*; *vdgydelsæ*; *vdlending*; *vdwalt*; *vtdraghen*; *vthen*; *vti*; *vtoffuer*. The two exceptions are occasional occurrences of *wthen* and *wti* (alongside the far more frequent *vthen* and *vti*). The negating prefix *ū-* is thus also written ⟨v⟩: *vbegribelighæ*; *vbehørlighe*; *vbekendt*; *vbeqwem*; *vblwffue*; *vbørlighæ*; *vgunsth*; *vhørlighæ*; *vkristelig*; *vmagh*; *vreenæ*; *vsighelighe*; *vwilghæ*; *vwiis*.

Only two words with ⟨u⟩ are found, *iomfru* (but also *iomfrw*) and *naturligt*, both of which are loanwords in Danish from Middle Low German (cf. MLG *junkvrowe* 'virgin' and *natûrlik* 'naturally').

/ў/   Old Danish /ў/ corresponds to ⟨y⟩; for example: *begyndilsæ*; *begyndæ*; *besyndherligen*; *bygghæ*; *byrd*; *dygdhelighe*; *dyræ*; *effterfylning*; *efftherfylghæ*; *fnysthæ*; *forfylghe*; *forfylning*; *frygd*; *gyllenæ*; *hyrnæ*; *mistyckæ*; *nedtryckæ*; *nygt, nyt*; *skyld*; *stycker*; *styrcker*; *syndhelig*; *syrgher*; *trycht*; *verdsckyld, werdsckyld*; *ypperstæ*.

---

15. Hansen 1962–71, I: 154.
16. *GG* I: 263–64 (§150) anm. 3; *GG* I: 319 (§167).

Before /r/ followed by a consonant, Old Danish /ȳ/ has sometimes been opened and corresponds to ‹ø›; for example: *førsther* 'princes'; *førstæ* 'first'; *spørghæ*; *tørræ*; but note, for example, *syrgher* and *syrghæ*. And so also in *køn* 'gender'; *løckesomt*; *løckæ*; *vløckæ*; *løgnafftig*.[17]

/ȳ/   Old Danish /ȳ/ corresponds to ‹y›; for example: *brydhæ*; *dyræ* 'expensive'; *fly*; *flydhendhes*; *hylæ*; *lydhæ*; *nydhæ*; *nylighen*; *scky*; *stryghæ*; *yderst*. We find ‹yg› in the words *nyg* and *nygt* 'new'; cf. GdO *nȳ*.

/ǽ/   Old Danish /ǽ/ commonly corresponds to ‹æ›: *blæss*; *brændæ*; *bædræ*; *forgæt*; *frælst*; *fæm*; *græmelsæ*; *hwær*; *hær*; *lærdt*; *læsæ*; *næsth*; *penninghæsæck*; *ræt*; *slæcht*; *thær*; *vbeqwæmt*; *wræghæ*; *wædheret*; *wæl*; *wærelsæ*; *ædhæ*.

However, Old Danish /ǽ/ also often corresponds to ‹e›: *belthestædh*; *gledscaff*; *henne*; *hwer*; *lessæ*; *med*; *mellom*; *men*; *mendhenæ*; *menniskis*; *offwertencht*; *omgengelse*; *penninghæsæck*; *predicken*; *pregedæ*; *prest*; *stemmæ*; *swerd*; *tencke*; *then*, *thet*; *ther*; *treffler*; *twennæ*; *vdlending*; *wegnæ*; *wenner*; *werdsckyld*; *wersthæ*.

The Old Danish verb *sǽghje* 'to say' is always written with ‹i›: *sighe(r)*, *sighæ*, *sigæ*. This spelling is typical of texts from Sjælland.[18] And note also the ‹a› in the present participle *nerwarendhes* (cf. GdO *nærværendes*, 'present') and past participle *varet* (cf. GdO *været*, 'been'), but the infinitive *wæræ*, 'to be'.[19]

/ǣ/   Old Danish /ǣ/ corresponds to ‹æ›: *æræ* 'honour'; *kær*; *blæsæ*; and in one word (in word-final position) to ‹æœ›: *fæœ*.

/ŏ̄/   Occurrences of Old Danish /ŏ̄/ are rather seldom, but where it appears, it corresponds to ‹ø›: *alsomstørst*; *børn*; *gør*, *goræ*, *gøris*; *røst*.

/ō̄/   Old Danish /ō̄/ corresponds to ‹ø›: *affløseræ*; *bedrøffuedhæ*; *bøn*; *død*; *forglømæ*; *høg*; *hønæ*; *købstædher*; *løbæ*; *pøl*; *øgnæ*. In word-final position, we find it doubled as ‹øø›: *døø*.

/ĭa̯/ and /īa̯/   In the vast majority of cases, progressive *i*-mutation has occurred in these diphthongs, which is reflected in their spelling. With few exceptions,

---

17. *GG* I: 313 (§164); Skautrup 1969, II: 181.
18. *GG* I: 51 (§15), 248–50 (§146.3).
19. On occurrences of *waræ* ~ *wæræ* in Ræff's publications of Reverend Michael's poems, see Brøndum-Nielsen 1914: 89.

these diphthongs correspond to ⟨ie⟩: *behielpes*; *dieffuelen*; *hielp*; *hielpæ*; *ieffncristen*; *iegh*; *sieldhen*; *sielæ*; *sielff*; *skiel*; *stierner*. But we find ⟨iæ⟩ in *siælen* (cf. GdO *sjal* 'soul'*)*; *tiæneræ*, *tiænisthæ* (cf. GdO *thjane* 'serve'); ⟨ighe⟩ in *fighendher*, *fighendæ* (cf. GdO *fjande* 'enemy'; cf. the MLG form *vîgende*); and ⟨ye⟩ in *tyenæ* (cf. GdO *thjane* 'serve').

There is, however, one word (GdO *hjarte* 'heart') in which progressive *i*-mutation does not appear to have taken place and Old Danish /iă/ corresponds to ⟨ia⟩: *hiarter*, *hiarthet*, *hiarthæ*, *hiartæ*. The lack of *i*-mutation in *hjarte* while occurring in other *iă*-words is apparently a dialect feature from Fyn.[20]

/iŏ/ and /iō/ Old Danish /iŏ/ usually corresponds to ⟨io⟩: *giordæ*, *giordhæ*, *giordhes*; *giort*; *iordhen*. The exception is the Old Danish word *jō* for which we find *iw*.[21]

/iŭ/ and /iū/ Old Danish /iŭ/ most usually corresponds to ⟨iw⟩; for example: *biwder*; *forbiwdæ*; *liwd*; *liwdhendis*; *liwss*; *sckiwdher*; *sckiwldt*; *siwdæ*; *siwgt*; *siwn*; *siwnghæ*; *vpliwsæ*. However, monophthongised forms with ⟨y⟩ are also to be found; for example: *vdgydelsæ*; *vdgydhæ*.[22]

Old Danish /iū/ corresponds to ⟨iø⟩ in the frequently occurring word GdO *juthe* 'Jew': *iøder*; *iødhætempel*; *iødisckæ*.[23] And Old Danish /iŭ/ has shifted to /iŏ/ before the nasal /m/ and corresponds to ⟨io⟩: *iomfru*. Note also ⟨io⟩ in *kiortlæ* (cf. GdO *kjurtel*, 'gown').[24]

Summary

The orthography for representing vowel sounds in stressed syllables is largely consistent and reflects the phonological changes that had taken place in the language by the beginning of the sixteenth century. Long vowels, in the case of /ā/, /ē/ and /ī/, are frequently marked by doubling in closed syllables (and with a ⟨w⟩

---

20. *GG* I: 52 (§16).
21. Hansen 1934–35: 232.
22. In accordance with the orthographical normalisation in *Gammeldansk Ordbog*, the words *brydhæ* (cf. GdO *bryte*; Old Norse *brjóta*), *flydhendes* (cf. GdO *flytendes*; Old Norse *fljótandi*); *nydhæ* (cf. GdO *nyte*; Old Norse *njóta*) and *stryghæ* (cf. GdO *stryke*; Old Norse *strjúka*) have been described in the section under /ȳ/. See *GG* I: 345–47 (§179).
23. *GG* I: 349 anm. 3 (§179).
24. *GG* I: 319 (§167); *GG* I: 344 anm. 4 (§178).

in the case of /ū/). In stressed final position, we also find ⟨aa⟩, ⟨ee⟩, ⟨ij⟩, ⟨oo⟩ and ⟨øø⟩.²⁵ A secondary diphthongisation of a vowel is marked by means of ⟨y⟩ for /e/: *arbeygd* (cf. GdO *arbejde*), *keyserens* (cf. GdO *kæjsere*), *reyser* (cf. GdO *rese*, *rejse*) and *weyeræ* (cf. GdO *væther*, *væjer*); and ⟨g⟩ for /ø/: *høgræ*, *høgt*, *nøges* and *øgnæ*. In this respect, the orthography is rather conservative.²⁶ It is possible to summarise the most common representation of phonemes (with graphemes in order of frequency):

/ă/	→	⟨a⟩, ⟨o⟩	/y̆/	→	⟨y⟩, ⟨ø⟩
/ā/	→	⟨aa⟩, ⟨o⟩, ⟨a⟩	/ȳ/	→	⟨y⟩
/ē/	→	⟨e⟩, ⟨ee⟩	/ǣ/	→	⟨æ⟩, ⟨e⟩
/ĭ/	→	⟨i⟩, ⟨y⟩, ⟨e⟩	/ǣ/	→	⟨æ⟩, ⟨æe⟩
/ī/	→	⟨i⟩, ⟨ii⟩, ⟨ij⟩, ⟨y⟩	/ø̆/	→	⟨ø⟩
/ŏ/	→	⟨o⟩, ⟨aa⟩	/ø̄/	→	⟨ø⟩, ⟨øø⟩
/ō/	→	⟨o⟩, ⟨oo⟩, ⟨aa⟩	/iǎ/	→	⟨ie⟩, ⟨iæ⟩
/ŭ/	→	⟨u⟩, ⟨w⟩, ⟨v⟩	/iŏ/	→	⟨io⟩
/ū/	→	⟨w⟩, ⟨v⟩	/iŭ/	→	⟨iw⟩

Each grapheme corresponds to one or more sounds (Grapheme used in *Iudeorum Secreta* → Phoneme [GdO]):

⟨a⟩	→	/ă/, /ā/	⟨o⟩	→	/ŏ/, /ā/, /ō/, /ă/
⟨aa⟩	→	/ā/, /ŏ/, /ō/	⟨oo⟩	→	/ō/
⟨e⟩	→	/ē/, /ĭ/, /ǣ/	⟨u⟩	→	/ŭ/
⟨ee⟩	→	/ē/	⟨v⟩	→	/ū/, /ŭ/
⟨i⟩	→	/ĭ/, /ī/	⟨w⟩	→	/ū/, /ŭ/
⟨ie⟩	→	/iǎ/	⟨y⟩	→	/y̆/, /ȳ/, /ĭ/
⟨ii⟩	→	/ī/	⟨æ⟩	→	/ǣ/, /ǣ/
⟨ij⟩	→	/ī/	⟨ææ⟩	→	/ǣ/
⟨io⟩	→	/iŏ/	⟨ø⟩	→	/ø̆/, /ø̄/, /y̆/
⟨iw⟩	→	/iŭ/	⟨øø⟩	→	/ø̄/
⟨iæ⟩	→	/iǎ/			

There are a couple of influences from 'south of the border' on the orthography of stressed vowels, such as the use of ⟨e⟩ to mark a preceding long vowel in *stoer*

---

25. Skautrup 1969, II: 180.
26. Skautrup 1969, II: 181, 185.

and *suaer*, and the appearance of ‹g› in *nyg(t)*, *frigbornæ* and *fighendher*. Similarly, the spelling *bedræghe* may be influenced from Low German. Otherwise the representation of stressed vowels in the text is typical of central Danish dialects of the period, particularly the islands of Sjælland and to a lesser extent Fyn.

Vowels (in unstressed position)

In weakly stressed syllables, the vowel is usually written ‹e› or ‹æ›. We also find examples of ‹i›, ‹o› and ‹u›, and, although most probably due to a type-setting error, even ‹a›.

‹æ›: (final position) *allæ*; *andræ*; *arbeydhæ*; *articlæ*; *begheræ*; *belackæ*; *blæsæ*; *brwghæ*; *baadhæ*; *dyppæ*; *effterfylgæ*; *enæ*; *foreldernæ*; *føffwæ*; *gantzæ*; *hwndhæ*; *læræ*; *manghæ*; *mennisckæ*; *meræ*; *myndræ*; *mynæ*; *penninghæ*; *plaghæ*; *propheternæ*; *sacramenthe*; *samæ*; *sckadhæ*; *suodanæ*; *synæ*; *traadæ*; *uidhæ*; *vhørlighæ*; *vildfarelsæ*; *ypperstæ*; *øffwæ*; *øgnæ*; (elsewhere) *arckæn*; *bethidælighen*; *firækant*; *gedhæbwckæ*; *gwdhælighedh*; *herrædømæ*; *iødhætempel*; *langæsiden*; *læræfeddræ*; *penninghæsæck*; *rindhænæ*; *sckriffthæfeddræ*; *sckriffthæmaal*; *strenghælighen*; *swodænæ*;[27] *vppæholdhæ*; *wædhæret*.

‹e›: (final position) *afftaghe*; *alle*; *article*; *atsckillighe*; *benedidelse*; *bliffue*; *cristne*; *drage*; *dricke*; *egne*; *ewindhelige*; *falscke*; *fattughe*; *forderffue*; *føffue*; *gantze*; *giffue*; *gudhelighe*; *gøre*; *haffue*; *hellighe*; *henne*; *hwilke*; *icke*; *kalffwe*; *kalle*; *komme*; *kunne*; *same*; *sckadhe*; *sculle*; *sighe*; *slemme*; *suodane*; *taghe*; *thenne*; *thette*; *ville*; *ware*; *wille*; (elsewhere) *affguder*; *affløseræ*; *affthenen*; *andhelighen*; *aszen*; *bedrøffuedhæ*; *begherer*; *bliffuer*; *bøgher*; *capitel*; *clogheræ*; *effther*; *eller*; *ether*; *folket*; *formindsckedhæ*; *landhenæ*; *leffendhæ*; *modher*; *maanedhen*; *noghen*; *offuer*; *qwindhernæ*; *sidder*; *sorgfwldheræ*; *tiæneræ*; *vsigherlighe*; *wsligheræ*; *wædheret*.

‹i›: *alterit*; *folkit*; *forklaris*; *framdelis*; *frwctsomeligt*; *giffwit*; *helffuedis*; *hemælighet*; *herris*; *hoffwit*; *huarledis*; *kirckis*; *loffwit*; *meenighæ*; *mennisckæ*; *noghit*; *sckreffuit*; *taknemmeligt*; *theris*; *tilsckickith*; *trolighen*; *vtwortis*; *aarith*.

---

27. The form *swodænæ* could be the result of a reduction in the vowel in the suffix; cf. *GG* I: 414 (§218).

Closing of the unstressed vowel before /s/ and /t/ is not unusual, and the ending ⟨is⟩ is more than twice as common as ⟨es⟩.[28]

⟨o⟩: *leghomæ* (cf. GdO *likeme*).[29]

⟨u⟩: *alsommegtugisthæ*; *fattugdom*; *fattughæ*; *ferdughæ*; *fordum*; *forplichtughæ*; *hannum*; *mangffoldug*; *mechtugæ*; *plichtug*; *retferdughæ*; *serdwghe*; *synduge*; *werdughe*; *werdughet*. The suffix ⟨ug⟩ is used after stems ending in the dentals ⟨d⟩ or ⟨t⟩ (for example, *ferdughæ* and *fattughæ*). There are, however, five occurrences where the suffix ⟨ig⟩ is used under these circumstances instead: *fornwfftig*; *offuerflødighen*; *retferdighet*; *tolmodighet*; *werdighe*. An unstressed ⟨u⟩ also appears in a number of loaned and foreign words and names (stressed vowel marked here by an accent): *Crístus*; *disputátz*; *disputéræ*; *fundamént*; *Ihésus*; *procurátor*; *pylátus*; *sánctus*; *studéræ*; *subtílig*; *tribulátz*.

⟨a⟩: *andha̱*; *bespotteda*; *ena*; *fattugha*; *myena*; *myena*; *Uara̱*; *wslighera*; *æra*. It has been suggested that such fluctuation between ⟨a⟩ and ⟨æ⟩ in word-final position in Ræff's printed works may be due to the influence of a dialect from eastern Denmark (such as Scanian/*skånsk*). In *Gammeldansk Ordbog*'s working papers for Ræff's publication of Michael's *Expositio pulcherrima super rosario beate marie virginis* from 1515, Jonna Dahl has written:[30]

> Det synes mig imidlertid ikke helt udelukket (omend tvivlsomt [< usikkert]), at det i en del af tilfældene kunde være sætterens sprogform, der giver sig til kende. I BrN. SF. 89f. påvises sætterformer af vb. 'være' med rodvokalen a. Hermed vilde det stemme, at sætterens, åbenbart østlige, mål havde a bevaret i tryksvag stavelse.
>
> *It does not seem to me to be entirely out of the question (albeit doubtful [< uncertain]), that in a number of cases it could be the typesetter's language, that is making itself felt. In Brøndum-Nielsen's* Sproglig forfatterbestemmelse. Studier over sprog i det sekstende århundredes begyndelse *(p. 89f.), he shows forms of the verb 'være'* [to be] *used by the typesetter with a* as the root vowel. In line with this, it would seem correct that the typesetter's evidently eastern dialect had a *preserved in weakly stressed syllables.*

---

28. Skautrup 1969, II: 194.
29. This form furthermore demonstrates labialisation of /a/ to /o/: Old Danish *likami* > *leghomæ*; *GG* I: 226 (§137).
30. Quoted in Skovgaard 2005: 66.

However, if we consider the typeface used in *Iudeorum Secreta*, it will be noted that ⟨a⟩ and ⟨æ⟩ are very similar, distinguishable only by means of a small diacritic mark,[31] and that they could easily have been confused by the typesetter. This and the fact that at least two of the examples (*bespotteda* and *wslighera*) look very odd even if viewed as Scanian (*skånsk*) or Swedish suggest to me that the appearance of ⟨a⟩ as a weakly stressed vowel in these words is a typographic error. Furthermore, the text is otherwise in a clearly central Danish dialect (*ødansk*) with forms consistent with the dialects of Sjælland. As such, they have been changed to ⟨æ⟩ in the edition and noted in the text critical apparatus.

Summary

As is typical of central Danish dialects, the unstressed vowels have been reduced but not lost entirely. Certain patterns can be detected in the orthographic representation of these unstressed vowels. For example, there are only two examples of ⟨æ⟩ being used in two consecutive weakly stressed positions: *rindhænæ* (elsewhere *rindhenæ*) and *swodænæ* (elsewhere *swodanæ*). Two consecutive weakly stressed vowels are occasionally written as two ⟨e⟩'s, or more frequently using a combination of two distinct graphemes. The distribution of ⟨e⟩ and ⟨æ⟩ in weakly stressed syllables can be summarised thus: By and large, but by no means always, ⟨e⟩ is used in closed syllables, and ⟨æ⟩ is used in open syllables (including in word-final position), unless this would result in two or more ⟨æ⟩'s occurring in consecutive weakly stressed syllables when another grapheme, typically ⟨e⟩, is used in the first position. There is, however, apparently no aversion to two ⟨e⟩s following one another:

-e-e-: *affthenen*; *bedrøffuedheræ*; *benedidelse(r)*; *bøgherne*; *dieffuelen*; *dieffuelsens*; *fiskene*; *fogheder*; *formaledidelser*; *frestelser*; *himmelen*; *himmelsens*; *holdendes*; *iødernes*; *kastedes*; *Keyserens*; *liwdendes*; *morghenen*; *maanedhen*; *propheterne*; *psaltheren*; *Raadhendes*; *tempelen*; *wædheret*.

-elsæ: *festtelsæ*; *fordømelsæ*; *forladelsæ*; *formaledidhelsæ*; *frestelsæ*; *gensighelsæ*; *græmelsæ*; *kommelsæ*; *lignelsæ*; *myndelsæ*; *omgengelsæ*; *vdgydelsæ*; *vildfarelsæ*; *vnderstandelsæ*; *wildfarelsæ*; *wærelsæ*. We

---

31. See, for example, *talæ*, the first word on fol. c1^r (p. 25) in fig. 7.

also find ‹ilsæ›, but this is far less frequent: *begyndilsæ*; *paamyndilsæ*; *vnderstandilsæ*; *wildfarilsæ*.

-*eræ*: *affløseræ*; *altheræ*; *bedræghеræ*; *bedrøffuedheræ*; *bittheræ*; *Borgmestheræ*; *clogheræ*; *forachteræ*; *fornwfftheræ*; *forspraakeræ*; *forstandheræ*; *kræseligheræ*; *sorgfwldheræ*; *stymperæ*; *tiæneræ*; *weyeræ*; *wiseræ*; *wsligheræ*; *wædheræ*.

-*isthæ*: *allenist(h)æ*; *alsommegtugisthæ*; *tiænisthæ*.

Consonants

This section accounts only for those consonants that had undergone qualitative changes by the sixteenth century in Danish, and that are of particular interest for an orthographic description of *Iudeorum Secreta*.

/p/ When the first letter in a word element or in combination with another consonant, Old Danish /p/ corresponds to ‹p›: *bespee*; *fodspor*; *forplictughæ*; *hielpæ*; *iødhætempel*; *penning*; *pynæ*; *paamyndhe*; *speghel*.

Intervocalic Old Danish /p/ most frequently corresponds to ‹b›: *beraabæ*; *døbes* (also *døbthæ*); *læber*; *løbæ*; *obenbarlighen*; *raabæ*; *swøbæ*; *taber*; *tilhobe*; *vbegribelighæ*. Note also *købstædher*. The only words with ‹p› are the verb *openbaræ* and the adverb *openbarlighen* (cf. MLG *openbâren* and *openbarliken*), as well as loanwords such as *biscoper* and *capitel*.

Weakening of /p/ to a fricative at the end of words can be seen by the use of ‹ff› in *bereffuenscaff*; *gledscaff*; *hoff*, *haaff*; *køpmanscaff*; *landsckaff*, *ondscaff*; *ræghenscaff*; but note the exceptions *dob* (GdO *dop* 'baptism'; cf. MLG *döpe*) and *vp* (GdO *up* 'up'; cf. MLG *op*). When words ending with a weakened fricative are inflected, and the Old Danish /p/ is no longer in final position, /p/ corresponds to the grapheme ‹p›; thus, *landsckaff+s* > *landsckaps* (not **landsckaffs*). Note also the form *sckapt* (not **sckafft*) that derives from the verb **sckabæ* (GdO *skape* 'create').[32]

/t/ Old Danish /t/ usually corresponds to ‹t›: *abstinentz*; *afftoo*; *atsckillighæ*; *besckickelighet*; *capitel*; *creatwræ*; *disputeræ*; *falskhet*; *forti*; *huat*; *institut*; *iødhætempel*; *latinæ*; *mandat*; *moltiid*; *møghet*; *nat*; *prophit*; *spot*; *taghe*; *til*; *tribu-*

---

32. Skautrup 1969, II: 184.

latz; *troo*; *twiffuel*; *vti*. It is by far the most common grapheme used in the definite ending on nouns (*-et* or *-et*). However, when Old Danish /t/ occurs in a post-consonantal position, it usually corresponds to ‹th›; for example, in combinations such as ‹bth› (for example, *døbthæ*; but ‹bt› in *subtilig*); ‹cth› (for example, *acthæ*; *dicther*; *encthen*; *tractheræ*; but ‹ct› in *actæ*; *forplictughæ*; *frwctsomeligt*; *tracteræ*); ‹fth› (for example, *affthen*; *effther*; *sckriffthæfeddræ*; but ‹fft› in *effter*; *løffter*; *offtæ*; *skrifftemol*; *vpløfftæ*); ‹lth› (for example, *altherit*; *belthestædh*; *bortelthæ*; *psaltheren*; *salth*; but ‹lt› in *alt; alterit*; *heltz*; *scalt*; *vdwalt*; *wilt*); ‹nth› (for example, *inthet*; *reenth*; *reghementhæ*; *testamenthæ*; but ‹nt› in the combination *–ntz(–)*; the suffix *–ment*; *blant*; *firækant*; *kant*; *reent*; *suodant, swodant*); ‹rth› (for example, *borthæ*; *forthi*; *giorth*; *hiarthæ*; but ‹rt› in *artickel*; *bort*; *clart*; *giort*; *hart*; *hiartæ*; *hwert*; *hørt*; *kiortlæ*; *lort*; *stort*; *uort, wort*; *vtwortis*); ‹sth› (for example, *allenisthæ*; *førsthæ*; *kasther*; *kunsther*; *mesthæ*; *presther*; *siisthæ*; but ‹st› always initially *st–*; often finally *–st*; *allenistæ*; *cristnæ*; *fnyster*; *fordrister*; *forkastæ*; *foster*; *frestelser*; *førstæ*; *kastedes*; *testamenthes*; *vkristelig*; *ypperstæ*), and ‹tth› (for example, *atther*; *besckatthæ*; *kettherij*; *nyttheligt*; *retthæ*; *setthæ*; *tretthæ*; but ‹tt› in *bespottedæ*; *fattughæ*; *festtelsæ*; *ketterij*; *lettelighen*; *settæ*; *thettæ*; *vnyttelighæ*).

Note that ‹dth› is only found in *ondth*; elsewhere ‹dt› is used (for example, *læsdt*; *sckedt*; *seedt*). Similarly, ‹gth› is found once (*langth*), and ‹ght› once (*langht*), with ‹gt› being used elsewhere, for example in the suffix *–(l)igt*, and in *hengt*; *høgt*; *lengtelighen*; *sagt*; *siwgt*; *vphengt*; *wegt*. In these combinations, ‹th› represents the pronunciation /t/ and does not represent a soundshift (for example, resulting in /ð/). The combination ‹th› represents /t/ after short vowels in the following words (often in word-final position): *ath*; *bethidælighen*; *eth*; *goth*; *mathe*; *mothe*; *nath(en)*; *plath*; *prelather*; *prophether*; *ræth*; *sæth*; *syth*; *vndersaathæ*; *vtsæth*. In the following words, the post-vocalic ‹th› may represent a shift from /t/ to /ð/: *gwdæligheth* (elsewhere *gwdhelighet* and *gwdhælighedh*); *horneth* (elsewhere *hornet*); *hwilketh* (elsewhere *hwilket* and *hwilkit*); *lyneth*; *aarith*; but it is difficult to know for sure.

In intervocalic and post-vocalic positions, where /t/ has been weakened to /ð/, we frequently find ‹dh›: *brydhæ*; *fliidh*; *flydhendhes*; *forladher*; *gedhæbwckæ*; *gwdhælighedh*; *hedher*; *hordhedher*; *hwedhemel*; *hwidhæ*; *ladhæ*; *lidhen*; *madh*; *modh*; *nydhæ*; *sckidhen*; *tilladhæ*; *uidhæ*; *vdgydhæ*; *widhæ*; *ædhæ*. Occasionally, this weakened consonant is written as ‹d›: *beddræ*; *brydæ*; *flijd*; *foradnæ*; *fødder*; *ladæ*; *mod*; *sckiød*; *vd*; *vdwalt*; *wed* (*vb.* 'knows'); *ædæ*. Note that GdO *vatn* 'water' appears as both *wadn* and *wand* in the text.[33]

---

33. *GG* II: 226 (§338).

/k/ Old Danish /k/ often corresponds to ‹k› (particularly when it is the first letter in a word-element): *arken; artikel; bagstak; bekwmræ; danskæ; falskhet; firækant; folk; forkastæ; forspraakeræ; Frankærighæ; huerken; hwilken; kagher; kalffwe; kalle; kirkis; klog; kommæ; omkring; sandkorn; scalkæ; silkæ; skadæ; skyld; sterkelighen; taknemmeligt; vbekendt; vkristelig.*

The grapheme ‹c› is found in *articlæ; bereffuenscaff; biscoper; cannick; capitel; clanck; clocken; clogheræ; dicther; frwctsomeligt; gledscaff; haarclædher; oc* (8 times more frequent than *och*); *procurator; ræghenscaff; sacramenther; scal; sculdæ; tracteræ.* The grapheme ‹c› is also used in combinations — ‹ch›, ‹ck› and ‹cki› — for /k/. The spelling ‹ch› is usually found in the combination ‹cht›: *acht; ansichtis; macht; mechtuge; offwertencht; plicht; slecht; vprachtæ; trycht;* but also in *och.* And ‹ck› is used in intervocalic position after a short vowel: *artickel; belackæ; beteckæ; bwckæ; drickæ; icke; løckæ; mistyckæ; predicken; streckæ; stycker;* or finally after a short vowel: *penninghæsæck; snack.* It is also found in *arck; folck; hwilcken; kirckis; styrcker; tancke; tenckæ.* The Old Danish combination /sk/ corresponds most frequently to ‹sck›: *ascken; atsckildhæ; besckatthæ; besckickæ; mennisckæ; omkringsckornæ; sckriffuer; tilsckickith.* But also ‹sk› in *danskæ; falskhet; menniske; ondskaff; skadæ; skeer; skyld;* and ‹sc› in *bereffuenscaff; biscoper; gledscaff; køpmanscaff; ondscaff; ræghenscaff; scal; sculdæ;* and ‹sch› in *mennischen* (once only; cf. MLG *minschen*); and finally the combination ‹cki› before a vowel is found in just one word: *sckiød* (GdO *skøt*, 'lap'). For Old Danish /sk/, ‹sck› is used just over 125 times, ‹sk› just under 100, ‹sk› about 30, and ‹sch› just once.

For /ks/ we find ‹x›: *exempel; moxen* (GdO *maksen* 'nearly'); *strax; text; vaxliwss.* Old Danish /kv/ corresponds either to ‹qu›, for example *qualdt; bequemt* (five times in total), or ‹qw›, for example *qwig; qwinder; qwædhæ; vbeqwemmæ* (sixteen times in total).

When /k/ has been weakened to the voiced fricative /ɣ/, it usually corresponds to ‹gh›: *afftaghe; allighewel; beswighæ; bogh; brwghæ; bøgher; clogheræ; forøghe; iegh; kagher; koghæ; leghomæ; møghel; møghet; noghen; orsaghæ; ransaghes; righæ; sagher; steghæ; stryghæ; tagher; teghen; tigh; sigh; vmaghæ; wræghæ; ydmyghe; aagher.* Occasionally, we find ‹g›: *bog; ieg; mig; nogræ; rigdom; tegner; tig; sig; swigefuldæ.* The Old Danish derivational suffix *–lik*, used to form adjectives, is usually written with ‹lig›: *atsckillig; daglig; ewindhelig; fulkommelig; idelig; løstelig; mangfoldelig; subtilig; syndhelig; vkristelig; ydmyghelig* (but *hemæligh*). The adverbial form is usually spelt with ‹lighen›: *andhelighen; bequemmelighen; besyndherlighen; bethidælighen; fuldkommelighen; gladlighen; hemelighen; høffuisckelighen; idelighen; indherlighen; lengtelighen; lettelighen; nylighen; openbarlighen;*

retthelighen; rolighen; snarlighen; stadhelighen; sterkelighen; strenghælighen; trolighen; visselighen; vsckellighen; warlighen (but as ‹ligen› in *besyndherligen; betideligen; fuldkommeligen; ideligen; mildheligen; snarligen; visseligen*).

For the Old Danish suffix *–aktig*, we find ‹afftig›: *løgnafftig* (GdO *lyghnaktigh*, 'deceitful'); *scalkafftighe* (GdO *skalkaktigh*, 'roguish'); *twrafftig* (GdO **thjuraktigh*, lit.: 'bull-like'; i.e. 'stubborn'? — see 'Hapax legomena and unusual words' below).

Note that /k/ appears as ‹g› in *ansigt* (GdO *ansikt*) and *wegt* (GdO *vækt*), and disappears altogether in *falst* (< *falsck+t*).

/d/ Old Danish /d/ often occurs in combinations with /l/ and /n/, and these are dealt with separately here. In other positions, Old Danish /d/ usually corresponds to ‹d›: *aldelis; bedriffuæ; dag; dieffuelen; ferdughæ; forderffue; framdelis; herrædømæ; lerdæ; løsdæ; middaghen; predicken; retferdighet; rigdom; studeræ; suodan; twungdæ; vtdraghen.* Occasionally, ‹dh› appears instead: *arbeygdhæ; framdheles; glømdhæ; gwddhommen; kedhæ; lærdhæ; nøddhæ; spreddhæ; swodhan; werdhen.*

For Old Danish /ld/, the text has ‹ld›: *foreldernæ; helder; holdendis; ild; mangffoldug: qualdt; sckyld*; and ‹ldh›: *foreldhernæ; gildhæ; heldher; holdhæ; mildheligen; sieldhen; sorgfwldheræ; weldhæ; ældherdom.*

Old Danish /nd/ corresponds to both ‹nd› and ‹ndh› in almost equal amounts. For example: ‹nd› in *affuend; andræ; blindæ; fighendæ; forhandling; forstandt; fundament; fwnd; hand; hender; hondæ; land; mandat; ondscaff; ondt; sandkorn; skinindæ; stander; stwnd; synd; sønder; vnderstandilsæ*; and ‹ndh› in *andheligen; bandher; besyndherligen; blindhæ; brandhen; fighendher; forbeneffndhæ; forstandheræ; grundhen; handhen; hendher; hwndhæ; hwsbondhen; landhenæ; ondhæ; samfundh; sendhæ; standher; stundh; syndhelig; syndher; søndher; vndher; wendhes; ændhæ.* Present participle forms are most frequently written using ‹ndh›: *hengendhæ; leffuendhæ; nerwarendhes; taghendhes.* In two instances of the same word, Old Danish /nd/ corresponds to ‹n›: *rindhænæ; rindhenæ* (cf. GdO *rinnende*).

/ll/ Old Danish /ll/ corresponds to ‹ll›: *alle; allighewel; atsckillig; collatz; eller; gyllenæ; heller; hellighe; kalle; lillæ* (< *litlæ*; cf. GdO *litel*); *mellom; sckillia; skilliæ; sculle; ville; vsckellighen.* Forms with ‹d› can be found in just a few words. For example: ‹ld› in *fald; falder; fuld; kelderhalss; rwldes; swigfuldæ*; and ‹ldh› in *faldher; lildhe; rwldhen.* Ræff's publication distinguishes fairly consistently between Old Danish /ld/ and /ll/.

/**nn**/ The text is less etymological in its realisation of Old Danish /nn/ compared with /ll/. In fact, /nn/ corresponds to ‹nn› in just a few words in intervocalic position (all of which are listed below), with ‹nd› and ‹ndh› being used elsewhere:[34]

‹nn›   *alminneligt; cannick; hannum; henne; konning; kunne; mannækøn; mennisckæ; penning; thennæ; twennæ; vwenner; wenner; wennyes.*
‹nd›   *anden, andet; begyndess; besindæ; brændæ; end; findæ; ind; inderlighen; mand; mend; offuerwindes; paamyndilsæ; qwinder; randsaghes; sand; sandinghen; spunden.*
‹ndh› *andhen, andhet; begyndhæ; brendher; endh; ewindhelig; findher; fwndhet; indherlighen; kwndhæ; mendhenæ; offuerwindhæ; paamyndhæ; qwindher; rindhænæ.*

The use of ‹d› after ‹n› may have been a way of assisting the reader in distinguishing between a series of minims that could have appeared confusing. We have already noted this with the use of ‹y› between ‹m› and ‹n›, and this may explain why unetymological occurrences of ‹ld› and ‹ldh› are less common — there are fewer minims in these graphemes and the possibility of confusion is smaller.

/**þ**/   For Old Danish /þ/, we find ‹th› used only for pronouns and articles: *forthi* (prep. + pron.); *the; them; then; thennæ; theris; thessæ; thet; thettæ; thi; thit; thu; thyn, thynæ*. And also in the adverbs *tha* and *ther*. Otherwise, /þ/ corresponds to ‹t› (occasionally also in pronouns, but such occurrences are few): *nedtryckæ; tancke; teckis; tenkæ; tig(h); tiid; tinghesth; tiænercæ; tiænisthæ; todhæ, toedt; tolmodighet; tordæ; trediæ; tree, try; trycht; trælæ; trøsser; traad; twingher; tyckis; tyenæ; tyt; tørræ*. Although ‹t› may be found for /þ/, ‹th› in initial position for /t/ is never found. Finally, we find ‹d› in the word *dess* (cf. GdO *thæs*).

/**ð**/   Old Danish /ð/ usually corresponds to either ‹d› or ‹dh›. They occur with similar frequency. For example, ‹d›: *affguder; bad; bedæ; biwder; baadæ; flood; forfeddræ; forhaanedhæ; fred; frygd; glæder; god; haffdæ; høgtiid; idelig; iøder; klædder; klæde; langæsiden; liwd; med; maaned; ord; pregedæ; sameledz; sedwanæ; siwdæ; swerd; sød; tiid; tolmodighet; trediæ; traad; vwighedæ*. And ‹dh›: *baddhet; bedhæ; biwdher; baadhe; flodhen; forhaanedhæ; forledhen; formindsckedhæ; fædherne; fødhæ; godh; haffdhe; iødhernæ; klædher; liwdh; modher; maanedh; qwædhæ; sagdhæ; sameledhes; sidhen; stadh; tidhen; todhæ; wordhæ;*

---

34. Skautrup 1969, II: 186.

wredhæ; wædheret. We also find ⟨th⟩ and ⟨t⟩, albeit rather seldomly. For example, ⟨th⟩: *ether, ethers* (cf. GdO *ither(s), ether(s)* 'your(s)'); *leffneth* (cf. GdO *livneth* 'life'); *meth* (cf. GdO *mæth* 'with'); and ⟨t⟩: *met* (cf. GdO *mæth* 'with'); *maanet* (cf. GdO *maneth* 'month'). Note also that /ð/ is ⟨dt⟩ in *mydtnat* (cf. GdO *mithnat* 'midnight'), and lost in *weyeræ* (cf. GdO *væther*).[35]

/g/ Old Danish /g/ corresponds to either ⟨g⟩ or ⟨gh⟩. The latter is often found after a vowel before an ⟨e⟩, or in the combination ⟨ngh⟩: *afftwinghæ; alstinghes; begheræ; bygghæ; endogh; fanghet; finghe; forhandlingh; faafenghæ; ganghen; gerningher; ghernæ; handlingher; henghæ; hwngher; ighen; inghen; konningh-elighæ; konninghers; langht; lenghe; ligghæ; manghe; nagghe; penninghæ; regh-el; reghementhæ; ringhen; sandinghen; siwnghæ; strenghælighen; tingh; tingh-esth; tingher; vnghæ; winghernæ.* Forms with ⟨g⟩ are the most common in other positions: *affgrwnd; affguder; begaffuæ; begyndæ; diligentz; figuræ; forgæffues; framgang; gaa; giffue; glædæ; igen; liggendhæ; modgang; pergament; vbegribe-lighæ; vdgydelsæ; vgunsth; wæg.*

/ɣ/ Old Danish /ɣ/ shows considerable variation in its realisation in *Iudeorum Secreta*. The most frequent is ⟨gh⟩: *almenighæ; almwghæ; atspørghæ; effterfylghæ; fogheder; forfylghe; galghen; gensighelsæ; helghen; hwgh; høghtidelighæ; dagh; middaghen, myddaghen; morghenen; mwghe; mwgheligt; Nørrenbergh; offuer-wæghe; plaghe; plæghæ; ræghenscaff; sighæ; speghel; spørghæ; syrgher; sørghen; vilghæ; vsighelighe; vwilghæ; wilghæ.* However, ⟨g⟩ can also often be found: *al-drig; dag; daglig; dog; drage; dygdhelighe; effterfylgæ; egnæ; endog; frygd; høg; højgræ; høgtiid; hwg; indseglæ; krig; log; løgnafftig; nøges; orlog; qwig; sagdhæ; slag; sorg; velsignæ; wegnæ; øgnæ.* The weakening of the consonant seems especially marked in these words, where /ɣ/ corresponds to ⟨ff⟩: *føffwæ, føffue* (cf. GdO *føghe* 'brief'); *gaffn* (cf. GdO *gaghn* 'gain', 'advantage'); *vblwffue* (cf. GdO *ublygh* 'shameless'). And in these words where /ɣ/ has disappeared altogether ⟨Ø⟩: *dwer* (cf. GdO *dughe* 'to be usable'); *effterfylning, forfylning* (cf. GdO *fylgh-ning*).[36]

/f/ Old Danish /f/ corresponds to ⟨f⟩ or ⟨ff⟩. For example, ⟨f⟩: *af; befalning; eff-terfylgæ; effterfylning; faa; falsck; findhes; frestelser; indføræ; iomfrw; læræfedd-ræ; mandfolckens; offuerfarit; paafwndhet; reformeræ; retferdighet; samfundh;*

---

35. Skautrup 1969, II: 184

36. On the realisation of /ɣ/ in early printed works, see Skautrup 1969, II: 185–86.

sorgfwldheræ; vildfarelsæ; and ⟨ff⟩: *aff; affthen; effther; fornwfftheræ; løffthæ; mangffoldug; offer; offræ; offtæ; sckrifft; sckrifftemol; straff; straffes; tilfforn; vpløffthæ; womkringsckiffthelighæ.* In these two loanwords, we find ⟨ph⟩: *prophetherneæ; prophit.*

/v/   Old Danish /v/ has by far the greatest variation of all consonants in the orthography of the text. It corresponds most frequently to the grapheme ⟨w⟩: *afftwinghæ; allighewel; beswaret; beswighæ; bewaræ; ewig; ewindhelig; forgæwes; forswaræ; forware; hwad; hwar; hwid; hwilken; ligherwiis; nerwarendhes; offuerwæghe; offuerwindes; Powel; qwædhæ; qwig; qwindher; sedwanæ; sweed; swerd; swig; swo; swodanæ; twennæ; two; vbeqwemmæ; vdwaldæ; vnderwisæ; vtwortis; vwiis; vwilghæ; wædheret; wæghæ; waræ; wed; wel; werdhen; wij; willæ; woræ; wredhæ.* However, ⟨u⟩ is also common and always used for a capital letter: *bequemmelighen, bequæmelighen; bequemt; qualdt; Uaræ; Ue; Uedh; Uerdhen; Uidhæ; Uillæ; Uort.* At the end of a word, or before another consonant, it corresponds to ⟨ff⟩: *bedriff; behoff; breff; dreffnæ; forbeneffndhæ; forderff; gaff; graff; haffdæ; haffens; heffnæ; ieffncristen; liiff; naffn; neffnæ; sckreffnæ; sielff; treffler; wtdreffnæ.* Between vowels, both ⟨ffu⟩ and ⟨ffw⟩ are found; for example, ⟨ffu⟩ with nearly 200 occurences: *affuend; bedriffuæ; begaffuæ; bereffuenscaff; bliffue; dieffuelen; fordeffue; forgæffues; giffue; haffue; helffuedis; leffuet; leffuæ; loffue; offuer; sckreffuit; twiffuel;* and ⟨ffw⟩ with just under 30 occurences: *bliffwe; forderffwæ; giffwer; giffwit; haffwe(r); hoffwed, hoffwit; kalffwe; Købmanhaffwen; loffwer; loffwit; offwertencht; sckreffwit; sckriffwer; øffwæ.* The grapheme ⟨v⟩ is only found in a small number of words, and always initially: *vaner; varæ; vaxliwss; ved; velsignæ; ville; visselighen.* Finally, we find ⟨f⟩ in *sielf* (just one occurrence).

/s/   Old Danish /s/ usually corresponds to ⟨s⟩: *alstingis; ansigt; fisckæ; glædis; hees; hworledhes; kasthæ; sagt; samæ; sckriffthemaall; siæls; syndher; theris; vdsla.* After a short vowel in an open syllable, the ⟨s⟩ is often doubled: *lessæ; messæ; thessæ; visselighen.* Note also *løssdæ.* Likewise ⟨s⟩ can often be found doubled in the final position of a word: *blæss; dess; hanss; hooss; huess; hwss; omgaass; oss; trooss.*

The grapheme ⟨z⟩ is found in combination with ⟨d⟩: *blodz; bordz; gwdz; inghenstedz; mendz; sameledz; syndz; verdzlighe.* The combination ⟨ds⟩ only occurs across derivational morpheme boundaries: *gledscaff* (= glæth-skap); *indseglæ* (= in-sighle); *ondscaff* (= ond-skap); *randsaghes* (= ran-sakes). And ⟨z⟩ is found in combination with ⟨t⟩: *artz* (GdO *ars*); *collatz; gantze; godtz; heltz; penitentz; pestilentzæ; tribulatz.* The combination ⟨ts⟩ only occurs across derivational morpheme boundaries: *altsamen* (= *alt-samen*); *vtsæth* (= *ut-sat*). We also find ⟨sz⟩ once: *aszen* (GdO *asen*). Note the loanwords with ⟨c⟩: *cerimonier*; *conscientier*; and forms with ⟨x⟩: *exempel*; *moxen*; *strax*; *text*; *vaxliwss*.

Summary

The orthography with regard to consonants is fairly stable with sounds being represented consistently by the same graphemes — the most widespread alternation being the addition or loss of an ⟨h⟩, and the realisation of Old Danish /v/. A rather noticeable, though not especially diffused, characteristic is the use of the grapheme ⟨g⟩ not only for the consonants /g/ and /ɣ/, but also for /j/ in *arbeygd*; *arbeygdhæ*; *forarbeygdhæ*; *fighendher*; *frigbornæ*; *nyg* and *nygt*. This feature probably comes from MLG and is typically found in early printed texts in Danish.[37] Other evidence of influence from MLG can be seen in the forms *openbaræ* (MLG *openbâren*) and *openbarlighen* (MLG *openbarliken*).

Style, translation and lexicon

In this section, certain aspects of style, translation and vocabulary in *Iudeorum Secreta* come under scrutiny. The focus is on how Ræff communicated his message and how he translated the text from Latin. The language of *Iudeorum Secreta* is on the whole simple and straightforward, but nevertheless there are several unusual words that require explanation.

Word pairs, doublets, tautologous constructions etc.

Ræff uses a great many word pairs in his language.[38] These formulaic constructions, also known as doublets or word couplings in English, are made up of two or more words and connected by 'and' or 'or'; for example, 'black and blue',

---

37. See Hansen 1962–71, II: 389; Lasch 1914: 82 (§124), 85 (§132), and 90 (§143). Cf. MLG *arbeydt* (= *arbeit*), GdO *arbejde*; MLG *vîgende* (= *vîent*), GdO *fjande*; MLG *vryg* (= *vrî*), GdO *fri*; MLG *nîge* (= *nüwe*), GdO *ny*.

38. On these types of construction, see Bendz 1965; also Scheel 1923: 68–70; Diderichsen 1931–37: 324 n. 1; Seip 1934: 159; Thorén 1942: 122–38, 130 nn. 1–2; Skautrup 1968, II: 68; Petersen 1991: 33–36.

'night and day', and 'sooner or later'. Rather like idioms, they sometimes form a whole unit of meaning that goes beyond the individual elements ('black and blue' means 'beaten and bruised all over'; 'night and day' means 'all the time', and 'sooner or later' means 'at some inevitable point in the future'). In Ræff's work, some of these phrases are translations of word pairs in the Latin original, but the majority are of his own creation. For example, the Latin word pair 'vociferantur et clamant [*cry out and call upon*]' is translated as 'raabæ oc bedhæ [*cry out and pray*, p. 4: 16]', whereas the single word 'penitenciam [*penance*]' in the Latin original becomes the pair 'plicht oc bod [*penitence and penance*, p. 4: 8]' in Ræff's translation. The use of such doublets in translated literature from Latin was, of course, not uncommon.[39] The doublets in *Iudeorum Secreta* can be grouped into three types: 1) synonyms, 2) antithetical words, and 3) enumerative words. They are connected by the word *oc* 'and' or *eller* 'or', and many of them alliterate.

1. Synonyms

Some of these synonym combinations may have arisen through Ræff using a *vocabularium* or glossary to look the words up in Latin and copying two or more of the translations. Indeed, most of his synonymous word pairs seem to be emphatic — the second element does not add much clarity or extra meaning to the first, but rather merely adds emphasis through repetition. For example:

> 'al ting wel oc inth*et* ildæ [*everything good and nothing bad*]', 'armod oc fattugdom [*wretchedness and poverty*]', 'armæ oc wslæ [*poor and wretched*]', 'atsckildhæ oc spreddhæ [*divided and dispersed*]', 'bedrægheræ eller then som sckadhe gør [*charlatan or one who does harm*]', 'begyndilsæ oc barndom [*beginning and childhood*]', 'behindrer oc forbiwdher [*prevent and forbid*]', 'belackæ oc bespee [*dishonour and mock*]', 'bewaræ oc gømæ [*hold and keep*]', 'bøner oc benedidelser [*prayers and blessings*]', 'clanck eller liwd [*tone or sound*]', 'falsckæ och swigefuldæ [*false and deceitful*]', 'fattugdo*m* och vselhet [*poverty and wretchedness*]', 'fly och scky [*flee and shun*]', 'forhaaning oc wanæræ [*spite and mockery*]', 'fornwfftig oc klog [*sensible and clever*]', 'frelsæ oc frij gøræ [*save and deliver*]', 'frælst oc løsdt [*delivered and freed*]', 'fwlæ oc slemme [*evil and bad*]', 'faafenghæ bøner oc formaledidelser [*vain prayers and curses*]', 'ghernæ eller met god wilghe [*willingly or intentionally*]', 'glædæ oc frygd [*joy and happiness*]', 'glædæ oc salighet [*joy and salva-*

---

[39]. On word couplings in medieval Swedish translations from Latin, see Bengtson 1947: 182–88, 207–11.

tion]', 'godhæ oc dygdhelighe [*good and virtuous*]', 'got oc nyttheligt [*good and useful*]', 'had oc affuend [*hate and envy*]', 'heffnæ oc wræghæ sig [*avenge and get back at*]', 'ketterij oc vildfarelse [*heresy and delusion*]', 'klarlighe oc skinindæ [*clearly and brightly*]', 'krig oc orlog [*war or war*]', 'macht oc besckickelighet [*ability and nature*]', 'modgang oc vløckæ [*hardship and misfortune*]', 'nw oc ewindhelig [*now and eternally*]', 'nøddhæ eller twungdæ [*have to or must*]', 'plicht oc bood [*penitence and penance*]', 'predicken oc gudz ord [*sermon and the word of God*]', 'røst eller stemmæ [*voice or voice*]', 'sacramenther oc cerimonier [*sacraments and ceremonies*]', 'scalkhet oc falscke fwnd [*roguery and deceitful inventions*]', 'en skær hwg oc eth reenth hiarthæ [*a clear mind and a pure heart*]', 'sorg oc græmelsæ [*sorrow and grief*]', 'spørghæ eller bedhæ [*ask and bid*]', 'stadt oc besckickelighet [*position and ability*]', 'en stoor storm oc eth stort wædher [*a great storm and a great wind*]', 'styrcker oc stadfesther [*strengthened and engrained*]', 'synd oc ondscaff [*sin and evil*]', 'syndher och ondhæ gerningher [*sins and evil deeds*]', 'sød oc kær [*sweet and dear*]', 'tilstaa eller vedtaghe [*admit or accept*]', 'tiæneræ eller trælæ [*servants or slaves*]', 'too oc gnidhæ sig reenæ [*wash or rub themselves clean*]', 'Twingher oc nødher [*force and compel*]', 'Uerdhen i hwset eller hwssbondhen [*male host or head of the household*]', 'vbegribelighæ oc vhørlighæ [*incomprehensible and senseless*]', 'vbesckickelighe wanæ oc wildfarilsæ [*inappropriate custom and delusion*]', 'vbørlighæ oc vhørlighæ [*shameful and senseless*]', 'vnyttelighæ oc faafenghæ [*fruitless and vain*]', 'vwighedæ oc formalediedhæ [*unconsecrated or cursed*]', 'wendes oc wemyes [*converted and turned away*]', 'werdughe oc hellighe [*venerable and holy*]', 'wændelighæ oc womkringsckiffthelighæ [*eternal and immutable*]', 'ydmyghe oc gudhelighe [*humble and devout*]', 'ærer oc loffwer [*honour and praise*]', 'æræ oc werdughet [*honour and dignity*]'.

Some of the doublets are used repeatedly in the text and seem to be rather empty set phrases where the second element has become redundant and does not add any special emphasis. For example:

akte ok/æller besinne	[*consider and realise*]: 'achtæ oc besindæ', 'acthæ eller besindæ'
liv ok sjal	[*life and soul*]: 'liif oc siæl' (3 times), 'lijff oc siæl'
rethe ok beskikke sik	[*prepare and get ready*]': 'redhæ och besckickæ sigh', 'redhæ [...] och besckickæ sig'
spot ok spe	[*mockery and ridicule*]: 'bespottedæ oc bespeedæ', 'spot oc spee', 'forhaaning/ spot oc spee', 'spee/ spot oc forhaaning', 'the fwlæ iødhers ondscaff/ farlighæ omgengelsæ/ falsck oc swig/ spee oc spot'

takke ok love	[*thank and praise*]: 'tacker oc loffwer', 'tackæ oc loffue' (2 times), 'at tackæ/ loffuæ/ oc benedidæ gud'
tith ok ofte	[*often and often*]: 'tiit oc offtæ' (2 times), 'tiit och offthe', 'tiith oc offthæ', 'tijt oc offte'
tillathe ok tilstæthje	[*allow and permit*]: 'tilladet oc tilstædt', 'tilladher oc tilstæder', 'tilladhæ och tilstædhæ'
tro ok mene	[*believe and are convinced*]: 'myenæ oc tro fuldkommeligen', 'tro oc myenæ fuldkommelighen'
ubekvæm ok ukristelik	[*malicious and unchristian*]: 'vbeqwem oc vkristelig', 'vbeqwæmæ oc vkristelighe'

Occasionally, the second element seems to explain the first which, if it appeared by itself, would not make much sense. The first element is perhaps a rather general word, such as the verbs 'gøre [*to do*]', 'haffue [*to have*]' or 'være [*to be*]', while the second element provides the semantic content for the word pair:

'faa oc afftwinghæ [*get and extort*]', 'giort oc offuerfarit [*done and finished*]', 'giort oc sckreffwit [*made and written*]', 'gøris eller bedriffues [*to be done or committed*]', 'gøræ eller ligghæ oss i mod [*do or set themselves against us*]', 'haffue eller brwghæ [*have or use*]', 'haffue oc lidhæ [*have and suffer*]', 'kommæ oc vdsendhes [*come and be sent*]', 'æræ oc boo [*are and live*]'.

It may also be a word that was thought to be unfamiliar to readers because of its exotic, unfamiliar or Jewish character. The second element is a reminder of this word's meaning and clarifies it. For example:

'theris affløsnings dag eller theris frælsen dag [*their day of atonement or their day of deliverance*]', 'rabier eller ypperste [*rabbis or leaders*]', 'rwldhen eller Moysi bøgher [*the scroll or the books of Moses*]'.

The final two items in these examples are Ræff's own expansions of the Latin (*viz.* 'Rabi' and 'libri moisi' respectively).

In the case of doublets, where one of the elements is a foreign word, the 'native' Danish word may be meant to explain the foreign word, although it is in fact often the foreign word that is the second element with the 'explanation' coming first. The reason for these synonyms may simply be Ræff's enthusiastic use of a *vocabularium*, a bilingual word-list or a dictionary rather than an attempt to be pedagogical, but the tendency is noteworthy. In fact, several of these foreign loanwords are not recorded in the citation catalogue of *Gammeldansk Ordbog* ('compositier', 'diligentz', 'tribulatz', 'tribwt'), Kalkar's *Ordbog over det ældre danske Sprog* from 1881–1918 ('compositier [except relating to music]', 'diligentz'), or in the twenty-seven volumes of the standard dicitonary of Danish, *Ordbog over det danske Sprog* ('diligentz', 'tribulatz').[40] This suggests perhaps, that the use of these words may not have been particularly widespread at the beginning of the sixteenth century, and the doublet constructions are intended for clarity and explanation. The foreign word, or the word that is presumably more difficult to understand, is underlined in the following examples:

'compositier eller dicther [*compositions and stories*]', 'flijd oc diligentz [*hard work and diligence*]', 'gaffn oc prophit [*benefit and profit*]', 'gildhæ eller collatz [*feast or dinner*]', 'glosæ och figuræ [*explanations and images*]', 'mandat eller befalning [*order and command*]', 'naturlighe log oc institut [*the law of nature and teaching*]', 'sckrifftemol oc penitentz [*confession and repentance*]', 'sermon oc talæ [*sermon and speech*]', 'sorg oc penitentz [*sorrow and repentance*]', 'tribulatz och forfylning [*tribulation and persecution*]', 'tribwt och sckat [*tribute and tax*]', 'vp retthæ oc reformeræ [*erect and rebuild*]'.

2. Antithetical

Antithetical pairings of words function to point towards something bigger than the individual elements. For example, when Ræff writes 'dag oc nat [*day and night*]', he means all the time, and by 'vnghæ oc gamblæ [*young and old*]' he means everybody without exception. Some of the phrases appear to be set expressions, and they have parallels in modern languages, including English:

dagh ok nat	[*day and night = the whole 24-hour period*]: 'dag oc nat', 'nat oc dag', 'nath oc dagh'
unge ok gamle	[*young and old = all the people*]: 'vnghæ oc gamblæ', 'vnghæ oc gamblæ'
æte eller drikke	[*eat and drink = feast*]: 'ædæ eller drickæ'

Less common antithetical word pairs include:

aften ok morghen	[*evening and morning*]: 'affthen och morghen'
haner æller høner	[*cocks or hens*]: 'haner eller høner', 'hanæ eller hønæ'

---

40. Skautrup 1969, II: 238.

3. Enumerative

There are quite a few enumerative listings in *Iudeorum Secreta*. The main role of enumeration is to emphasise and to suggest completeness, that is that there are no exceptions or intervening items. Their function is thus similar to that of antithetical pairs. Some of these enumerating words are so similar they could be considered synonyms:

> 'bedræghæ/ beswighæ/ forderffue/ formaledidhæ och nedtryckæ [*to deceive, trick, corrupt, curse and oppress*]', 'clart/ hwith oc sckinindæ [*bright, white and luminous*]', 'eth frwctsomeligt/ eth saligt/ oc eth løckesomt [...] aar [*a fruitful, blessed and fortunate year*]', 'fald/ frestelsæ/ eller vildfarelsæ [*sin, temptation or error*]', 'faræ/ skadæ/ oc frestelser [*danger, harm and temptations*]', 'Forhaanedhæ/ forsmaaedhæ/ plath inthet achtedhæ/ forladnæ aff gwd forwthen al løckæ [*mocked, rejected, not respected at all, abandoned by God and without any happiness*]', 'hwg/ wilghæ oc sind [*thoughts, intention and mind*]', 'loffwet/ æret oc benedidhet [*praised, honoured and blessed*]', 'penninghæ/ rigdom/ gwld oc godtz [*money, wealth, gold and goods*]', 'reen/ pwr oc skær [*clean, pure and cleansed*]', 'stoer tretthæ/ stor sckadhæ/ stor vwilghæ och stor vgunsth [*great tumult, much damage, much ill will and much displeasure*]', 'wiseræ/ clogheræ/ eller fornwfftheræ [*wiser, cleverer or more sensible*]', 'wsligheræ/ bedrøffuedheræ/ sorgfwldheræ/ eller meræ beswaret met tiænisthæ [*more wretched, more sad, more sorrowful, or more oppressed by servitude*]'.

Other enumerative listings contain words that are not synonyms:

> 'Cristo gwdz søn/ iomfrw Marie hanss velsignedhæ modher oc alle gwdz werdughe helghen [*to Christ, the son of God, Mary, his blessed mother, and all of God's worthy saints*]', 'gud oc hanss werdighe modher Marie met alle hanss helghen/ [*God and his venerable mother Mary and all his saints*]', 'gudz/ then hellighe cristelighæ troes/ then hellighe kirckis/ oc fattughe cristnæ mennisckis retferdughæ fogheder oc forstandheræ [*the rightful governors and representatives of God, the holy Christian faith, the holy Church and poor Christian people*]', 'møghet nyttheligt/ bequemt oc gud taknemmeligt [*very useful, apt and godly*]', 'med pestilentzæ/ met hwngher/ met swerd oc met fengsel [*with pestilence, with famine, by sword and with imprisonment*]', 'noghet aff theris qwig (encten aszen eller koo eller noghet andhet creaturæ) [*one of their cattle (either an ass or a cow or some other creature)*]', 'settæ sig til bordz/ ædhæ oc dricke oc gøre sig gantze gladæ [*sit at their tables, eat and drink and make merry*]', 'stædhes/ høres eller lidhes [*be allowed, heard or tolerated*]', 'theris store sckriffthemol/ abstinentz oc fasthæ [*major confession, abstinence and fasting*]',

'til stocke oc steenæ oc til affguder [*to sticks and stones and to idols*]', 'vti en pøl/ vti en graff/ vti en kelderhalss/ eller i noghen andhen farlig stæd [*into a pool, into a ditch, into a cellar-shaft or into some other dangerous place*]', 'werdzens macht/ wold oc weldhæ/ oc stor rigdom [*world power, domination and might, and great wealth*]'.

Word pairs and verbs of utterance

Particularly interesting are the combinations with 'raabæ [*to shout*]', where 'to shout' has been paired with another verb of utterance. With the exception of 'siwnghæ oc raabæ' to translate Latin 'ordiuntur carmen [*a song is begun*]', these 'shout pairings' are all found in Pfefferkorn's original:

> 'raabæ the och hylæ alle met en røst oc sighe [*they shout and all yell with one voice and say*]', 'raabæ oc sighæ [*shout and say*]', 'raabæ oc bedhæ [*shout and pray*]', 'raabæ the alle høgt oc sighæ [*they all shout loudly and say*]', 'siwnghæ oc raabæ [*sing and shout*]'.

The emphasis on shouting is presumably because, as we have seen in chapter 1 of this book, shouting is a stereotypical Jewish behaviour. Other pairings of verbs of utterance include:

> 'han suaredæ hannum oc sagdhæ [*he answered him and said*]', 'Han tal til them oc paamyndher [*He speaks to them and reminds them*]'.

Omissions and simplifications

The preface to the book is quite dissimilar in Pfefferkorn's Latin original and the Danish version (pp. 1: 3–3: 14):[41]

Original (Cologne version)	→	Ræff
A booklet about the Confession of the Jews or the Sabbath of Suffering published by Johannes Pfefferkorn, a recently converted Jew.		Recently brought out into the light: The secrets of the Jews

---

41. Only the English translations are provided here to avoid extensive repetition; please refer to the edition in ch. 5 for the original language versions.

If you wish to know who I am, I shall tell you: a booklet, brief and easy,

about the sacred time of purification for Jews,

the day on which they rid themselves of their sins and by what rites of purification.

I make public the vain fantasies of the Jewish people,

who cannot obtain for themselves hope of salvation.

Oh, condemn them — thus God the judge of what is right will save you.

In honour and praise of Jesus Christ, his blessed mother the eternal Virgin Mary and the entire host of heaven.

It is my intent to explain and carry forth into the light the synagogical confession of the Jewish people — who wander and stumble in blindness — the method and preparation for this confession, and at which time of the year it is done (for they solemnly perform it once every year), and to whom they confess or who absolves and frees them of sin, so that men possessing discernment and correct reasoning can recognise and examine the abuses and empty rituals of those who are without a solid foundation. For the latter have nothing that may disprove the former. And I, poor man, have for a long time (as a madman) together with the rest my people clung to these and other delusions, led by a common delusion which has been accepted from the cradle, in the belief that a great deliverance was preserved in them, but later, by the grace of God, I have abandoned this, and as if a cloud had been driven away and a cataract had been removed from my eyes, I have come

This book is taken from Latin and translated into Danish to meet the needs of those who cannot understand Latin. It deals with and contains all the secret affairs that the bad Jews keep between themselves both in their Jewish temple and in their own houses. Thus shall Christian people know to punish them. Johannes Pfefferkorn.

I, Johannes Pfefferkorn, born a Jew and now a Christian, greet all of you who keep that promise and those articles of faith that you promised when you received baptism and the Christian faith. And I advise you all to keep yourselves away from the Jews and Jewish affairs, particularly because by not doing so people forsake the salvation of their souls. May God protect you all.

A cleric, who is in Cologne and is called Johannes Pfefferkorn, has made and written this book for the benefit of common Christian people, so that they will know to flee and shun the bad Jews who continually — day and night — try to corrupt Christian people's lives as well as their souls. The aforementioned Johannes Pfefferkorn was born a Jew and circumcised, but has now had himself baptised and is a good Christian learned man; he knows best their secret which he makes public in this little book; so that Christian people, when they come to hear such bad things spoken against the Christian faith, will know to punish them for their error.

closer to the light and clarity of the Christian religion, to Jesus Christ, who is the true light — as close as the feeble eyes of my mind could when I cast my thoughts upon him, humbly praying — If I can pray for something and eventually obtain it — that this light may increase and become stable for me so that by walking in it without turning away from it, I shall not stumble [i.e. be tempted to do evil]. I also beseech all of you, my faithful brothers in Christ, not to deign to pray on behalf me, the sinner, to the Lord God that he forgive my sins, grant me and preserve the true splendour of faith, and give me understanding and a strong and constant spirit to fight those bloody enemies and blasphemers of Jesus Christ and Holy Mary, his mother, and so that I can (as I very much want to) persuade my brothers and fellow tribesmen according to the flesh, in proportion to my smallness, following the practice of the teachers and superiors in the Holy Church, to whom I humbly subject myself with all veneration, in every way (as is right, pious and even due), to give up their blindness and, preceded by the true light, enter the road by which they may arrive at the celestial Jerusalem, for which the one in Palestine was a model. Now therefore, with God's help, I embark upon my proposed enterprise, which is not arduous but easy, and which, so I believe with a survey and a method has something of interest in it. This should be known so that the Jews become aware of their vain deception, and not just they alone, but also foreigners, so that eventually, when it is no secret any more, they will be driven by their shame to cast it away in a hurry. And likewise by means of such a comparison, the Christians should understand, with expressions of thanks to God the Father and Jesus Christ, how different their ceremonies and rites, and even the grace and goodness in their confessions, are from those of the Jews, not to mention the other new sacraments in this book when the first have passed.

The Danish version is not only much shorter than the Latin, it is quite different. In the prefatory matter of the Latin book, we find a poem, a dedication, an account of the book's contents, of Pfefferkorn's past, as well as his intentions with regard to the book — that the Jews will convert. In Ræff's Danish version, we have no poem or dedication, but again a (short) account of the book's contents and of Pfefferkorn's Jewish credentials, and the purpose of the book is also clearly spelt out here — that Christians will punish Jews for their error. The two introductions thus demonstrate the two sides of the coin of Christian anti-Judaism: conversion or persecution. Ræff's introduction may be different because either he did not have access to this part of the Latin text, or he wanted to reshape the text to make it more applicable to the situation in Denmark, where there were no resident Jews to be converted.

At one point in the original Latin text, where Pfefferkorn describes the Jews' attitude towards and terms of abuse for the eucharistic Host, the language switches to German with a couple of Hebrew words thrown in. Although Ræff clearly had difficulty understanding the German and Hebrew words in this section, he succeeds in providing his readers with a graphic interpretation in Danish (p. 24: 4–5) based on the Latin explanatory sentence 'id est ille defedatus est'. However, he does not translate the German text, nor does he include the three Hebrew words *metame'* [מטמא, 'defiling', 'making impure'], *zevel* [זבל, 'dung', 'manure'] and *tame'* [טמא, 'defiled', 'impure']:

Original (Cologne version) →	*Ræff*
men hat mettamme gewest.	See/
off men hat den zeueltamme gegeuen.	then haffue the varet borthæ
id est ille defedatus est.	oc besckit
They have been 'defiling',	Look!
or they have given the 'impure dung'.	That's one that they have just gone
That is, it is defiled.	and defiled with shit!

The accusation of referring to the sacramental bread as 'impure dung' reflects the Jews' supposed desire to desecrate the Host and inflict physical and verbal abuse on the body of Jesus Christ contained therein.

Additions

There are a few instances where Poul Ræff has added to the original text and expanded it in his translation. Although there are very few such places, they provide us with an insight into his own thoughts on the subject and about his intended public. For example, on p. 6: 23–27, Ræff underlines the fact that the Jews when talking about Christians mean his readers whom they hold in very little regard. Thus:

Original (Cologne version) →	Ræff
Deinde precatur deum […]	han bedher ath gwd
vt populum hunc suum	wil frelsæ
seruet et custodiat	syt folk
ab hominibus impudentibus.	fran vblwffue me*n*nisckæ/
a malis cogitationibus.	af ondhæ ta*n*ker/
ab incircumcisis sub eo	fran the folk som ickæ æræ omkringsckornæ/
nomine christianos precipue	oc ther met myen han besyndherligen
notans tanquam immundos.	oss cristnæ me*n*nisckæ
[- - -]	(han regner oss at wæræ møgh*et* vreenæ)
a diabolica tentatione et potestate.	Aff dieffuelsens macht oc frestelser *etc*.
Next [he] begs God […]	*He prays that God*
to keep and protect	*will save*
his people	*his people*
from shameless people,	*from shameless people,*
from evil thoughts,	*from evil thoughts,*
from the uncircumcised	*from those people who are not circumcised,*
(meaning in particular	*and here he means in particular*
such impure Christians),	*us Christian people*
[- - -]	*(he considers us to be very unclean),*
and from the Devil's temptations and power.	*and from the Devil's power and temptations etc.*

Here we can see that Poul Ræff has chosen to expand his translation with an entire parenthetic sentence 'he considers us to be very unclean' not found in the original.

This shows how Ræff was not averse to adding to his material if it emphasised the message of *Iudeorum Secreta*.

On p. 15: 17–25, we find a short theological addition by Ræff where he draws attention to how the blindness of the Jews is sending them to damnation whilst Christians look forward to eternal salvation:

Original (Cologne version) →	*Ræff*
Inter ceteras autem precationes	Blant suodanæ theris bøner
orationem habent et dictionem	oc scalkafftighe sedwaner/
qua aiunt reliquas gentes omnes (quo	belackæ the oc bespee
nomine nos christianos significant maxime)	oss cristne menniske
adorare venerarique	oc sighæ at wij bedæ til
idola/ et inuocare deos mutos et surdos/	stocke oc steenæ oc til affguder
qui nemini adiumento esse/	som inthet kunnæ hielpæ oss
a nemine malum propulsare queant.	oc ey taghæ oss noghet ondt fran/
iactant preterea	men the rosæ ther aff
in hac gratulatione et gaudio et laude.	oc forrummæ sig
[- - -]	at the bedæ til then sandhæ gud/
[- - -]	en dog at the icke ville
[- - -]	achtæ oc besindæ
[- - -]	at theris bøn er them sielf
[- - -]	til ewig fordømelsæ
[- - -]	oc vor bøn er oss
[- - -]	til ewig salighet
se adorare	The bedhæ til then
regem regum	som er en konning offuer alle konninger
However, among other prayers	*In their prayers*
they have words and phrases	*and roguish customs,*
that say that other people	*they dishonour and mock*
(with which words they mean us Christians)	*us Christians*
pray to and worship	*and say that we pray to*
idols and invoke deaf and mute gods	*sticks and stones and to idols*
who cannot be of help	*who cannot help us*
and cannot keep us from evil.	*and do not keep us from anything evil.*
Furthermore, they praise themselves	*But they praise themselves*
in thanksgiving and joy and glory	*and boast*
[- - -]	*that they pray to the true God,*
[- - -]	*even though they do not want*

[- - -]	to see and realise
[- - -]	that their prayer sends them
[- - -]	to eternal damnation
[- - -]	and our prayer sends us
[- - -]	to eternal salvation.
for praying to	They pray to the one
the 'king of kings'.	who is 'king of kings'.

In the example above, Ræff has expanded the text and also changed the Latin 'among other prayers they have words and phrases that say...' to the far more contentious 'In their prayers and roguish customs, they dishonour and mock...'. Finally, there is an addition that clearly shows us whom Ræff had in mind as the readers of his book (p. 25: 13–21):

Original (Cologne version) →	Ræff
¶ Particula quinta admonitoria ad christianos principes populos ciuitates/ qui iudeos recipiunt/ et tuentur in sua illos nequicia viuere sinentes. […] principes/ nobiles et populos prefatus et veniam paucis alloquar atque respublicas christianas/ sub quibus et vbi iudei morantur et agunt/	¶ Thet v artickel er en paa myndelsæ til herrer/ Førsther. Prelater. Købstædher oc alle andræ cristnæ me*n*nisckæ/ som tilladhæ oc tilstædæ at iødernæ sculle suodan theris herrenscked bedriffue oc fuldko*m*mæ vti theris la*n*d och stædher. HErrer Førsther Prelater Frigbornæ mend Borgmestheræ Raad oc Meenæ almwghæ vti cristhe*n* hedhen/ huar som heltz och vndher huess herredømæ Iøder the æræ oc boo.
The fifth chapter: An admonition to Christian princes and common citizens who accept Jews and permit them to live from their wickedness. [...] princes, noblemen and common people [- - -] and Christian lands under whom and where Jews are not detained and do business.	The fifth chapter is an admonition to <u>lords</u>, princes, <u>prelates</u>, <u>cities</u> and other Christian people who allow and permit the Jews to pursue and fulfil such villainy in their countries and towns. <u>Lords</u>, princes, <u>prelates</u>, <u>freeborn men</u>, <u>mayors</u>, <u>councils</u> and common people in Christendom wherever you may be and under whose dominion the Jews exist and live:

Ræff has added *købstædher* 'market towns' or 'cities', *borgmestheræ* 'mayors', *raad* 'councils', *herrer* 'lords' and *prelater* 'senior members of the clergy' to his list of addressees. In his view, the Jewish threat was to arrive in Denmark through the country's trading centres, and unless the leaders of these towns were vigilant, the Jews would be able to oppress and corrupt the Danish people.

Native elements

In one place, Ræff has clearly changed the text in order to make it more natively Danish and familiar to his readers (p. 15: 6–10):

Original (Cologne version) →	*Ræff*
quemadmodum et nos peana	ligherwiis som wor sedwanæ er
(vt vocant)	ath wij qwædhæ noghen løstelig wisæ
nostrum annum nouum ingredientes	nyt aars affthen oc nyt aars dag som er/
canimus in laudes iesu	war wel kommen nygt aar war wel kommen hær.
vt romanis erant per illud tempus	The ladæ sig waræ forplichtughæ
saturnalia eum diem letum auspicantes	at holdæ then dag met stort gledscaff/
just as it is also our custom	*just as it is our custom*
to sing a song of praise	*to sing a joyous song*
when our new year begins,	*on New Year's Eve and New Year's Day, namely*
we sing in praise of Jesus;	*'Welcome New Year! Welcome here!'*
just like Saturnalia was for the Romans	*They are obliged*
their happy and auspicious day.	*to celebrate the day with much happiness.*

The song that Ræff mentions here is still popular in Denmark, in a version penned by Nikolaj Frederik Severin Grundtvig (1783–1872) under the title 'Vær velkommen, Herrens år, og velkommen herhid' (1849). The final part of Ræff's translation ('They [...] happiness') is either a mistake or an intentional change in the translation. The reference to Saturnalia in the Latin version is also interesting because the Jews are often related to Saturn. St Augustine thought him to be a Jewish God, and the planet Saturn was identified as the star of Israel.[42]

---

42. On the interrelationship between the Jews and Saturn, see Zafran 1979.

Mistranslations and errors

There are a few mistranslations and errors in Poul Ræff's book. For example, on p. 3: 16–17, the title is incorrect. It reads:

Original (Cologne version)	→	*Ræff*
De preparatione Iudaice confessionis. et quo tempore fiat et quo ritu.		¶ Then første artickel er om iødhernæ. Hworledhes the redhæ och besckickæ sigh modh then tiidh the scwllæ goræ theris høghtidelighæ sckriffthæmaal. <u>Om hwad tiidh the goræ samæ theris sckrifftæmaal. Och hwarledhes the goræ thet.</u>
On the Jews' preparation for their confession and what time they prepare and with what ceremony.		*The first chapter is about the Jews: How they prepare and get ready for the time when they make their ceremonial confession;* <u>*about the time when they make their confession, and how they do so.*</u>

The chapter in *Iudeorum Secreta* does not deal with how Jews confess, so the last part of the Danish chapter heading (underlined in the quotation above) is irrelevant and is also not in the original Latin title. The incorrect part of the chapter heading also appears correctly in the heading for chapter 2 (p. 10: 24–26). This is clearly a type-setting, not a translation, error.[43]

Ræff has, however, mistranslated several sections on Jewish ritual. It is very unlikely that such mistakes were intentional, but Ræff's version of events certainly places his contemporary Jews in an even worse light than Pfefferkorn's original (pp. 6: 27–7: 2):

Original (Cologne version)	→	*Ræff*
[- - -] Recolitur quoque magna deuotione latissime ad aras eorum prisca immolatio holocaustomatum [- - -]		Paa samæ tiid goris stort offer til theris altheræ met stor gwdhelighet/ effther thet gamblæ testamenthes sedwanæ.

---

43. See Lausten 1992: 132 n. 21.

et ceterarum victimarum	Som er m*et* kalffwe/ met weyeræ/
in bobus arietibus et hircis.	met bwckæ oc swodant meræ.
[- - -]	*At the same time,*
It is remembered how with great devotion	*a great sacrifice is made*
in days of old to ancient altars	*on their altar*
a burnt offering was brought	*with great devotion*
[- - -]	*in accordance with Old Testament custom*
and other beasts for sacrifice	*by sacrificing a calf, a ram,*
oxen, rams and he-goats	*a he-goat or something else,*

In *Confession of the Jews*, Pfefferkorn writes that the Jews remember the great sacrifice of cattle, rams and goats that their forefathers offered with great diligence on the altar, but Ræff in his *Iudeorum Secreta* writes that sixteenth-century Jews were in fact still performing these animal sacrifices in their synagogues. Likewise he continues that (p. 7: 2–4):

Original (Cologne version)	→	*Ræff*
libaminumque		Sameledhes
farris triticei		met kagher giort aff hwedhemel/
olei vini mellis salis		olliæ/ wyn och salth
a sacerdotibus suis peragi solita		som the plæghæ at offræ theris presther.
And a libation of		*Similarly*
cakes made of wheat flour,		*with cakes made of wheat flour,*
oil, wine, honey, salt		*oil, wine [- - -] and salt*
was custom for the priests to perform		*which they usually offer to their priests.*

Contrary to what Ræff writes, Jews did not give cakes of wheat flour, oil, wine and salt to their priests. Pfefferkorn wrote correctly that these cakes were offered by the priests at the time of the Temple. Again, Ræff's mistranslation paints an even more ridiculous picture of Jewish rituals than that found in Pfefferkorn's work. There have of course been no priests or Temple or sacrifices in Judaism since the destruction of the Second Temple in 70 CE.

Ræff's translation of Pfefferkorn's description of the Priestly Blessing is also wrong. Rather than the *kohanim* ascending to the ark and raising their hands, they lift the ark up with their hands (p. 16: 15–17):

Original (Cologne version)	→	Ræff
Accedunt supplices		the gaa til arken
et magna deuotione arcam/		me*t* stor gudelighet/
tendunt in altum manus suas		taghæ oc løfftæ he*n*ne høgt vp m*et* theris hendher
benedicunt populo		oc benedidæ folkit

They ascend to the ark in	They go to the ark
supplication and great devotion.	with great devotion
They raise their hands high	take it and raise it up high with their hands
(and) bless the people	and bless the people

Taking the weight of a Torah-scroll ark into consideration, this would require superhuman powers! Ræff, having no first-hand knowledge of Jewish rituals, has simply misunderstood Pfefferkorn, and not intentionally altered the meaning of the text. Ræff appears to have read the accusative plural 'manus suas [*their hands*]' as an ablative plural ('manibus suis [*by means of their hands*]'). Furthermore, the similarity between 'he*n*ne [*it*]' and 'hendher [*hands*]' may also have confused Ræff. These mistakes create an even more disparaging and ludicrous account of the Jews' religious practices than presented in Pfefferkorn's Latin version.

Hapax legomena and unusual words

The word 'forgheræ' (p. 11: 15) is a *hapax legomenon*, a word that is not attested in any other Danish text. The Latin original has 'lacinia', which in Latin-Danish dictionaries from the early modern period is translated as 'talle paa kleder [*waist on clothes*]' (Pedersen 1510 [1973]); 'Talie [*waist*]' (Hingelberg 1576 [1995])', and 'Flig [*shirt tail, flap*]', 'Kiltning [*tucked up piece of cloth*]', 'Opslag [*cuff, turn-up*]', 'Side Flasker [*sides that hang down on clothes*]', 'Skød paa Klæde [*tails or skirt on clothes*]', 'Svøb [*swaddling-clothes*]' (Colding 1626). Pfefferkorn's German version has 'klaider' which means 'clothes'. It seems most likely to me, that the word 'forgheræ' is related to the German word *G(h)er* as in 'Geren der kleyderen' and 'kleyderGheren' (my emphasis), which are used to translate the Latin 'laciniæ' in Dasypodius' Latin-German dictionary of 1536.[44] This German word is derived from Middle High German *gêr* meaning 'keilförmiges zeug-

---

44. See Dasypodius 1995: fols 106va and 342ra.

stück, das unten an ein gewand zur verzierung oder erweiterung eingesetzt ist [*a wedge-shaped piece of cloth, which is inserted under a garment in order to adorn or extend it*]'.[45] The Danish word *forgheræ* thus means the 'front wedge-shaped piece of cloth on or under a garment'.[46]

There are a number of unusual words in Ræff's translation that are not particularly common in Old Danish works. These include *compositier* ('compositions'), *diligentz* ('diligence'), *tribulatz* ('tribulation'), and *tribwt* ('tribute') which are all loanwords and discussed above (under 'Word pairs: 1. Synonyms'). Another unusual word is *fnyster* (or *fnysthæ* as it also appears in the text). Its meaning is 'sneeze', but the word does not appear in any modern reference work. It can, however, be found in Henrik Smith's *Libellus Vocum Latinarum* from 1563:[47]

>   **Sternutamentum, ti.** Lægedom som giør at fnyste/ eller pruste

> *'Snuff'. A medication that causes one to sneeze or snort.*

The verb *hurle* 'to hurl, swing' is also not found in GdO or any medieval text. The verb *wræghæ* (GdO *vrækje*, 'to avenge, get back at') is also rather uncommon in Old Danish literature, usually occurring only in legal texts and charters from the time of the Union of Kalmar, although rather suprisingly also in the chivalric poems *Ivan Løveridder* and *Hertug Frederik af Normandi* found in the first part of the manuscript Stockholm, Royal Library, K 47 from *c*. 1500. It is most likely a form influenced by Swedish. The word *forspraakere* (GdO *forsprokkere*, loaned from Middle Low German *vorsproke* 'spokesman') and *gomp* (GdO *gump* 'backside') are also rather rare in Old Danish but begin to occur more frequently from the sixteenth century.

---

45. West 1989: 324.

46. Alternatively, Ræff's word may be a printing error for Old Danish *forklæthe*, the usual word meaning 'an item of clothing that covers the front of the body' as can be seen from the following dictionary equivalents: 'feminale [*thigh-bandages*]', 'linteum [*girdle*]', 'semisintium [*semi-girdle, apron*]' (Pedersen 1510); 'Fœminale [*thigh-bandages*]', 'Præcinctorium [*girdle, apron*]' (Tursen 1561 [1975]); 'Ventrale [*belly-band*]' (Smith 1563 [1974]); 'Semicintorium [*semi-girdle, apron*]' (Hingelberg 1576 [1995]); 'castula [*kind of petticoat*]' (Colding 1626). However, this interpretation seems unnecessary to me. Note also, that the Swedish translation of *lacinia* provided by the Latin-Swedish dictionary *Variarum rerum vocabula* of 1538 is 'bieffza [*border, edging; trim*]' (Andersson 1890: 18[b]), which is not much help for our discussion of 'forgheræ'.

47. Smith 1974: 86.

A most unusual word in the text is *twrafftig* which is not registered in any dictionary. The phrase 'man er suo twrafftig vti syndhen' corresponds to 'floccifacientes peccata'. The verb *floccifacio* means 'to consider unimportant'. Although the Latin verb is rather rare, it does, for example, occur in Pedersen 1510 [1973]: fol. 66ᵛ, *s.v.* 'flocifacio' with the translation 'ath forsmaa [*disdain; reject*]'. It seems to me that there are three possible origins of the word *twrafftig*:⁴⁸

1. *thjuv-aktigh*, lit.: 'thief-like', with the meaning 'secretive', 'clandestine'; cf. Old Swedish 'thiuflika', and Old Icelandic 'þjófligr'.
2. *thvær-aktigh*, lit.: 'contrary-like', perhaps with the meaning 'stubborn', 'pig-headed' (cf. Lower Saxon *dwērig* 'perverse', 'stubborn', 'truculent'; MLG *dwer(s)*, *dwars*, *dwass* 'thwart', 'contrary');
3. *thjur-aktigh*, lit.: 'bull-like', perhaps with the meaning 'stubborn' or 'foolishly optimistic' (cf. 'bullish' in English).

The word *thjuvaktigh seems at a first glance to be the most likely, but the meaning 'secretive' is quite different to 'floccifacientes' and does not make a great deal of sense in the context. Furthermore, the word is unattested in Old Danish, the closest form to it being *thjuvlik*: *thiyfligh* (*c.* 1300); *tiffuelege* (*c.* 1480); *tiøffuege* (1509).⁴⁹ The final two words, *thværaktigh and *thjuraktigh, are phonologically close to *twrafftig*, and they can also be interpreted as close in meaning to 'floccifacientes'. However, neither word has been recorded anywhere else which does weigh rather heavily against these interpretations.

A final point of interest concerning Danish lexical items in *Iudeorum Secreta*, is the use of two different suffixes for the same word. For example, the words for 'common' appear as *almenighæ* (p. 14: 3) and *alminneligt* (p. 20: 12); 'eternal' as *ewig* (p. 15: 23) and *ewindhelig* (p. 31: 3); 'multiple' as *mangfoldug* (p. 7: 21) and *mangfoldelig* (p. 15: 10); 'truth' as *sandinghen* (p. 10: 7) and *sandhet* (pp. 19: 17; 26: 6); 'sinful' as *syndugt* (p. 5: 3) and *syndhelig* (p. 26: 13); and 'worthy' as *werdighe* (p. 28: 8–9) and *werdughe*

---

48. Other possible, but to my mind less likely, explanations are:
    1. an error for *thurftelik* or *thurftigh*, 'needy' (cf. the German word *dürftig* 'wretched', 'miserable', 'poor'), but the meaning does not fit well here;
    2. related to the MLG words *ture* 'bold', 'brash', and *turen* 'to venture', 'be audacious';
    3. a type-setting error for *daraktelik* 'foolish'. However, there are no other instances where /d/ corresponds to ⟨t⟩;
    4. a type-setting error for *foraktelik* 'contemptible; contemptuous, disdainful' (cf. Dasypodius 1995: fol. 74ᵛᵃ⁻ᵇ: 'Floc|cifacere & Floccipendere, Verachte*n*').
49. See the GdO citation-slip collection.

(p. 23: 24). These are perhaps evidence of a language in transition where newer forms or more common forms (typically those influenced by or loaned from Low German) compete with more unusual, old-fashioned or stylised variants.

Conclusion

The text includes a number of words that have not been recorded elsewhere or are rather rare: *fnysthæ*; *forgheræ*; *forspraakere*; *gomp*; *hurle*; *twrafftig*. Other such unusual words occur in word-pair constructions: *compositier*; *diligentz*; *tribulatz*; *tribwt*. The translation from Latin to Danish is largely accurate and includes just a few additions by Ræff that either elucidate the text in some way or directly address the intended public for the book in Denmark. However, on the whole, the changes in the translation appear to be accidental rather than intentional. The style of the piece is almost always idiomatic, but rather unsophisticated and folksy. In places, there are short, abrupt sentences and some repetitive language. That said, the piece is rhetorically effective with difficult terms and concepts put into clear language, or reinforced through the use of doublets, that cannot to be misunderstood enabling the message to be put across clearly to the book's intended audience: 'common Danes'.

Hebrew words in *Secreta Iudeorum*

Pfefferkorn lists a number of words and phrases, best described as invectives, that he says are used by the Jews when referring to Christians and aspects of their religion.[50] These words are of great interest as it is the first time discussions of non-Biblical Hebrew words are to be found in print in a Danish work. The words and phrases in question are:

- **Gymach schinophe sichroe** (p. 23: 25)   *Yimaḥ šemo wezichro*, ימח שמו וזכרו
  'May his name and memory be obliterated'

---

50. On anti-Gentile (including anti-Christian) expressions form the Middle Ages, see the extensive list in Zunz 1855: 437–55, and Dalman 1893: 21*–28*, 40*–47*; and also the shorter descriptions in Breuer 1978: 195; Abulafia 1985. Anti-Christian invectives from the early modern period are discussed in Deutsch 2010. On the Hebrew words in Ræff's translation, see also Adams 2010.

Translation in *Iudeorum Secreta*:	'Ue wordhæ tig/ oc we wordhæ hannum som noghen tiidh kommer thet naffn i hwgh eller gør thet æræ oc werdughet [*Woe betide you and woe betide him who ever remembers that name and does it honour and treats it with dignity*]'[51]
• **iesche nozore** (p. 24: 17)	*Yešu (ha)nozri*, ישו (ה)נוצרי 'Jesus of Nazareth'
Translation in *Iudeorum Secreta*:	'en bedræghèræ eller then som sckadhe gør [*a charlatan or one who does harm*]'
• **kendeschim** (p. 24: 20)	*qedešim*, קדשים 'whoremongers', 'sodomites'
Translation in *Iudeorum Secreta*:	'vwighedæ oc formalediedhæ [*unconsecrated or cursed*]'
• **Olenu laschabeha** (p. 16: 10–11)	*ʿaleinu lešabeaḥ*, עלינו לשבח 'it is our duty to pray' (a Jewish prayer)
Explanation in *Iudeorum Secreta*:	'thet er theris daglighæ bøn [*this is their daily prayer*]'
• **talmot** / **Talmot** (pp. 11: 20; 21: 2)	*talmud*, תלמוד 'The Talmud'
Explanation in *Iudeorum Secreta*:	'en theris bog [*one of their books*]' and 'iødernes bog [*the Jews' book*]'
• **tholoi** (p. 24: 15–16)	*taluy*, תלוי 'hanged', 'suspended'
Translation in *Iudeorum Secreta*:	'then som war hengt i galghen [*he who was hanged in a gallows*]'

---

51. See Spanier 1936: 212.

- **thlue** (p. 24: 19)　　　　　　*teluyah*, תלויה
　　　　　　　　　　　　　　　'hanged', 'suspended'

　Translation in *Iudeorum Secreta*:　'hwn som war vphengt [*she who was hanged, strung up*]'

- **tifflos** (p. 24: 21)　　　　　　*tiflut*, תפלות
　　　　　　　　　　　　　　　'absurdity'

　Translation in *Iudeorum Secreta*:　'eth hwss som er forsmæligt oc dwer inth*et* [*a house that is worthy of contempt and good for nothing*]'

- **toifos** (p. 24: 22)　　　　　　*tofet*, תופת or *tofes*, תופס
　　　　　　　　　　　　　　　'hell', 'inferno'; or 'imprisoned'

　Translation in *Iudeorum Secreta*:　'eth hwss som er forsmæligt oc dwer inth*et* [*a house that is worthy of contempt and good for nothing*]'

Misreadings

Some of the words have been rendered in an incorrect form, because either (1) Poul Ræff misread the original Latin source, or (2) Pfefferkorn (or the Dominicans who assisted him in producing the pamphlet) made the mistake in the original work.

An example of (1):

	Danish:	Gymach sch<u>in</u>ophe sichroe
	Latin:	Gymach sch<u>m</u>ophe zichroe
Cf.	German:	gymach sch<u>mo</u> phesichroe
	Hebrew:	*yimaḥ š<u>emo</u> wezichro*, ימח שמו וזכרו
	[English:	May his name and memory be obliterated]

In the example of (1), Ræff has incorrectly analyzed the three minims in 'm' as an 'in'.

An example of (2):

	Danish:	Olenu laschabe<u>ha</u>
	Latin:	Olenu laschabe<u>ha</u>
Cf.	German:	olen[n>u] laschabe<u>ha</u>
	Hebrew:	*'aleinu lešabe<u>ah</u>*, עלינו לשבח
	[English:	It is our duty to pray]

The rendering of the *ḥet* in final position as ⟨ha⟩ rather than *⟨ach⟩ reflects a pronunciation error that is actually rather surprising, particularly if Pfefferkorn, as he claims, was familiar with Jewish prayer and the Hebrew language (and presumably its correct vocalisation and pronunciation). Perhaps this is due to someone other than Pfefferkorn, such as a Dominican, writing this. It is more likely that it is the result of a poor transliteration of Hebrew letters than a transcription of a spoken word in Hebrew.

Phonology and orthography

Generally, Pfefferkorn's transliterations appear to be based on spoken forms in the local Ashkenazi pronunciation German/Polish Jews of central and eastern Europe. For example, the *qamaẓ* vocalisation of the *'ayin* in *'aleinu*, עלינו is rendered ⟨o⟩ reflecting the standard Ashkenazi pronunciation ('<u>O</u>lenu', /o'le⁽ʲ⁾nu/); so also in 'th<u>o</u>loi' in *taluy*, תלוי. The *ḥolam maleh* and *waw* in *tofet*, תופת are pronounced as the diphthong /oj/ ('toifos'), while the final *tet* is pronounced /s/ (as is also the case in 'tiffl<u>o</u>s', cf. *tiflut*, תפלות).[52] The letter ⟨o⟩ may also be being used in some cases to represent the schwa-like vowel found in Ashkenazi (and Yiddish) pronunciations of unstressed vowels in Hebrew words (for example, in 'tiffl<u>o</u>s' and 'toif<u>o</u>s'); compare, for example, modern Ashkenazi transliterations of *šabat*, שבת

---

52. Unless, of course, that Pfefferkorn's 'toifos' is meant to represent תופס. Spanier (1934: 585; 1936 214 n. 12) notes that in German — particularly in publications from Cologne — ⟨i⟩ is used to mark a long vowel, so that ⟨oi⟩ and ⟨ei⟩ are not diphthongs, but long monophthongs. This may also be the case in how the Hebrew words are transliterated here in *Iudeorum Secreta*.

('Shabbat' or 'Sabbath') as *Shabbos* or *Shabbes* for /ˈʃabəs/. Ræff's Germanised spelling (for example, ⟨s⟩ for /z/ in 'sichroe', ⟨z⟩ for /ts/ in 'nozore', ⟨ch⟩ for /χ/ in 'Gymach', and ⟨sch⟩ for /ʃ/ in 'iesche') is no doubt due to the spellings used in the Latin original, but it should be noted that these spellings are typical of sixteenth-century transliterations of Hebrew words in Danish works too.[53] The initial ⟨g⟩ in 'Gymach' may be an attempt to reproduce a glottal stop, which, although not actually present in the Hebrew *yimaḥ*, ימח, occurs at the beginning of all words in German that start with a vowel and thus may be due to influence from German or even Yiddish on the pronunciation of the Hebrew here.[54] Similarly, the devoicing of the final *dalet* in 'talmot' (*talmud*, תלמוד) may be due to interference from German (but note that the Latin version also has 'talmoṯ').

Morphology and syntax

Pfefferkorn's words reflect correct Hebrew grammatical forms. For example, the infinitive is prefixed with *l* ('laschabeha') and the masculine plural ends in *im* ('kendeschim'). Note also that the past participle of the verb 'to hang' (*letalot*, לתלות from the root *t-l-h*) is a term used for both the crucified Jesus and his mother Mary. When referring to Jesus it should be in a masculine form (*taluy*, תלוי) which indeed is the case in Pfefferkorn's text ('tholoi'). Similarly, the feminine form that should be used for Mary (*teluyah*, תלויה) is also reflected in his spelling 'thlue'. However, in the phrase 'Gymach schinophe sichroe', the *waw* conjunctive meaning 'and' has been suffixed to the preceding word as '-phe', rather than prefixed to the following word as it should be: *šemo wezichro*. In Pfefferkorn's original German version, he writes: 'gymach schmo phesichroe' with correct word division; the mistake in word division has arisen during the translation from German into Latin. The transliteration of ו as ⟨phe⟩, presumably corresponding to the pronunciation /fe/, reveals that the *waw* conjunctive has acquired a Germanised pronunciation whereby the /v/ in initial position has become /f/. These examples of phono-graphemic spellings show that Pfefferkorn probably learnt these words from the spoken rather than the written language (although compare the point about 'laschabeha' above).

---

53. Cf., for example, Jakob Villumsen who in his *Elementale Ebraicvm* (1569) gives the pronunciation of שׁ as 'sch' (and mistakenly also as 's'), ח as 'ch latinum [*Latin ch*]', כ as 'ch', ע in final position as 'ch vel gh [*ch or gh*]', and צ as 'z' (as well as 'tz' and 'ts').
54. On the somewhat sporadic evidence for a weak glottal stop in vowel-initial words in Yiddish, see Jacobs 2005: 122 (with references).

Pfefferkorn's translations

The translations are clearly not always accurate or reliable. Pfefferkorn sometimes appears to know the gist of or the general sentiment behind the phrase (for example, 'Gymach schinophe sichroe' and 'tholoi' above), but he is unaware of the words' individual or actual meanings. By considering the forms of Jewish anti-Christian curses in the Middle Ages, particularly the use of the pun, it is, however, possible to make sense of and understand Pfefferkorn's translations.

Pfefferkorn gives the meaning of the words 'tifflos' and 'toifos' as 'a house that is worthy of contempt and good for nothing'. Clearly, both of his words are missing the first element in the compound, viz. the construct form 'house-of' (*beit*, בית). With regard to 'tifflos', his translation is evidence of a pun. The use of wordplay in anti-Christian insults is well documented and, for example, can be seen in *'awen gilayon* (עון גליון, 'page of wickedness/emptiness'), not used by Pfefferkorn but found elsewhere, to mean 'the gospels'.[55] Here, the Hebrew word sounds almost identical to the Greek word *evangelion* (Εὐαγγέλιον, 'gospel'), and the curse is in fact a pun: 'page of emptiness' ~ 'gospel', *'awen gilayon* ~ *evangelion*. In Hebrew, the words for prayer (*tefilah*, תפילה) and 'pointlessness, folly' (*tiflut*, תפ-לות, or *tiflah*, תפלה) are similar as they have the same three root letters: *t-f-l*, ת.פ:ל. They are also close in pronunciation to the unrelated Hebrew word for 'secondary importance' (*tfelut*, טפלות), and the Yiddish word for 'devil' (*tayvl*, טײװל; cf. Early Modern German *Teuf(f)el*), although this probably has no bearing on the matter here; however, the coincidence certainly does not detract from the insult. It would seem that the Hebrew word for 'prayer-house' (*beit tefilah*, בית תפילה) was purposely mispronounced to give *beit tiflah* or, as Pfefferkorn probably means, *beit tiflut* (*beis tiflos* in Ashkenazi pronunciation) meaning 'house of folly', or as it says in *Iudeorum Secreta*, 'a house that is good for nothing'.[56] This is recorded as a derogatory Jewish term for a church in Johannes Buxtorf's *Synagoga iudaica*:[57]

> Ita solum ipsorum Templum, sanctum, solæ ipsorum Synagogæ, sanctæ, & בית אל *Domus Dei*; omnium verò cæterorum populorum, præsertim Christianorum, Templa,

---

55. For example in *Sefer Niẓaḥon Yašan* (Berger 1979: 167 §154). See also Kirn 1989: 24; Sapir and Zuckermann 2008: 32.

56. The disrespectful term *beit tiflah* to refer to a church is not unknown from other sources, some modern. For example, Marc Shapiro (2003: 9 n. 38) mentions the famous *poseq* Rabbi Moshe Feinstein (1895–1986) who regularly used the term when talking of churches [*identification via pers. comm. with author*]. See also Deutsch 2010: 46, 56.

57. Buxtorf 1989: *Ad lectorem*, fol. 5ʳ.

non vocant בית אל, sed בית אלילים vel בית אבודת אלילים *Domus Idololatriæ*, בית התורפה [...], בית התפילה, *Bes hattiphlah*, non *hattephillah*, &c.

> *Thus, only their temple is holy, only their synagogues holy, and* beit 'el, *the house of God. But they do not call other people's, especially Christians', temples* beit 'el, *but rather* beit 'elilim, *or* beit 'avodat 'elilim, *house of idolatory,* beit haturpah, [...], beit hatiflah, *and so on*]

It is likely that Pfefferkorn's 'toiffos' is another variation of this same insult and represents Ashkenazi Hebrew *beis toyfes* (< *beit tofet*, בית תופת) 'hell-house', where a Hebrew word for 'hell' or 'inferno' is used in place of the word for prayer. The word 'Topheth' (תופת, *tofet*) appears in the Bible as a place-name: a pagan sacrificial site outside Jerusalem that later became a refuse dump with permanently burning bonfires (II Kings 23: 10; Isaiah 30: 33; Jeremiah 7: 31–32; 19: 6, 11–14). In Jeremiah, 'Topheth' is identified as a place where the Canaanites sacrificed their children to their God Moloch. From these original meanings, it became a synonym for 'hell'. Another very likely meaning of the phrase is '(house, place or state of?) imprisonment', this time taken from the Yiddish word *toyfes*, תּוֹפֶס meaning 'captured', 'imprisoned'.[58] If this is the case here, it would make 'toiffos' the earliest occurrence of a Yiddish word in a text from Denmark.

Pfefferkorn writes that 'kendeschim' means 'unconsecrated or cursed'. The word is very similar to the masculine plural nominal *qedošim* (קדושים), which means precisely the opposite of Pfefferkorn's 'kendeschim', *viz*. 'consecrated', 'set apart', 'holy' or 'sainted'. The similarity of Pfefferkorn's 'cursed' word to the Hebrew word for 'holy' points once again to a pun based on similar sounding words, 'kendeschim' ~ *qedošim*, but what then is the word meant by Pfefferkorn's 'kendeschim'? The Latin version of the text, from which Ræff made his translation, also has 'ke*n*deschim', but in Pfefferkorn's original German text, *Ich heyß eyn buchlijn der iuden beicht* (1508), we find 'kedeschim' with no 'n' after the first vowel. Either the translator of the German work into Latin or the printer who set the first Latin version probably thought he saw a nasal stroke over the first 'e' and added this extra letter in his word. The fact that the mistake was not corrected in the Latin translation tells us something about Pfefferkorn's ability or role (or

---

58. Cf. the Yiddish phrase *toyfes zayn*, תּוֹפֶס זײַן, 'to be imprisoned' (cf. Hebrew *tofes*, תופס 'to catch'), but also 'to grasp' in the metaphorical sense of 'understand' (cf. Hebrew *tofeś*, תופש 'to comprehend'). See Lötzsch 1992: 170, *s.v.* 'tójfeß' [= *imprison*]; 168, *s.v.* 'táfßn' [= *dungeon-master*]; 169, *s.v.* 'tfißße' [= *prison*], and Weinreich 1968: 417, *s.v.* 'תּוֹפֶס'.

rather lack thereof) in translating his material from German to Latin and checking it. The word 'kendeschim' in the Danish *Iudeorum Secreta* is thus a mistake copied from its Latin source and should read 'kedeschim' as in the German text. It represents a transliteration of the Biblical Hebrew word *qedešim*, plural of *qadeš*, קדש, the precise meaning of which, however, is not certain.[59] The usual translations of the word in the Bible are:

Deuteronomy 23: 18
JPS: קדש, 'cult prostitute'
Greek Septuagint: πορνεύων, 'male prostitutes'
Latin Vulgate: *scortator*, 'whoremonger', 'fornicator'
King James Version: *sodomite*
Young's translation: *whoremonger*

I Kings 14: 24
JPS: קדש, 'male prostitutes'
Greek Septuagint: σύνδεσμος, 'sodomy'
Latin Vulgate: *effeminati*, 'effeminate men
                            (who submit to homosexual acts)'
King James Version: *sodomites*
Young's translation: *whoremonger*

I Kings 15: 12
JPS: הקדשים, 'the male prostitutes'
Greek Septuagint: τελετάς, 'spirits presiding over the initiation rites
                            of Bacchic orgies'
Latin Vulgate: *effeminatos*, 'effeminate men
                            (who submit to homosexual acts)'
King James Version: *sodomites*
Young's translation: *the whoremongers*

I Kings 22: 47
JPS: הקדש, 'male prostitutes'
Greek Septuagint: - - - -

---

59. See Boswell 1981: 98–99 for a discussion of the meaning and (mis)translation of this word, which he though mistakenly spells 'kadash' (plural 'kadēshim'), and to what extent it implies homosexuality. Cf. also the section 'Who were the *Kedeshim*?' in Crompton 2006: 39–43.

Latin Vulgate:	*effeminatorum*, 'of effeminate men (who submit to homosexual acts)'
King James Version:	*of the sodomites*
Young's translation:	*of the whoremongers*

II Kings 23: 7

JPS:	הקדשים, 'the male prostitutes'
Greek Septuagint:	καδησιμ, 'male temple prostitutes'
Latin Vulgate:	*effeminatorum*, 'of effeminate men (who submit to homosexual acts)'
King James Version:	*of the sodomites*
Young's translation:	*of the whoremongers*

Although the translations vary, the word apparently implies either men who engage in sexual acts of a cultic or homosexual nature, or in the selling and pimping of prostitutes, and as such 'ke[n]deshim' (*qedešim*) would be a strong insult to refer to the Christian saints and would also function as a stinging pun on the Hebrew word for 'saints' (*qedošim*).

In his transliteration 'iesche nozore', the name *Yešu*, ישו ('iesche') is a form of *Yešu'a* (ישוע), the name Jesus in Hebrew. The use of *Yešu* as an insult may be connected to the fact that it is also an acronym for the phrase *Yimaḥ šemo wezichro* ('May his name and memory be obliterated'), the phrase that Pfefferkorn says is used after mentioning Jesus' name (p. 23: 25). The word *nozri*, נוצרי ('nozore') means 'Nazarene', 'of Nazareth', and by extension also 'Christian' (cf. Matthew 2: 23). However, 'nozore' is also similar to the Hebrew word for 'shoot', 'sprig', 'branch' *nezer*, נצר. By using it with the name *Yešu*, the insult in *Iudeorum Secreta* mirrors this passage in *Toledot Yešu HaNozri*:[60]

ואמרו עוד מה שמך אמר נצר אמרו מהכן ראייה אמר לו ונצר משרשיו יפרה אמרו לו ואתה השלכת מקברך כנצר נתעב וכאלה רבות שהיה אומר לעצמו שמות רבות

And they [i.e. the Jewish priests] say to him [i.e. Jesus] again, 'What is your name?' He says, 'Nezer.' They say, 'And how do you make it so?' And he says, 'A branch [nezer] shall sprout from his roots.' They say to him, 'You have been thrown out of your grave like an abominable branch.' And much else like this, while he stated many other names for his own sake.

---

60. Krauss 1977: 45, ll. 6–8; cf. also *Sanhedrin* 43a.

This is an allusion to Isaiah 14: 19 *'kenezer nit'av* [like an abominable branch]'. The fact that the stem *n-z-r* in *nezer* ('branch') is the same as in *nozri* ('Christian') lies at the heart of the pun. Pfefferkorn's translation of the name as 'fraudster' or 'charlatan' is not a literal translation, but rather an interpretation. Either Pfefferkorn does not understand the meaning of the Hebrew that he has written (that, *nozri* means 'Nazarene'), or he is intentionally mistranslating it, or he is unaware of the real reason behind the use of *Yešu nozri* as an insult and assumes that it means someone who cheats. There is also plenty of evidence elsewhere that Jesus of Nazareth was referred to as fraudster in Jewish anti-Christian works. *Sefer Nizahon Yašan* contains several warnings against believing his pretensions of divinity, while the *Toledot Yešu HaNozri* portrays Jesus as a fraudulent magician.[61] In his book *The Enemy of the Jews* (1509), Pfefferkorn translates 'Jescheynozere' as 'a seducer of the people'. It was apparently also a widespread practice to use the name *Yešu hanozri* as an insult in Jewish circles, for example to refer to naughty children.[62]

The term *taluy*, תלוי ('tholoi') to refer to Jesus is common in anti-Christian works from the Middle Ages. By stressing the method of killing and his 'hanged' body, Jews were focusing on Jesus 'the man' rather than Jesus 'the son of God', and thus negating his divinity.[63] The scholar Israel Yuval has offered an exegetical explanation for the constant use of the word *taluy* to refer to the Christians' messiah:[64]

> Note that, in the Middle Ages, Jews were insistent in referring to Jesus as 'the hanged one', a fact that may be based on the Jewish exegesis of the Biblical verse 'for a hanged man is accursed by God' — that is, that one who is 'hanged' is also accursed.

Conclusion

The Hebrew words in *Secreta Iudeorum* have not been invented by Pfefferkorn for the occasion, but represent genuine Hebrew words and phrases as used by Jews. Although they do not appear in perfectly inflected forms and often as rather poor written representations of Ashkenazi pronunciation, these words are any-

---

61. See, for example, Berger 1979: 147, 238–39.
62. See Carlebach 2001: 99.
63. Cf. Deuteronomy 21: 23.
64. Yuval 2006: 117.

thing but nonsense and provide us with evidence of both Pfefferkorn's Hebrew skills, the translation process of the original German into Latin, and also more generally of anti-Christian formulations in use in the spoken language of sixteenth-century Jews living in Germany.

Pfefferkorn includes these Hebrew phrases to add evidence for and authenticity to his claims that Jews curse Christians and various aspects of their religion. He is also making use of the sinister connotations that the Hebrew language already conjured up for Christian readers. Hebrew, the language of a despised people, was believed to be the secret language among the Jews containing hidden mysteries and full of magical potency.[65] Medieval magical amulets, for example, tended to rely on sacral languages (Latin, Greek and Hebrew) which may not have been understood by the wearer. As the original 'primal language' and the language used by Adam to name the animals, Hebrew in particular enjoyed a special status and was believed to be endowed with mystical properties and magical pre-eminence. The legendary association of King Solomon with magic probably reinforced popular suspicions about the use of Hebrew and the involvement of Jews in magic.[66] Knowledge of Hebrew in Denmark was practically nil during the Middle Ages, and xenophobic ideas about it and other unintelligible tongues were probably widespread.[67] The power of unknown tongues was taken very seriously as were the dangers associated with them. The dark use to which Hebrew could be put is exemplified in a number of the European versions of *Mandeville's Travels*, in which Hebrew is the oral channel by which the Jews will be able to destroy all Christendom.[68] The words in *Secreta Iudeorum* thus provide us with an ethnographical record, they act as evidence of authenticity for the readers, and they give Pfefferkorn an opportunity to exploit pre-existing popular fears and beliefs.

---

65. See Carlebach 1996: 124–25; Gilman 1986: 22–86.
66. See Skemer 2006: 75–124 (especially 113–14).
67. See Adams 2010: 42–43.
68. Braude 1996: 145–46.

CHAPTER 4

The extant copies of Iudeorum Secreta

A physical description

Si queris: qui sim curtus facilisque libellus:
Dicam. judeis que sint lustralia sacra
Quove die culpas/ et quo purgamine ponant:
Prodo. leges in me gentis phantasmata vana:
Quis nullam poterit sibi spem fecisse salutis.
Vt damnes. saluet te sic deus arbiter equi.
Johannes Pfefferkorn (1508)[1]

The quarto that goes under the title of *Nouiter in lucem data: iudeorum secreta* was printed in 1516 by Poul Ræff on his press in Copenhagen. The colophon on fol. c4^r (p. 31) reads 'Aar effther gwdz byrd M.d.xvi [*year after God's birth 1516*]'. It is one of the oldest extant printed books in Denmark, and one of just four extant books in Danish printed by Ræff during his time in the capital city. It exists today in just two identical copies, one housed in the Hielmstierne-Rosencroneske Collection at the Royal Library in Copenhagen (with catalogue number Hielmst. 242, 4°), and the other in the Bielke Collection in the library at Skokloster Castle in Uppland, Sweden (with catalogue number IV 82.

---

1. Johannes Pfefferkorn, *Libellus de Iudaica confessione* (1508), fol. a1^r (translation into English in Rummel 2002: 79–80): 'If you wish to know who I am, I shall tell you: a booklet, brief and easy, about the sacred time of purification for Jews, the day on which they rid themselves of their sins and by what rites of purification. I make public the vain fantasies of the Jewish people, which cannot obtain for itself hope of salvation. Oh, condemn them — thus God the judge of what is right will save you.'

549). In the description that follows the two copies are dealt with separately where necessary.[2]

Binding

Royal Library, Copenhagen:
The present binding is not original but dates from the eighteenth century. It comprises brown leather stretched over board and measures 140 mm x 190 mm. On the front cover, the title 'Judaeorum | Secreta. | Danice. s. 1. & a.' has been tooled in gold lettering. There is blind tooling around the outer edge in the form of a wavy line. On the back, there is the same decorative line and a gold-tooled *super ex libris* (a shield with three lions with a crown on top and an elephant beneath flanked by cherubs with clubs). The binding is in good condition with little wear.

Inside the binding there is a pastedown of coloured patterned paper, with Royal Library stamps and an *ex libris* plate pasted in. It comprises the book-collector Henrik Hielmstierne's coat of arms with an escutcheon (shield) containing three six-pointed stars in a vertical line, on top of which is a mantled helm with a crest of bird wings and a star. The shield supporters are crowned eagles and the compartment below contains a face. The motto is empty.[3] Printed at the bottom of the plate are the words 'M. Tuscher fecit', referring to the famous artist and engraver Marcus Tuscher (1705–51).

The cords are all intact and the spine is divided into six sections, each with decorative gold floral patterns. The title section (second from the top) reads, 'NOU | IN | LUC | DAT'.

There are flysheets at the front and back of the book which are not original. They are clean with some marking at the edges. The watermark is partially visible with a crown and what appears to be the bottom part of a capital M.

Bielke Library, Skokloster Castle:
Poul Ræff's publication is bound in a volume together with theological material from the time just after the Reformation in Denmark:

---

2. The following works include mention of the book: LN 219; Langebek 1764–65, I: 73; Graesse 1859–69, VIII [suppl.]: 445; Bruun 1870–98, I: 239–41; Nielsen 1934: 9, xi (reproduction of woodcut); Edelmann 1948; Birkelund *et al.* 1949: 6–7 (no. 10); Koch-Olsen 1968: 510 (reproduction of woodcut); Dal 1982: 73 (reproduction of woodcut on the cover); Lausten 1991–92; Lausten 1992: 108–32; Dahlerup 2010: 157–59, and Adams 2010.
3. Weber 1782–85, I: 126–27 (no.14).

Folios	Contents	LN
1ʳ–23ᵛ	Hans Tausen, *A Short Answer to the Bishop of Odense's Open Letter* (Viborg: Hans Vingaard, 1529)	263
24ʳ–55ᵛ	Hans Tausen, *An Answer to the False and Unchristian Teaching which Lecturer Poul Wrote to the Council in Copenhagen about the Papist Mass* (Malmö: Oluf Ulricksøn, 1531)	264
56ʳ–106ᵛ	[Peder Laurentsen], *A True and Correct Christian Teaching about the Office of The Priests and Their Lives, Marriages and Correct Chastity etc.* (Malmö: Joh. Hoochstraten, 1533)	128
107ʳ–34ᵛ	[Peder Laurentsen], *A Short Teaching with God's Own Words and the Holy Scripture against The Pope, Bishops and Their Disciples' Statutes, Laws, Commandments and Customs* (Malmö: Joh. Hoochstraten, 1533)	127
135ʳ–50ᵛ	Johannes Pfefferkorn, *Iudeorum Secreta* (Copenhagen: Poul Ræff, 1516)	219

The current binding is a typical sixteenth-century white leather binding without any ornamentation or tooling, and with paper pastedowns inside. On the pastedown on the inside of the front cover, we read, '3 st 89 m 18 — p. 25. — IV, H. 82, 549 | C55691 | IV 82 549 | Skoklosters Bibliothek.' All four cords that bind the book together are intact. Written on the spine is '15 9 E in 1511'.

There are flysheets at the front and back of the book. Both sides of the front flysheet contain a list of the book's contents in a nineteenth-century hand and signed with the initial 'M', after which someone (in the twentieth century) has written 'anderström' in pencil. The name Manderström almost certainly refers to the Swedish count Christofer Rutger Ludvig Manderström (1806–73), who was a member of the Swedish parliament, a diplomat and the minister of foreign affairs (1858–68). Manderström had diplomatic assignments in Denmark and in his various roles was involved in Swedish-Danish relations. He was also elected to the Royal Swedish Academy of Sciences in 1848, and to the Swedish Academy in 1852, for which he was secretary 1869–72. He moved in the same circles as the owners of Skokloster Castle: Nils Magnus Brahe (1790–1844), Nils Frederik Brahe (1812–50), and Nils Claes Brahe (1841–1907).[4] The handwritten description of the book's contents reads:

> Detta band innehåller några här undan upräknade Danska theologiska skrifter af stor sällsynthet och af stort wärde Såsom skriftprof på det äldsta tryckta Danska språket.

---

4. I should like to thank Elisabeth Westin-Berg for her help in identifying Ludvig Manderström as the most likely author of the notes on the flysheet.

Nº. 1 saknar Titel och de 3 första bladen, — (Sign. A–Aiv) — men synes innehålla Lector Powells Undervijsning om then Papistiske Messe. Det återstående, (23 blad, Sign. Bi till Giii i quarternioner) utgör 23 blad. Prendth*et* i Wiborgh aff migh Hans Wingarthener, fridagh effter Kiørmøss Anno Domini MDXXIX (1529.)

Nº. 2 är: Suar til then fallske oc vchristelige vnderviisning Som Lector Powell screff til Raadet y Københaff*en* Om then Papistiske Messe ved Hanss Thomsøn. 31 blad, (Sign A–Hiij i quarternioner) Sista bladet, som troligen warit hwitt, bortskuret, likasom en del af marginalerne, men Tractaten fullständig. Tryckt i Mallmø wedt Olaff Vlrickssøn, anden dagen effter Sancte Pederss och Sancte Pouells apostelerss dag. Gutz aar tusinde femhundrede tjuffue och paa det elløffte. (1531.)

Nº. 3 är: En sand oc ret christe*n* vnderuisning om presteembede och om deriss leffnit, Gifftermaal oc ret Kysscked &c. Sat i Malmø. 52 blad, (Sign. A–N i quaternioner,) fullständig. In fine: Denne Bog er prentet i Malmø aff Johan Hogstrate Aar effter Gudz Byrd MDXXXIII (1533) &c fredag nest hellige tre Kongers dag. A tergo å sista sidan Hogstratens Märke Tiden på ett wingadt hjul, med ordskriften: Occasio. ||

Nº. 4 är En stacket vnderuisning aff Gudz egne ord och den hellige Scrifft Emod Pawe*n*s, Bispers och deris disciplis Statuter, Lower, bwd och skickelser (Författad af Peder Laurentsen) Sat i Malmø. 28 blad (Sign. A–J i quatern*ioner*.) In fine: Sat i Malmø, aar effter Gudz byrd MDXXXIII (1533).

Nº. 5 är: Nouiter in lucem data: iudæorum Secreta. Thenne bog er vthdraghen aff latinen oc vdsæth paa dansckæ, til theris behoff som icke kwunne forstaa latinæ. Hwn tracterer oc indhæholdher, alle the hemilighæ stycker som the fwlæ iøder haffue mellem sig sielff baadhe i theris iødhæ tempel, oc i theris egre(ne) hws. Paa thet at cristnæ me*n*niskæ sculle widhæ ath straffæ them. A tergo tituli: Träsnitt föreställande den upgifne författaren: Joha*n*nes Pfefferkorn. En iødhæ føddher, oc nw eth cristhen me*n*nisckæ. — 16 blad (Sign Ai–vi, Bi–vi, Ci–iv. Fullständig, ehuru sista bladet kring- och afskuret. In fine: Trycht vti Købmanhaffwen, hooss Her Powel Ræff Ca*n*nick thersamestedz Aar effther Godz byrd M.d.xvi. (1516)

Detta är den enda kända exemplar af denne skrift. Boken har 1867 warit sänd som lån till det stora Kong. Biblioteket i Köpenhamn, der den sista Tractaten blifvit afskrifna, för att i ny uplaga utgifvas.

M(anderström)

This volume contains some Danish theological writings, listed below, of great rarity and great value as specimens of the earliest printed Danish language.

No. 1 is missing its title and three first folios (fols a1–a4) but seems to comprise **Lecturer Poul's Teaching about the Papist Mass**.[5] *The remaining part (23 folios b1–g3 in quarto) comprises 23 folios. 'Printed in Viborg by me, Hans Vingaard, Friday after Candlemas, AD MDXXIX [1529]'*

No. 2 **An Answer to the False and Unchristian Teaching which Lecturer Poul Wrote to the Council in Copenhagen about the Papist Mass** *by Hans Thomsen. 31 folios (a–h3 in quarto). The final folio, which presumably had been white [i.e. empty], has been excised just like many of the margins, but the treatise is complete. 'Printed in Malmö by Oluf Ulricksøn, on the second day after the feast of the apostles St Peter and Saint Paul. The year of our Lord one thousand five hundred twenty and eleven [1531]'.*

No. 3 is **A True and Correct Christian Teaching about the Office of The Priests and Their Lives, Marriages and Correct Chastity etc. Printed in Malmö**. *52 folios (A–N in quarto) complete. At the end: 'This book is printed in Malmö by Johan Hoochstraten. Year of our Lord 1533 etc. Friday just after Epiphany'. On the back of the final page Hoochstraten's mark time [i.e. Kairos] on a winged wheel, with the text 'Occasio'.*

No. 4 is **A Short Teaching with God's Own Words and the Holy Scripture against The Pope, Bishops and Their Disciples' Statutes, Laws, Commandments and Customs** *(Authored by Peder Laurentsen) Printed in Malmö. 28 folios (A–J in quarto). At the end: 'Printed in Malmö, the year 1533 after the birth of God'.*

No. 5 is **Recently brought out into the light: The secrets of the Jews. This book is taken from Latin and translated into Danish to meet the needs of those who cannot understand Latin. It deals with and contains all the secret affairs that the bad Jews keep between themselves both in their Jewish temple and in their own houses. Thus shall Christian people know to punish them**. *On the back of the title page: A woodcut depicting the mentioned author: 'Johannes Pfefferkorn: born a Jew and now a Christian'. 16 folios (A1–6, B1–6, C1–4). Complete, although the final page has been circumcised and partially excised. At the end: 'Printed in Copenhagen by Mr Poul Ræff, canon in that same place 1516 years after the birth of God'.*

This is the **only** known copy of this publication. In 1867, the book was sent on loan to the great Royal Library in Copenhagen, where this final treatise was copied in order to be published in a new edition.

Ludvig Manderström

---

5. This is an incorrect identification. The work is Hans Tausen's *A Short Answer to the Bishop of Odense's Open Letter.*

Unfortunately, the archive for the Royal Library in Copenhagen does not contain any mention of the book being borrowed. It could be that Manderström's note actually refers to the copying of the final folio in the book which appears as a pasted-in addition in the Copenhagen copy. There is certainly no record of Poul Ræff's edition of Pfefferkorn's book being published again after 1516.

Damage and condition

Royal Library, Copenhagen:
There is some damage due to cutting along the outermost edge of fol. a6 (pp. 11–12). On fols b1–b3 (pp. 13–18), a section measuring 3 mm x 55 mm has been cut from midway up the outermost edge of the folio. The paper is in fairly good condition, but there is some water damage, damp spots and tearing particularly towards the end of the book. The final folio is missing. A copy of the folio from the book in the Bielke Library has been glued onto the rear flysheet, and a photo plate has also been inserted.

Bielke Library, Skokloster Castle:
The Bielke Library copy is in very good condition. The pages are clean with just some darkening and spotting, and there is little sign of wear. However, the final folio has been cut down to 110 mm x 60 mm; the section of folio without text has been excised. The binding has also been slightly damaged by fire. This fire damage has resulted in darkening of the leather binding and two small burn holes, and the spine has also cracked near the top.

Foliation, collation and layout

The folios measure 135 mm x 185 mm and are collated thus:

Quire	Page number	Folio (Copenhagen)	Folio (Skokloster)
flysheet	i	0^r	0^r
flysheet	ii	0^v	0^v
$a1^r$	1	1^r	135^r
$a1^v$	2	1^v	135^v
$a2^r$	3	2^r	136^r
$a2^v$	4	2^v	136^v

a3^r	5	3^r	137^r
a3^v	6	3^v	137^v
a4^r	7	4^r	138^r
a4^v	8	4^v	138^v
a5^r	9	5^r	139^r
a5^v	10	5^v	139^v
a6^r	11	6^r	140^r
a6^v	12	6^v	140^v
b1^r	13	7^r	141^r
b1^v	14	7^v	141^v
b2^r	15	8^r	142^r
b2^v	16	8^v	142^v
b3^r	17	9^r	143^r
b3^v	18	9^v	143^v
b4^r	19	10^r	144^r
b4^v	20	10^v	144^v
b5^r	21	11^r	145^r
b5^v	22	11^v	145^v
b6^r	23	12^r	146^r
b6^v	24	12^v	146^v
c1^r	25	13^r	147^r
c1^v	26	13^v	147^v
c2^r	27	14^r	148^r
c2^v	28	14^v	148^v
c3^r	29	15^r	149^r
c3^v	30	15^v	149^v
c4^r	31	[16^r (photo repr.)]	150^r
c4^v	32	[16^v (photo repr.)]	150^v
flysheet	iii	17^r	151^r
flysheet	iv	17^v	151^v

The following signatures can be found in the bottom right-hand corner of the relevant recto pages: Aij, Aiij, Bi, Bij, Biij, Ci and Cij. There are no catchwords.

Note that fol. c4 (pp. 31–32) is only extant in the Bielke Library copy. This damaged folio has been photo-reproduced and glued into the Royal Library Copenhagen copy from which the folio is missing.

There are on average 28 lines per page, with a text field measuring 98 mm x 139 mm. Chapter headings are indented by approx. 10 mm, and have spacing above and below.

Typeface and abbreviations

The book is printed in a blackletter typeface, with larger textura (*missal*) type used for the title on fol. a1^r (p. 1) and roman type (*antiqua*) for the name 'Iohannes pfefferchorn' on fol. a1^v (p. 2).[6] Initials are of three types of Lombard capitals; two with simple rounded dots resembling decorative leaves and foliage, and one with no decoration but closed chambers. A rounded paraph resembling a large 'g' is used for rubrication.

There are a number of abbreviations in use. A much used abbreviation is ʒ ('z'), in word-final position only:

thʒ	th*et*	'it', 'the', 'that'
møghʒ	møgh*et*	'very'
mʒ	m*et*	'with'
inthʒ	inth*et*	'nothing', 'not'
fwndhʒ	fwndh*et*	'found'

A stroke over a vowel (*a, e, i, o, u* only) marks a following nasal:

tāker	ta*n*ker	'thoughts'
anāmedhæ	ana*m*medhæ	'received'
diligētz	dilige*n*tz	'diligence'
bequēt	beque*m*t	'comfortable'
Salomōis	Salomo*n*is	'Solomon's'
welkōmen	welko*m*men	'welcome'
stūdh	stu*n*dh	'while'
hānū	ha*n*nu*m*	'him'

The same stroke can also be found over *m* and *n* to mark a preceding vowel:

thn̄	the*n*	'the'
middaghn̄	middaghe*n*	'the dinner'
affthn̄	affthe*n*	'evening'
inghn̄	inghe*n*	'nobody'

---

6. Lauritz Nielsen refers to the types as Type 1 (M 30), Type 5 (M 32), and Type 6 respectively. See Nielsen 1996, I: 105, 178. The two words in roman type (*antiqua*) are the first use of this typeface for letters in text rather than numerals in Denmark. Roman type for text was not to be used again until 1538. See Dal 1982: 73, and Birkelund *et al*. 1949: 7.

thm̄	them	'them'
cristhn̄	cristhen	'Christian'
høffuisckelighn̄	høffuisckelighen	'politely'
forwthn̄	forwthen	'besides'

Strokes are also found in abbreviations in Latin words to mark a contraction:

sctūs	s*anc*tus	'saint'
dn̄s	d*omi*n*u*s	'lord'
Ihūs	Ih*esus*	'Jesus'

Other Latin abbreviations used are:

ꝛc.	*et*cetera	'and so forth', 'etcetera'
Ihrĩm	Ih*erusa*lem	'Jerusalem'
ne3	ne*que*	'and not'
Xpi	Crist*i*	'(of) Christ'

Generally, the abbreviations are rather few and straightforward; many abbreviations commonly found in contemporaneous works (including others by Poul Ræff) are not to be found in *Iudeorum Secreta*, where the words are written in full instead:

Iudeorum Secreta has:	not:	
alius	ali⁹	'other'
Augustus	August⁹	'August'
pylatus	pylat⁹	'Pilate'
deus	d̄s	'God'
Cristus	xps, xpus	'Christ'
compositier	9positier	'compositions'
conscientier	9sciētier	'consciences'
Leuiticorum	Leuiticoꝛ	'Leviticus' (genitive plural)

Indeed, even common words appear in unabbreviated forms: 'Cristi' (as well as 'Xpi'), 'Ihesus' (as well as 'Ihūs'), 'Iherusalem' (as well as 'Ihrĩm'), and 'Sanctus' (as well as 'sctūs'). Poul Ræff's simple system of abbreviation in *Iudeorum Secreta* (compared, for example, with his publication of Michael's *Expositio*) may be evidence of his endeavours to make the book as accessible to those he describes as 'meenighæ Cristhnæ menniscke [*common Christian people*]' as possible. Even people of limited learning would be able to read the text — including most of the Latin which would have been familiar from attending mass and instruction in catechism.

Woodcut

One important point where Poul Ræff's edition of Pfefferkorn's book and the editions in German and Latin differ is that unlike in these other versions, Ræff's does not include woodcuts to illustrate the text. The text of the German and Latin versions is interspersed with woodcuts illustrating the author, a synagogue interior during Rosh Hashanah, the malqot ceremony, kaparot with feasting, bathing, and the tashlich ceremony.[7] These are among the earliest and most popular illustrations of Jewish rituals, and were, for example, reproduced in Antonius Margaritha's *Der gantz Jüdische glaub* (Augsburg: Heinrich Steiner, 1530). Ræff clearly did not have access to these woodcuts. Instead, he used a woodcut to portray Pfefferkorn that he found among the printing equipment he had bought in 1512 from the German Matthæus Brandis.[8] Brandis had used the woodcut in his edition of Jacobus de Cessolis' *Dat schakspel to dude* (Lübeck, c. 1490), where it was used to represent the knight chess-piece. Ræff had also used the same woodcut on fol. a1^v (p. 2) in his *Manuale Curatorum secundum vsum ecclesie Rosckildensis* which was printed in 1513.[9]

Marginalia

Royal Library, Copenhagen:
There are a numerous marginalia in the Royal Library copy. The majority of them are pen trials and scribblings, but some of them do relate to the text of *Iudeorum Secreta*. They are on the whole faded and rather difficult to read.

Position	*Marginalia*
Front binding inside top)	'DA *[in pencil]* No. 242 *[in black ink]* BOX *[in pencil]*'

---

7. See figs 9–12.
8. See fig. 5.
9. The title page is thus not a portrait of Pfefferkorn as suggested by Bent Blüdnikow and Harald Jørgensen in Jørgensen 1984: 18, 19.

Front binding (inside bottom)	'LN 219 M' *[in pencil]*
ii, top	'29 4º'
a1r, bottom	*Illegible scribbling*
a1v, top	'Lau Michaelis.' *[presumably an* ex libris *('Lau, son of Michael'); there is also smudging on the right-hand side of the page]*
a1v, in woodcut	'A a a | b c d e | f g' *[pen trial, with scribbling in Pfefferkorn's hat]*
a1v, bottom	'a b b c d d e f g h i k l m n s t' *[pen trial]*
a5v, bottom	'A a a b c d e f g h i k l m n o p q r ß t u u x ÿ z' *[pen trial; the ink has blotted above the 'A' and been transferred onto the page surface opposite]*
b3v, outer margin	'En lignelse | \<m\>ed 2ne sagher' *[with underlining of l. 20 in text: 'A comparison with two things']* 'Samelunde' *[uncertain; with underlining of l. 22 in text: 'Similarly']*
b4r, outer margin	'nota .j.' *[with underlining of l. 2 in text: 'Note 1']* '2m.' *[with underlining of l. 8 in text: '2nd']*
b4v, outer margin	'lex naturalis' *['natural law']*
b4v, bottom	*Scribbling/illegible letter forms; pen trial?*
b6r, outer margin	'<u>officium</u> ju|<u>d</u>eorum' *[with underlining of l. 11 in text: 'the Jews' works']* '<u>officium</u> |sathane' *[with underlining of l. 17 in text: 'Satan's works']* 'nota' *[with underlining of l. 21 in text: 'note']*
b6v, outer margin	'nota | om siuge | menniske' *[with underlining of l. 2 in text: 'note about sick people']* 'de cruce' *[with underlining of l. 5 in text: 'about the Cross']* 'nomen ihesu | <u>quid</u> *['name of Christ that']* 'Exempla' *['Examples']*

b6ᵛ, bottom	'A a a b c d'
c2ᵛ, top	'Iniqui narrauerunt mihi fabulationes' *[Psalms 118: 85: 'The proud have digged pits for me']* '*Et* Legem tuam non sum oblitus' *[Psalms 118: 61: 'but I have not forgotten thy law']* 'Jüder i gudtz | fredtt' *['Jews in God's peace']*
c2ᵛ, bottom	'<.>esid<..> in lapide magnæ ingens pietat*is* aliu<…> | Carolus q*ui* domino seruit | insignis religione de <…>| Marmoreo lapide | insignis pietate <…> | <..>ustans | Pictus qui' *[difficult to read: 'On a stone of marble, Charles, a man of great piety, who serves the Lord; of great religiosity; Depicted on a stone of marble a man of great religiosity who']*
c3ᵛ, bottom	'Non Bone Caliope dicto mihi carmina | tristis | sed ser | Sed spero ipsam | Ipsam Sed spero tempore fore ser' *['It is not the sad muse Caliope who dictates poems to me, but I hope, that she will at some later point in time be'; other illegible and deleted text]*
iv, bottom	'foto. 156047' *[in pencil]* ' " 185320' *[in pencil]*

Bielke Library, Skokloster Castle:
There are very few marginal additions. On fol. a1ʳ (p. 1 of *Iudeorum Secreta*), there is a small ink cross penned in the right-hand margin. At the bottom of fol. c3ᵛ (p. 30 of *Iudeorum Secreta*), we find a small illegible scribbling, possibly a capital letter ('B'?), written in black ink.

There is no *ex libris* in the book, but we know that it once belonged to Carl Gustaf Bielke (1683–1754), and most probably also his father Nils Bielke (1644–1716). The fire damage to the cover suggest that it once belonged to the library of Salsta Castle in Västra Götaland (owned in the sixteenth century by the Bielke family), as several books at Skokloster that have been acquired from Salsta show damage by fire. There has never been a fire in the library at Skokloster Castle and no other books in the collections, other than those from Salsta, are damaged in this way.

Figure 5
Woodcut in *Iudeorum Secreta* (Bielke Library, Skokloster Castle).
Photograph by author.

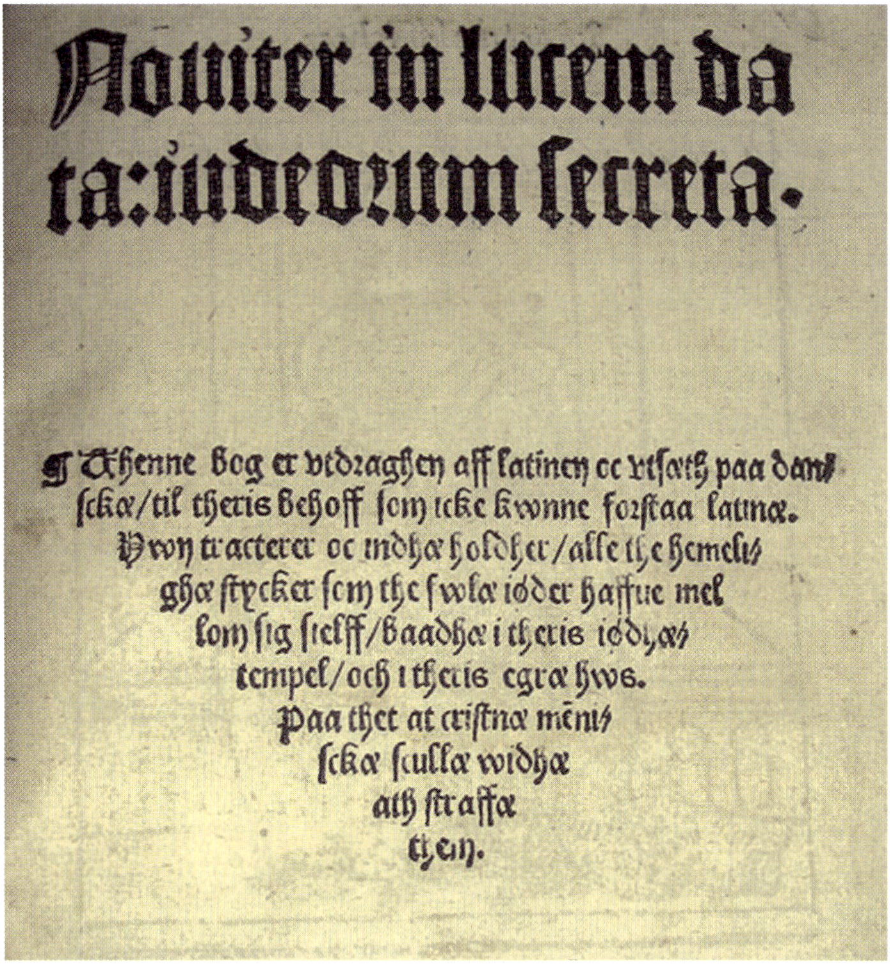

Nouiter in lucem data: iudeorum secreta.

¶ Thenne Bog er vtdragsen aff latinen oc vtsat paa dan∫ka/til theris behoff som icke kwnne forstaa latine. Hwn tracterer oc indhæholdher/alle the hemeli∫ ghæ stycker som the fwlæ iöder haffue mel lom sig sielff/baadhæ i theris iödi∫æ tempel/och i theris egræ hws. Paa thet at cristnæ meni∫ ckæ sculæ widhæ ath straffæ then.

Figure 6
Title page of *Iudeorum Secreta* (Bielke Library, Skokloster Castle).
Photograph by author.

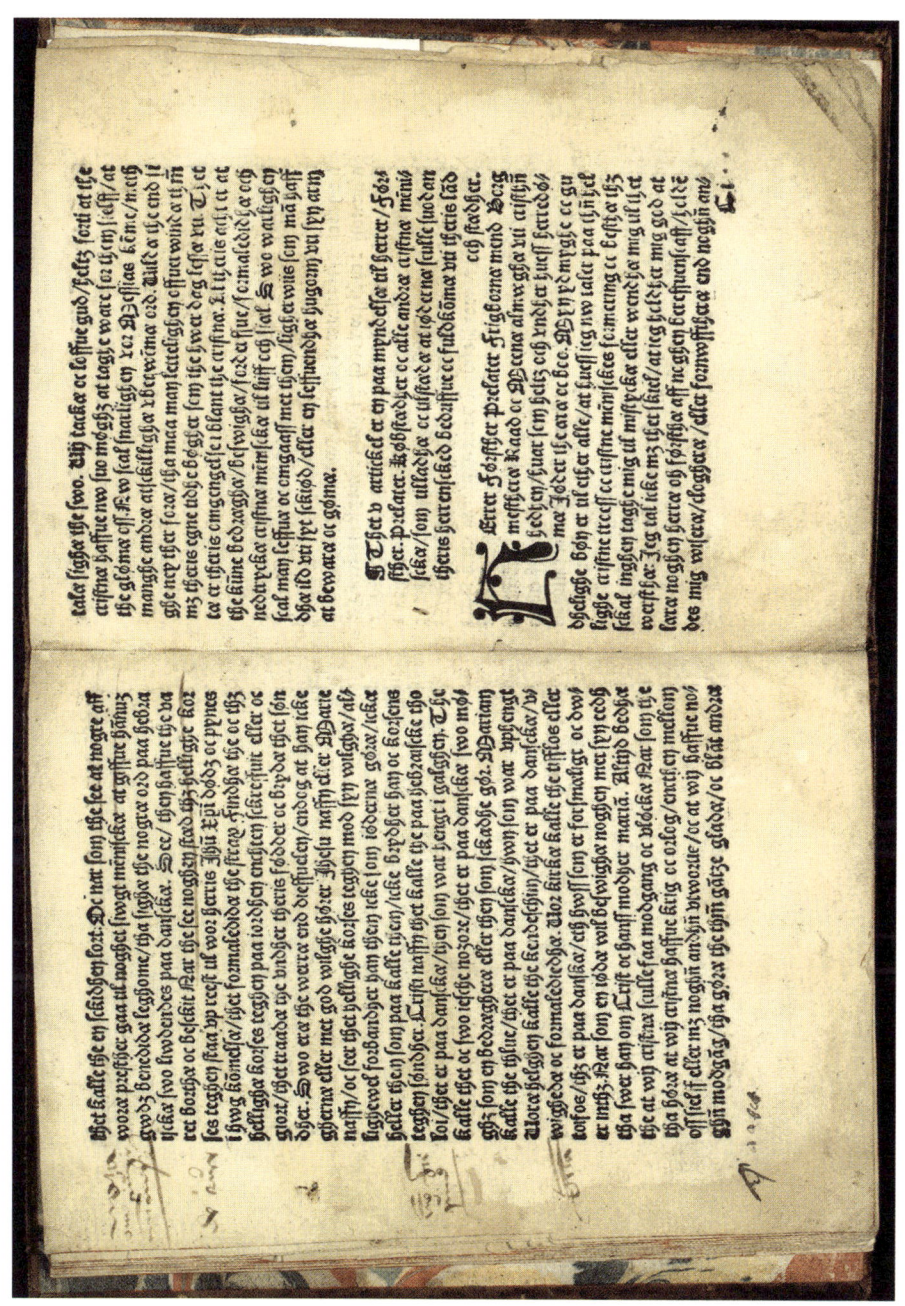

Figure 7
Fols b6ᵛ–c1ʳ of *Iudeorum Secreta* (Royal Library, Copenhagen).
With permission of the Royal Library.

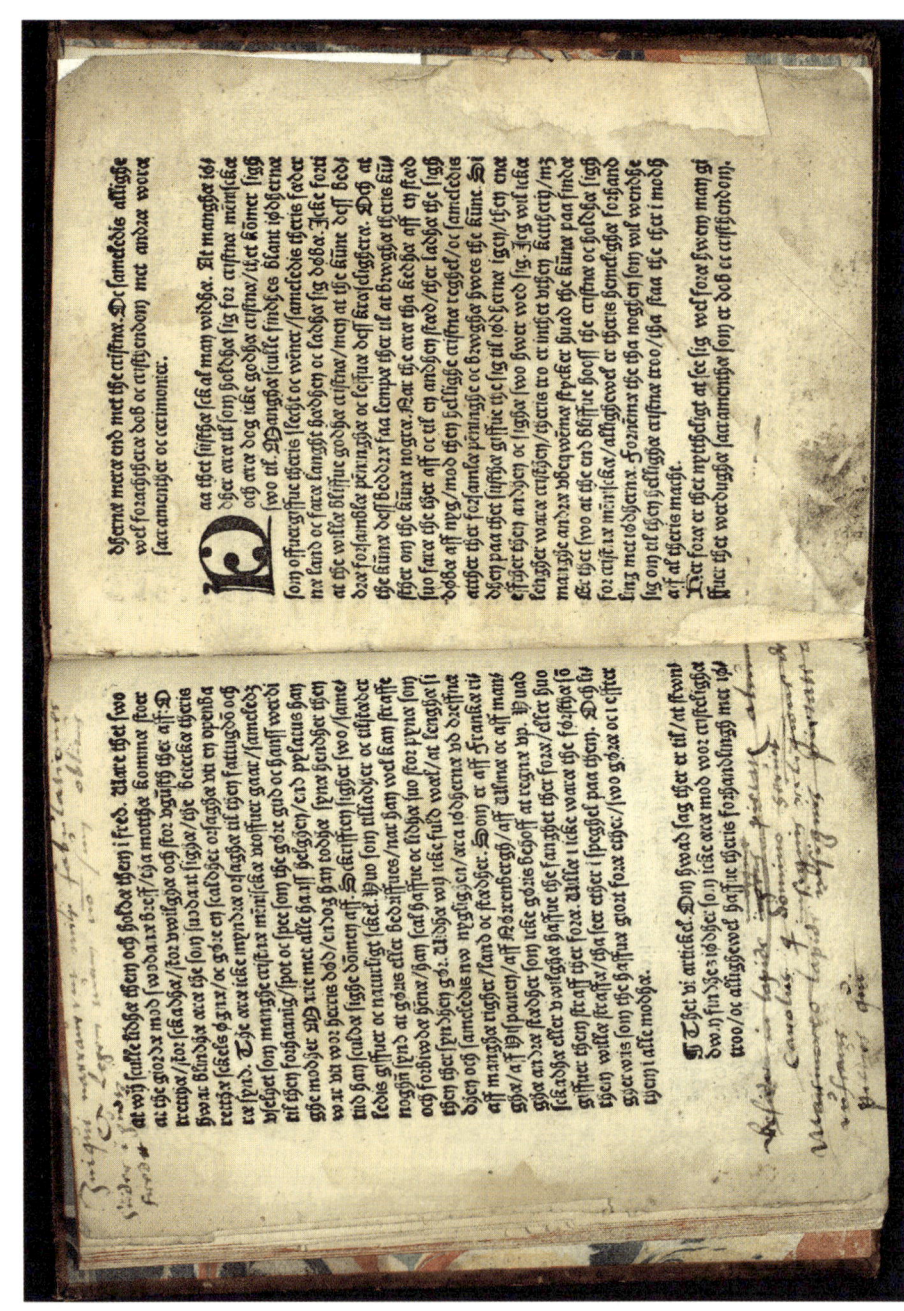

Figure 8
Fols c2ᵛ–3ʳ of *Iudeorum Secreta* (Royal Library, Copenhagen).
With permission of the Royal Library.

CHAPTER 5

Iudeorum Secreta

An edition of the text with a description of editorial principles, critical apparatus, English translation and Latin original

> *...bedhendes indherlighen oc ydmyghelig alle them som henne lessæ. Om ieg haffuer noghet vbeqwæmt sæth her vti/ at the thet mildheligen willæ offuer see oc forbeddræ.*
> Poul Ræff (1516)[1]

The text as presented here is a diplomatic edition of Poul Ræff's *Nouiter in lucem data: iudeorum secreta* printed on his press in Copenhagen in 1516. The principal aim of the edition has been to indicate to the reader precisely what appears in the original work. Every attempt has been made in the transcription to show which parts of the text contain errors or are questionable. The original Latin text is provided for comparison and an English translation of the Danish work accompanies the edition. The following conventions have been observed.

The Danish transcription

The original lineation, pagination, word division, punctuation (the *virgula*, full-stop and paraph), capitalisation and initial letters have all been retained in the transcription. Abbreviations have been expanded in accordance with the spelling used by Ræff elsewhere in the book, and these expansions are printed in italics.

---

1. *Iudeorum Secreta*, p. 30: '...sincerely and humbly asking all those who read it: If I have translated something unsuitably here, that they will kindly scrutinise it and improve upon it.'

Allographs have not been differentiated, so that long and short ‹s›, and tall and rotunda ‹r› have not been distinguished. However, ‹i› and ‹j› are always distinguished.

The Danish critical apparatus

Amendments in the transcription made by the editor are noted in the apparatus under the transcription. Errors and *loci desperati* are also discussed here.

The English translation

The translation is as literal as good usage allows, but may appear repetitive or stilted in places as it attempts to reproduce the language of the Danish original precisely. There is a note (superscript Roman numeral) in the few places where the translation is uncertain because either the Danish text is corrupt or its meaning is difficult to ascertain.

The sources of individual biblical quotations mentioned in *Iudeorum Secreta* are recorded in the English translation italicised in square brackets, for example '[*Genesis 22: 3*]'.

The Latin original text

The text edited here is the Cologne 1508 print of *Libellus de Iudaica confessione siue sabbato afflictionis* by Johannes Landen. This text is most likely the one used by Ræff for his translation. The presumption builds on Ræff's use of the doublet 'faa oc afftwinghæ' to translate the phrase 'emunxerunt/ et exuxerunt', which is also a doublet in Cologne 1508 (but is merely a single word in Nuremberg 1508, 'emunxerunt'). The proposition is admittedly not without its problems and for this reason, the edition printed by Johannes Weissenburger in Nuremberg in 1508 has been carefully compared with Cologne 1508, and any differences are noted in the comparative apparatus (by means of a superscript Arabic numeral). However, where the two editions differ in trifling matters such as punctuation, layout or variant spelling (of the type *quattuor* ~ *quatuor*, *gratia* ~ *gracia*, *auctoritate* ~ *autoritate*, *charitatis* ~ *caritatis*, etc.), there is no note in the apparatus.

All abbreviations have been expanded without any specific typographical indication. No standardisation in the use of small or capital letters has been made.

Page breaks are marked by square brackets with the page number inserted, for example '[p. 1; fol. a1ʳ]', and refer to the page breaks in Cologne 1508. Note that the Latin transcription may repeat several words from the previous page across page breaks, as I have endeavoured to present the Latin in understandable segments of text that are complete and do not suddenly break off. In this way, they can be used for comparison with the Danish text on each page.

Abbreviations used in the apparatuses

    Col.   Cologne 1508 print of *Libellus de Iudaica confessione siue sabbato afflictionis* by Johannes Landen;

    Cph.   Copenhagen 1516 print of *Nouiter in lucem data: iudeorum secreta* by Poul Ræff;

    Nur.   Nuremberg 1508 print of *Libellus de Iudaica confessione siue sabbato afflictionis* by Johannes Weissenburg.

Judaeorum Secreta

Danice. s. 1. & a.

The text here is the title on the front cover of the copy of *Iudeorum Secreta* at the Royal Library in Copenhagen.

Nouiter in lucem da
ta: iudeorum secreta.

¶ Thenne bog er vtdraghen aff latinen oc vtsæth paa dan-
sckæ/ til theris behoff som icke kwnne forstaa latinæ.
Hwn tracterer oc indhæ holdher/ alle the hemeli-
ghæ stycker som the fwlæ iøder haffue mel
lom sig sielff/ baadhe i theris iødhæ-
tempel/ och i theris egnæ hws.
Paa thet at cristnæ mennisckæ scullæ widhæ
ath straffæ
them.

1: 8   eghnæ] eghræ, *Cph.*

English translation:
Recently brought out into the light: The secrets of the Jews
This book is taken from Latin and translated into Danish to meet the needs of those who cannot understand Latin. It deals with and contains all the secret affairs that the bad Jews keep between themselves both in their Jewish temple and in their own houses. Thus shall Christian people know to reproach them.

Latin original:
[p. 1; fol. a1ʳ] Libellus de Iudaica confessione siue sabbato afflictionis. per Iohannem Pefferkorn[2] factum ex iudeo christianum nuper editus.

> Si queris: qui sim curtus facilisque libellus:
> Dicam. judeis que sint[3] lustralia sacra
> Quove die culpas/ et quo purgamine ponant:
> Prodo. leges in me gentis phantasmata vana:
> Quis nullam poterit sibi spem fecisse salutis.
> Vt damnes. saluet te sic deus arbiter equi.

---

2. Pefferkorn] Pfefferkorn, *Nur.*
3. sint] sine, *Nur.*

Iohannes pfefferchorn.

[*Woodcut*]

Ieg Iohannes Pfefferkorn. En iødhe føddher/ oc nw eth cri
sthen menniskæ. Helser ether alle som wed macht holdhæ/ thet
løffthæ oc the articlæ som i haffue loffwit then tiid i anammedhæ
dob oc cristhendom Raadhendes ether alle/ at i forware ether 5
wel for iødher oc iødisckæ stycker. Heltz forti/ at menniscken
ther met forkasther syn siæls salighet. Gud bewaræ ether alle

---

English translation:

Johannes Pfefferkorn. [*Woodcut*] I, Johannes Pfefferkorn, born a Jew and now a Christian, greet all of you who keep that promise and those articles of faith that you promised when you received baptism and the Christian faith. And I advise you all to protect yourselves from the Jews and Jewish affairs, particularly because by not doing so people forsake the salvation of their souls. May God protect you all.

Latin original:

AD honorem et laudem ihesu christi/ benedicte matris sue marie virginis perpetue/ totiusque celestis exercitus Animus mihi est judaici populi in sua gradientis seque offendentis cecitate/ synagogicam confessionem/ confessionis morem et apparatum/ quoque tempore anni fiat (nam singulis annis semel eam solenniter peragunt) et cui confiteantur/ quive eos absoluat et liberet exponere. et in lucem proferre. vt possint intellectu et recta[4] ratione vtentes homines abusiones et ritus vanos ipsorum/ qui absque solido quodam[5] fundamento sunt. agnoscere et considerare. agnitosque contemnere. Nam vt refellantur hij. nihil eis digni inest Et ego quidem misellus prohdolor (tanquam vesanus) diu in his alijsque vanitatibus hesi cum gentilibus meis communi et a cunabulis errore accepto ductus. reputans magnam in ijs[6] salutem contineri cum postea per graciam dei hec reliqui/ et velut nube depulsa glaucomaque ab oculis detracta. ad lumen et claritatem religionis christiane. ad christum iesum. qui vera lux est accessi propius quantum mentis mei oculi debiles [p. 2; fol. a1ᵛ] ferre potuissent in eum iactans cogitatum meum. orans suppliciter/ si quid orare atque tandem exorare queo. vt hoc lumen mihi increscat et stabiliatur. vt in illo ambulans/ ab illo non declinans/ non scandalizer. Vos etiam in christo fratres meos christifideles omnes obsecro. precari pro me peccatore dominum deum dignemini. vt veniam det peccatis meis. verum fidei iubar mihi tribuat et conseruet intelligentiamque concedat et spiritum fortem et constantem. ad certandum contra cruentos illos inimicos et blasphemos christi iesu et sancte matris sue marie. quo possim et ipsos (quod maximopere cupio) fratres meos et tribules secundum carnem pro paruitate mea/ ex institutis doctorum et superiorum meorum ecclesie sancte/ quibus me in maximis et minimis (vt equum pium immo et debitum est) cum omni veneratione humiliter subijcio/ adducere/ vt suam deponant cecitatem. ingrediaturque viam vero lumine preeunte. qua ad celestem hierusalem cuius hec in palestina figura erat. valeant peruenire. Nunc igitur auxiliante deo rem propositam non arduam sed planam. et quantum puto sub eo quo dicitur respectu et formula salis aliquantulum in se habentem aggrediamur. que ita noscenda est. vt et iudeis sua futilis patescat vanitas. et non eis tantum/ sed et de eis apud exteros/ vt aliquando pudore adacti cum res in secreto non est. eam ocius abijciant. intelligantque christiani cum graciarum actione deo patri et christo iesu oblata per huiusmodi comparationem. quam dispares ab illorum sue cerimonie et ritus gracia etiam et virtus in confessione sint. vt de alijs taceam in hoc libello sacramentis nouis. quando priora illa transierunt.

---

4. recta] recte, *Nur.*
5. quodam] quidam, *Col. & Nur.*
6. ijs] his, *Nur.*

[p. 3; fol. a2ʳ]

Thennæ bogh haffuer giort oc sckreffwit en clerck
som er vti Colnæ oc hedher Iohannes Pfeffer-
korn/ til meenighæ Cristhnæ mennisckes nytthæ
At the scwllæ widhæ ath fly och scky the fwlæ Iødhæ/ som
trolighen legghæ sig effther nath oc dagh/ at forderffwæ cri 5
stnæ mennisckæ baadhæ til liiff oc siæl. Forbeneffndhæ Iohan
nes Pfefferkorn/ han er en iødhæ føddher oc om kring skaa
ren. Men nw haffwer han ladt sig døbæ/ oc er en godh Cristhen lærdt man/ thi wed han bæsth theris hemæligh leglighet
hwilcken han obenbarlighen sckriffwer vti thennæ lildhe bog 10
Paa thet at Cristhnæ mennisckæ/ nar the kommæ til talæ met
swodhanæ fwlæ hondæ modh then hellighæ Cristhælighæ
troo. Tha scwllæ the widhæ at straffæ them for theris wildfa
relsæ. Oc er thennæ bogh deeldt vti sex articlæ

¶ Then førstæ artickel er om iødhernæ. Hworledhes 15
the redhæ och besckickæ sigh modh then tiidh the scwllæ
gøræ theris høghtidelighæ sckriffthæmaal. Om hwad
tiidh the gøræ samæ theris sckrifftæmaal. Och hwarledhes the gøræ thet.

Modh then tiidh som Iødhernæ skwllæ gøræ theris 20
høgthidelighæ sckrifftæmaal effther theris sedwanæ. Tha redhæ the och besckickæ sig ther til
meth aldssomstørsth gwdhælighedh/ som them ty
ckes. Och thet begyndhæ the paa Kalendas Augusti. Thet
er then førstæ dagh wti then maanedh som hedher Augustus 25
Samæ dagh staa the bethidælighen vp/ wedh two stwndhæ

3: 27   Augustus] Augnstus, *Cph.*

English translation:
A cleric, who is in Cologne and is called Johannes Pfefferkorn, has made and written this book for the benefit of common Christian people, so that they will know to flee and shun the bad Jews who continually — day and night — try to corrupt Christian people's lives as well as their souls. The aforementioned Johannes Pfefferkorn was born a Jew and circumcised, but has now had himself baptised and is a good Christian learned man; therefore he knows best their secret affairs which he makes public in this little book; so that Christian people, when they come to speak to such vile dogs, [who are] against the Christian faith, will know to reproach them for their error. And this book is divided into six chapters.

The first chapter is about the Jews: How they prepare and get ready for the time when they make their ceremonial confession; about the time when they make their confession, and how they do so.

Leading up to the time when the Jews must make their ceremonial confession according to their custom, they prepare and get ready with the greatest devotion that they can think of. And it begins on *Kalendas Augusti*, that is the first day in the month called August. On this day, they rise early, two hours […]

Latin original:
¶ Partiemur itaque hoc opusculum in partes sex vt subiecta lectio monstrabit De preparatione Iudaice confessionis. et quo tempore fiat et quo ritu.

[p. 3; fol. a2^r; *woodcut*]

[p. 4; fol. a2^v] Cvm sollennem de peccatis suis ex more confessionem facturi sunt iudei. incipiunt kalendis augusti cum quanta possunt pro opinione sua. ad eam se parare deuotione Surgunt[7] e stratis mane horis ferme duabus ante lucanis ingrediuntur[8] synagogam.

---

7. Surgunt] Surgent, *Nur*.
8. ingrediuntur] ingrediunter, *Col*.; ingredientur, *Nur*.

207

[p. 4; fol. a2ᵛ]

før end thet daghes oc gaa til theris Synagogam/ thet er
til theris Iødhæ tempel. Ther øræ the theris gwdhelighe bø
ner en thymæ eller two. Sidhen gaa the hiem ighen hwar til
syth hwess/ øræ theris arbeygd/ hwær effther syn besckickelighet Samæ dagh om affthenen/ gaa the ighen til theris iø-   5
dhæ tempel. Tha er ther en tilsckickith/ som affthen och morghen blæss wti eth bwcks horn. Han tal til them oc paamyn-
dher/ ath the sckwllæ syrghæ/ oc øræ plicht oc boodh for theris syndher/ och forlighæ sig meth gwd ath the haffwe dra-
ghet hannum til wredhæ meth theris syndher och ondhæ ger-   10
ningher. Ligherwiis som woræ biscoper/ prelather/ læræfed-
dræ/ oc sckriffthefeddrer the paamyndhæ oss cristnæ menniscæ
om fasthen besyndherlighen/ at øræ plicht oc bood for woræ
synder. Swodan paamyndilsæ met thet bwcks horn/ oc swodan gudhelighet blant iødhernæ/ warer then heelæ maanet i gem   15
men. At the hwer dag raabæ oc bedhæ til gwd/ at han scal for
ladhæ them theris syndher. At han scal frelsæ them fran allæ
theris fighendher. At han scal vndhæ them at komme til theris
stadh igen Iherusalem/ oc hielpæ them at reformeræ salomonis
tempel ighen. At the ther vti/ mwghæ øræ hannum swodan of-   20
fer som theris forfeddræ haffue giorth/ met wædheræ/ gedhæ-
bwckæ/ och andræ swodanæ creatwræ.
¶ Then siisthe dag vti maanedhen som er theris nyg aars aff
then Tha redhæ the them alle samen til (mend oc qwindher af
hwad som heltz køn the æræ) at badæ/ suo wel the vnghæ som   25
the gamblæ/ oc too sigh gantzæ reenæ. Men nar the swo haffue badt/ tha gaa the alle sammen tiid som the vidhæ eth rindhæ
næ wadn oc dyppæ sig ther vti/ mend/ qwindher/ vnghæ oc gam

English translation:
[…] before daybreak and go to their *Synagogue*, that is their Jewish temple. There they say their pious prayers for an hour or two. Then they go home again each to his own house, do their

work, each according to his lot. In the evening of that same day, they return to their Jewish temple. At that time someone has been appointed to sound a ram's horn morning and evening. He talks to them and reminds them that they should grieve, do their penitence and penance for their sins and reconcile themselves with God as they have made him angry with their sins and evil deeds, just as our bishops, prelates, teachers and confessors admonish us Christian people particularly during Lent to do our penitence and penance for our sins. Such reminders with the ram's horn and such devotion among the Jews continue throughout the entire month, so that they cry out and pray to God every day that he might forgive them their sins, that he might deliver them from all their enemies, that he might allow them to return to their city Jerusalem and help them rebuild Solomon's temple, so that they will be able to make him the sorts of sacrifices there that their ancestors did, rams, he-goats and other such creatures.

On the last day of the month, which is their New Year's Eve, they all, men and women (of whichever sex they are), both young and old, prepare to bathe and wash themselves clean. However, when they have thus bathed, they all go to that place where they know [there is] running water and immerse themselves in it — men, women, young and […]

Latin original:

ingrediuntur[9] synagogam. orant corde et verbo prolata vsque in vnam aut duas horas diei oratione. abeunt domum ad curandum corpus et reliqua sua negocia exercenda Ad vesperum redeunt in synagogam Ibi flatu hircini cornu per cornicinem ad hoc lectum. quo mane et vesperi tunc sonari consuetum est. admonentur vt doleant de peccatis suis. penitenciam agant. curentque reconciliari deo quem ad iracundiam prouocauerunt. vt et nos christianos maxime per tempus ieiunij quadragesime[10]. nostri concionatores et predicatores sacerdotes pontifices relligiosi aut seculares cohortantur. Huiusmodi admonitio per sonitum cornu. etcetera. et animi hec preparatio durat hunc quem dixi mensem totum. Quo mense cum omni dilegentia et studio vociferantur et clamant ad deum. vt dimittat eis peccata ipsorum. liberet eos ab inimicis[11] suis. reducat eos in ciuitatem suam ierusalem. adiumentoque sit ad restaurandum templum salomonis. vt in eo tandem sacrificare et immolare possit deo in bobus arietibus et hircis more patrum et progenitorum[12] suorum. Postremo die mensis prenominati. quem velut preuium anni noui colunt atque obseruant. omnes cuiuscumque sexus aut etatis fuerint. parant se ad balneas lauantur. perfricantur totum corpus. post quam ablutionem ingrediuntur flumen viuum seu aqua profluentem. atque in eo viri femine iuuenes[13] senes totum corpus demergunt ter clamantes et dicentes

---

9. ingrediuntur] ingrediunter, *Col.*; ingredientur, *Nur.*
10. quadragesime] quodragesime, *Col.*; quadragesime, *Nur.*
11. inimicis] inimis, *Col.*; inimicis, *Nur.*
12. progenitorum] progenitor, *Col.*; progenitorum, *Nur.*
13. iuuenes] iuuines, *Col.*; iuuenes, *Nur.*

[p. 5; fol. a3ʳ]

blæ hwer i syn stæd iij reyser/ raabæ oc sighæ suo hwer for sig
Dess wær. Ieg er en aff them. Thet er. At hwer aff them teg
ner sig at wæræ eth syndugt menniscke. The myenæ at nar the
swo haffue toedt leghomet reent/ tha er oc siælen reen. Thettæ
fwnd taghæ the aff thet gamblæ testamentæ Leuiticorum vti thet   5
xxiij capitel. Men andhen daghen ther næst/ som er then førsthæ dag vti maanedhen/ oc then førstæ dag vti aarith effther
theris log/ hannum holdhæ the vti stor høgtiid. Tha staa the beti
delighen vp om morghenen/ oc gaa wti theris iødhæ tempel
Thet fwnd haffue the aff texten Genesis vti thet xxij capitel   10
ther staar sckreffwit/ at abraham/ then tiid gwd bød hannum
at han sculdæ offræ syn søn/ tha stod han betidhelighen vp om
morghenen oc wildhe lydhæ gwdz bwd. Swo myenæ oc the
at the wille gaa vti abrahams fodspor/ oc staa betideligen vp
The myenæ at the villæ øræ gud eth taknemmeligt offer som   15
Abraham giordhæ. Nar the tha æræ gangnæ vti tempelen/ tha
beteckæ the theris hoffwit met eth hwith reenth lyneth klædhæ
Uedh en modhæ som voræ presther/ nar the foræ them i theris
messæ klædher. Thet klædhe er firækant/ oc haffuer nogræ hen
gendhæ treffler vti hwert hyrnæ/ hwilkæ treffler the holdhæ   20
samen met theris hendher Met samæ klædæ stryghæ the them
oc tørræ sig/ ligherwiis som the ther wed sculdæ i hwg kommæ
the bwd oc then log som gud gaff them wed Moysen/ oc ide
lighen holdhæ hennæ Nar som the tha æræ swo forsambledhæ i
theris iødæ tempel/ i hwilken mendhenæ æræ atsckildæ fran   25
qwindhernæ/ swo at hwer haffwer syt besyndherligæ stædh
at øræ synæ gwdhelighæ bøner vti. Tha vpstaar then ypper
sthæ offuer theris tempel/ hwilken them alle offuergaar/ baa-

---

5: 3   the] the-, *Cph.*

English translation:
[…] old — each in his or her own spot three times. They cry out and say each to him- or herself, 'Unfortunately, I am one of them'; that is, they each declare themselves to be a sinful person. They believe that when they have thus washed their bodies clean, then their souls are also clean.

This idea they take from the Old Testament, chapter 23 of the Book of Leviticus [*Leviticus 23: 6*]. However, the following day, which is the first of the month and according to their law is the first day of the year, they celebrate with great solemnity. They rise very early in the morning and go to their Jewish temple. This idea they have taken from chapter 22 in the Book of Genesis [*Genesis 22: 3*], where it is written that when God asked him to sacrifice his son [*Isaac*], Abraham rose early in the morning and wanted to obey God's command. Thus they believe that they are walking in Abraham's footsteps and rise early. They believe that they will make God an acceptable sacrifice like Abraham did. When they go into the temple, they cover their heads with a white clean linen cloth, in a way like our priests when they put on their vestments for Mass. The cloth is square and has some hanging fringes at each corner; they hold these fringes together in their hands. They stroke and dry themselves with this very cloth, apparently so that they will remember the commandments and the law that God gave them through Moses and always keep it. When they have thus assembled in their Jewish temple, in which the men are separated from the women so that each has their own special area in which to say their prayers, then the most important man in their temple who surpasses them all […]

Latin original:

atque in eo viri femine iuuenes[14] senes totum corpus demergunt ter clamantes et dicentes Prohdolor et ego vnus ex eis sum. innuentes scilicet ex numero peccatorum se esse Putantes cum corpus ita lauerint Animam quoque mundatam esse. hunc ritum sumentes ex Leuiticorum capitulo xxiij [p. 5; fol. a3ʳ] a medio ferme vsque ad finem vbi de sabbato sancto memoriali agitur siue afflictionis festoque tabernaculorum. sic quod ibi nominatur varijs nominibus. Postridie eius diei. qui primus est mensis septembris. atque ipsis inicium anni magna celebritate et veneratione festus. surgunt mane luce vix dum certa in ipsa aurora. ingrediuntur synagogam. sumentes illud ex textu Genesi. capittulo .xxij. Vbi legitur. cum Abraham iussus fuisset a deo immolare filium suum. quod mane surrexerit pariturus diuino precepto. creduntque se vestigia abraham sequi surgendo mane. et deo gratam facere oblationem et acceptam. quemadmodum fecit abraham. cui non est inuentus similis qui seruaret legem excelsi. Ingressi synagogam operiunt capita sua casula (vt ita dicam) seu panno lineo candido. quemadmodum nostri christiani sacerdotes faciunt dicturi officium misse. qui pannus in quattuor angulis et quasi inicijs philacteria et fimbrias habet stragulatas. quas manibus suis tenent. aspiciunt illis se tergunt. tanquam recordantes preceptorum dei per moysen illis datorum. vt ea obseruent iugiter Cum vero ita congregati sunt in synagoga sua. que distincta est. vt viris separatim. et feminis separatim cuique suus locus orandi et mansio sit. surgit archisynagogus siue diuicijs siue auctoritate alia prepollens.

---

14. iuuenes] iuuines, *Col.*; iuuenes, *Nur.*

[p. 6; fol. a3ᵛ]

dhæ i macht oc i rigdom. Han gaar til then arck i hwilken fæm
Moysi bøgher the ligghæ bewæredhæ. Han gør syn sermon
oc talæ til gud/ som en forspraakeræ for alt folkit. Han tacker
oc loffwer gwd/ som wildæ werdhes hellighæ at gøræ them
wed synæ bwdord oc reensæ theris hendher. Oc then som ha-   5
ffuer giffwit hanen then forstand/ at han sckillia daghen
fran natthen. Oc at gwd haffuer sckapt them mend oc ickæ
qwindher. At the ickæ æræ wordnæ cristnæ mennisckæ/ oc at the
icke æræ andræ landsckaps tiæneræ eller trælæ Thettæ sigher
han altsamen paa mandfolckens wegnæ. O hwar lidhen vn-   10
dherstandilsæ haffuer thette armæ oc wslæ folk. I al werdhen
er inthet folk wsligheræ/ bedrøffuedheræ/ sorgfwldheræ/ eller
meræ beswaret met tiænisthæ. Fordwmæ æræ the wtdreffnæ
aff theris sædher/ oc nw atsckildhæ oc spreddhæ offuer then gan
tzæ werdhen. Forhaanedhæ/ forsmaaedhæ/ plath inthet ach-   15
tedhæ/ forladnæ aff gwd forwthen al løckæ. The driffuæ the
ris leffneth forwthen alt hoff i stor wslighet/ aff hwilken the
kwnnæ aldrig behielpes/ met myndræ end the bliffuæ cristnæ
mennisckæ. Ther næst gør samæ procurator som han staar foræ
arcken en myenlig bøn/ for alle them som tha æræ forsamble   20
dhæ vti tempelen/ och for alt theris folk som ickæ tha nerwarendhes æræ/ men swo langth borthæ eller i thet forfald/ ath
the icke kwnnæ kommæ til tempelen. han bedher ath gwd wil
frelsæ syt folk fran vblwffue mennisckæ/ af ondhæ tanker/ fran
the folk som ickæ æræ omkringsckornæ/ oc ther met myen han   25
besyndherligen oss cristnæ mennisckæ (han regner oss at wæræ
møghet vreenæ) Aff dieffuelsens macht oc frestelser etc. Paa samæ tiid gøris stort offer til theris altheræ met stor gwdhelig-

---

6: 12   wsligheræ] wslighera, *Cph.*
6: 18   bliffue] bliffne, *Cph.*
6: 21   som] fom, *Cph.*

English translation:
[…] in terms of power and wealth rises to his feet. He goes to the ark in which the five books of Moses are kept. He delivers a sermon and speech to God as the representative of all the people.

He gives thanks and praise to God for sanctifying them with his commandments and cleansing their hands; and for having given the cockerel the intelligence to distinguish between the day and the night; and to God for having created them men and not women; and because they have not become Christians nor the servants or slaves of some other nation. All this he says on behalf of the men. Oh, how little understanding this poor and wretched people have! In the entire world there is no other people more wretched, more sad, more sorrowful, or more oppressed by servitude. In the past they were driven out of their homeland, and now they are divided and dispersed over the entire world, mocked, rejected, not at all respected, abandoned by God without any happiness. They live their lives without any hope in great wretchedness from which they cannot be helped unless they become Christians. Next, the same representative whilst standing in front of the ark says a communal prayer for all those who have gathered in the temple and for all their people who are not present but who are far away or inconvenienced so that they were unable to come to the temple. He prays that God will save his people from shameless people, from evil thoughts, from those people who are not circumcised, and here he means us Christians in particular (he considers us to be very unclean), and from the Devil's power and temptations etc. At the same time, a great sacrifice is made on their altar with great […]

Latin original:

surgit archisynagogus siue diuicijs siue auctoritate alia prepollens. accedit arcam. in qua asseruantur quinque libri moysis[15]. orditur sermonem ad deum tanquam orator et nuncius totius populi. gracias agit deo. et laudes eius pronunciat. qui dignatus est sanctificare eos preceptis suis ad abluendas et mundandas manus eorum. quique gallo dederit intelligentiam. vt diem a nocte discriminet. quod viri creati ipsi a deo sint non femine (id enim pro virorum parte femineo sexu posthabito pronunciat) quod non sint christiani [p. 6; fol. a3ᵛ] quod non sint serui nationum O quam paruo intellectu et sine omni scrutinio inconsideratus est populus iste misellus et pauper. In omni mundo non est miserior/ non tristior[16]/ non molestior/ non onerosior seruitus quam iudeorum est. sedibus olim suis pulsi per orbem terrarum profugi vagantur. disturbati. dissipati. sine estimatione. sine fortunis derelicti a deo. sine re. sine spe miseram ducentes vitam. a qua nunquam nisi per christianam religionem liberari poterunt. Deinde precatur deum quasi omnium qui conuenere/ quique longius absunt ex gente sua/ procurator stans coram arca. vt populum hunc suum seruet et custodiat ab hominibus impudentibus. a malis cogitationibus. ab incircumcisis sub eo nomine christianos precipue notans tanquam immundos. a diabolica tentatione et potestate. Recolitur quoque magna deuotione latissime ad aras eorum prisca immolatio holocaustomatum

---

15. moysis] Moysi, *Nur.*
16. tristior] tristinor, *Col.*; tristior, *Nur.*

[p. 7; fol. a4ʳ]

het/ effther thet gamblæ testamenthes sedwanæ. Som er m*et*
kalffwe/ met weyeræ/ met bwckæ oc swodant meræ. Same
ledhes met kagher giort aff hwedhemel/ ølliæ/ wyn och salth
som the plæghæ at offræ theris presther.
¶ Tha lesses oc psaltheren met stor gwdhelighet/ dog forw- 5
then al forstandt/ men allenisthæ effther texten som hwn standher bloth i sigh sielff/ ligherwiis som the goræ i manghæ andræ handhæ tinghesth oc stycker. Nar som the bedhæ/ tha forarbeygdhæ the och goræ sig stor vmagh paa theris gantzæ le-
ghomæ/ meesth oc besyndherligen nar the beraabæ thessæ ord 10
som Esaias han sckriffuer. Sanctus s*an*ctus s*an*ctus do*mi*nus deus sa-
bahot. The streckæ theris hendher/ the bwckæ til iordhen/ the
goræ sig stor vmaghæ oc myenæ at Moyses wildhæ swo haffue thet/ then tiid han bød at man scullæ tyenæ gwdh aff all
syn macht. Endog at hanss myening war om en skær hwg oc 15
eth reenth hiarthæ. the actæ icke at the æræ the som Esaias
taler om oc sigher. Thettæ folck/ th*et* ærer oc loffwer mig allenisthæ meth synæ læber *etc*. Sidhen ther næsth paa myndhes
gwd aff same procuratore/ at han scal i hwg kom*m*æ th*et* lofftæ
oc then eedh han giordhæ Abraham/ som sckriffues Genesis i 20
thet xxij capitel swo liwdhendis. Ieg sckal mangffoldug goræ thyn sædh offuer alle landsckaff som hi*m*melsens stierner och
haffens sandkorn. Han bedher oc framdelis indherlighen/ at
Messias scal ko*m*mæ oc vdsendhes/ then som scal frelsæ oc frij
goræ hanss folk. Oc ligherwiis som the*n*næ forbeneffndhæ pro- 25
curator han bedher hoos arcken for alt folckit/ swo bedhæ oc
alle iødhernæ besyndherligen hwer i syn stæd/ oc haffwe theris bøgher at lessæ vti Men theris boner/ the æræ forwth*en* al

---

7: 7   sielff] s elff, *Cph.*

English translation:

[…] devotion in accordance with the custom of the Old Testament by sacrificing calves, rams, he-goats or something else of the same kind, and similarly also with cakes made of wheat flour, oil, wine and salt which they usually offer to their priests.

Then the Psalter is read with great devotion, but without any understanding, but solely according to the text, as it plainly stands, just as they also do in many other kinds of things and acts. When they pray, they perform and make energetic movements with their entire bodies, mostly and especially when they proclaim these words written in Isaiah [*6: 3*]: 'Sanctus, sanctus, sanctus Dominus Deus Sabaoth [*Holy, holy, holy is the Lord God Almighty!*]' They stretch out their hands, they bow to the ground, they make a great effort and think that this is what Moses meant when he commanded that they should serve the Lord with all their might, even though he actually meant a clear mind and a pure heart. They do not realise that they are the ones whom Isaiah [*29: 13*] speaks about when he says, 'This people do honour and praise me solely with their lips, etc.' Next, the same representative reminds God to remember the promise and the pledge to Abraham as is written in Genesis chapter 22 [*: 17*] where he says, 'I shall multiply your seed over all nations like the stars of heaven and the sands of the sea.' He also prays particularly fervently that the Messiah may come and be sent, the one who will save and deliver his people. Just as the aforementioned representative prays before the ark on behalf of all the people, so also do all the other Jews pray each by himself in his own place and they have their prayer books to read from. But their prayers lack all […]

Latin original:

Recolitur quoque magna deuotione latissime ad aras corum prisca immolatio holocaustomatum et ceterarum victimarum in bobus arietibus et hircis. libaminumque farris triticei olei vini mellis salis a sacerdotibus suis peragi solita et legitur psalterium magno quodam animi feruore. verum sine intellectu. tantummodo secundum litteram quemadmodum et multis alijs in rebus et actionibus faciunt cum orant/ perpetuo gestu et corporis motu laborant. maxime cum illud esaie proclamant. sanctus sanctus sanctus dominus deus/ subsiliunt plaudunt. tanquam hoc voluisset moises cum iubet omnibus viribus seruiri deo ac non magis de mente dixerit vt et esaias ostendit populus hic labijs me honorat etcetera. Admonetur postea per hunc eundem deus sponsionis et iuramenti sui/ quod fecit ad abraham. vt legitur Genesi .xxij. cum inquit. multiplicabo semen tuum super omnes nationes quasi stellas celi et sicut arenam maris/ oratque pectore supplici. vt mittatur aliquando messias saluator et liberator populi sui. Quo autem modo prefatus procurator multitudinis orat coram arca. sic ceteri quoque iudei orant multis precationibus. qui[p. 7; fol. a4ʳ]bus refertos habent libros/ quos oculis suis subijciunt Sed he preces absque intellectu. absque ratione sunt.

[p. 8; fol. a4ᵛ]

vndherstandelsæ oc forwthen alt sckæl. Heltz forti/ at the inthet andhet begheræ/ atspørghæ eller bedhæ/ wthen om werd
zens macht/ wold oc weldhæ/ oc stor rigdom/ oc at the mwæ
heffnæ oc wræghæ sig offuer oss cristnæ/ oc fwldkommæ theris
vilghæ/ had oc affwend paa oss. The bedhæ fast at gwd scal   5
sendhæ them Messiam/ men the wille icke forstaa at then san
dhæ Messias som er Cristus Ihesus gwdz søn/ han er langæsiden vtsændt gwd oc mand/ føddher aff theris eghen slæcht
oc nw begheræ the at han scal kommæ. Men thet er forgæffues
oc eth falst haaff/ the faræ wild ligherwiis som theris forfed-   10
dræ/ hues fodspor the efftherfylghæ. Suodanæ theris bøner
the begyndess om morghenen nar clocken er moxen wed try
oc forfylghes swo til clocken er wed viij.
¶ Nar som thettæ er giort/ tha taghes the v. Moysi bøgher
aff arcken/ the æræ reenlighæ sckreffnæ paa got pergament/ til   15
altherit/ oc lesses nogræ capitel i them for folkit som tha forsambledhæ æræ. Sidhen er en tilsckickit som thet haffuer i mandat
eller befalning/ han tagher same bøgher i baadæ synæ hender och
løffter them vp paa syn herdæ/ suo at the kunnæ bequæmelighen
sees aff alle/ han vendher sig trennæ reyser omkring for folkit/ tha 20
raabæ the alle høgt oc sighæ. Thet er then log som moyses gaff
israels børn/ oc bød at holdhes met altsomstørst fliidh. Ther
effther rwldes bøgherne til samen igen/ oc en aff theris rabier
setther sig for alterit/ haffuer rwldhen paa syn høgræ arm/ hun
er vel suaer Suo blæss han igen i hornet som tilfforn er sagt han   25
holder sig vp til altherit met stor reuerentz Folkit thet giffuer sig
till stoor gwdhæligheth for synæ syndher aff swodhan liwdh

English translation:
[…] understanding and all reason. Particularly because they desire, ask and pray for nothing but world power, domination and might, and great wealth, and that they might avenge and get back at us Christians and exercise their will, hatred and jealousy over us. They fervently pray that

God will send them the Messiah; but they do not want to understand that the true Messiah, who is Jesus Christ, the son of God, has already been sent — God and man — a long time ago, born of their own people, and now they desire for him to come. But it is in vain and a false hope. They are deluded just like their ancestors whose steps they imitate. This is what their prayers are like, which begin in the morning at almost three o'clock and continue until the time is around eight.

When this is over, the five books of Moses are taken out of the ark (they are written clearly on good parchment) and placed onto the altar, and several chapters from them are read to the people who are assembled at that time. Then someone is appointed, who has been ordered and commanded to this task: he carries these very books in both of his hands and lifts them up onto his shoulders so that they can be easily seen by everyone. He turns around three times in front of the people, while they all shout loudly saying, 'This is the law that Moses gave the children of Israel and commanded to be observed with utmost diligence' [*Deuteronomy 4: 44*]. Then the books are rolled together again and one of their rabbis sits by the altar and has the scroll on his right arm. It is very heavy. Then the man who was mentioned earlier blows into the horn. He stays by the altar with great reverence. The people are moved to great devotion, [repenting] for their sins by such a noise.

Latin original:

Sed he preces absque intellectu. absque ratione sunt. hoc enim solum querunt. cupiunt et orant. vt terrenam et mundanam potestatem. imperium diuicias. adipiscantur. et vlciscantur se in christianos. ac in illos odium suum expleant Orant vt mittatur[17] eis messias/ quoniam missus verus deus et homo est ex ipsorum stirpe prognatus. quem mittendum frustra expectant vana delusi spe. quemadmodum et patres eorum quorum ipsi vestigia persequuntur. hec prenarrata precatio continuatur mane ab hora ferme tercia vsque ad octauam. Tum promuntur quinque libri moisi ex arca scripti mundule in pargameno bono inuoluti in formam rotuli. deponuntur super altare. recitanturque nonnulla capitula ex ijs[18]./ turbe illic congregate Tum quidam est qui munus hoc sibi mandatum habet. is acceptum ambabus manibus rotulum eleuat supra verticem suum. vt possit ab omnibus commode videri ter circumgirans se. conclamat totus ibi tum populus clara voce hoc est institutum. hec lex est quam moises dedit maioribus nostris filijs israhel et mandauit omni studio obseruari. post hec conuoluitur in rotulum lex. et rabi quidem aliquis collocat se ad aram. habetque rotulum reclinatum in brachium dextrum. est enim non modici ponderis. prodit tum iterum ille cum cornu hircino. de quo dixi et ipse quoque cum multa reuerentia se iuxta altare recipit. et populus est intentus deuotioni[19] sue et penitencie pro peccatis suis. huic cornicini

---

17. mittatur] mittat in, *Nur*.
18. ijs] his, *Nur*.
19. deuotioni] deuotione, *Nur*.

[p. 9; fol. a5ʳ]

Then rabi som sidder for altherit met rwldhen/ han sigher til
hannum som hornet haffuer Blæss vti hornet Swo blæss han
effther then rabies bwdord x reyser vti hornet Sidhen biwdher samæ rabi/ at han scal vppæholdhæ en føffwæ stund och
icke blæsæ. Icke møghet lenghe ther effther/ tha biwder samæ 5
rabi/ at han scal blæsæ x reyser igen i hornet/ oc atther scal vppeholdhæ en føffue stwnd oc icke blæsæ. Sameledz blæss han
trediæ tiid oc x reyser. tha myenæ alle iødhernæ visselighen
at theris syndher gaa bort met then clanck eller liwd aff horneth. Nar han tha swo blæss/ och hornet giffwer en sckarper 10
oc reen clanck aff sig/ swo at thet er icke heest/ tha glædis alle
iødhernæ ther wed The tro tha fuldkommelighen/ at the sculle
faa eth frwctsomeligt/ eth saligt/ oc eth løckesomt tilkommen-
dhæ aar. Men giffuer hornet en hees clanck fran sig/ tha bliffue the alle samen bedrøffuedhæ/ taghæ sigh stor sorg oc græ- 15
melsæ til. Troo stadhelighen/ at thet aar sckal bliffue them til
stor modgang/ besyndherlighen/ at the cristnæ sculle gøre them
stor tribulatz och forfylning/ them oc alt theris folck. Nar som
thettæ er swo giort oc offuerfarit/ swo legghæ the rwldhen eller Moysi bøgher vti arcken vel til ighen. Strax ther eff- 20
ther/ raabæ the och hylæ alle met en røst oc sighe. O fader oc kon
ning/ wij haffue syndhet i thit ansigt. O thw wor gwd/ for tyt
hellighæ naffn gør oss effther thyn vilghæ. Tagh fran oss och
sckil oss ved alle ondhe frestelser oc ondhe tancker. Heffnæ oss
offuer alle woræ vwenner. Forderffuæ them alle som begheræ 25
at goeræ eller ligghæ oss i mod. Forfylghæ och forderffwæ them
med pestilentzæ/ met hwngher/ met swerd oc met fengsel. Ladh

English translation:

The rabbi who is sitting by the altar with the scroll says to the man who has the horn, 'Blow into the horn!' He blows into the horn ten times in accordance with the rabbi's orders. Then the same rabbi orders him to rest for a brief moment and not to blow. Not very long after that, the same rabbi orders him again to blow ten times into the horn, and again he must rest a brief moment and not blow. In this way he blows ten times for a third time. All the Jews truly think that their sins disappear with the tone or sound of the horn. So when he blows and the horn makes a sharp and clear tone so that it is not harsh, then all the Jews are joyful, as they are convinced that they have a fruitful, blessed and fortunate year ahead. But if the horn makes a harsh noise, then they are all aggrieved, filled with great sorrow and grief. They believe firmly that the year will bring them much hardship, in particular that the Christians will create much tribulation and persecution for them and all their people. When this is thus done and finished, they put the scroll or the books of Moses safely back in the ark again. Immediately afterwards, they all shout and howl with one voice and say, 'O Father and King! We have sinned before your face. O you, our God, for the sake of your holy name fashion us according to your will. Take from us and keep us from temptations and evil thoughts. Take revenge on our behalf over all our enemies. Destroy all those who wish to do us evil or who set themselves against us. Persecute and destroy them with pestilence, with famine, by sword and with imprisonment. Let [...]

Latin original:

Rabi qui assidet altari cum rotulo. dicit infla cornu. Atque ita inflatur decies et clangitur ex iussu huius rabi Iubet deinde rabi vt cornicem paulum[20] cesset canere. nec ita multo post iterum iubet inflari cornu decies. atque iterum cessatur. similiter tercio inflatur decies. suntque omnes constanti et integra fide peccata sua hoc canore deleri atque auferri Si autem cum inflatur cornu clarum edit sonum absque raucedine. gaudent audientes et letantur. confiduntque se faustum et felicem ac fortunis multis refertum annum eum habitu[p. 8; fol. a4ᵛ]ros. at si cornu raucum ediderit sonum. dolent atque tristantur ominantes sibi annum aduersum fore. et a christianis persecutiones et mala genti sue imminere. hijs peractis reponuntur libri mosis[21] in arcam vnde sumpti fuerant et includuntur in ea Subsequitur dissona voce et incomposito clamore aut potius vlulatu omnium vox dicentium. O pater et rex peccauimus in conspectu tuo fac nobiscum voluntatem tuam deus noster secundum nomen tuum Aufer a nobis et depelle omnes prauas tentationes cogitationesque malas. vindica nos et vlciscere de inimicis nostris. perde omnes qui male cupiunt nobis. persequere eos peste gladio fame captiuitate ingere super eos

---

20. paulum] paulo, *Nur.*
21. mosis] Moysi, *Nur.*

[p. 10; fol. a5ᵛ]

alle handhæ plaghæ offuergaa them for thynæ omkringsckor
næ børns sckyld/ hwilkæ thw haffuer vdwalt tigh *etc*.
¶ Wildhe ma*n* gøræ th*et*/ tha mothe ma*n* snarlighe*n* offuerwin
dhæ them met theris egnæ bøgher/ i hwilke suodanæ oc man
ghe andræ oc fleræ vbørlighæ oc vhørlighæ tingh the findhes.
Hwilkæ the alle samen gøræ oc bedhæ mod oss cristnæ me*n*nisckæ oc mod inghen andhen. ther foræ ræth sandinghen at si-
ghæ/ tha tyckes mig th*et* varæ stor verdsckyld/ at taghæ swodænæ bøgher fran them/ oc icke tilstædhe them at haffue eller
brwghæ swodanæ bøgher. Icke forti at swodanæ vbeqwæ-
mæ oc vkristelighe bøner icke kunne sckadhæ oss/ eller vti no
græ modhæ høres aff gwd/ som wij lessæ Esaie vti th*et* førstæ
capitel. Th*et* er dog en vbeqwem oc vkristelig ting/ som ickæ
bør at stædhes/ høres eller lidhes. thet varæ wel iødhernæ
the armæ stymperæ eth got oc nyttheligt raad/ at the icke haff
dhe swodanæ bøgher/ oc icke heldher tilsteddes at haffue them
the wandhes wel tha met tidhen aff swodane stycker och
glømdhæ them/ m*et* swodane theris ondhæ sedwaner. Swo
at then had oc affuend som the haffue paa oss cristnæ/ formi*n*d-
sckedhæ sig wel med tidhen. Thessæ stycker som ieg nw siisth
haffuer sagt/ them forfylghe iødhernæ wel til clocken er wed
xij om myddaghe*n*. Oc swo er thet nog sagt aff samæ iødher
hworledhes the redhæ sig til at gøræ theris sckriffthemaall.

¶ Then andhen artickel om Iødhernæ. Hwarledhes
the gøræ theris sckriffthæmaal. Oc til hwem the sckriff-
thæ. Oc om hwem them løser aff theris syndher.

English translation:

[…] every kind of plague befall them for the sake of your circumcised children whom you have chosen for yourself, etc.'

If you want to do so, then you may quickly defeat them with their own books in which these sorts of things and many others and numerous shameful and senseless things are to be found. All of this they do and pray against us Christians and not against anyone else. So to tell the truth, it seems to me that it would be just deserts to take such books from them and not permit them to have and use such books. Despite the fact that such malicious and unchristian prayers cannot harm us or be heard by God in any way, as we read in the first chapter of Isaiah [*1: 15*], it is nevertheless a malicious and unchristian thing that should not be allowed, heard or suffered. It would be a good and useful remedy for the Jews — the poor wretches! — if they did not have such books and were not permitted to have them either. In time, they would be weaned off such passages and forget them, and likewise their evil customs. So that the hate and jealousy they hold towards us Christians would be vastly reduced in time. The Jews pursue these things that I have described above until around twelve o'clock midday. And so enough has been told of how these Jews prepare for their confession.

The second chapter about Jews: How they confess, and to whom they confess, and about who delivers them from their sins.

Latin original:

ingere super eos plagas omnes propter circumcisos filios tuos quos elegisti tibi etcetera. Quod si forte inficiari hec velint facile suismet libris conuincentur. in quibus huiusmodi pluresque alie execrationes perscripte continentur. quas omnes inprecantur nobis christianis[22]. nec fere alij cuiquam. Quare si quid ex fide sincera dicere licet non ab re putarem fore quinimo pium crederem et sanctum. hos execrationum libros auferre ab eis. nec sinere[23] eos tale quid habere vel dicere. Et quamuis nefarie iste optationes et abominande. nobis nocere non possint. et a deo non exaudiantur vt Esaie primo legimus. est tamen quodammodo inhumana res et non ferenda auribus et animis. Illis autem salubriter et bene consultum esset si libros harum execrationum non haberent. nec habere permittentur. desuescerent enim paulatim ab hac malignitate. obliuiscerentur praue consuetudinis. nec ita refricarent maledictis odium. quod aduersum nos christianos gerunt. Que nuperrime nunc dicta sunt. continuantur per iudeos modo prenarrato vsque in duodecimam horam meridiei. Atque hec sufficiant de preparatione iudaice confessionis

¶ Particula .ij[24]. ostendens cui et quomodo confiteantur. et quis eos absoluat a peccatis.

[p. 9; fol. b1ʳ; *woodcut*]

---

22. christianis] christiani, *Nur.*
23. sinere] sincere, *Nur.*
24. .ij] secunda, *Nur.*

[p. 11; fol. a6ʳ]

Som clocken er tha ved xij om middaghen som tilfforn
er sagt. tha gaa iødhernæ alle aff theris iødhæ tem
pel/ och gaa til eth wadn som noghet flydhendhes er
i hwilcketh the kwnnæ faa nogræ fisckæ ath see. the wendhæ theris ansigt til flodhen/ oc løffthæ vp nogræ theris klædher foræ til oc vdsla theris sckiød. Swo talæ the til fisckene
med en høg stemmæ/ indherlighen aff alt theris hiarthæ oc sighæ
Alle voræ syndher them kasthæ wij til ether/ tagher them til
ether. the æræ alstingis vti then myening/ at fisckenæ visseligen
taghæ theris syndher til sig/ oc at iødernæ swo scullæ bliffwe
skildt ved theris slemme syndher. men er thet suo/ at the boo
wti noghit righæ/ then stædh som ickæ kwnne kommæ met
godhæ lempæ til swodan en flood. Tha forbidhæ the en stoor
storm oc eth stort wædher. Swo vendhæ the sig i mod wædhe
ret/ taghe theris forgheræ vp/ vdsla theris sckiød modh wæ-
dheret/ oc talæ lighæ swodanæ ord til wædhæret som tilfforn
staar sckreffuit om fisckenæ. Thenne vbesckickelighe wanæ oc
wildfarilsæ/ haffue the inghenstedz taghet eller fwndhet i thet
gamblæ testamenthæ/ icke heldher aff nogræ hellighæ mendz
exempel/ men aff en theris bog som the kalle talmot/ oc aff an
dræ falsckæ løgnafftighæ compositier eller dicther/ som theris
rabier eller ypperste haffue tilhobe sæt oc paafwndhet. Paa
hwilkæ the wille heldher tro/ end the wille efftherfylghæ then
hellighæ sckrifft. Thet sckrifftemol kalle the at varæ theris
lillæ sckrifftemol. Oc thet gøre the then førsthæ dag vti then maa
ned som hedher September/ som foræ er sagt.
¶ Nar som the swo haffue giort theris lillæ sckrifftæmol/ sidhen begyndæ the at gøre penitentz vti ix daghæ met wegt och

11: 15 theris] therrs, *Cph.*

English translation:

As said earlier, the time is around twelve o'clock midday when all the Jews leave their Jewish temple and go to some water that is flowing and in which they can see some fish. They turn their faces to the river and lift up some of their clothes in front and shake out the tails of their garments. Then they talk to the fish from the bottom of their hearts saying in a loud voice, 'We are casting all our sins to you. Receive them!' They are entirely of the opinion that the fish do indeed receive their sins and the Jews are thus relieved of their ugly sins. However, if it is the case that they live in some place where it is not possible to reach such a river with ease, then they wait for a great storm and a great wind. They then turn into the wind, pull up the front hanging flaps of their clothes, shake out the tails of their garments into the wind and speak the same words to the wind as were written before about the fish. This inappropriate custom and delusion has not been taken from nor been found in the Old Testament nor in the example of holy men, but from their book, which they call the Talmud, and from other false, deceitful compositions and stories which their rabbis or leaders have cobbled together and fabricated, which they prefer to believe rather than follow holy scripture. This confession they call their 'minor confession' and they do it on the first day of the month called September as is said above.

When they have performed this minor confession, they then start to do penance for nine days with night-time vigils and [...]

Latin original:

[p. 10; fol. b1^v] Consequens est vt aliam particulam subnectamus/ de eo scilicet cui et quando peccata sua iudei ritu suo sollenni confiteantur/ et quis eos absoluat Accedente meridiano tempore de quo supra/ egrediuntur omnes synagoga[25]/ accedunt aquam limpidam profluentem/ in qua et pisces cernere possent/ conuertunt facies suas ad fluuium subleuant vestimenta sua ab anteriore parte/ excutiunt sinum eorum/ alloquunturque pisces[26] sonora voce ex imo cordis sui dicentes/ proijcimus ad vos peccata nostra/ ea recipite vobis/ Suntque omino in ea opinione/ quasi pisces eorum putida[27] ac fetencia peccata ad se capiant/ illique sic ab eis liberentur. Quod si forte aliquam regionem habitent/ in qua commode ad aquam fluentem accedere nequeant/ expectant tempestatem ventorum flatumque vehementem/ ibi tum conuersi in uentum subleuata lacinia priore vestimentorum/ eaque commota et excussa alloquuntur ventum quo modo supra de piscibus expositum est. Roget nunc quispiam/ quam ob causam ad pronum flumen et non aduersum/ nec auersi ipsi sed[28] aduersi/ itemque in uentum facies vertant/ quod ea ratione faciunt/ vt videatur deferre flumen peccata ipsorum et ventus abigere non referre. inordinatum hunc morem et incompositum abusum nulla auctoritate veteris testamenti assumpsere sibi/ nullisve sanctorum[29] exemplis/ sed ex eo libro quem talmot appellant/ alijsque falsis et inanibus institutis suorum Rabi/ quibus obsequuntur[30] magis et inherent/ quam diuinis et probatis auctoribus et scripturis. Hec confessio a iudeis parua confessio nuncupatur Fit autem vt diximus prima die mensis septembris [p. 11; fol. b2^r; *woodcut*]

[p. 12; fol. b2^v] Post huiusmodi vero confessionem per dies nouem magnam (vt aiunt) penitentiam agunt id est vigilias.

---

25. synagoga] synagogam, *Nur.*
26. pisces] piscibus, *Nur.*
27. putida] putrida, *Nur.*
28. sed] se, *Nur.*
29. sanctorum] sauctorum, *Col.*; sanctorum, *Nur.*
30. obsequuntur] obsequuntut, *Col.*; obsequuntur, *Nur.*

[p. 12; fol. a6ᵛ]

fasthæ. The føræ them i haarclædher oc legghe sig hart om na
then Pynæ theris leghomæ met manghæ andræ atsckillighæ
hordhedher. icke alle eens/ men hwer effter syn macht oc be-
sckickelighet/ oc thet kalle the then storæ penitentz oc thet storæ
sckrifftæmol. I thenne theris hellighæ tiid/ gaa the huer dag vti   5
the ix daghe vti theris iødæ tempel Men then ix dag som the
gaa aff tempelen/ tha gaa the alle hiem hwer til syt hwss vnghæ oc gamblæ. The som æræ aff mannæ køn/ the taghæ wti
theris hand/ huer en hwid hanæ. Men the som æræ aff qwin-
dæ køn/ the taghe huer aff them en hwid hønæ/ om thet er mw   10
gheligt at the kwnnæ faa swo manghe hwidhæ høns. Er tha
noghen aff qwindhernæ som er met foster/ hwn scal haffue en
hanæ oc en hønæ for sig oc syt fosther som hwn er met och ickæ
end nw haffuer giort noghen synd. Uerdhen i hwset eller hwss
bondhen/ han tagher syn hanæ vti handhen/ staar myt i blant   15
syt folck/ tencker indherlighen paa synæ syndher aff eth gw-
deligt hiarthæ. Nar hannum tha tyckis at han haffuer fwldkommelighen offwertencht synæ syndher/ swo tagher han hanen
om baadhæ synæ been/ oc hwrler hannum tree reyser om syt ho
ffwit/ swo at hanen nødhis til at sla met winghernæ paa iø-   20
dhens hoffwit. Sidhen tal han til hanen oc sigher. Thw æsth
then som forladher mig mynæ syndher/ the faræ aff mig och i
tig Nw er ieg frælst oc løsdt aff alle mynæ syndher. Thu æst
plichtug at lidhæ pynæ for mynæ syndher. Thu gaar i dødhen
oc ieg scal gaa til thet ewindhelige liiff. Ther næsth gaa the al   25
le fram/ then eenæ effther then andhen/ huer met syn hanæ eller hønæ/ gøræ i alle modhæ ligherwiis som hwssbondhen han
giordhæ/ met stor sorg oc penitentz for theris syndher/ oc troo

English translation:

[…] fasting. They dress in hairshirts and sleep on a hard surface at night. They punish their bodies with many other different forms of harshness, not all in the same way, but each according to his ability and nature, and they call this the 'major penance' and the 'major confession'. During this their holy time, they go to their Jewish temple every one of the nine days. But on the ninth day, when they leave the temple, they all return home, young and old, each to his or her own house. Those who are male each take a white cockerel in their hands, but those who are female each take a white hen, if it is possible for them to procure so many white fowl. If one of the women is pregnant, then she should have a cockerel and a hen for herself and the unborn child inside her which is yet to commit any sin. The male host or the head of the household takes his cockerel in his hand, stands in the midst of his family and, with a devout heart, contemplates his sins. When he thinks that he has fully considered his sins, he takes the cockerel by both of its legs and swings it three times about his head so that the cockerel is forced to beat its wings on the Jew's head. Then he speaks to the cockerel and says, 'You are the one who delivers me from my sins. They transfer from me into you. I am now delivered and freed of my sins. You are obliged to suffer the punishment for my sins. You meet death and I shall go on to eternal life.' Then they all step forward, one after the other, each with his cockerel or with her hen, and do just as the head of the household did with great sorrow and repentance for their sins, and they are […]

Latin original:

ieiunia in cilicio et cinere iacentes ceterasque corporis afflictiones adhibent sibi/ quisque secundum propositum suum aut vires/ nec enim par omnibus super his obseruatio est que et magna penitentia seu confessio etiam dicitur. Ingrediuntur quotidie per id sacrum nouendiale synagogas Nono tandem die huius penitencie cum egressi sacra ede redeunt domum judei omnes iuuenes et senes masculini sexus gallum album tenent habentque/ femine gallinam eiusdem coloris/ si modo eis possibile sit hec indipisci[31]. Si qua mulier pregnans est ex ipsis ea gallum et gallinam vt habeat/ iubetur/ pro fructu quem in vtero gerit qui nec dum peccauit. Paterfamilias autem suum tenens manu gallum stat in medio familie intento animo deuotoque corde/ suorum adhuc memor peccatorum. Vbi iam eorum satis sibi recordatus videtur/ apprehendit gallum per pedes et ter girat eum circum caput suum/ ita vt gallus cogatur concutere alas suas et quasi caput hominis diuerberare tum ille ad gallum/ tu es qui peccata mihi mea dimittis/ que a me transferuntur in te. Iam ego a peccatis meis solutus et liberatus sum/ tu debitor culpe es/ tu in mortem is/ ego in vitam eternam. Tum procedunt singuli alius post alium quisque cum gallo suo/ ac imitantur ritum et mores obtestationum et cerimoniarum patrisfamilias cum dolore grandi et penitencia peccatorum suorum/ animo intento et cogitabundo/ pro comperto et certo habentes sua illis a deo peccata omnia dimissa esse.

---

31. indipisci] adiscipi, *Nur.*

[p. 13; fol. b1ʳ]

fwldko*m*meligen at gwd haffuer tha forladt them alle theris
synder. Sidhen taghe the strax oc brydhæ halsen sønder paa
haner oc høner/ siwdæ them/ steghæ them/ eller oc anderledis
koghæ them/ hwer som ha*n*num sielff teckis effther syn eghen vil
ghæ. Strax ther effther gaa the vti bastwen igen/ too oc gni 5
dhæ sig reenæ met alsomstørst flijd och myenæ/ at waræ ther
noghen synd igen hooss them som haffdæ sckiwldt sig eller oc
ware forgæt/ tha sculle the ther m*et* afftoo he*n*ne. Sidhe*n* strax
effther baddhet gaa the til thet rindhenæ wand igen oc dyppæ sig ther vti/ swo at ma*n* kan plat inth*et* see aff theris legho- 10
mæ/ sidhen føræ the sig (hwer i syn stædh) vti eth reent hwit li
ned klædhebonæ. Er ther tha noghen i blandt som tyckis ath
han icke end tha er fwldko*m*meligen ree*n*set aff syndhen/ han ta
gher til sig synæ naboer oc synæ we*n*ner oc gaar ind vti tempelen. Han faldher paa synæ knæ oc kasther strax syt hoffwed 15
ned mod iordhen. Hwilken som tha stander ha*n*num næst/ han ta
gher hanss klædder och kasther them vp til hanss belthestædh
swo at hanss artz staar aaben Han slar ha*n*num i hanss bagstak
met eth belthæ oc wendher ringhen til/ eller met e*n* andhen swø
bæ wel xxxix serdelwghe slag i then myening/ at er ther noge*n* 20
synd igen vti thet me*n*nisckæ/ tha scal hwn swo vd driffues aff
hanss gomp/ oc sidhen regner han sig at waræ alsamen reen/
pwr oc skær aff alle syndher. Nar som thettæ er swo sckedt oc
then dag er forledhen/ tha om affthenen setthæ the sig gladeli-
ghen til theris bord oc faa them madh. Tha ædhæ the baadæ 25
theris affløseræ oc theris sckriffthæfeddræ oc sameledhes allæ
theris synder som the haffue sæt fran sig oc sændt i them/ tha
ædhæ the sig al dørghen metthæ oc plæghæ sig wel.

13: 6   myenæ] myena, *Cph.*
13: 11 syn] syu, *Cph.*
13: 20 serdelwghe] serdwghe, *Cph.*
13: 28 dørghen] *possibly a mistake for* dørghend(h)es.

English translation:
[…] entirely convinced that God has forgiven them all their sins. Immediately afterwards they
break the necks of the cockerels and hens, boil them, roast them or cook them in some other

way as he or she each wishes. Immediately afterwards they go to the bath-house again, wash and scrub themselves clean with great diligence, and they believe that if any sin should remain that has hidden itself or been forgotten, then they must wash it off in this manner. Directly after their bath, they return to the running water [*i.e. the mikvah*] and submerge themselves so that absolutely nothing can be seen of their bodies. Then they get dressed (each in his or her own spot), putting on a clean white linen gown. If there is anyone among them who thinks that he is still not completely cleansed of his sins, he assembles his neighbours and friends and goes to the temple. He falls to his knees and immediately throws his head to the ground. Whoever is standing beside him lifts up the man's clothes and tucks them up above his belt so that his backside is exposed. He beats him on the behind with a belt using the end with the buckle or with some other scourge, lashing him a good thirty-nine individual times in the belief that if there is any sin left in the man, then it can be driven out of his rump. And then he considers himself to be completely clean, pure and cleansed of any sins. When this has taken place, and the day has turned to evening, they sit joyfully at their dinner tables and have a meal. In this way they eat both their saviour, their confessor and at the same time all the sins that they had rid themselves of and transferred into them [*i.e. the fowl*]. Thus they audaciously eat their fill and they fare well.

Latin original:

et certo habentes sua illis a deo peccata omnia dimissa esse. iugulum tum frangunt gallis et gallinis/ coquunt igne aqua/ assos elixosve pro libitu parant. Ingrediuntur iterum balneas et baptismata. lauantur/ fricantur/ strigiles adhibent. [p. 13; fol. b3ʳ] omni cura et sollicitudine omne perluunt et mundant corpus/ vt si forte adhuc peccatum aliquod residuum sit/ et velut se occuluerit[32] vel obliuione vel incuria/ sic quoque abluatur. Adeunt iterum aquam post hec balnea profluentem/ totos se vt nulla corporis emineat aut conspici possit pars immergunt/ induunt se tum vestem lineam candidam. Si quis autem se a peccatis non mundatum satis et expiatum forte putaret/ is cum vicinis et proximis suis ingreditur Synagogam/ procumbit in genua/ capite in terram prone demisso. subleuat qui astat illi vestes ad nates vsque a tergo/ verberat eum cum corigia seu cingulo aut alio huiusmodi flagro ad ictus vsque xxxix. super clunibus/ tanquam si aliquod adhuc residuum in eo homine peccatum est/ ita abigatur/ expellatur/ et abeat per posteriorem corporis partem obscenam. tum totus mundus est/ et ab omni peccatorum sorde purus His ita procuratis cum tandem in vesperum inclinatur dies/ leti accumbunt mensis Vescuntur et de illis/ imo et illos vorant suos confessores absolutoresque[33] simul cum peccatis suis que in eos transmiserunt/ vsque ad plenam saturitatem etcetera.

[p. 14; fol. b3ᵛ; *woodcut*]

---

32. occuluerit] occultauerit, *Nur.*

33. absolutoresque] absulotoresque, *Col.*; absolutoresque, *Nur.*

[p. 14; fol. b1ᵛ]

Nar the haffue tha giort thette gildhæ eller collatz/ tha føræ
the them vti andræ reenæ kiortlæ offuer bremmedæ met silkæ som
æræ allenistæ ther til bereddæ oc icke til theris almenighæ wa
næ/ Sidhen tagher hwer aff them oc tender eth vaxliwss/ the
liwss sculle ideligen brændæ then affthen eller nat oc then andhen   5
dag i gemmen/ oc then dag kalle the theris affløsnings dag eller
theris frælsen dag. Ther til scal sckickes eth cristen mennisckæ/
eller oc en hedning som icke er vnder giffuen theris log at taghe
waræ paa thessæ liwss at the icke sculle gøre skadæ. Men iøder
næ sielff the gøre plat inthet/ icke swo møghet at the taghe bran   10
dhen aff eth liwss/ paa thet at the icke sculle brydæ theris helligæ
dag. Skeer thet paa same dag at noghet aff theris qwig (encten
aszen eller koo eller noghet andhet creaturæ) falder vti en pøl/
vti en graff/ vti en kelderhalss/ eller i noghen andhen farlig stæd
Tha løbæ the alle samen/ then enæ at hielpæ then andhen at hans   15
qwig scal icke bliffue at skadæ/ men hielpæ thet vp aff pølen.
Thet regnæ the for inghen synd/ oc myenæ at the icke ther met
brydhæ theris hellighe dag. Dog er then ypperstæ sag ther til
girighet at the swodant villæ gøre paa then dag/ endog at the
met theris smegring villæ/ at thet gøres aff ræt kerlighet som   20
then enæ haffuer til then andhen. Thenne samæ affthen effter mol-
tiid/ gaar alle rabiernæ til samen enæ for them sielff til iødæ tem
pelen/ oc bliffue ther i for sig sielff til klocken er ved try effther
mydtnat oc bedhæ gud om syn nadæ The haffue samtale om
theris log oc om propheterne/ oc huorledis the sculle giffue fol   25
kit foræ/ at tackæ/ loffuæ/ oc benedidæ gud/ oc hwad helder
the villæ framdelis forfylghe theris gamblæ sedwanæ/ eller om
the kunne findæ nogræ nyg scalke fwnd at vnderwisæ folket

14: 5   affthen] affthn, *Cph.*
14: 7   cristen] crinsten *or* crimsten, *Cph.*
14: 15 enæ] ena, *Cph.*
14: 22 alle rabiernæ] allerabiernæ, *Cph.*

English translation:

When they have had this feast or dinner, then they dress in other clean gowns edged with silk and that are only used for this occasion and not for general everyday use. Then each of them takes and lights a candle. These candles should keep burning that evening or night, and through the following day, and that day is called their 'day of atonement' or 'day of deliverance'. They appoint a Christian or even a pagan who is not subject to their laws to take care of these candles so they do no harm. But the Jews themselves do absolutely nothing, not even trim the wick of a candle so as not break their holy day. Should it come to pass on this day that one of their cattle (either an ass or a cow or some other creature) falls into a pool, into a ditch, into a cellar-shaft or into some other dangerous place, then they would all come running, each helping the other so that his cattle would not be harmed, and help it up out of the pool. They do not consider this to be a sin and do not think that they have thereby broken their holy day. However, the principal reason why they would do such a thing on this day is greed, even though, flattering themselves, they insist that they act out of the pure love that they have for one another. That same evening after the meal, all the rabbis go by themselves to the Jewish temple and stay there alone until about three o'clock after midnight praying to God for mercy. They discuss their laws and the prophets and how they should instruct the people to thank, praise and bless God, and whether they will still follow their old customs, or whether they can find some new roguish creation of the imagination to teach the people […]

Latin original:

[p. 15; fol. b4ʳ] Post id conuiuium eamque coenam induuntur alias tunicas candidas ex bombace[34] contextas filo ad hoc preter ceterum vulgarem vsum preparato et incendit quisque eorum candelam ceream/ que eo vespere/ et die postero qui dicitur dies remissionis seu liberationis/ iugi igne et flamma ardere iubetur. circa quod lumen christianus aut gentilis non eorum religionis homo adhibetur/ qui illis ferijs et superstitioni addictus non est/ qui curet nequid damni forte lumen id afferat. ipsi non contingunt vel lichnum quidem purgaturi/ ne suum violent festum diem opere aliquo. Si tamen illorum cuiuis per eum diem quem sanctissime colunt/ asinus aut bos in puteum aut foueam seu penarium caderet/ concurrerent omnes totis cetibus adiutorio iumento ipsi/ et damno vicini/ pereque vt suo prospicerent/ sub specie caritatis. nequaquam putantes suam religionem obseruantie sabbati eo opere violauisse vt appareat huiusmodi supersticionem apud eos pre religione/ et auariciam damnique metum pre sanctitate pollere et pietate. Eodem vespere Rabbi fere omnes ingrediuntur synagogam finita coena/ manentque illic vsque ad terciam fere horam post noctis medium soli/ tanquam vel diuinum posituri atque accepturi oraculum/ collaturi etiam de preceptis legis et mysterijs prenunciationibusque prophetarum/ et ritibus et sacris deo gratiis populo iubendis et siue prisco siue suo noue efficto more peragendis

---

34. bombace] bambace, *Nur.*

[p. 15; fol. b2ʳ]

oc giffue them foræ at retthæ sig effter. nar som clocken er tha
wed iij som sagt er/ tha kommer thet myenæ folk til tempelen/
mend oc qwinder/ icke til hobæ/ men mendhenæ for sig oc qwin
dernæ for sig/ oc iomfruernæ the bliffue hiemme tha begyndæ the
at siwnghæ oc raabæ met glædæ oc frygd/ thi at thet er then før- 5
stæ dag i theris nyg aar/ ligherwiis som wor sedwanæ er ath
wij qwædhæ noghen løstelig wisæ nyt aars affthen oc nyt aars
dag som er/ war wel kommen nygt aar war wel kommen hær.
The ladæ sig waræ forplichtughæ at holdæ then dag met stort
gledscaff/ the tackæ oc loffue gud mangfoldelig paa samæ tiid. 10
The bedhæ inderlighen til gud/ allenistæ om thessæ verdzlighe
ting/ men the glømæ oc villæ icke widhe the ting som eræ til frel
sens salighet/ wændelighæ oc womkringsckiffthelighæ. The
bedæ vor herræ indherlighen at han wil draghæ them til Iherusalem
igen/ at vp retthæ oc reformeræ Salomonis tempel/ eller end 15
helder at bygghæ hannum vp aff nyg/ met suodanæ andræ mangæ
vnyttelighæ oc faafenghæ bøner. Blant suodanæ theris bøner
oc scalkafftighe sedwaner/ belackæ the oc bespee oss cristne men
niske oc sighæ at wij bedæ til stocke oc steenæ oc til affguder som
inthet kunnæ hielpæ oss oc ey taghæ oss noghet ondt fran/ men the 20
rosæ ther aff oc forrummæ sig at the bedæ til then sandhæ gud/ en
dog at the icke ville achtæ oc besindæ at theris bøn er them sielf
til ewig fordømelsæ oc vor bøn er oss til ewig salighet The be
dhæ til then som er en konning offuer alle konninger/ och thet konnin
ghelighæ naffn neffnæ the trøssuer vti theris gwdelighe bøner 25
Oc tha tilstaa the thet i samæ theris gwdhelighæ bøner/ at vti
gwddhommen æræ tree personer/ endogh at the thet icke willæ
openbarlighen tilstaa eller vedtaghe for theris ondskaff skyld

---

15: 20 inthet] nthet, Cph.

English translation:
[…] and instruct them to follow. When it is three o'clock, as has been said, the common people arrive at the temple, men and women, not together but men by themselves and women by themselves, and virgins [*i.e. unmarried young women*] stay at home. Then they begin to sing and shout

with joy and happiness, as it is the first day in their New Year; just as it is our custom to sing a joyous song on New Year's Eve and New Year's Day, namely 'Welcome New Year! Welcome here!' They are obliged to celebrate the day with much happiness. They thank and praise God many times all at once. They pray fervently to God solely for worldly things, but they forget and do not want to accept the things that concern the joy of salvation, eternal and immutable. They pray fervently to our Lord that he will lead them back to Jerusalem to erect and rebuild Solomon's Temple or preferably even construct it anew, and many other fruitless and vain prayers. In their prayers and roguish customs, they dishonour and mock us Christians and say that we pray to sticks and stones and to idols who cannot help us and do not keep us from anything evil. But they praise themselves and boast that they pray to the true God, even though they do not want to see and realise that their prayer sends them to eternal damnation and our prayer sends us to eternal salvation. They pray to the one who is 'king of kings', and this king's name is mentioned three times in their pious prayers. And thus they admit in their own pious prayers that there are three persons in the Godhead, even if they do not want to admit so publicly or accept this because they are evil [...]

Latin original:
et siue prisco siue suo noue efficto more peragendis Ad horam eam ineunt synagogam reliquum vulgus mares et femine/ separatim autem non promiscue discalciati nudipedes preter virgines que domi manent[35] etcetera. Ordiuntur ibi carmen leticie et hylaritatis/ vtputa in sui noui anni principio [p. 16; fol. b4ᵛ] quemadmodum et nos peana (vt vocant) nostrum annum nouum ingredientes canimus in laudes iesu vt romanis erant per illud tempus saturnalia eum diem letum[36] auspicantes vociferantur aduersus deum et resonant laudes. orantque semper terrenis intenti celestium immemores et immutabilium/ vt reducat eos hierosolimam ad edificandum restaurandum aut potius dirutum omnino instaurandum[37] templum salomonis cum multis alijs inanibus et superuacuis precibus Inter ceteras autem precationes orationem habent et dictionem qua aiunt reliquas gentes omnes (quo nomine nos christianos significant maxime) adorare venerarique idola/ et inuocare deos mutos et surdos/ qui nemini adiumento esse/ a nemine malum propulsare queant. iactant preterea in hac gratulatione et gaudio et laude se adorare regem regum[38]. qua particula[39] orationis sub regis nomine ter repetito manifestissime eorum confessione/ quamuis sibimet contradicentes. nec constantes sibi/ eam negent duricia et pertinacia sua trinitatis personarum in vnitate essentie diuine predicatio apud eos est et palam proditur/ vt vel inviti vel phanatici verum fateri cogantur.

---

35. manent] maneant, *Nur.*
36. letum] letem, *Col.*; letum, *Nur.*
37. instaurandum] instaurundum, *Nur.*
38. regum] regem regum, *Col.*; regum, *Nur.*
39. particula] paricula, *Nur.*

[p. 16; fol. b2ᵛ]

meth myndræ endh the bliffuæ strenghælighen nøddhæ eller
twungdæ ther til. Nar som the lessæ themnæ artickel wti theris bø
ner met en høg røst eller stemmæ. Tu es deus noster neque alius
preter te etc. Thet er swo møghet paa dansckæ. Thw æst wor
gwd oc inghen forwthen tig/ tha beslwthæ the ther vti oc willæ 5
fuldkommelighen/ ath Cristus Ihesus iomfrw Marie søn (then
som swo dyræ løssdæ oss igen met syt hellighæ blodz vdgydelsæ oc syn bittheræ død oc pynæ/ oc striddæ sterkelighen for oss
som en løffuæ aff Iuda slecht) han er icke sand gwd. Thet si
ghæ the swo fram paa theris hebraisckæ maal. Olenu lascha 10
beha/ thet er theris daglighæ bøn.
¶ Nar som thessæ stycker haffue en endæ/ tha forsamblæ sig
besynderligen hooss arckæn vnghæ oc gamblæ/ alle the som kal
les at varæ aff Aarons slecht hwilken ther var then ypperstæ prest
i fordum/ endog at hanss afkommæ icke nw suo eræ/ the gaa til ar 15
ken met stor gudelighet/ taghæ oc løfftæ henne høgt vp met theris hendher oc benedidæ folkit effter then modhæ som sckreffuit
staar Numeri vti thet vi capitel oc sighæ suo. Gud han scal velsignæ ether oc i sculle bliffue salighæ/ herren han scal vpliwsæ syt
ansigt mod ether oc i sculle rolighen bliffue i hanss nadhæ/ gwdh 20
han scal vpløfftæ syt siwn offuer ether oc scal giffue ether fred.
Suodanæ theris bøner oc benedidelser som ieg nw haffuer aff
sagt/ them gøre the trøsser paa then dag: Oc al then stundh som
the aff aarons slecht staa suo met vprachtæ hender at giffue folkit
benedidelse/ tha fordrister sig inghen aff iødernæ at see vp til the 25
ris hender/ icke helder prester sielff. the myenæ oc tro fuld-
kommeligen/ at offuer theris hender scal siddæ gud eller gwdz
and/ oc hwilken aff them som vpløffthæ synæ øgnæ oc soghæ

16: 6   iomfrw] ionfrw, *Cph*.
16: 15   i] in, *Cph*.
16: 26   myenæ] myena, *Cph*.

English translation:
[…] unless they absolutely must or are forced to do so. When they read this passage in their books with a loud voice, 'Tu es Deus noster neque alius præter te, etc.' In Danish, this means 'You are our God and there is no-one but you etc.', they include and mean completely that Jesus Christ, the Vir-

gin Mary's son (who has lovingly saved us through the spilling of his holy blood and his bitter death and suffering, and who fought for us as strongly as a lion from the tribe of Judah) is not the true God. This they say directly in their Hebrew language ' *'Aleinu lešabeaḥ*', which is their daily prayer.

When these acts have finished, they gather by the ark, young and old, all those who can be said to have been born of the family-line of Aaron, who was once the most important priest even though his descendants are not now. They go to the ark with great devotion, take it in their hands, and raise it up high and bless the people after the method described in Numbers in the sixth chapter [*Numbers 6: 24–26*], and they say, 'May God bless you, and you shall be joyful! May the Lord make his face shine upon you, and you shall be calm in his grace! May God lift up his face over you and give you peace.' They repeat these prayers and blessings of which I have told three times on this day. And the entire time while those from the family-line of Aaron stand with outstretched hands to give the people a blessing, not one of the Jews, not even the priests themselves, dare look up at their hands. They believe and are convinced that God, or the spirit of God, is resting on their hands and anyone who was to raise his eyes and look in that direction [...]

Latin original:

vt vel inviti vel phanatici verum fateri cogantur. Cum autem in oratione sua dicunt alta et canora voce/ tu es deus noster/ neque alius preter te/ et insinuant per hec verba/ quod christus filius marie/ quando nos omnes illo[40] dolore et liuore ac precioso rosaceo sanguine suo in ligno sancte crucis a diabolica potestate et eterna damnatione fortiter vt leo de tribu iuda liberauit/ non sit deus In hebreo ita dicunt. olenu laschabeha. et est hec quotidiana eorum oratio Post finem rerum omnium harum conueniunt extra reliquam multitudinem/ et congregantur iuniores et seniores omnes orti ex stirpe et genere aaron ordine et officio sacerdotali olim functi. nunc autem minime. Accedunt supplices et magna deuotione arcam/ tendunt in altum manus suas benedicunt populo secundum formam et prescriptum Numeri .vj. capituli. [p. 17; fol. c1ʳ] dicentes Deus benedicet vobis/ et vos saluabimini[41]. dominus illuminabit faciem suam aduersum nos vt requiescatis in gratia eius. Deus eleuabit vultum suum super vos et dabit pacem vobis. Tales iudeorum quas nunc diximus orationes simul et benedictiones fiunt et dicuntur eo ipso die ter. Et quam diu illi ex stirpe aaron stant extentis ac porrectis supra se manibus ad populo[42] benedicendum/ audet aliorum nemo iudeorum qui in synagoga sunt/ suspicere ad manus eorum sed nec ipsimet[43] putant[44] enim/ aut potius credunt integra fide hac ducti ratione. quod requiescat super eas manus spiritus domini quem qui aspexerit homo viuens/ mox ei moriendum sit.

---

40. illo] illi, *Col.*; illo, *Nur.*
41. saluabimini] saluabamini, *Col.*; saluabimini, *Nur.*
42. populo] populum, *Nur.*
43. nec ipsimet] ne ipsimet, *Col.*; nec ipsimet, *Nur.*
44. putant] putaut, *Col.*; putant, *Nur.*

[p. 17; fol. b3ʳ]

ther til/ han sculle visselighen døø Hær taghe the effterfylning aff
Exodi bog vti thet xxxiij capitel thær wij suo lessæ. Moyses han
bad til gud at hannum matthe sømæ at see gudz ansigt. Gud han
suaredæ hannum oc sagdhæ. Inghen menniske scal see mig oc leffuæ
Item/ hwilken aff iødernæ paa same dag om affthenen ther 5
fnyster trolighen/ eller ee hues liwss ther klarlighe oc skinindæ
brendher/ han glæder sig aff alt syt hiartæ/ oc troer fulkommelig
at thet er eth wist teghen ther til at gud haffuer hørt hanss bøner
Thenne theris sedwanæ (effter som mig kan mindhes ath haffue
læsdt/ oc som ieg haffuer hørt aff mynæ ypperstæ blant iøder- 10
næ the som haffue wæret lerdhæ mend) haffue the icke aff thet
gamblæ testamentæ/ swo at forti at menniscken kunne fnysthæ/ tha
sculle hanss syndher ware hannum forladnæ. Men wel findhes
ther om en rød spunden silkæ traad etc. At nar folket om affthe
nen effter theris gudelighe bøner fwndhe suodant clart/ hwith 15
oc sckinindæ/ thet scildæ waræ eth got teghen til theris syndz for
ladelsæ/ som ther standher screffuit Esaie i thet førsthæ capitel.
Suo bliffue tha alle iødernæ vti tempelen met them som æræ
aff Aarons slecht oc gøre suodane bøner for folkit then hele dag
i gemmen/ huerken ædæ eller drickæ til soo lenghæ the see natthen 20
paa himmelen. Sidhen gaa the hiem/ settæ sig til bordz/ ædhæ oc
dricke oc gøre sig gantze gladæ. Oc huat som leffnet er aff for-
neffndhæ haner eller høner/ thet settæ the fram paa bordhet oc æ-
dhæ suo huess igen er aff theris sckrifftæfeddrer/ oc tro fuldkommelighen at theris synder oc alt theris ondscaff er them forladt 25
aff then alsommegtugisthæ gud. Oc suo er thet nw sagt aff theris
store sckriffthemol/ abstinentz oc fasthæ.

17: 2   xxxiij] xx, *Cph.*
17: 14 spunden] spundeu, *Cph.*
17: 15 fwndhe] *the letter f is misshapen*, *Cph.*

English translation:

[…] would surely die. They take this from the book of Exodus in the thirty-third chapter [*Exodus 33: 20*] where we read that Moses asked God to be allowed to see his face. God answered him and said, 'No one may see me and live.' In the evening of the same day, whichever Jew sneezes for certain[i] or whose candle burns clearly and brightly is happy with all his heart and is convinced that it is a sure sign that God has heard his prayers. It is not from the Old Testament that they take this custom of theirs, namely that because people can sneeze then they are free of their sins (about which I remember having read and have heard about from my eminent men among the Jews who were learned men). But there [in the Old Testament] is found the one about a spun thread of red silk etc. When people in the evening after their devout prayers find such [a thread] bright, white and luminous, it could be a good sign that their sins have been pardoned, as it is written in Isaiah in the first chapter [*Isaiah 1: 18*]. All the Jews remain in the temple with those of the family-line of Aaron and say prayers like this for the people throughout the entire day. They neither eat nor drink until they see the night in the sky. Then they go home, sit at their tables, eat and drink and make merry. And they put out whatever is left of the aforementioned cockerels and hens on the table and thus eat what is left of their confessors and are convinced that their sins and all their evilness have been taken from them by God Almighty. And so it has now been told of their major confession, abstinence and fasting.

---

[i] for certain] *The Danish* trolighen, *which can also mean 'faithfully', seems to make little sense here. The Latin version has* acriter, *meaning 'bitterly', 'harshly', 'sharply'*.

Latin original:

mox ei moriendum sit. Sumunt argumentum ad eam rem Ex libro Exodi. capitulo .xx. Vbi legimus. Orauit moises dominum vt liceret sibi videre faciem domini. Cui respondit deus. Non videbit me homo et viuet Quisquis tamen eodem die ad vesperum sternutauerit acriter/ aut cuius candela lucide et clare arserit is gaudet Et velut pro indicio certo habet et signo quod eius preces exaudiuerit deus Huiusmodi obseruationes quantum ego legisse aut a maioribus meis in iudaismo viris doctis audiuisse memini/ in vetere testamento non fuere/ vt scilicet per sternutationem remissio peccatorum significaretur et ostenderetur/ quin potius per filum sericum rubrum seu coccineum. netum et conglomeratum/ si illud post orationem eorum vesperi candidum compertum fuerit/ secundum Esaiam capitulo primo[45]. si fuerint peccata vestra vt coccinum. quasi nix dealbabuntur et si fuerint rubra quasi vermiculus. velut lana alba erunt. Ita autem ad preces illorum aaronitarum[46] perseuerant ieiuni abstinentes cibo et potu eum diem totum quousque appareant in celo plene clareque ad vesperum et noctem sidera Tum redeunt domum/ Accumbunt mense/ come[p. 18; fol. c1ᵛ]dunt/ bibunt/ epulantur cum magna hilaritate et gaudio vescunturque reliquijs suorum confessorum (vt ita dicamus gallorum. scilicet. quibus sua imposuere peccata) cum peccatis suis omnino credentes illis omnia peccata delicta et malefacta sua a deo vero et viuo optimo maximo dimissa esse. Ita finitur eorum maior tandem confessio. abstinencia. ieiunium plurimorum dierum.

---

45. primo] j, *Nur.*
46. aaronitarum] araonitarum, *Col.*; Aaronitarum, *Nur.*

[p. 18; fol. b3ᵛ]

¶ Thet iij artikel. huar fore ieg openbarer suodane iø
dhernes hemmelighe handlingher. Oc huorledis man skal kun
næ bestøræ oc afftaghe them theris vildfarelsæ.

Ieg haffuer nw sagt vti thesse forbeneffndæ article
om iødernæ oc theris vhørlighe vaner som the ha 5
ffue nar the gøre theris sckrifftemol oc penitentz.
Thet haffuer ieg giort forti/ at nar som swodant
bliffuer them openbarlighen kast for øgnæ/ oc the ther met tiith
oc offthæ bliffuæ bespottedæ oc bespeedæ/ tha mathe thet end
swo kunne skee/ at the dess snaræ mothe om kring wendhes aff 10
theris ondhæ wæghæ oc til then helligæ cristnæ troo som alsom
bæst fundament haffuer. Nw mothe noghen suo sighe. Iøderne
the æræ suo hordæ i theris sind/ oc er theris ondæ sedwane them
suo sød oc kær/ at ware thet suo at thette oc meræ kastedes them
end foræ met spot oc spee som sagt er. Alligeuel sculdæ the ville 15
bliffue ved theris ondæ waner oc i theris ondscaff/ oc icke scul
dæ ville acthæ eller besindæ theris salighet/ suo waræ thet men
altsamen forgæwes. her til wil ieg swaræ. Moxen thet kan
wel suo varæ. Alligewel som mig tyckis vti myt sind/ wil ieg
fram settæ en lignelsæ met twennæ sagher/ som vthen twiffuel 20
styrcker oc stadfesther menniscken synd oc ondscaff. Dess wær
man findher manghe cristne mennisckæ som møghet vsckellighen le-
ffuæ/ mod gud forwthen al retferdighet/ forwthen mildhet/ for
wthen misckundelighet/ oc forwthen al tolmodighet. Tractheræ
paa manghe atscklighe falscke fwnd/ som er met aagher/ met 25
falsck køpmanscaff oc manghe andræ vsighelighe vbehørlighæ
syndher oc falscke fwnd/ met hwilke the fortørnæ gud oc for-

18: 9   bespottedæ] bespotteda, *Cph.*
18: 12 Iøderne] Iød rne, *Cph.*
18: 14 thette] tehtte, *Cph.*
18: 22 som] son, *Cph.*
18: 23 retferdighet] retferd ghet, *Cph.*

English translation:
The third chapter: Why I am exposing these Jews' secret acts, and how we can lead them and remove from them their error.

In the previous chapters, I have now told of the Jews and their absurd customs that they have when they make their confession and repent. I have done this because when the Jews are publicly reproached for this sort of thing and are frequently mocked and ridiculed for it, then perhaps they will more quickly be turned from their evil ways and to the holy Christian faith which has the best foundation. Now it might be said that the Jews are so determined and that they hold their evil customs so near and dear, that even if this and more still were thrown at them with mockery and ridicule as mentioned above, they would nonetheless keep to their evil customs and remain in their evilness and would not consider or think of their salvation, and the whole thing would have been in vain. To this I answer that that may well be the case. Yet to make my opinion clear, I will present a comparison with two reasons why people's sins and evilness are without doubt strengthened and ingrained. Unfortunately, one comes across many Christians who live very immodestly, against God, without any justice, without kindness, without mercy and without patience. They engage in many deceitful activities such as usury, fraudulent commerce and many other unmentionable shameful sins and deceitful activities with which they spurn God and [...]

Latin original:

¶Particula tercia huius opusculi quare ego huiusmodi propalauerim[47] atque in lucem (vt aiunt) produxerim. et quo pacto ab huiusmodi erroribus et nequicijs abduci queant Iudei.

Dixi prioribus duabus partibus et explicui iudeorum quod modo satis esse putaui prauam et vanam abusionem in hoc genere confitendi penitencieque peragende si forte ipsi hoc ridiculo[48] palam prodito/ ac illis exprobrato et contemptim obiecto/ relictis ijs[49] supersticiosis et vanis ritibus ad religionem christianam solido innixam fundamento conuerti possint Sed dicet aliquis tanta inest eis duricia et sue consuetudinis tanta dulcedo. vt si hec etiam illis exprobrentur. nihilominus in suo errore et cecitate pertinaciter manere velint/ nec agnoscere curent ineptias suas/ vt superuacuum sit hec prodidisse. His ita respondebo. fortasse ita est. Verum ex mei animi sententia/ si tamen recte sentio/ afferam similitudinem/ in qua duas contingam causas (vt puto) rationabiliter editas/ que firmant et augent peccata hominum Inueniuntur prohdolor multi christiani qui reprobam et diuinis contrariam[50] preceptis vitam degunt/ contra religionem pietatem iusticiam/ tractantes vsuras fraudulentas mercaturas aliaque multa peccata scelera et flagicia peragentes/ que non est necesse memorare sigillatim/

---

47. propalauerim] pro palauerim, *Nur.*
48. ridiculo] ricudulo, *Col. & Nur.*
49. ijs] hijs, *Nur.*
50. contrariam] contraria, *Col. & Nur.*

[p. 19; fol. b4ʳ]

derffue theris ieffncristen. Swodant theris syndughe leffnet ha
ffuer syt fundament aff twennæ stycker. Thet førstæ er/ nar som
børn the æræ i theris vngæ aar oc see møghet ondt aff theris for
eldernæ/ oc myenæ at alle theris gerningher æræ godæ oc wel
giordæ/ forthi at the icke end tha kunne skilliæ ondt fran goth   5
for sckellig alders brøst sckyld. Oc ther met paa theris ældher
dom/ settæ the sig foræ at ville effterfylgæ theris foreldhernæ
oc gaa i theris fodspor. Thet andet er en daglig sedwane/ suo
at dag fran dag oc aar fran aar øffuer eth menniske sig vti ondhæ gerningher/ suo at tiit oc offtæ ther met menniscken taber syn   10
retthæ vnderstandelsæ/ suo at hannum tyckis ondth ware got och
got ondt/ oc thet er forti at man er suo twrafftig vti syndhen.
Dog suo/ Sckeer thet at suodane synduge mennisckæ (huat hel
der the haffue nw theris fundament aff theræ foreldernæ eller
aff theris eghen ondscaff) the finghe at høræ predicken oc gudz   15
ord/ i hwilke the kunne høræ theris ondhæ gerninger straffes. I
sandhet thet sculde strax nagghe them vti theris ondscaff/ at the
haffdæ fortørnet gud oc varit mod cristnæ mennisckis samfundh
Oc sculdæ the wel offuerwæghe huarledis the met suodant eth
leffnet icke kunne komme til then glædæ oc salighet/ som gud ha-   20
ffuer bereedt til alle synæ vdwaldæ/ oc tiit oc offtæ aff suodanæ tancke haffdæ hørdt theris ondhe gerningher straffes vti predicken
Then wiisæ mand Salomon han sigher. En wiis man/ nar han
hører tha bliffuer han wiseræ/ ende sig en vwiis man om han hører. Suo er thet ligherwiis met iødernæ. the æræ iw suo na-   25

19: 1   ieffncristen] ienffcristen, *Cph.*
19: 3–4   foreldernæ] forelderuæ, *Cph.*
19: 24   sige] sig, *Cph.*

English translation:

[…] corrupt their fellow Christian. This sinful life of theirs has its basis in two things. The first is, when, in their young years, children see a lot of bad behaviour in their parents and think that all their [*parents'*] deeds are good and done well, because they [*the children*] are still unable to distinguish evil from good because of their young age; and then, when they grow older, they try to imitate their parents and follow in their footsteps. The second reason is daily habits, by which someone performs evil deeds day in, day out, year in, year out, so that very often the person loses his proper understanding, so that he thinks bad is good and good is bad, and that is because he is so stubborn in his sin. Nevertheless, if such sinful people (whether their sin has its roots in their parents' or their own evilness) hear a sermon and the word of God in which they can hear that their evil deeds are being blamed, then truly it should immediately pain them in their evilness that they have spurned God and acted against the Christian community. And they should consider how with such a way of life they are unable to obtain the joy and salvation that God has prepared for his chosen, and to hear often in sermons how their evil deeds are blamed. The wise man Solomon says, 'When a wise man listens, he becomes wiser, let alone when a fool listens.' [*cf. Proverbs 9: 9*] So it is also with the Jews. They are of course just as […]

Latin original:

quorum reproba vita duabus maxime occasionibus accedit et increscit. prior est cum a parentibus liberi a teneris annis vi[p. 19; fol. c2ʳ]cia et scelera vident/ ea tanquam recte acta cum adhuc nullum habeant iudicium ad discernendum a bono malum vtpote a maioribus auctoritate annis prudencia contemplantes. ac reputantes/ imitantur/ et maiorum suorum vestigia prosequuntur. Altera est diuturna in vicijs consuetudo et velut exercitatio/ que habitum inducit. vnde quodammodo perdunt recte rationis sentimen/ estimantes malum bonum et bonum malum. floccifacientes peccata quibus longo vsu obcalluerunt Si tamen huiusmodi homines siue prauis inducti exemplis siue suamet consuetudine in vicijs obfirmati. audiant concionantes et predicantes verbum dei. in quorum sermonibus vicia ea quibus laborant recenseantur/ arguantur/ et tanquam oculis subijciantur/ profecto scintilla interioris hominis et cordis sinderesis commouetur ad agnoscendum iniquos actus suos aduersus instituta diuina ac formulam religionis christiane/ cogitantque se eo viuendi genere ad eternam (que pie iuste sancteque versantibus/ promissa christianis est) vitam peruenire non posse. ex qua admonitione ac motu/ deinde cogitatione/ sepe inordinatam/ et sancte pieque religioni reluctantem vitam abijciunt. aliud viuendi genus adsumunt reformant in melius mores/ quos si non audissent sermones serios/ ad eas nunquam venissent cogitationes/ nunquam erroris sui meminissent/ imo recte se agere et egisse opinarentur omnia. quandoquidem illud ex sapientissimo salomone legimus/ audiens sapiens sapientior erit/ quid ergo insipiens/modo docibilis sit/ faciet Ita apud iudeos est/ sunt illis vt ceteris gentibus rationalia ingenia/

[p. 20; fol. b4ᵛ]

turlighe aff læræ oc vnderstandilsæ som andræ mennisckæ. Then
sedwanæ som the haffue fanghet oc seedt aff theris foreldernæ
Then efftherfylghe the/ the tro oc myenæ fuldkommelighen/ at the
gøre al ting wel oc inthet ildæ. Uaræ thet suo at thessæ oc swodanæ stycker kasthes them fore vti predicken eller andhen stedz 5
huar man fwndæ them/ met spee/ spot oc forhaaning/ vthen al twi
ffuel the komme til them sielff/ swo at then ild som liggher qualdt
vndher ascken/ han sculle wel tendhes igen. The sculle wæl
tencke huer wed sig See then naturlighe log oc institut/ hwar
høffuisckelighen oc huar bequemmelighen biwder hwn oc paamin 10
dher huad man scal gøre oc huad man scal ladhæ. See/ wij ha
ffue eth alminneligt budord/ thu scalt aldrig gøre noghen andhen
then deel som thu icke wilt haffue aff hannum/ huar foræ bandher
thu huer dag oc formaledider the cristnæ mennisckæ/ effther thi
thw wilt ickæ thet haffuæ aff them. Oc wedst thw wel/ ath 15
the hwer dag bedhæ for tig til gwd. Sidhen sculdhe the wel
swo tenckæ vti theris hiarthæ huer wed sig. See the fæm mo
ysi bøgher. Offuersøg alle prophethernæ. Offuer wæg thyn
eghen stadt oc reghementhæ/ thynæ rabier the liwffuæ at tigh
oc at oss alle om wor messia/ heltz forti/ at then tiid som the ha 20
ffue sagt oss aff i hwilken wij scudæ frelses/ hwn er fram gan
ghen. O hwar vslighen æræ wij beswegnæ. Hwar æræ wore
prophether/ inghen aff them haffuer waret blant oss i manghæ
aar/ oc swo framdhelis.
Uaræ thet end suo/ at the icke aldelis strax kwnnæ wendes 25
oc wennyes aff theris ondhæ wæghæ oc wildfarilsæ/ tha scullæ
the wel allighewel suo lengtelighen met tidhen tenkæ them ræt
om kring och wendæ sig til gudh/ nar som theris conscientier

20: 3   oc] ac, *Cph.*
20: 10 bequemmelighen] bequemmeligheu, *Cph.*
20: 18 thyn] thyn e, *Cph.*

20: 21 hwilken] hwillen, *Cph.*
20: 25 Uaræ] Uara, *Cph.*
20: 26 ondhæ] andha, *Cph.*

English translation:
[...] naturally able to learn and understand as other people. They follow the custom that they have taken from and seen in their parents. They believe and are convinced that they are doing

only good and nothing bad. If they are reproached for these and similar things in a sermon (or in some other place where they are to be found) using mockery, ridicule and insults, then they will without doubt come to their senses, just like it is possible for the fire that lies smouldering under ash to reignite by itself. They will each think to him- or herself: See the natural law and teaching! How it modestly and rightly instructs and reminds us what we should do and what we should avoid. Look! We have a common commandment, 'Do not do unto others what you would not want them to do to you' [*Leviticus 19: 18*], so why then do you curse and condemn Christians every day when you do not want the same treatment from them? And you know very well that every day they pray for you to God. Then they will each think in his or her heart: Look into the books of Moses! Search through all the prophets! Consider your own situation and regime. Your rabbis are lying to you and all of us about our Messiah, not least when they talk about the time in which we are to be saved, it has already passed! Oh, how unkindly we have been deceived! Where are our prophets? None of them has been among us for so many years, and so forth.

If it happens that they cannot be converted straightaway and weaned from their evil ways and error, they will still in good time come to their senses and turn to God when their consciences […]

Latin original:

sunt illis vt ceteris gentibus rationalia ingenia/ neque tanta barbaries/ qualis vel lestrigonum vel ciclopum aut triballorum huiusmodique hominum apud historias describitur. que a parentibus eis et maioribus tradita est consuetudo/ eam sectantur/ credunt eos recte omnia/ nihil praue aut perperam egisse. Si autem illis in sermonibus et concionibus hec obijcerentur [p. 20; fol. c2ᵛ] commemorarentur cum ridiculo etiam et contemptu/ haud dubium redirent ad cor/ incenderetur igniculus pressus cinere/ apud semetipsos dicerent/ aspice naturale ius et institutum/ quam rationabiliter quam honeste iubeat et vetet/ que facienda/ que fugienda sint doceat et moneat Vnum communione omnibus generale sine scripto notum preceptum est quod tibi non vis fieri/ alteri ne feceris/ quid ergo quotidie maledicis christiano/ quando minime velles a christiano tibi id fieri/ qui et ipse orat pro te vt scis. Postea quoque apud animum suum reuoluerent et cogitarent/ loquerenturque in cordibus suis apud se quisque. Aspice quinque libros moisis[51]/ scrutare[52] prophetas omnes/ status et regimen tuum Rabi tui mentientur tibi/ et omnibus nobis de messia nostro/ quando tempus de quo locuti sunt. id est in quo liberandi essemus/ preterijt. O quam misere et miserabiliter decepti sumus. Vbi sunt prophete nostri/ quorum nemo intra annos plures inter nos fuit etcetera. Etsi fortasse non omnino mox a suis prauis consuetudinibus abusionibus/ ritu/ perfidia desisterent/ ac descicerent/ paulatim tamen in dies stimulante eos consciencia monitis et preceptis informata/

---

51. moisis] Moysi, *Nur*.
52. scrutare] scutare, *Nur*.

[p. 21; fol. b5ʳ]

swo pregedæ them. The*t* vare forti møghet nyttheligt/ bequem*t*
oc gud taknem*m*eligt/ at iødernes bog som the kalle Talmot
Sameledis theris Rabiers falsckæ och swigefuldæ bøgher i
hwilke the haffue suodanæ faafe*n*ghæ bøner oc formaledidel-
ser/ m*et* ma*n*ghe vbehørligæ stycker/ the toghes fran th*em* oc for   5
derffuedæs plat i gru*n*dhen. Forwthen al twiffuel the sculdhæ
wel met tidh*en* alstinges forgløm*æ* suodanæ theris vwaner so*m*
ieg nogh*et* haffuer sagt aff tilfforn. Myt hoff er alstinghes til
gud/ at vti en stacket tijd (om suoda*n* flijd oc dilige*n*tz giordhes
wed th*em*) tha sculle the fuldkom*m*eligen om kring wendes til   10
then hellighæ cristelighæ troo.

¶ The*t* iiij artickel/ om huad ondt/ huat forfa*n*g oc ska
dhæ ther kan hendhæ cristnæ me*n*nisckæ baadhæ till lijff
oc siæl/ om the boo oc omgaass for møgh*et* m*et* iødherne

Effther the articlæ som nw sagt eræ/ vil ieg talæ om   15
then store faræ cristnæ me*n*niskæ staa om the idelige*n*
haffue omge*n*gelsæ m*et* iødernæ. Er th*et* swo at then
slem*m*æ vbørlighæ sedwanæ som iødernæ haffue kan sckadhæ
th*em* suo møgh*et* (thi at then brøst som the haffue i th*et* at the icke
høræ prediken hwn gør th*em* then skade) at the bliffue alstædis   20
suo i theris ondscaff. Huat scal ieg tha sighæ om th*em* som altijd haffuer omge*n*gelsæ m*et* th*em*/ huar møgh*et* ondt oc stor faræ mwnæ th*em* vpaa henghæ. Effther thi at iødernes mesthæ
studiu*m* er/ at the ku*n*ne forstøræ then hellighæ cristnæ troo aff all
theris macht m*et* subtilighæ argume*n*t mod simplæ cristnæ me*n*ni-   25
sckæ/ eller i hues andræ modhæ the kwnnæ. Ieg troer fulkom-

English translation:
[…] have pricked them. It would therefore be very useful, apt and godly to confiscate the Jews' book which they call the Talmud as well as their rabbis' false and deceitful books in which they have such vain prayers and curses with many shameful passages, and to destroy them completely. Without any doubt they would then in time completely forget their bad habits as I have mentioned earlier. My hope is entirely in God, and, if we use hard work and diligence on them, they will before long be completely converted to the holy Christian faith.

The fourth chapter: About what evil, what injury and harm can physically and spiritually happen to Christians if they live and associate too much with the Jews.

Having told these chapters, I now want to talk about the great danger Christians are in if they associate freely with the Jews. If it is the case that the evil shameful custom that the Jews keep can harm them so much (as it is their failure to listen to sermons that does them this harm) that they will forever remain in their evil, what then shall I say about those [Christians] who always have dealings with them? So much evil and danger hangs over them, as Jews study for the most part so that they can confuse the holy Christian faith with all their might using fancy arguments against simple Christian people or in whatever other way they can. I am [...]

Latin original:

paulatim tamen in dies stimulante eos consciencia monitis et preceptis informata/ magis magisque vie salutis appropinquarent[53]. Esset preterea vtile certe honestum et deo gratum opus/ vt iudeorum talmot[54]/ Rabique ipsorum falsi ac deceptorij libri/ item in quibus inanes et friuole[55] precationes et execrationes perscripte sunt/ abusionesque varie/ ab eis auferrentur/ et delerentur ac exstirparentur[56] omnino. Haud dubium cuiquam/ quin tempore/ abusionum suarum obliuiscerentur penitus vt et alijs locis aliquando dixi. Integra mihi spes est et fiducia in deum saluatorem meum/ eos breui opitulante diuina gracia his adhibitis humanitus curis et [p. 21; fol. c3ʳ] studijs/ que dicta sunt/ relictis tenebris errorum suorum ad lumen christiane religionis et fidei venturos esse.

¶ Quarta particula in qua ostenditur quid mali offense et damni ijs[57] immineat christianis in anima et corpore/ qui iudeis cohabitant et nimis familiariter cum eis conuersantur

Attingamus nunc rem aliam. expositi sunt vani ritus nonnulli iudeorum de confessionis preparatione/ de ipsa confessione et absolutione. postea quare hec proposita sunt/ quibus subijciendum videtur/ quid periculi instet christianis nimis familiariter cum iudeis agentibus. Nam si illis sua praua consuetudo tantum (vt diximus) obest/ abstinentia audicionis verbi diuini ex ore doctorum et probatorum in religione christiana virorum sic induratos aut reddit/ aut deserit/ quid putabimus cum illis verbo et opere versantibus imminere mali/ cum eorum studium sit profligare pro viribus christianam fidem siue suasibus/ siue verisimilibus[58] apud simplices argumentis/ siue quo alio modo. Credo ego/

---

53. appropinquarent] approquinquarent, *Col.*; appropinquarent, *Nur.*
54. talmot] talmut, *Nur.*
55. friuole] freuole, *Col.*; friuole, *Nur.*
56. exstirparentur] ex/|stirparentur, *Col.*; exstirparentur, *Nur.*
57. damni ijs] damnijs, *Nur.*
58. verisimilibus] virisimilibus, *Col.*; verisimilibus, *Nur.*

[p. 22; fol. b5ᵛ]

melighen at hwar som iøder the boo vti nogræ cristnæ købstæ
der eller stæder/ tha sculle the meræ faræ/ skadæ/ oc frestelser
indføræ paa cristne menniske end dieffuelen sculle gøre/ thi ath
dieffuelsens festtelsæ hun kan aldrig varæ suo idelig som iødernes. Er hun end suo idelig/ tha kan man snarligen bort elthæ hen- 5
næ met thet hellighe korsis teghen/ met hwilkit man icke kan bort
elthæ theris indbondhenæ sckalkhet The ladæ sig varæ møghet
hellighe/ oc met suodan løgnafftig hellighet haffue the huer dag
theris omgengelsæ met the cristnæ oc eræ dog øgnæ scalkæ The
haffue manghe samtalæ met them om troen oc om eth gudeligt le 10
ffnet Fornemme the tha noghen cristhen som wil bindæ sig til ordet
met them oc er icke fornwfftig oc klog/ eller oc then som icke vil
oc the dog kunne drage ther til met subtilig snack/ suo taghe the
manghe stycker aff biblien i thet gamble testamentæ oc settæ fram
for hannum/ hwilke ther neest liwdæ paa theris log. Oc paa suo 15
danæ manghe article eræ the møghet ferdughæ/ heltz forti at af
førstæ begyndilsæ oc barndom tha læræ the theris børn i swo
dane articlæ/ at the sculle widhe at disputeræ met cristnæ. Thi
skeer thet tijt oc offte at manghe cristnæ som icke wel eræ lerdæ
the offuerwindes lettelighen aff suodane iødernes argument oc 20
faldæ i kettherij mod troen/ suo at mangæ aff them tracteræ hemelighen met iødernæ/ endog at the tordæ icke openbarlighen for
liiffs faræ skyld Men er thet suo at the komme i disputatz met no
ghen cristhen som wel er lærdt oc wed biblien som thet sig bør/
tha sighe iødernæ suo. Uij ville icke disputeræ/ wij ville ladhe 25
huer bliffue vti then troo som gud sckiwdher hannum i hiarthet. O
huar møghet ketterij oc huar møghel vildfarelse gøre the scalkæ i blant thet cristnæ folk. O huar manghæ sielæ forraadhæ the

---

English translation:
[…] completely convinced that wherever Jews live in Christian cities or towns, they cause more danger, harm and temptations for Christians than the Devil does, because the Devil's hold can never be as complete as the that of the Jews. If it is ever that strong, then it can quickly be driven away with the sign of the Holy Cross, with which one cannot drive away their [*the Jews'*] sly

malicious behaviour. They pretend to be very holy and using this deceitful holiness they associate every day with Christians, and yet they are blatant scoundrels. They [*the Jews*] have many discussions with them [*the Christians*] about faith and a godly life. If they sense that some Christian wants to engage in conversation with them and he is not sensible or clever, or even someone who does not want to but who they can draw into conversation using fancy talk, then they take many passages from the Bible (in the Old Testament) and expound them in accordance with their law. And they are prepared in these many passages since they teach these passages to their children from earliest childhood, so that they will be able to dispute with Christians. So it very often happens that many Christians who are not very learned are easily defeated by these Jews' arguments and fall into heresy against the faith; many of them secretly do deals with the Jews even though they would not dare do so publicly as they hold their lives dear. But should it happen that they [*the Jews*] start a dispute with a Christian who is very learned and is familiar with the Bible as is proper, then the Jews say, 'We do not want to argue. We want each man to remain in the faith that God has shot into his heart.' Oh, how much heresy and how much delusion do these villains cause among the Christians! Oh, how many souls do they betray […]

Latin original:

Credo ego/ vbi iudei in christianis vrbibus et vicis habitant/ maiore eos damno afficere periculoque maiore illis quibus commorantur esse/ quam diabolus sit/ cuius tentatio neque tam sedula est et si sit/ facilius signo crucis in qua passus est saluator noster disturbari potest/ quam horum blandi nequamque sermones sibilis proximi serpentinis Offerunt se in specie quidem et vmbra sanctitatis/ subque ea hipocrisi/ quotidie cum christianis versantur/ agunt cum illis familiaria colloquia/ preter cetera que communiter (vt fit) negocia inter eos tractantur/ de religione et fide tractant. si tamen comperiunt christianos seu plures seu vnum quemuis indoctum volentem cum eis disceptare/ aut nolentem pellicientes/ afferunt loca ex biblio/ que pro ipsis ipsorumque religione sint/ quorum copiam habent/ illisque ea in promptu sunt/ quando etiam iuniores et liberos suos a primis (vt aiunt)[59] vnguiculis docent [p. 22; fol. c3ᵛ] et diligenter instituunt in lectione veteris instituti/ ad disputandum et disceptandum cum christianis. vnde euenit vt huiusmodi christiani facile vincantur argumentis eorum/ coganturque cedere/ et in heresim dilabantur ex eorum verisimilibus apud indoctos scilicet allatis pro ipsis aduersum nos testimonijs/ incipiantque cum iudeis clam/ quod palam non audent penarum metu sentire Si autem doctum quem christianum sacrarum litterarum atque in biblio exercitatum offenderint et de religione et fide oratio suscepta sit/ aiunt/ nolumus disputare et argumentari/ maneat quisque in fide sua/ quam menti sue[60] inseruit deus. O quot hereses et errores excitant/ et mouent hi inter christianos/ pluresque ad infernum seducunt animas/

---

59. aiunt)] aiunt, *Nur.*
60. sue] suo, *Nur.*

[p. 23; fol. b6ʳ]

til helffuedis affgrwnd. The æræ verræ end dieffuelen/ thi at
han forstører icke menniscken met then hellighæ sckrifft oc ickæ
gør falsck forclaring paa hennæ/ men thet gøre iødernæ. Dieffue
len han kommer icke mennischen i fald/ frestelsæ/ eller vildfarelsæ
i thet han tagher sig noghen menniskes røst til vthen thet skeer siel- 5
dhen/ thi troer ieg fwlkommelighen i blandt manghe andræ stycker som ieg troer/ at dieffuelen kan icke fuldelighen faa macht
offuer eth cristhen menniscke vthen han haffuer noghen iødes hielp
ther til/ besynderlighen i suodanæ modhæ. Thw kant wel ten
kæ huar møghet ondt oc huar møghet got leffuendhæ røst oc dag 10
lig omgengelsæ the kwnne gøræ. Item. Iødernæ them nøges
icke ther met allenisthæ/ at the kunnæ forkastæ cristnæ menniskis
siæl/ men the studeræ dag oc nat ther paa at the kunnæ gøre them
sckadhe paa theris tymelighe godtz/ met aagher oc al andhen
falskhet i huat modhe the kunnæ met altsomstørsth subtilighet/ 15
hwilkit dieffuelen icke gør/ endog at han er alsomstørst fighen
dæ. Han leggher sig alleniste effther at fortabæ sielen/ men i huat
modhe han yderst kan tha hielper han at formeræ oc forøghe pen-
ninghæ/ rigdom/ gwld oc godtz. Item/ end haffue iødernæ en
andhen ondscaff i them/ met hwilken the offuergaa dieffuelen/ 20
thet er at the ingeledz mwghe høre Ihesu benedidæ naffn/ icke hel
der iomfru Marie naffn. The forsmaa woræ kirker/ the haffue huer dag nogræ besynderlighe formaledidelser nar the hø
ræ thesse forbeneffndæ werdughe oc hellighe naffn som liwdæ
swo paa hebraisckæ. Gymach schinophe sichroe. Thet er swo 25
møghet paa dansckæ Ue wordhæ tig/ oc we wordhæ hannum
som noghen tiidh kommer thet naffn i hwgh eller gør thet æræ
oc werdughet. Uort sacramenthæ Ihesu benedidæ leghemæ/

23: 5   noghen] nohhen, *Cph.*
23: 16–17 fighen|dæ] figheu|dæ, *Cph.*

English translation:

[…] to the abyss of hell! They are worse than the Devil, because he does not corrupt people using the Holy Scriptures and does not expound them deceitfully, but this is what the Jews do. The Devil does not lead people into committing sin, into temptation or error by using a human's voice — that happens but rarely. Therefore, along with many other articles which I believe, I am convinced of this: that the Devil cannot acquire full power over a Christian unless he has the help of some Jew to do so, especially in these ways. You can well imagine how much evil and how much good a living voice and daily contact can do. Likewise, the Jews are not satisfied with just damning Christians' souls, but they study day and night so that they can cause damage to their worldly goods by means of usury and all other kinds of trickery in whatever way they can with the greatest subtlety, which the Devil does not do even though he is the greatest enemy of all. He seeks only to damn souls, but in whatever way he can he helps to augment and increase money, wealth, gold and goods. Furthermore, the Jews contain yet another evil in which they exceed the Devil: they cannot bear to hear Jesus' holy name or the Virgin Mary's name. They disdain our churches. Every day when they hear the aforementioned venerable and holy names, they use special curses which sound like this in Hebrew, '*Yimaḥ šemo wezichro.*' In Danish it means, 'Woe betide you and woe betide him who should ever remember that name and do it honour and treat it with dignity!' Our sacrament, the holy body of Jesus […]

Latin original:

pluresque ad infernum seducunt animas/ quam diabolus/ qui scripturas non exprimit et declarat falso Non humana nisi rarissime loquitur voce/ vt sermonis ei cum homine communio sit non comi et amico gestu/ affectibusve vtitur ad hominem decipiendum. Et ego quidem inter cetera non puto verum fidelemque christianum/ ex diabolica tantummodo tentatione/ absque adiumento iudei in totum sensum reprobum et perfidiam et desperationem cadere posse. quid enim credis/ quid viua vox et quotidiana consuetudo potest. Sed iam non solum iudei querunt christianorum animas perdere/ sed et rebus et facultatibus eorum damna inferre student noctes et dies/ ac inferunt per vsuras alias fraudes et dolos quoscunque comminisci possunt/ quod diabolus quamquam sit prauissimus non facit animam magis ille cupit perdere/ etiam si queat augendo pocius opes. inest iudeis et alia pre diabolo malignitas naturaque prauior Nomen iesu et benedicte matris sue marie audire nullatenus sustinent/ ecclesias nostras abhorrent habent execrationes quotidianas/ quas efferunt/ vbi hec sacra nomina audierint hebraice ita sonantes gymach schmophe sichroe quod latine dicitur/ ve tibi et ve illi qui [p. 23; fol. c4^r] nominis eius vnquam meminerit. quin etiam cum eucharistie sacramento/

[p. 24; fol. b6ᵛ]

thet kalle the en sckidhen lort. Oc nar som the see at nogre aff
woræ presther gaa til noghet siwgt mennisckæ at giffue hannum
gwdz benedidæ leghome/ tha sighæ the nogræ ord paa hebra
isckæ swo liwdendes paa dansckæ. See/ then haffue the va
ret borthæ oc besckit Nar the see noghen stæd thet hellighe kor 5
ses teghen staa vp reest til wor herris Ihesu Cristi død oc pynes
i hwg kommelsæ/ thet formaledidæ the strax Findhæ the oc thet
hellighæ korses teghen paa iordhen encthen sckreffuit eller oc
giort/ thet traadæ the vndher theris fødder oc brydæ thet søn
dher. Swo eræ the werræ end dieffuelen/ endog at han icke 10
ghernæ eller met god wilghe hører Ihesu naffn eller Marie
naffn/ oc seer thet hellighe korses teghen mod syn wilghæ/ allighewel forbandher han them icke som iødernæ øræ/ ickæ
heller them som paa kalle them/ icke brydher han oc korsens
teghen søndher. Cristi naffn thet kalle the paa hebraiscke tho 15
loi/ thet er paa dansckæ/ then som war hengt i galghen. The
kalle thet oc swo iesche nozore/ thet er paa dansckæ swo møghet som en bedrægheræ eller then som sckadhe gør. Mariam
kalle the thlue/ thet er paa dansckæ/ hwn som war vphengt
Uoræ helghen kalle the kendeschim/ thet er paa dansckæ/ v- 20
wighedæ oc formalediedhæ. Uor kirkæ kalle the tifflos eller
toifos/ thet er paa danskæ/ eth hwss som er forsmæligt oc dwer inthet. Nar som en iødæ wil beswighæ noghen met syn eedh
tha swer han om Crist oc hanss modher mariam. Altijd bedhæ
the at wij cristnæ sculle faa modgang oc vløckæ Nar som the 25
tha høræ at wij cristnæ haffue krig oc orlog/ encthen mellom
oss sielff eller met noghen andhen vtwortis/ oc at wij haffue noghen modgang/ tha øræ the them gantze gladæ/ oc blant andræ

English translation:

[…] they call 'a filthy shit'. And whenever they see some of our priests going to [*the home of*] a sick man to give him the blessed body of God, then they say some words in Hebrew that in Danish mean, 'Look! That's one that they have just gone and defiled with shit!' Whenever they see a site on which the sign of the Holy Cross has been raised in remembrance of the death and suffering of our Lord Jesus Christ, they curse it immediately. And if they see the sign of the Holy Cross either drawn or made on the ground, they tread it underfoot and smash it up. Thus they are worse than the Devil. Even though he does not like to hear Jesus' name or Mary's name and only looks at the sign of the Cross against his will, he still does not curse them in the way that the Jews do, nor [*does he curse*] those who invoke them [*Jesus, Mary and the Holy Cross*], nor does he smash up the sign of the cross. They call the name of Christ in Hebrew, '*taluy*', which in Danish means 'he who was hanged in a gallows'. They also call him '*Yešu (ha)noẓri*', which in Danish means the same as a 'charlatan' or 'one who does harm'. They call Mary '*teluyah*', which in Danish is 'she who is hanged'. They call our saints '*qedešim*', which in Danish is 'unconsecrated' and 'cursed'. They call our church '(*beit*) *tiflut*' or '(*beit*) *tofet/toyfes*', which in Danish is 'a house that is worthy of contempt and good for nothing'. Whenever a Jew wishes to trick someone with his oath, then he swears on Christ and his mother Mary. They are always praying that we Christians should have hardship and misfortune. Whenever they hear that we Christians are in a conflict or at war, either amongst ourselves or against someone from outside [*Christendom*] and that we are experiencing hardship, they are greatly pleased and among other […]

Latin original:

quin etiam cum eucharistie sacramento/ quod ipsi immundum stercus blasphemissime nominant/ ad egrotum aliquem christianum cibo illo spiritali comfortandum itur/ dicunt omnes hec verba prescripta men hat mettamme gewest. off men hat den zeueltamme gegeuen[61].[62] id est ille defedatus est. Cum forte eos crucem preterire necesse est in memoriam crucis christi positam. quouis loco/ quam perosi maxime sunt/ et eius conspectum non ferunt/ ei maledicunt/ si in terra compererint figuram crucis ex stramine aut ligno/ quod interdum euenit fictam procalcant et perfringunt. quare deteriores diabolo sunt[63]/ qui licet iniquo animo audiat et ferat nomen christi iesu benedicte matris sue marie et signum sancte crucis aspiciat inuitus/ non tamen execratur et maledicit ijs[64]/ qui hec sancta nomina inuocant/ nec cruces ipse perfringit. Nomen christi hebraice tholoi id est suspensum vocant item iesche nozore quod est nocens seu damnificans aut seductor mariam nominant thlue/ id est eam que suspenderit. sanctos nostros nuncupant prophanos et execrabiles/ quod hebraice dicitur kendeschim. Edes nostras sacras dicunt tifflos seu toifos id est domum contemptibilem et perituram. Si quando fallere et peierare volunt iudei/ asseuerant verba et iuramento firmant per nomen christi et matris sue marie. Ad hec optant et precantur omni christiano populo et nomini omne infortunium. cum audiunt nos christianos inter nosmet/ aut aliunde bella persecutiones tribulationes et aduersa queuis pati vrgerique malis/ tum ipsi gaudent et exultant inter cetera dicentes gracias agimus deo/

---

61. gegeuen] gegeben, *Nur*.
62. men hat mettamme gewest. off men hat den zeueltamme gegeuen] 'one has been defiling or one has given the impure dung'. See discussion in ch. 3.
63. sunt] suut, *Col.*; sunt, *Nur*.
64. ijs] hijs, *Nur*.

talæ sighæ the swo. Uij tackæ oc loffue gud/ heltz forti at the
cristnæ haffue nw suo møghet at taghe ware for them sielff/ at
the glømæ oss. nw scal snarlighen vor Messias komme/ meth
manghe andræ atsckillighæ vbeqwemmæ ord. Uildæ the end si
ghe ney ther foræ/ tha maa man lettelighen offuerwindæ them
met theris egne tidhe bøgher som the hwer dag lessæ vti. Thet
tæ er theris omgengelse i blant the cristnæ. Al theris acht er at
the kunne bedræghæ/ beswighæ/ forderffue/ formaledidhæ och
nedtryckæ cristnæ mennisckæ til liiff och siæl Swo warlighen
scal man leffuæ oc omgaass met them/ ligherwiis som man haff
dhæ ild vti syt sckiød/ eller en leffuendhæ hugorm vti syn arm
at bewaræ oc gømæ.

¶ Thet v artickel er en paa myndelsæ til herrer/ Førsther. Prelater. Købstædher oc alle andræ cristnæ menni-
sckæ/ som tilladhæ oc tilstædæ at iødernæ sculle suodan
theris herrenscked bedriffue oc fuldkommæ vti theris land
och stædher.

HErrer Førsther Prelater Frigbornæ mend Borg
mestheræ Raad oc Meenæ almwghæ vti christhen
hedhen/ huar som heltz och vndher huess herredø-
mæ Iøder the æræ oc boo. Myn ydmyghe oc gu
dhelighe bøn er til ether alle/ at huess ieg nw taler paa then hel
lighe cristne trooss oc cristne mennisckes formering oc besthæ thet
sckal inghen taghe mig til mistyckæ eller wendhæ mig til thet
wersthæ Ieg tal icke met thet skiel/ at ieg holdher mig god at
læræ noghen herræ oc førsthæ aff noghen bereffuenscaff/ holden
des mig wiseræ/ clogheræ/ eller fornwfftheræ end noghen an-

English translation:

[…] utterances they say, 'We thank and praise God, especially because the Christians now have so much to occupy themselves with that they forget about us. Our messiah will now soon come', and many other malicious words. If they ever deny this, then they can easily be defeated with their own prayer books that they read every day. This is how they deal with Christians. Their sole intention is to be able to deceive, trick, corrupt, curse and oppress Christians, both as regards their lives and their souls. One should live and deal with them as one would hold and keep a fire in one's lap or a living viper in one's arms.

The fifth chapter is an admonition to lords, princes, prelates, cities[ii] and all other Christian people who allow and permit the Jews to pursue and fulfil such villainy in their countries and towns.

Lords, princes, prelates, freeborn men, mayors, councils and common people in Christendom wherever you may be and under whose dominion the Jews exist and live: my humble and devout request to you all is that what I now speak for the growth and best of the holy Christian faith and Christians, no-one shall treat me unworthily or distort my words. I am not speaking because I think myself in a position to lecture a lord or prince on any situation nor do I consider myself wiser, cleverer or more sensible than anyone […]

[ii] cities] *Literally 'market towns'; Presumably city-leaders, councillors or such people are meant here.*

Latin original:

gracias agimus deo/ christiani ita suis impliciti et grauati curis et negocijs sunt/ vt nostri nunc obliuiscantur Nunc breui veniet messias noster/ cum multis alijs verbis in hanc et deteriorem sentientiam. que si negare velint/ facillime conuincentur et coarguentur ex quotidianis libris oratorijs/ quibus vtuntur. hec est eorum inter christianos con[p. 24; fol. c4^v]uersatio/ hic fauor/ hic amor/ deceptionum fraudum execrationum maledictorum in anime corporis et rerum perditionem plena perniciosaque cupido. sic illis conuiuitur/ vt siquis ignem in sinu aut serpentem in gremio foueat

¶Particula quinta admonitoria ad christianos principes populos ciuitates/ qui iudeos recipiunt/ et tuentur in sua illos nequicia viuere sinentes.

Cvm omni veneratione honorem prefatus et veniam paucis alloquar principes/ nobiles et populos atque respublicas christianas/ sub quibus et vbi iudei morantur et agunt/ quod religionis et hominim christianorum amore/ a me dictum misello nemo iniquo animo ferat/ supplex oro.

[p. 26; fol. c1ᵛ]

dhen sig/ men allenisthæ at paa myndhæ herrer/ førsther/ och
andræ cristnæ menniscka the fwlæ iødhers ondscaff/ farlighæ om
gengelsæ/ falsck oc swig/ spee oc spot/ met atsckillig forderff
som the nat oc dag haffue i hwg/ wilghæ oc sind/ at wille be
kwmræ oc forderffue cristnæ menniscka met baadhæ til liiff oc 5
siæl. Swo er thet i sandhet i godhæ herrer/ ath iødhernæ the
haffuæ theris wærelsæ vti ethers herrædømæ/ endog at i wel
widhæ the æræ gwdz oc then hellighæ kirkis fighendæ. Ickæ
taler iegh end swo møghet om iødhernæ i sigh sielff/ men iegh
myen thet storæ vbegribelighæ oc vhørlighæ herrenscket som 10
the bedriffuæ vti ethers land/ herrædømæ oc stædher. I taghæ
them til ether/ i forswaræ them mod gwd oc troen/ thet goræ i
altsamen for en føffwæ oc en syndhelig penning som i kwndhæ
haffue aff them oc nydhæ them ath/ hwilken penning the fwlæ
oc slemme hwndhæ faa oc afftwinghæ ethers egnæ fattughe vn 15
dherdaner cristnæ menniske/ met aagher oc andræ manghæ at
sckillighe falsckæ fwnd. Thi at the haffue inthet at giffue/ v-
then allenisthæ hwes the swo kwnnæ atspørghæ meth theris
scalkhet oc falscke fwnd tenker ether om vti ethers hiarter
at hwar som the giffue ether en gyllenæ for theris tribwt och 20
sckat/ ther besckatthæ the igen eth hundredæ gyllenæ aff ethers
fattughæ vndersaathæ/ swo at baadæ landhenæ oc fattughæ
cristnæ the forderffues ther aff/ och tiit och offthe komme til swo
stor armod oc fattugdom at gud maa sig ther offuer forbarme
Giffuer inderlighen acth ther vpaa/ om i æræ gudz/ then helli- 25
ghe cristelighæ troes/ then hellighe kirckis/ oc fattughe cristnæ
mennisckis retferdughæ fogheder oc forstandheræ/ nar i see suo
gemmen fingræ met them/ oc tilstædhæ suodane vbehørlighe the

26: 16   andræ] audræ, *Cph.*
26: 28   vbehørlighe] vbehørlenghe, *Cph.*

English translation:

[…] else, but I do so *[i.e. speak out]* only to remind lords, princes and other Christian people of the sordid Jews' evilness, dangerous association, deception and fraud, mockery and ridicule, numerous acts of harm that they commit day and night and have in their thoughts, intention and mind that they wish to oppress and corrupt Christians both physically and spiritually. So, good sirs, it is the truth that the Jews are present in your dominions, even though you know well that they are the enemies of God and the holy Church. I am not talking so much about the Jews themselves, but rather I mean the great incomprehensible and senseless villainy that they pursue in your countries, provinces and towns. You take them in; defend them against God and the faith. You do all this for a few sinful pennies which you can take from them and enjoy. These unclean and evil dogs obtain and extort this money from your own poor Christian subjects by means of usury and many other deceitful tricks. As they have nothing to give except whatever they can acquire through their roguery and deceitful inventions, think again in your hearts: for each guilder they give you in tribute and tax, they in turn tax your poor subjects a hundred guilders. In this way, countries and poor Christian people are harmed, and very often they end up in such wretchedness and poverty that God must have mercy on them. Consider deeply whether you are the rightful governors and representatives of God, the holy Christian faith, the holy Church and poor Christian people when you turn a blind eye to them [*the Jews*], and allow such improper […]

Latin original:

non enim vt docens aut precipiens loquor/ sed inimicus[65] non iudeis sed iudaice nequicie peruicacie et rabide auaricie blasphemeque[66] lingue/ nostramque vicem dolens/ quibus noctes et dies insidiantur/ vt rapiant ac diripiant/ quod partim nostro permissu fit Vos inquam christiani principes ciuitates ceterique quando quidem in vestris dominijs dicionibus et locis iudei hostes dei et fidei ac religionis nostre commorantur/ vosque illos recipitis/ defenditis/ et tuemini propter paruum temporalium bonorum lucrum et commodum scelestum/ quod ab illis consequimini/ quod sanguinarij illi canes ex sudoribus et laboribus pauperum subditorum vestrorum emunxerunt/ et exuxerunt/[67] neque enim aliunde quod dent acipiunt/ quam per questum vsurarum et fraudes/ cogitate in cordibus vestris vbi vobis illi vnum porrigunt aureum et dant quasi pro tributo/ ipsi a vestris subditis centum extrahunt et accipiunt/ qua ex re terre et homines ita depauperantur et exhauriuntur/ vt vel ipse in celis deus condicionem pauperum hominum quos fenore suo iudei premunt et perdunt/ miseretur. Attendite preterea/ si modo fideles estis [p. 25; fol. c5ʳ] prefecti ecclesie christiane. contumelias contemptus blasphemias execrationes maledicta. que ingerunt.

---

65. inimicus] in mi cos, *Nur.*
66. blasphemeque] blasphemieque, *Nur.*
67. emunxerunt/ et exuxerunt/] emunxerunt., *Nur.*

[p. 27; fol. c2ʳ]

ris gerningher/ met suodan forhaaning oc wanæræ som the gøre
Cristo gwdz søn/ iomfrw Marie hanss velsignedhæ modher
oc alle gwdz werdughe helghen. Encthen driffuer them vd af
ethers land/ eller oc behindrer oc forbiwdher at swodan the‑
ris formaledidhelsæ och ondscaff icke fram gangher. Heffner
swodant vpaa them/ och stædher them icke at bedriffuæ swo‑
dant aagher och ondscaff. Twingher them til at arbeygdhæ
oc vdgydhæ theris ansichtis sweed for theris fødhæ/ som wij
fattughæ cristnæ mennisckæ gøræ for wort brødh/ hwer effther
syn stadt oc besckickelighet. Twingher oc nødher them til at
høræ gwdz ord (som er predicken) met ydmyghet forwthen al
gensighelsæ/ the motthæ end en tiid kommæ til them sielff. Flier
thet swo/ at i ickæ scullæ waræ forplictughæ at gøræ ræghen‑
scaff paa then ydersthæ domæ dag for theris gerningher.
Ieg syrgher wed thet ieg nw scal sighæ. Ieg wed manghæ
stædher oc købstædher/ i hwilkæ iødhernes bedriff haffuer bæ
dræ framgang end cristnæ mennisckes. The orsaghæ sig oc sigæ
the som foræ oss haffue warit/ the haffue swodant tilladet oc
tilstædt. the kalle iødhernæ icke andhet end theris penninghæ
sæck/ oc sighæ at the æræ en kisthæ/ i hwilken the haffue for‑
waret theris liggendhæ fææ. the nødhæ thet meenæ folk til
at lidhæ them. The tilladhæ och tilstædhæ/ ath the forsamblæ
storæ penninghæ met aagher oc andræ scalkæ fwnd i then mye
ning/ at om behoff giordhes/ tha scullæ theris penninghæ kommæ
theris myenæ stad til gaffn oc prophit.
The orsaghæ sig framdheles och sighæ. Hwad scullæ wij gø
ræ ther til: Iødhernæ the haffwe Keyserens/ Konninghers/ oc
manghæ andræ oc fleræ mechtugæ førsthers breff oc indseglæ

27: 9   fattughæ] fattugha, *Cph.*

English translation:

[…] acts from them with such spite and mockery that they do to Christ, the son of God, Mary, his blessed mother, and all of God's worthy saints. Either drive them out of your lands or also prevent and forbid their cursing and evil from advancing. Take revenge upon them and do not allow them to engage in usury and evil. Force them to work and pour sweat from their faces for their food, as we poor Christians do for our bread each according to his or her position and ability. Force and compel them to hear the word of God (that is preaching) with humility, without any contradictory remarks — at some point they will come to their senses. See to it that you will not be obliged to account for their deeds at the Final Judgement. It saddens me to say what I now must: I know of many towns and cities in which the Jews' exploits are more successful than the Christians'. They [*the city's leaders*] excuse themselves and say, 'Those before us allowed and permitted this to happen!' They call the Jews nothing other than their 'money-bag' and say that they are a 'treasure chest' into which they have placed their treasure. They force the common people to put up with them. They allow and permit them to collect much money through usury and other deceitful tricks in the belief that if it were necessary then their money would benefit and profit the community.

They excuse themselves further and say, 'What can we do about it? The Jews have letters and seals from the emperor, kings and many other powerful princes […]

Latin original:

contumelias contemptus blasphemias execrationes maledicta. que ingerunt. et prophanissimo ore dicunt in christum iesum/ virginem mariam matrem eius sanctos omnes/ ac totum populum christianum/ vna nobiscum Ista scilicet paciemini/ et conniuentibus oculis dissimulabitis. aut pellite eos finibus vestris/ aut hec posse prohibete[68]/ impedite/ vindicate non sinite illos vsuris viuere. facite eos laborare manibus suis/ vt nos christiani quisque pro statu suo facere cogimur. Cogite illos audire verbum dei humiliter/ sine refragatione/ si fortasse aliquando conuertantur ad cor Ne vobis necesse sit in die seueri et districti iudicij apud deum super his et horum causa reddere rationem. dolens refero/ scio ego ciuitates multas et loca in quibus firmius cum iudeis res geritur quam christianis. dicunt/ priores nobis admiserunt eos/ appellantque iudeos erarium suum/ et quasi repositorium thesaurorum. communi populo pretendunt eos sustineri/ pecunias vsuris et nequiciosis modis colligere sini/ vt si forte necessitas aliqua ingruat/ eorum pecunie in vtilitatem publicam dispensentur/ et expendantur Ad hoc aiunt/ Iudeos litteras et sigilla habere regum et imperatorum super admissione et tuicione eorum/

---

68. prohibete] prohibere, *Nur*.

[p. 28; fol. c2ᵛ]

at wij sculle lidhæ them och holdæ them i fred. Uare thet swo
at the giordæ mod swodanæ breff/ tha motthæ kommæ stoer
tretthæ/ stor sckadhæ/ stor vwilghæ och stor vgunsth ther aff: O
hwat blindhæ æræ the som suodant sighæ/ the beteckæ theris
retthæ sckels øgnæ/ oc gøre en scaldhet orsaghæ vti en openba
ræ synd. The æræ icke myndræ orsaghæ til then fattugdom och
vselhet som manghe cristnæ menniskæ vtoffuer gaar/ sameledz
til then forhaaning/ spot oc spee som the gøre gud oc hanss werdi
ghe modher Marie met alle hanss helghen/ end pylatus han
war vti wor herris død/ endog han todhæ synæ hendher then
tiid han sculdæ sighe dommen aff. Sckrifften sigher swo/ sameledis giffuer oc naturligt sckel. Huo som tilladher oc tilstæder
noghen synd at gøris eller bedriffues/ nar han wel kan straffe
och forbiwdæ hennæ/ han scal haffue oc lidhæ suo stor pynæ som
then ther syndhen gør. Uidhæ wij icke fuld wæl/ at lenghæ si
dhen och sameledis nw nylighen/ æræ iødhernæ vd dreffnæ
aff manghæ righer/ land oc stædher. Som er aff Frankæ ri-
ghæ/ aff Hispanien/ aff Nørrenbergh/ aff Ulmæ oc aff manghæ andræ stædher som icke gøris behoff at regnæ vp. Huad
sckadhæ eller vwilghæ haffue the fanghet ther foræ/ eller huo
giffuer them straff ther foræ. Uillæ i icke waræ the førsthæ som
them willæ straffæ/ tha seer ether i speghel paa them. Och li-
gher wiis som the haffuæ giort foræ ether/ swo goræ oc i effter
them i alle modhæ.

¶ Thet vi artickel. Om hwad sag ther er til/ at stwndwm findhes iødher som icke æræ mod wor cristelighæ
troo/ oc allighewel haffue theris forhandlingh met iø-

28: 16   æræ] æra, *Cph.*

English translation:

[... *stating*] that we should put up with them and leave them alone!' If they violated these letters, it would result in a great tumult, much damage, much ill will and much displeasure. Oh! How blind are those who speak like this! They cover their eyes of justice, and make a poor excuse for a blatant sin. They bear no less responsibility for the poverty and wretchednness which affect many Christians as well as the contempt and mockery that are done unto God and his venerable mother Mary and all his saints, than [*Pontius*] Pilate did for the death of our Lord, even though he washed his hands when he gave his verdict. The scripture says this, and natural reason also judges likewise: Whoever allows and permits any sin to be done or committed, when he can reproach or prevent it, is to be punished just as much as the one who committed the sin. Do we not know perfectly well that long ago, and likewise more recently, Jews were driven out of many provinces, lands and towns, such as from France, from Spain, from Nuremberg, from Ulm and from many other towns which need not be listed? What harm or ill will they have had from this? Or who has reproached them for this? Do you not want to be the first to reproach them? Then see them in a looking-glass, and as they have done before you, so you do following them in every way.

The sixth chapter: On the reason why there are sometimes Jews who are not opposed to our Christian faith, and nevertheless associate with [...]

Latin original:

super admissione et tuicione eorum/ si eas violarent posse inde oriri et excrescere non paruam indignationem. motus/ perturbationes/ damna. O hi sunt occecati/ obtegentes[69] oculos rationis recte/ excusantes excusationes in peccatis metuoque illos non minus reos esse destructionis et depauperationis misellorum per iudeos Blasphemie et irrisionis in deum. quam fuerit pilatus mortis christi. quamuis manus lauerit sentenciam capitalem pronunciaturus. Scriptum est enim et naturalis ratio id ita esse iudicat. qui peccatum cum prohibere possit. et im[p. 26; fol. c5ᵛ]-pedire/ fieri permittit/ pari est afficiendus pena vt is qui opere illud perpetrauit. Sed nonne scimus et olim et nuper in multis regnis terris et vrbibus habitauisse iudeos et pulsos[70] esse vt in Francia Hispania Nuremberga Vlma alijsque locis plurimis que nominare non opus est. quid (rogo) his ob eam causam dedecoris aut damni obuenit/ si potestis/ afferte testimonium. quod si recte illi pellendo iudaicam prauitatem egerunt/ vestrum certe est eos imitari/ si priores esse noluistis.

¶ Particula .vj.[71] super eo/ quid sit in causa cum comperiantur iudei qui non auersantur fidem christianam/ tamen in iudaismo perseuerant refugientes baptisma nostrum et aliquid remedij.

---

69. obtegentes] ob te|gentes, *Col.*; ob tegentes, *Nur.*;
70. et pulsos] expulsos, *Nur.*
71. .vj.] sexta, *Nur.*

dhernæ meræ end the cristnæ. Oc sameledis allighe
wel forachtæ dob oc cristhendom met andræ woræ
sacramenther oc cerimonier.

Paa thet siisthæ sckal man widhæ. At manghæ iødher æræ til som holdhæ sig for cristnæ mennisckæ
och æræ dog icke godhæ cristnæ/ thet kommer sigh
swo til. Manghæ sculle findhes blant iødhernæ
som offuergiffue theris slecht oc wenner/ sameledis theris fæder
næ land oc faræ langht hædhen oc ladhæ sig dobæ. Icke forti
at the willæ bliffue godhæ cristnæ/ men at the kunne dess beddræ forsamblæ penninghæ oc leffuæ dess kræseligheræ. Och at
the kunnæ dess beddræ faa lempæ ther til at brwghæ theris kunsther om the kunnæ nogræ. Nar the æræ tha kedhæ aff en stæd
suo faræ the ther aff oc til en anden stæd/ ther ladhæ the sigh
døbæ aff nyg/ mod then hellighe cristnæ reghel/ oc sameledis
atther ther forsamlæ penninghe oc brwghæ hwes the kunne. Si
dhen paa thet siisthæ giffue the sig til iødhernæ igen/ then enæ
effther then andhen oc sighæ swo hwer wed sig. Ieg wil ickæ
lengher waræ cristhen/ theris tro er inthet vthen kettherij/ met
manghe andræ vbeqwemmæ stycker huad the kunnæ paa findæ
Er thet swo at the end bliffue hooss the cristnæ oc holdhæ sigh
for cristnæ mennisckæ/ allighewel er theris hemmelighæ forhand
ling met iødhernæ. Fornemmæ the tha noghen som wil wendhe
sig om til then hellighæ cristnæ troo/ tha staa the ther i modh
aff al theris macht.
Her foræ er thet nyttheligt at see sig wel foræ hwem man gi
ffuer thet werdughæ sacramenthæ som er dob oc cristhendom.

29: 2   forachtæ] forachteræ, *Cph*.

English translation:

[…] *the Jews more than Christians; and yet similarly who despise baptism and Christianity along with our other sacraments and ceremonies.*

Finally, you should know that there are many Jews who pretend to be Christians, but who are not good Christians. This happens in this way: There are many among the Jews who leave their family and friends and likewise their country of birth, and travel from here and have themselves baptised — not because they want to become good Christians, but because by doing so they will be better able to accumulate money and live in greater luxury. And so they can have greater opportunity to use their skills, if they have any. When they tire of one place, then they leave and go to another town. There they have themselves baptised anew against holy Christian rules and likewise accumulate money again and use what they can. Then, in the end, they return to the Jews, one after the other, each saying to himself, 'I don't want to be Christian anymore. Their religion is nothing but heresy,' along with many other improper phrases, whatever they can come up with. If it happens that they stay with the Christians and pretend to be Christians, they still have secret dealings with the Jews. If they learn of someone who wishes to convert to the holy Christian faith, then they oppose this with all their might.

This is why it is useful to be wary of to whom one gives the worthy sacrament that baptism and Christianity are.

Latin original:

tamen in iudaismo perseuerant refugientes baptisma nostrum et aliquid remedij.

Ad postremum hoc quoque adnectendum huic opusculo est. Sunt multi iudei qui in cordibus suis christianam fidem complexi sunt/ nec tamen sacramentum baptismi christiani recipiunt hac maxime occasione Inueniuntur inter iudeos nequam homines/ qui suam deserentes patriam et notos baptizantur alibi/ non vt vere et ex animo christiani esse velint/ sed ad acquirendas pecunias/ viuendum laute et delicate/ exercendas commodius ad questum artes siquas nouere. Vbi in loco vno defatigati sunt/ migrant in alium/ tacitoque priore baptismo iterum ibi baptizantur contra religionis christiane legem et normam Ad coaceruandos nummos. Redeunt iterum tandem ad iudeos. dicit vnus et alter ex istis/ nolo diutius christianus esse Fides eorum nihil est aliud/ quam idololatria[72] cum alijs multis conuicijs et probris. Quod si etiam tales cum christianis maneant/ et speciem religionis nostre pre se ferant/ occulte tamen communicant iudeis/ et coutuntur/ auertuntque ceteros a nostra fide/ si forte aliquibus animus esset ad eam se conertendi. Quare necesse est diligenter intendere/ cui sacramentum baptismi conferatur.

---

72. idololatria] idolatria, *Nur.*

[p. 30; fol. c3ᵛ]

Kommer noghen vdlending som er vbekendt oc begherer at dø
bes/ tha maa man wel forsckriffue hannum til syth fædhernæ
land ther som han er bekendt. Er han oc bekendt/ tha scal man
dog ickæ ladhæ sig forhasthæ/ men ladhæ hannum offuer høris
oc randsaghes wed godhæ lerdhæ mend. Icke scal man oc be- 5
gaffuæ them offuerflødighen nar the swo døbes/ men ladhæ
them læræ at ødhæ sig met erligt arbeygd som wij øræ The
som æræ døbthæ/ oc icke øffwæ them i godhæ oc dygdhelighe
gerningher/ som er at høræ messæ/ predicken/ at fasthæ/ at læsæ theris gwdhelighæ bøner etc. the æræ icke retthæ cristnæ men 10
nisckæ/ oc haffue icke ræt fundament vti troen. Swodhanæ
øgnæ scalckæ som swo ladhæ sig waræ godhæ cristnæ oc ickæ
æræ/ the æræ then hellighæ kirckæ møghet til sckadhæ. Oc iw
meræ the æræ lærdhæ/ iw meræ wildfarelsæ saa the blant fol
ket. hwad the icke kwnnæ openbaræ/ thet øræ the hemeli- 15
ghen. Icke forti at the widhæ møghet vti thet gamblæ testamentæ i biblien/ allighewel bliffue the wed then blothæ text
The kwnne icke forstaa henne andhelighen effther syn glosæ
och figuræ/ forti at the aldrig høræ eller willæ høræ noghen
predicken aff thet nyg testamentæ/ aff hwilket loghen oc pro 20
phethernæ the retthelighen forklaris.

¶ Nw wil ieg øræ en ændhæ paa thennæ bog/ bedhendes
indherlighen oc ydmyghelig alle them som henne lessæ. Om ieg
haffuer noghet vbeqwæmt sæth her vti/ at the thet mildheligen
willæ offuer see oc forbeddræ. Oc at hwer i syn stæd (som hanss 25
macht er til) wil hielpæ oc øræ syn fliid. At thet armæ blindæ
iødhesckæ folk/ maa noghen tiidh omkring wendhes til thet

English translation:
If some foreigner arrives, who is unknown and desires to be baptised, then one ought to banish him to his country of birth where he is known. If he is known, then one should still not let one-

self be hurried, but have him interrogated and questioned by good learned men. One should not inundate them with gifts when they are baptised, but let them learn to feed themselves through honest labour as we do. Those who are baptised but who do not practise good and virtuous deeds, that is hearing mass and sermons, fasting, reading their devout prayers etc., are not real Christians and do not have a real foundation in faith. Such hypocrites who pretend to be good Christians, but who are not, are of much harm to the holy Church. And the more learned they are, the more error they sow among the people. What they cannot do publicly, they do secretly. Even though they know much in the Old Testament, they keep to the plain text. They cannot understand it spiritually according to its explanations and prefigurations, because they never listen to or want to listen to a sermon from the New Testament by which the law and the prophets are correctly explained.

Now I shall finish this book by sincerely and humbly asking all those who read it: If I have translated something unsuitably here, that they will kindly scrutinise it and improve upon it. And each in his own town (in accordance with his power) will help and work diligently so that the poor, blind Jewish people may some day be converted to the […]

Latin original:
Si alienigena quis et ignotus po[p. 27; fol. c6ʳ]stulet se baptizari/ remittatur in patriam suam et ad notos. si notus est/ non tamen accelerandum est/ sed per probos et discretos viros tentandus primum/ et studiose perscrutandus est. Neque illis abunde largiendum baptizatis/ discant laborare manibus suis et honestis rationibus victum sibi parare/ vt nos facere vrgemur. Qui autem baptizati sunt/ et post baptismum[73] non exercent se in sanctis operibus/ ieiunijs orationibus auditione frequenti verbi dei/ ij[74] non sunt vere christiani. sermonibus quippe euangelicis et alijs per sacerdotes christiano populo prepositos editis ceterisque doctrinis sanis et institutionibus nos in religione et fide christiana stabilimur. Tales verbo simulati christiani magno damno sunt ecclesie christiane/ et quo doctiores sunt/ plus zizanie seminant in populo/ et palam quantum audent/ et occultis susurris. qui licet in biblio veteris instituti docti sint/ satisque in eo sapiant/ manent tamen in occidente littera/ nude eam intelligentes cum non possunt spiritum eius et mentem accipere et elicere cum non audiunt noui testamenti sermones. ex quo lex et prophete clare monstrantur et intelliguntur

¶ Hic nunc libello huic finem imponam/ humili prece orans omnes et singulos qui eum legerint/ si fortasse male aliquid aut inconuenienter insertum sit. id benigne corrigere velint/ et quantum cuique possibile est/ eniti/ vt cecus ille iudaicus populus aliquando ad verum lumen christiane fidei perueniat/

---

73. baptismum] baprismum, *Col.*; baptismum, *Nur.*
74. ij] hi, *Nur.*

sandhæ liwss som er gwdh. Taghendhes løn och stor werdsckyld/ aff hannum som er loffwet/ æret oc benedidhet aff allæ creatwræ nw oc ewindhelig Amen.

¶ Trycht vti Købmanhaffwen/ hooss
her Powel Ræff Cannick ther samestedz
Aar effther gwdz byrd. M.d.xvi.

English translation:

[…] true light that is God, and take their reward and just deserts from the one who is praised, honoured and blessed by all creatures now and forever more. Amen.

Printed in Copenhagen by
Rev. Poul Ræff, canon in that same place
1516 years after the birth of God.

Latin original:

ad verum lumen christiane fidei perueniat/ vnde haud dubium[75] non paruam consequentur a deo optimo maximo mercedem et premium in christo iesu domino nostro

¶ Hoc opus editum a Johanne pefferkorn olim iudeo nunc christiano. Et impressum per me Johannem Landen ciuem felicis ciuitatis Coloniensis. in platea sancti Gereonis in domo facultatis artium rubea porta nominata. moram gerentem feliciter explicit. Anno domini .M.ccccc.viij. etcetera.[76]

---

75. haud dubium] haudubium, *Col.*; haud dubium, *Nur.*

76. Et impressum … etcetera.] Et impressum Nurnberge. per me dominum Joannem Weyssenbur-|ge presbiterum. Anno octauo.

CHAPTER 6

Commentary

Notes to the edition of Iudeorum Secreta

Les faits et gestes des Juifs, ainsi que leurs mœurs, sont choses inconnues du monde. On croît les connaître parce qu'on a vu leur barbe, mais on n'a vu d'eux que cela et, comme au moyen âge, ils sont toujours un mystère ambulant.

Henrich Heine (in Drumont 1886)[1]

The principal aim of the commentary is to provide notes that explain terms and factual matters in the text. Drawing a satisfactory line in determining the criteria for these explanatory comments has not been easy, but the guiding principle has been to provide a note wherever the text might not be understood by the reader or where further background information might be of particular interest. These notes concern in particular historical circumstances, aspects of Jewish and Christian religion, ritual and beliefs, as well as textual uncertainties and problems. References to secondary sources have now and again been provided and include both introductory works to the ritual, event or act under discussion, as well as those works in which a scholar makes a substantive comment on a specific point of detail. References to *Iudeorum Secreta* are by page and line number and refer to the original Danish text.

1: 8–9 **iødhætempel:** Just like today, the synagogue during the Middle Ages fulfilled a number of varied roles in Jewish community life. It was the place of communal worship, religious services and weddings. There

---

1. Henrich Heine (quoted in Drumont 1886: 1): 'The Jews' deeds and gestures even their morals are things unknown to the world. One thinks that one knows them because one has seen their beards, but one has not seen any more of them than that, and just as in the Middle Ages, they are always a wandering mystery.'

were three daily services with the largest congregations on Shabbat and other religious holidays. The synagogue was also the venue for community meetings, for meetings of the Jewish religious court (בית דין, *beit din*) as well as for social events. The building would have included a library, a ritual bath or mikvah (מיקוה, *miqwah*), a storeroom, living quarters for the caretaker and maybe even one or more guestrooms for visitors from other communities. The surrounding Christian communities placed severe restrictions on the construction of synagogues, which often required ingenious innovations in building techniques and styles to ensure that the synagogue was both legal and kosher (*kašer*, כשר, 'in accordance with Jewish religious law').

Several words were used to refer to the Jews' place of worship in Danish texts from the Middle Ages: *juthekirkje* ('Jews' church', the most common word which could also refer to the Jewish community as a whole); *juthetempel* ('Jews' temple'); *mynster* ('minster'): *jøtherne bønehus* 'the Jews' prayer-house', and *synagoge* ('synagogue'). The term 'synagoge' (from Greek *synagōgē*, συναγωγή, 'congregation'), although used exclusively in modern Danish, was probably unfamiliar to most laypeople in medieval Denmark; indeed, when the word 'Synagogam' is used in *Iudeorum Secreta* (p. 4: 1–2), Ræff glosses it with 'til theris Iødhæ tempel [*to their Jews' temple*]'. In extant Danish dictionaries from the sixteenth-century, *synagoga* is translated as 'church' or 'gathering place'. In the Jewish languages, the synagogue is called *beit kneset* (בית כנסת, 'meeting house') in Hebrew; *shul* (שול < Middle High German *schuol* 'school') in Yiddish, and *esnogah* (אסנוגה < Latin *synagoga*) in Ladino.

On the history of the synagogue, see Wigoder 1986; *EJ*, XIX: 352–83, *s.v.* 'synagogue'; Roth 2003: 620–31, *s.v.* 'Synagogues'. And on synagogues in Denmark, see Jørgensen 1981; Linvald 1982; Blüdnikow 1983; Hampton Frosell 1987.

2: 1–2   **[Woodcut]:** The woodcut is discussed in ch. 4 and reproduced as fig. 5.

2: 4   **the articlæ:** The twelve articles of faith in the Apostolic Creed as used in the Catholic Church as the profession of faith, for example during the rite of baptism. See *Catechism of the Catholic Church* 1994: 45–242 (§§185–1065).

3: 1   **en clerck:** Pfefferkorn was not a clergyman, but a layman who acted as a shill for the Dominicans in Cologne. However, this title alludes to a

	solid educational background for the author and creates a sense of his good reputation and an air of authority and trustworthiness.
3: 2	**Colnæ:** Cologne (Köln), a town in north-western Germany. Under the Dominicans, who had established their headquarters in the city, Cologne was turned into a centre of the Inquisition and anti-Judaism. The Jews were expelled from the city in 1424/26. On Cologne's Jewish history, see Roth 2003: 176–80, *s.v.* 'Cologne' (with references).
3: 7–8	**han … skaaren:** His trustworthiness and authority to tell the readers about the Jews' secrets are proven by his credentials as a born Jew, of which his circumcision is mentioned here as the ultimate proof. However, although circumcision is often referred to as a physical mark that sets Jews apart from Christians, the act of circumcision does not make a man Jewish. It is merely the fulfilment of one of hundreds of *mizwot* (Genesis 17: 1–14; Leviticus 12: 3). A Jew is someone who is born of a Jewish mother or who converts to Judaism according to the *halachic* requirements of the community he or she is joining.
3: 17–19	**Om … thet:** These three lines in the chapter title are presumably a typesetting error. The chapter only deals with the preparatory period, not the confession itself, so the text is not relevant here. The lines also appear in the heading for chapter 2 (p. 10: 24–26) which is in fact about the confession itself. On this error, see 'Mistranslations and errors' in ch. 3.
3: 24	**Kalendas Augusti:** The Jewish month of *'Elul* (אלול), usually beginning in August, is the month that precedes the Jewish New Year, known as Rosh Hashanah (ראש השנה, *ro'š hašanah*). It is a time when one assesses one's deeds and the condition of one's soul, an act known as 'accounting for the soul' (חשבון הנפש, *ḥešbon hanefeš*). See Eisenberg 2004: 182–84.
4: 7	**eth bwcks horn:** The ram's horn, known as a shofar (שופר, *šofar*), is used ritually during the month of *'Elul* and to mark the conclusion of the period of fasting on the Day of Atonement or Yom Kippur (יום כפור, *Yom Kipur*). A shofar can in fact be made from any kosher animal, but within Ashkenazi Judaism it became traditional to use a ram's horn. See Eisenberg 2004: 190–96.

4: 16	**At ... gwd:** These penitential poems (פיוטים, *piyuṭim*) and prayers, known as *seliḥot* (סליחות), are said during the period leading up to the High Holy Days. See Eisenberg 2004: 178–82.
4: 19–20	**salomo*n*is tempel:** The First Temple (בית המקדש, *beit hamiqdaš*) was constructed in Jerusalem around 960 BCE by King Solomon and was destroyed by the Babylonians in 586 BCE. The Second Temple, built to replace it, was destroyed by the Romans in 70 CE. The desire to rebuild the Temple is expressed in the central daily prayer of traditional Jews, the Standing Prayer or *'Amidah* (תפילת העמידה, *tefilat ha'amidah*), also called the Eighteen (שמנה עשרה, *šemoneh 'eśreh*).
4: 23–24	**theris ... affthen:** The evening before New Year (ערב ראש השנה, *'erev ro'š hašanah*) is on the twenty-ninth day of the month *'Elul*.
4: 24	**mend oc qwindher:** Pfefferkorn includes the participation and role of women in rituals in his descriptions; see Carlebach 2001: 185–92 on descriptions of the role of Jewish women in rituals. Pfefferkorn's aim here with describing the bathing (and, one must assume, the accompanying sinful nudity) of Jewish men and women together regardless of their age may well be to show Jews as being lacking in modesty and dignity, and thus to cause outrage among his readers. This contrasts with their separation in the synagogue (p. 5: 26–27). Cf. also p. 4: 28. On Jewish women in the Middle Ages, see Roth 2003: 657–63, *s.v.* 'Women' (with references).
4: 27–28	**eth ri*n*dhænæ wadn:** The evening before New Year is a traditional time to immerse oneself in a ritual bath, called a mikvah (מקוה, *miqwah*) in order to achieve ritual purity (see *Rosh Hashanah* 16b in the Talmud). The mikvah must be connected to a source of 'living water' such as a spring or river in order to be kosher, which is described here as 'running water' in which the Jews can ritually bathe.
5: 5–6	**Leuiticorum ... capitel:** In Leviticus 22: 3, 6 it says: 'Say to them: Throughout the ages, if any man among your offspring, while in a state of uncleanliness, partakes of any sacred donation that the Israelite people may consecrate to the LORD, that person shall be cut off from me: I am the LORD. [...] the person who touches such shall be unclean until evening and shall not eat of the sacred donations, unless he has washed his body in water.'

5: 6–7	**then ... maanedhen:** The month of *Tišrei* (תשרי) is the first month of the Jewish civil year, and the seventh month of the religious calendar. The name is Talmudic; the Bible calls it *'Etanim* (אתנים, 'steady flowings'; Leviticus 23: 23–43; Leviticus 25: 9; I Kings 8: 2; Ezra 3: 1, 6).
5: 10	**Genesis ... capitel:** Genesis 22: 3: 'So early next morning, Abraham saddled his ass […]'.
5: 11	**abraham:** Abraham (אברהם, *'Avraham*), the founding patriarch of the Jews (and subsequently of the Christians and Muslims).
5: 12	**syn søn:** Isaac (יצחק, *Yizḥaq*). The story of the binding of Isaac (known as עקדה, *'aqedah*) is found in Genesis 22: 1–24. It forms part of the *parašat Wayer'a* (Torah portion; see commentary note for p. 6: 1–2) and is read at Rosh Hashanah.
5: 17	**eth ... klædhæ:** The prayer shawl or tallit (טלית, *ṭalit*) worn by men during religious ceremonies and prayer is a rectangular piece of cloth with twined, knotted fringes (ציצית, *ẓiẓit*) in each of its four corners. It is usually draped over the shoulders, but during prayer can be drawn up over the wearer's head (as described here).
5: 20–21	**hwilkæ ... hendher:** The *ẓiẓit* of the prayer shawl are gathered and held in the hands during certain parts of the service (for example during the *šema'* prayer: 'Hear, O Israel!').
5: 21–22	**Met ... sig**: As it is used in the performance of a *miẓwah*, a tallit is treated with respect. It seems rather odd that Pfefferkorn says that the Jews rubbed and dried themselves using their tallitot. The Latin has 'aspiciunt illis se tergunt [*they inspect them and wipe themselves clean*]'. The 'wiping' [*tergunt*] in the Latin could have the meaning of expiation in this context, rather than cleaning and drying.
5: 23	**the ... Moysen:** The Ten Commandments are the list of moral laws authored by God and given to Moses who delivered them to the people of Israel (Exodus 20: 2–17; Exodus 34: 11–27, and Deuteronomy 5: 6–21).
5: 26–27	**swo ... vti:** Women and men were seated separately, as they still are in Orthodox and some Conservative congregations. This is in accordance

with the Talmud (*Sukkah* 51b–52a), which describes the Temple in Jerusalem (see commentary note for p. 4: 19–20) with separate-sex worship during the 'water-drawing celebrations' (שמחת בית השואבה, *śimḥat beit hašo'evah*). The aim of separating female and male worshippers was to increase the level of concentration and devotion (כוונה, *kawanah*, 'intention') during services and prayer. The two sexes are divided either by a screen, called a *meḥizah* (מחיצה, 'dividing wall'), or by different floor levels with the women seated in a balcony away from the men. The women's part of the synagogue is called the *'ezrat našim* (עזרת נשים, 'women's gallery).

5: 27–28 **then ... tempel:** According to Pfefferkorn the scroll is removed from the ark by the most prominent member of the community, known in Hebrew as the *parnas* (פרנס). The Latin version further specifies that that this man's importance can lie in his religious role (*archisynagogus*), his wealth (*diuicijs*), or his authority (*auctoritate*).

6: 1 **arck:** The Torah ark (ארון קודש, *'aron qodeš*) is an ornamental receptacle which contains the synagogue's Torah scrolls. It is placed on the eastern wall (nearest Jerusalem) which is also the direction the congregation faces during prayer.

6: 1–2 **fæm Moysi bøgher:** The Pentateuch, in Judaism called the Torah (תורה, 'teaching'), forms the first part of the Hebrew Bible. The Torah comprises the five books of Moses: Genesis (בראשית, *Bere'šit*), Exodus (שמות, *Šemot*), Leviticus (ויקרא, *Wayiqra'*), Numbers (במדבר, *Bamidbar*), and Deuteronomy (דברים, *Devarim*). The Torah scrolls are used for public reading, and each week and on holidays a Torah portion (פרשה, *parašah*) is read aloud. In this way, the entire Torah is read from start to finish during the course of a year.

6: 2–3 **sermon oc talæ:** It seems that what is meant here is that a sermon is given to the people and a 'speech' to God. In Latin, the word *sermo* is usually understood to mean 'speech', but in Danish it was often used with a more specific meaning, viz. 'sermon', just as in English. Thus, the phrase 'Han gør syn sermon' means 'he delivers a sermon'. The 'speech to God' probably refers to some sort of direct petition appealing to God for forgiveness on behalf of the community. On the history of Jewish preaching, see Zunz 1932 (revised edition 1954); Bettan 1939; Elbogen 1993: 156–58, and especially Saperstein 1989 and 2010.

6: 3–9 **Ha*n* ... trælæ:** This is a paraphrase of the morning blessings (ברכות השחר, *birchot hašaḥar*) in which thanks are given for several things in a series of fifteen blessings. These include the blessing for not having been born a gentile — Christians are not mentioned specifically. In the beginning of the fourteenth century, this part of the prayer was disingenuously translated by the inquisitor Bernhard Gui in Toulouse as 'qui non fecisti christianum vel gentilem [*who did not make me a Christian or a non-Jew*]'. From that time on, the prayer was considered as proof of the Jews' enmity towards and hatred of Christians. Subsequent Christian violence towards Jews in the thirteenth century resulted in a number of changes to the text of the prayer, and the reference to non-Jews was dropped. See Yerushalmi 1970: 357; Lausten 1991–92: 71; Elbogen 1993: 36, 51.

6: 6 **hanen:** The appearance of a cockerel here is due to the use of the word *śechwi* in the blessing: אֲשֶׁר נָתַן לַשֶּׂכְוִי בִינָה לְהַבְחִין בֵּין יוֹם וּבֵין לָיְלָה ('*'ašer natan laśechwi vina lehavḥin bein yom uvein laylah*, 'Blessed art thou, O Lord our God, King of the universe, who hast given the heart/cockerel understanding to distinguish between day and night'). The meaning of *śechwi* is uncertain. The Bible commentator Rashi (Rabbi Šelomo Yizḥaqi, 1040–1105) translates the word as 'cockerel', but this meaning makes no sense at the one place in the Bible where it occurs (Job 38: 36). Here it must mean something like 'heart' or 'mind'. The blessing is thus interpreted to be thanks to God who has given us the ability to hear ('cockerel') or the power of discernment ('heart').

6: 13–14 **Fordwmæ ... sædher:** After a doomed revolt against the Romans, the Jews were expelled (for the second time) from their land in 135 CE.

6: 27–7: 2 **Paa ... meræ:** This bizarre image of sixteenth-century Jews sacrificing animals on the synagogue *bimah* (see note for p. 6: 28) is in fact due to a mistranslation into Danish on Poul Ræff's part. The Latin has 'Recolitur quoque magna deuotione latissime ad aras corum prisca immolatio holocaustomatum et ceterarum victimarum in bobus arietibus et hircis [*Then they remember the great sacrifice their forefathers offered of cat-*

tle, rams and goats with great diligence on the altar]'. See 'Mistranslations and errors' in ch. 3.

6: 28 **altheræ:** The 'altar' in a synagogue is a podium called a *bimah* (בימה, from Greek βῆμα) among the Ashkenazim. It is an elevated platform from which the Torah is read and is usually situated in the middle of the synagogue.

7: 2–4 **Sameledhes ... presther:** Ræff's Danish translation is also wrong here: the Jews do not give cakes of wheat flour, oil, wine and salt to their priests. The text in the Latin original is describing the cakes that were once offered '*a sacerdotibus suis [by their priests]*' in the Temple during ancient times. See 'Mistranslations and errors' in ch. 3.

7: 5 **psaltheren:** By the time Pfefferkorn was writing, the prayers and form of the prayer book or siddur (סידור, *sidur*) were fixed. Pfefferkorn mentions three types of prayer book in his works: *tefilah* (general prayer book), *maḥzor* (the prayer book for the High Holy Days) and *seliḥot* (the book of penitential prayers for the period leading up to Yom Kippur). The first printed siddur appeared in Italy at the end of the fifteenth century. See Elbogen 1993: 271–85.

7: 5–7 **dog ... sielff:** Pfefferkorn is referring to the Jews' alleged blindness to the truth: they do not have the New Testament to interpret their prayers and their relationship with God, and therefore only read the text literally 'as it stands written'. The Church Fathers had developed a system of biblical interpretation based on two principal meanings: *sensus literalis* (a literal meaning) and *sensus spiritualis* (a spiritual meaning). Jews were believed to read the Bible with just *sensus literalis*.

7: 8–10 **Nar ... leghomæ:** *Shokling*, from the Yiddish verb *šoklen zich* (שאָקלען זיך, 'to shake, rock, sway'), also known as *shuckling* or *shuckeling*, is the ritual swaying of worshippers during services, usually forward and back but also from side to side. This practice can be traced back to at least the eighth century CE, and possibly as far back as Talmudic times. It is thought by some to increase concentration and emotional intensity, known as *kawanah* in Jewish practice (Unterman 1991: 192, *s.v.* 'Swaying in prayer'; Eisenberg 2004: 360; see also note for p. 7: 5).

During High Holy Days, male worshippers may also prostrate themselves fully with their body flat to the ground during prayer.

The phenomenon of *shokling* during religious study was conspicuous enough to be addressed by the *Zohar*, the classic of Jewish mysticism composed in thirteenth-century Spain. In it, Rabbi Šimʿon bar Yoḥai is asked by his students why it is only the Jews who move back and forth when learning Torah. Rabbi Šimʿon begins his reply by observing that the soul of a Jew derives mystically from the celestial Torah. Thus, through hearing a word of Torah the soul is immediately ignited like the wick of a lamp as it is joined with its supernatural source. By swaying during Torah study, the Jew's body is actually quivering to the flame-like rhythm of his soul. No other people, says Rabbi Šimʿon, possesses such a mystical connection to the divine Torah.

The twelfth-century Jewish philosopher and poet Yehudah Halewi (*c.* 1075–1141) had a rather mundane explanation and wrote that the habit began as a result of a shortage of books, forcing people to hover over a single codex laid on the ground, each one bending in turn to read a passage (*The Kuzari* II, § 80).

During the thirteenth century, Abbot 'Iohannes de Brach' wrote a series of notes in the margin of a manuscript of Petrus Comestor's *Historia scholastica* (Oxford, Bodleian Library, MS Rawlinson C 46). On fol. 47ᵛ, when he had reached the description of the revelation at Mount Sinai (Exodus 19: 18 'and the whole mountain trembled violently'), he wrote (Smalley 1964: 341):

> Inde est quod Iudei adhuc in orationibus suis tremunt, representantes illum tremorem montis

> *Thence it is that the Jews still quake at their prayers representing the quaking of the mount*

There seems to be no Jewish tradition of interpretation to this effect. There is, however, a reference to this biblical scene in the commentary *ʾArbaʿah Ṭurim* by Rabbi Yaʿakov ben 'Ašer (1270 – *c.* 1340), in which he links the custom of *shokling* to Exodus 19: 16: 'And all the people who were in the camp trembled'.

Whatever the history behind *shokling*, it is permitted by the ruling that whatever helps one concentrate on prayer is the correct thing to do (*Oraḥ Ḥaim* 48; *Mišnah Berurah* 5; *Magen ʾAvraham* 4).

| 7: 11–12 | **Sanctus ... sabahot:** At the words 'Holy, Holy, Holy! The LORD of hosts' (Isaiah 6: 3), the congregation traditionally rises to their toes in order to lift themselves symbolically to the level of the angels. |

| 7: 13–16 | **Moyses ... hiarthæ:** Cf. Deuteronomy 6: 5 which forms the beginning of the *we'ahavta* section of the *šema'* prayer. |

| 7: 17–18 | **Thettæ ... etc:** Isaiah 29: 13: '[...] Because that people has approached [Me] with its mouth And honoured Me with its lips, But has kept its heart from Me, And its worship of Me has been A commandment of men, learned by rote.' |

| 7: 20–21 | **Genesis ... capitel:** Genesis 22: 17: 'I will bestow My blessing upon you and make your descendants as numerous as the stars of heaven and the sands of the seashore.' |

| 7: 27–28 | **theris bøgher:** Presumably referring to prayer books; see note for p. 7: 5. |

| 8: 15 | **the ... pergament:** A Torah scroll (ספר תורה, *sefer Torah*) must meet very strict requirements concerning its production to ensure that it is kosher. The clean parchment mentioned by Pfefferkorn is known as *gewil* (גויל), an animal hide that has been specially prepared in accordance with requirements laid out in various Jewish books. See *JE*, XI: 126–34, *s.v.* 'Scroll of the Law'. |

| 8: 16 | **nogræ capitel:** The entire Torah is read aloud through the course of a year at synagogue services to the assembled congregation. Each weekly Torah portion (called פרשה, *parašah*) comprises several chapters and is chanted in Hebrew using a traditional *trop* (טְרָאפ) or cantillation. |

| 8: 18–20 | **han ... folkit:** At the conclusion of the Torah-reading part of the service, the scroll is held aloft in such a way that the portion that has been read aloud is visible to the entire congregation. This raising of the scroll is known as *hagbahah* (הגבהה). In *Iudeorum Secreta*, Pfefferkorn describes the ceremony as including a procession of the scroll three times around the congregation. The scroll procession usually takes place either at the beginning of the Torah service or at the end after the scroll has been dressed and just before it is returned to the ark. Pfeffer- |

	korn's description may reflect some local practice or is simply a conflation of the *hagbahah* and scroll-procession ceremonies.
8: 22	**oc ... fliidh:** At this point in the service, the congregation says, 'And this is the Torah given by Moses to the children of Israel at the command of God by the hand of Moses' (Deuteronomy 4: 44). The Torah contains hundreds of commandments, or *miẓwot*, which Jews follow. The precise number is open to discussion, but traditionally, since Maimonides (Rambam) in the twelfth century, there are said to be 613 *miẓwot* in the Torah: 248 positive commandments ('thou shalt...') and 365 proscriptions ('thou shalt not...').
8: 23	**rabier:** In the Middle Ages, Jewish communities appointed a rabbi (רבי, *rabi*) to act as their religious leader. The rabbi preached, admonished the community, answered questions on Jewish law and philosophy, and taught Torah.
9: 2	**hornet:** The shofar is blown after the Torah readings. There are three different types of blast: *teqi'ah* (a long tone, which, if made very long, is called *teqi'ah gedolah*), *ševarim* (three short blasts), *teru'ah* (nine very short blasts). The order of the blasts is: *teqi'ah, ševarim, teru'ah, teqi'ah, teqi'ah, ševarim, teqi'ah, teqi'ah, teru'ah, teqi'ah gedolah* (giving thirty tones in total). This series is repeated twice during the service which ends with ten blasts of the shofar. In German tradition, as in *Iudeorum Secreta*, distinguished members of the society were honoured by being asked to recite the series of blasts to be made (Cohen 1998: 17–18).
9: 8–10	**tha ... horneth:** The idea that one is cleansed of one's sins at the sounding of the shofar is not a sanctioned belief in Judaism, but could reflect some sort of folk tradition. Alternatively, Pfefferkorn could be fabricating superstitious aspects in Jewish ritual.
9: 10–18	**Nar ... folck:** That the tone of the shofar somehow predicts future events is certainly not a tenet of Judaism. Again it may reflect a local belief or be an invention on the part of Pfefferkorn to represent the Jews as superstitious. If it is indeed genuine, then it provides us with an insight into the Jewish community's fears and how it felt threatened and persecuted by the majority Christian population.

9: 21–10: 2 **O ... etc.:** These lines are a Danish rendering of the Hebrew prayer *'Avinu malkeinu* ('Our father, Our king'). The prayer is mentioned in the Talmud (*Ta'anit* 25 b) and can be traced back to Rabbi Akiva (*'Aqiva ben Yosef*, c. 50 – c. 135 CE), and the text has been altered through the years (Elbogen 1993: 216, 283). As the prayer includes the request that God thwart the plans of the Jews' enemies, it was considered by Christian theologians, who identified themselves as the Jews' enemies, as anti-Christian. Pfefferkorn makes an interesting mistranslation of the prayer which is repeated by Ræff:

Hebrew text of *'Avinu malkeinu*	→ Poul Ræff's translation (via Pfefferkorn)
אָבִינוּ מַלְכֵּנוּ כַּלֵּה דֶּבֶר וְחֶרֶב וְרָעָב וּשְׁבִי וּמַשְׁחִית (וְעָוֹן) וּשְׁמָד מִבְּנֵי בְרִיתֶךָ.	Forfylghæ och forderffwæ them med pestilentzæ / met hwngher / met swerd oc met fengsel. Ladh alle handhæ plaghæ offuergaa them for thynæ omkringsckornæ børns sckyld/ hwilkæ thw haffuer vdwalt tig
Our Father, our king! Save us, the members of your covenant, from plague and sword, and hunger and captivity, destruction (and transgression), and annihilation.	*Persecute and destroy them [i.e. the Christians] with pestilence, with famine, by sword and with imprisonment. Let every kind of plague befall them for the sake of your circumcised children whom you have chosen for yourself.*

The translation transforms the supplication for protection into a threatening curse against non-Jews, which is not the intention of the original. See also Kirn 1989: 44–45; Lausten 1991–92: 71–72; Yuval 2006: 136; Deutsch 2012: 105.

10: 4 **theris egnæ bøgher:** Their books are the Jewish books, such as the Talmud, that Pfefferkorn wanted so keenly to be destroyed. In his publications, Pfefferkorn condemns the Talmud and Jewish prayer books, but he does not specify which books he considers false and should be confiscated. He considers some books as being anti-Christian and others as deviating from biblical (Mosaic) law. In this latter group, he seems to want to place all post-biblical literature.

10: 6–7	**Hwilkæ ... andhen:** Pfefferkorn repeatedly writes that Jews view Christians as their prime enemies.
10: 8–20	**tha ... tidhen:** Here we read about one of Pfefferkorn's main aims, *viz.* the confiscation and destruction of Jewish books, which he believed to be the cause of the Jews' hatred towards and jealousy of Christians.
10: 12–13	**Esaie ... capitel:** Isaiah 1: 15: 'And when you lift up your hands, I will turn My eyes away from you; Though you pray at length, I will not listen.'
11: 1–4	**Som ... see:** The tashlich ceremony in which one casts away one's sins by emptying the dust of one's pockets into a river or the sea is described here. Despite Pfefferkorn's statement, the ceremony does not build on a Talmudic interpretation, but builds on the Bible. In Micah 7: 19, we read 'You will hurl all their sins into the depths of the sea' (cf. also Nehemiah 5: 13). In Hebrew, *tašliḥ* (תשליח) means 'you will cast', whence the ceremony takes its name. See *Shabbat* 153a; Agnon 1965: 92–100; Kirn 1989: 40–41; Lausten 1991–92: 72–74; Lausten 1992: 121; Lauerbach 1936 (Pfefferkorn's description is discussed on pp. 296–97, 299, 303–04); *EJ*, XIX: 524–25, *s.v.* 'tashlikh'. The tashlich ceremony is, however, not an ancient custom and is first mentioned in the fifteenth century by Ya'akov ben Mošeh Halewi Mulin (known as Maharil). In *Sefer Maharil* ('the book of the Maharil'), a compendium of Ashkenazi ritual and liturgical customs recorded by his disciple Rabbi Zalman, there are several interpretations concerning the ceremony (see Spitzer 1989: 277–78 [§9]). For example, there is a midrash that Satan transformed himself into a river to block Abraham's path when he was leading Isaac to be sacrificed, but Abraham prayed to God, who rebuked the river. Fish are also seen as being symbolic of God's eye that sees everything, and also as creatures that are caught in a net in the same way as humans are caught in the severe net of divine judgement.
11: 15	**forgheræ:** The word 'forgheræ' is a *hapax legomenon* (a word unattested in any other Danish text) and in all likelihood means 'front wedge-shaped piece of cloth on or under a garment', 'front flap(s) of a garment'. The Latin has 'lacinia [*flap, corner (of dress)*]'. See 'Hapax legomena and unusual words' in ch. 3.
11: 20–21	**a*n*dræ ... dicther:** Cf. pp. 7: 27–28; 10: 4–5.

11: 22	**rabier…paafwndhet:** Pfefferkorn is casting the rabbis as the villains here. The superstitious practices of the Jews are their fault and invention. Cf. pp. 14: 21–15: 1.
12: 8–9	**The … hanæ:** *Kaparot* (כפרות, 'expiations') is a ritual in which one recites texts from Psalms 107: 10, 14, 17–21 and Job 33: 23–24 before symbolically transferring one's sins to another object (typically a chicken) by swinging it around one's head three times. Preferably, a man should use a rooster, and a woman should use a hen for the ritual. The description of the ceremony as well as of the words cited by Pfefferkorn as being said during the swinging of the chicken (p. 12: 21–25) is accurate (cf. also Deutsch 2012: 83, 89). After the ritual, the chicken is slaughtered and eaten at the feast preceding Yom Kippur (as described here). The ritual has been much disputed through the ages and probably has its origins in superstition and pagan practice. It is not mentioned in the Talmud, and first described in the ninth century (*EJ*, XI: 781–82, *s.v.* 'kapparot'; Lausten 1991–92: 73–74; Agnon 1965: 147–50). Today *kaparot* is only performed in the traditional version by ultra-Orthodox Jews. Many others have replaced the chicken with money and wave bank notes over their heads before donating them to a charity. Pfefferkorn is implicitly comparing the ritual to the Christian doctrine of Jesus' atonement where he bears and removes the sin of humanity from those who believe in him.
12: 11–14	**Er … synd:** Pfefferkorn's description of the ceremony of *kaparot* especially for a foetus may, as suggested by Yaacov Deutsch (2004: 212; 2012: 89), reflect Christian ideas of original sin and a projection of Christian beliefs and practices onto this 'other' religion. However, there are references in earlier Jewish sources to the separate use of a chicken for the foetus. The earliest is in the early fifteenth-century *Sefer Maharil*, where, in the section on rituals during *'erev yom kipur*, it says (Spitzer 1989: 314): אמר מהר"י סג"ל אשה מעוברת תקח שתי כפרות והאחד בשביל העובר. *Our teacher and rabbi, Ya'akov Segal [Maharil] said, 'A pregnant woman performs two* kaparot; *one of them is for the sake of the foetus.'*
13: 9	**rindhenæ wand:** Cf. note for p. 4: 27–28.

Figure 9
Woodcut of a synagogue interior; Johannes Pfefferkorn, *Libellus de Iudaica confessione siue sabbato afflictionis* (Nuremberg: Johannes Weissenburger, 1508), fol. a2[r]. With permission of Bayerische Staatsbibliothek.

Figure 10
Woodcut of the tashlikh ceremony; Johannes Pfefferkorn, *Libellus de Iudaica confessione siue sabbato afflictionis* (Nuremberg: Johannes Weissenburger, 1508), fol. b1[r.] With permission of Bayerische Staatsbibliothek.

Figure 11
Woodcut of the kapparot ritual and bathing; Johannes Pfefferkorn, *Libellus de Iudaica confessione siue sabbato afflictionis* (Nuremberg: Johannes Weissenburger, 1508), fol. b2ʳ. With permission of Bayerische Staatsbibliothek.

Figure 12
Woodcut of a synagogue interior with the malqot ritual and a 'shabbes goy' lighting candles; Johannes Pfefferkorn, *Libellus de Iudaica confessione siue sabbato afflictionis* (Nuremberg: Johannes Weissenburger, 1508), fol. b3ᵛ. With permission of Bayerische Staatsbibliothek.

13: 15–23 **Han … syndher:** Previous scholars who have worked with Pfefferkorn's book have written that the ceremony described here is invented (for example, Kirn 1989: 41; Lausten 1991–92: 74; Lausten 1992: 121–22; Cohen 1998: 20: 'Pfefferkorn concocted this entire ritual, farcically relating how the Jew falls to his knees, rolls up his pants, and is subsequently whipped thirty-nine times with a belt by his neighbour'). However, what we have here, is in fact a fairly accurate description of the ceremony of *malqot*, 'lashes of a whip'. This ceremony, that takes place on the eve of Yom Kippur, involves the ritual beating of penitential community members by the 'beadle' (שמש, *šamaš*), or some other pious man, as a symbolic punishment for their sins. The Talmud also lists one of the purposes of undergoing lashes as a means of gaining atonement (*Temurah* 3a–b). Each penitent is struck thirty-nine times across the back. The custom came about because the Torah calls for punishment by 39 lashes for certain sins during the time of the Temple. During his beating, the penitent recites Psalms 78: 38: 'But He, being merciful, forgave iniquity and would not destroy; He restrained His wrath time and again and did not give vent to His fury'. This verse has thirteen words in the Hebrew, so by repeating it three times, it was possible to keep count of the number of lashes (Deutsch 2004: 215). See also Deutsch 2012: 90–92.

In addition to Pfefferkorn's account, there are a number of other descriptions from the period, although they do not usually mention the one being whipped exposing his behind. For example, the fifteenth-century rabbi Abraham Klausner wrote in his Book of Customs or *Sefer Minhagim* (Dissen 1978: 25):

לד: ונהגו העם להתפלל וללקות, והלוקה לא יושב ולא עומד אלא מוטה ואומר בשעת
ההלקה אשמנו בגדנו וכו'. המכה אומר ג"פ והוא רחום וברצועה של עגל מכהו, שנאמר
ארבעים יכנו לא יוסיף וסמיך ליה לא תחסום שור בדישו.

> §34. And the people would pray and beat. And the person being beaten would not sit or stand, but would be bent over and say while being beaten, 'we have trespassed, we have dealt treacherously, and so on [i.e. the alefbet-*acrostic* Widui *confession from the Yom Kippur service*]'. The beater would say three times, 'and he is merciful,' and would beat him with a calf's leash. As was said, 'He may be given up to forty lashes, but not more [Deuteronomy 25: 3]. You shall not muzzle an ox while it is threshing [Deuteronomy 25: 4].'

The first ever description by a Christian writer who was not a convert is found in *Synagoga iudaica* (1603) written by the Protestant professor of Hebrew at Basle, Johann Buxtorf (1564–1629). See the readily available reprint of the 1680 Latin translation in Buxtorf 1989 [1680]: 521–23 'De Malkus, sive flagellatione & ejus modo'.

The custom of *malqot* has continued uninterrupted into the modern era as can be seen, for example, from an image under the words ע"י יום כפור (*'e[rev] yom kipur*, 'the evening of Yom Kippur') on an eighteenth-century German *mizraḥ* plaque that depicts a man in a synagogue using a leather strap to beat another man, who is on his knees, crouched forwards, face against the ground (the plaque is housed in the Feuchtwanger Collection, Israel Museum, Jerusalem, and is reproduced in Wigoder 1986: 53). Nowadays, the annual performance of the ceremony is largely restricted ultra-Orthodox communities.

13: 25–28 **Tha ... wel:** Pfefferkorn is using satire here to ridicule the Jews. Having transposed their sins and cleansed themselves, the Jews then consume their sins once more and are no longer pure. This stands in sharp contrast to the Christian doctrine of sacramental grace bestowed by consuming the Host.

14: 7–12 **Ther ... dag:** Pfefferkorn notes that the congregation hires a Christian or gentile to take care of the lit candles and make sure that they are not extinguished or cause a fire. The Jews are too pious (although the implication is that they are too foolish) to do this themselves in case they break the rules concerning Yom Kippur. An illustration of this Christian candle-keeper can be seen on the left-hand side of the woodcut in fig. 12, and this is probably the first visual representation of a 'Sabbath gentile' or *shabbes goy* (Cohen 1998: 20). Jewish *minhag* literature also mentions employing a Christian to watch over the candles. In the *Yosef 'Omeẓ* by Rabbi Josef Juspa Nördlinger Hahn (Frankfurt am Main, 1570–1637), first published in 1723, we read (Hahn 1928: 224):

ההדלקה רק יאמרו קודם יום כפורים לנכרי המיוחד להיות בבית הכנסת לשום כך שבכל
שעה או חצייה יסבב בבית הכנסת מעצמו מפנה לפנה לעיין אחרי הנרות הכבויים שיחזור
להדליקם מעצמו.

Before Yom Kippur, they would tell a gentile who was designated to be in the synagogue for this reason that every hour or half an hour he

> *should go around the synagogue on his own from corner to corner to look for extinguished candles and relight them on his own.*
> (Translation from Deutsch 2012: 94 n. 18).

14: 12–16   **Skeer ... pølen:** This is a clear parallel to Luke 14: 5, where Jesus questions the Pharisees about their own observance of Shabbat after they challenge him for curing a man on the day of rest:

> And [Jesus] answered them [the Pharisees], saying, Which of you shall have an ass or an ox fallen into a pit, and will not straightway pull him out on the sabbath day?

The narrative is used to show the Pharisees' cynical flexibility in contravening Shabbat customs when they can derive benefit by doing so. Pfefferkorn uses the same accusation to demonstrate the Jews' lax observance and greed.

14: 21–15: 1   **The*nn*e ... eff*t*her:** It is the rabbis who mislead the Jews. They have secret meetings to create superstitious beliefs and rituals to prevent the Jews from joining Christendom.

15: 8   **war wel ko*m*men nygt ... hær:** This is the title of a Danish song, and is not a translation of the Latin. See 'Native elements' in ch. 3.

15: 27   **tree personer:** The Hebrew text reads מלך מלכי המלכים (*melech, malchey hamelachim*, 'king, the king of kings'), which is interpreted by Pfefferkorn as a reference to or recognition of the Christian Trinity. See Kirn 1989: 46; Lausten 1991–92: 72.

16: 10–11   **Olenu laschabeha:** The prayer *'aleinu lešabeaḥ* is ascribed to 'Aba 'Arika, who lived in Babylon in the third century CE, but it is possibly older. The prayer praises God for having chosen the Jewish people to serve him, expresses the hope that non-Jews will recognise him and abandon their own idolatry (Isaiah 30: 7 and 45: 20). Originally the text included these lines:

> For they worship vanity and emptiness   שֶׁהֵם מִשְׁתַּחֲוִים לְהֶבֶל וָרִיק,
> and pray to a god who cannot save.   וּמִתְפַּלְלִים אֶל אֵל לֹא יוֹשִׁיעַ.

Even though the prayer was composed in a non-Christian land (and probably originates form a pre-Christian era), it was considered by Christians as being explicitly anti-Christian. Peter of Bohemia in the fourteenth century was the first to claim that the Jews thought of Christians as those worshipping vanity (Trachtenberg 1993: 182–83). In the manual he prepared for the Inquisitors, the Dominican Bernhard Gui in Toulouse explained the lack of an explicit mention of Christians by making the distinction between the language of the prayer and its contextual intent (Kirn 1989: 46). Israel Yuval (2006: 192–204), however, has argued that at least as far as the twelfth century is concerned, the *'aleinu* prayer was in fact perceived by some Jews as an anti-Christian prayer of opposition, and particularly in the early Middle Ages, it often contained scathing additions directed at Christians. The passage was censored, but accusations of anti-Christianity continued. See Lausten 1991–92: 72; Deutsch 2012: 105.

16: 13–14 **alle … slecht:** The *kohanim* (כהנים) are Jews in direct patrilincal descent from Aaron, Moses' elder brother. It is an honoured status and *kohanim* are bound by a number of special rules. One of the duties of *kohanim* is to deliver the Priestly Blessing (*birkat kohanim*, ברכת כהנים) during the prayer service. This is described below.

16: 15–17 **the … hendher:** The *kohanim* gather in the front of the synagogue to perform the blessing, but they do not — as described here — lift up the ark. Ræff has mistranslated the Latin here, which reads: 'Accedunt supplices et magna deuotione arcam/ tendunt in altum manus suas benedicunt populo [*They go up to the ark in entreaty and great devotion, they raise their hands in the air, they bless the people*]'. See 'Mistranslations and errors' in ch. 3.

16: 18–21 **Gud … fred:** The text is biblical (Numbers 6: 24–26):

יְבָרֶכְךָ יְהוָה, וְיִשְׁמְרֶךָ
יָאֵר יְהוָה פָּנָיו אֵלֶיךָ, וִיחֻנֶּךָּ
יִשָּׂא יְהוָה פָּנָיו אֵלֶיךָ, וְיָשֵׂם לְךָ שָׁלוֹם

> The Lord bless you and protect you!
> The Lord make His face to shine upon you and be gracious to you!
> The Lord lift up His countenance upon you and grant you peace!

See Horowitz 1986–87.

16: 24–17: 1   **m*et* ... d*øø*:** While chanting the Priestly Blessing, the *kohanim* stretch out both arms at shoulder height with their hands touching at the thumbs and with their palms facing forwards. The first two fingers of each hand are separated from the other two, thus producing the appearance of a fan. The custom derives from Song 2: 9 and is called *nesi'at kapayim* (נמיעת כפיים, 'raising of the hands').

The Talmud forbids a person from looking at the hands of a *kohen* while he is delivering the Blessing, lest his or her 'eyes become dimmed' (*Ḥagigah* 16a). The great Bible commentator Rashi (Rabbi Šelomo Yiẓḥaqi, 1040–1105), explained that this is due to the bright glow of the Divine Presence in the synagogue that radiates from the fingers of the *kohanim*.

17: 2   **xxxiij:** The German has 'xxiij', the Latin 'xx', and the Danish 'xx'. However, it is, in fact, in Exodus 33: 20 that God says 'You cannot see My face, for man may not see Me and live.'

17: 5–13   **Item ... forladnæ:** There is a folk belief expressed by the Yiddish expression, 'sneezed at the truth' (*gnosen oyfen emes*, גנאָסן אויפֿן אמת), that whenever someone sneezes, the sneeze proves that whatever the person said immediately before it is true. In central and eastern Europe, a sneeze — especially during a conversation discussing the future or something that is unknown or unclear — can be answered with a phrase such as the Russian phrase на правду! (*na pravdu*, 'for truth'), in addition to phrases expressing a wish for good health. The idea is that whatever was said immediately preceding is true, will come true or should be recognised as true. It is difficult to know whether the tradition started in the Yiddish- or the Slavic/Hungarian-speaking community.

That sneezing is a salutary accompaniment to prayer comes straight from the Talmud into standard Jewish law through Dawid 'Abudirham (fl. 1340) and Ya'akov ben 'Ašer (1270 – c. 1340). We read in the Talmud (*Berachot* 24a–b; translation from Simon 1948: 145–46):

> R. Ḥanina also said: I saw Rabbi [while saying the *Tefillah*] belch and yawn and sneeze and spit [...] The following objection was cited: '[...] if he sneezes during his prayer it is a bad sign for him — some say, it shows that he is a low fellow' [...] There is no contradiction between sneezing and sneezing either; in the one case it is above, in the other below.[i] For R. Zera said: This dictum was casually imparted to me in the

school of R. Hamnuna, and it is worth all the rest of my learning:[ii] If one sneezes in his prayer it is a good sign for him, that as they give him relief below [on earth] so they give him relief above [in heaven].

i. That is, 'sneezing above' *vs.* 'sneezing below', the latter, the note in the Soncino edition of the Talmud delicately informs us, is a 'euphemism'.

ii. Rashi's comment on this is: 'For it praises one who sneezes, and I am one who sneezes often!'

In *Oraḥ Ḥaim* 103, Yaʿakov ben ʾAšer — an alleged habitual sneezer himself — codifies Rabbi Zera's dictum about physical relief from the pressure to sneeze signalling a parallel Heavenly forgiveness. It seems that what is driving these ideas is that needing to sneeze is a terrible feeling, and its relief is both outside of our control and totally transforms our embodied experience. It thus makes for a charming, folkloristic model for Divine answer to prayer. The idea is that 'relief' is a forgiveness from sins — internal pressure being released, a burden of contaminants ejected. While this makes sense all year, there is something particularly timely about stressing the supernatural ramifications of sneezing during prayer before Yom Kippur. Sneezing thus appears to have been considered a positive sign. Cf. however Deutsch 2012: 93.

The verb *fnysthæ* 'to sneeze' is unusual, but found, for example, in the sixteenth-century dictionary *Libellus Vocum Latinarum* (Copenhagen, 1563) by Henrik Smith. See 'Hapax legomena and unusual words' in ch. 3.

As far as the section concerning the way a candle burns is concerned, it seems to be a folk belief as well. However, *Sefer Maharil*, a Jewish source, does mention that the way candles burn is an indication of the future (Spitzer 1989: 322):

אמר מהר״י סג״ל טעם הנרות שמדליקין ביה״כ, משום שכתב המרדכי מי שרוצה לידע
אם יעלה לו שנתו יקח נר וידליק מן ר״ה עד יו״כ.

Our teacher and rabbi, Yaʾakov Segal [Maharil] stated that the reason for lighting candles on Yom Kippur is because the Mordechai wrote that someone who wants to know whether he will make it through the year should take a candle and light it from Rosh Hashanah until Yom Kippur. (Translation adapted from Deutsch 2012: 93 n. 16).

17: 13–14	**Men ... *et*c:** A red string, or *royṭe bendel* (ראיטע בענדל) as it is called in Yiddish, is customarily worn by some Jews as a kind of talisman to ward off the evil eye (see Teman 2008). Here, however, it refers to another tradition whereby a red silk thread turns white if one's prayers are heard.
17: 17	**Esaie ... capitel:** Isaiah 1: 18: 'Come, let us reach an understanding, — says the LORD. "Be your sins like crimson, They can turn snow-white; Be they red as dyed wool, They can become like fleece."'
17: 18	**tempelen:** Cf. note for p. 1: 8–9.
17: 18–19	**th*e*m ... slecht:** Cf. note for p. 16: 13–14.
17: 19–21	**th*e*n ... hi*m*melen:** There are a number of prohibitions on Yom Kippur: eating, drinking, engaging in sexual relations, bathing, dealing with money, anointing with perfume or lotions, and wearing leather shoes. The last meal before the fast, known as *se'udah mafseqet* (סעודה מפסקת, 'meal of separation'), is an important and festive meal that ends shortly before sunset. The subsequent fast lasts just over 24 hours.
17: 22–23	**forneffndhæ ... høner:** Cf. note for p. 12: 8–9.
17: 24	**theris sckrifftæfeddrer:** Cf. note for p. 13: 25–28.
19: 23–25	**Th*e*n ... hører:** Proverbs 9: 9: 'Give instruction to a wise man, and he will be yet wiser'.
20: 9	**th*e*n ... institut:** Pfefferkorn is here suggesting that Judaism is a violation of both natural law (*lex naturalis*, a sort of self-evident truth) and man-made teachings (*institutum*).
20: 11–13	**wij ... ha*nn*u*m*:** The ethical principle called the Great Principle (a variation of the Golden Principle) is best summarised with this short story from the Talmud (*Shabbat* 31a; translation from Hertz 1992):

> On another occasion it happened that a certain heathen came before Shammai and said to him. 'Make me a proselyte, on condition that you teach me the whole Torah while I stand on one foot.' Thereupon he

289

repulsed him with the builder's cubit which was in his hand. When he went before Hillel, he said to him, 'What is hateful to you, do not do to your neighbour: that is the whole Torah, while the rest is the commentary thereof; go and learn it.'

Cf. Leviticus 19: 18 (and also Tobit 4: 15; Ecclesiasticus 31: 15). It has a parallel in Christian tradition: 'Do unto others as you would have them do unto you' (Matthew 7: 12; and also Luke 6: 31, 10: 25–28). The connection to Hillel's rule is underlined by Jesus' next comment: 'for this is the Law and the Prophets' (Matthew 7: 12).

20: 20   **wor messia:** Jesus of Nazareth, the central figure of Christianity.

21: 2   **iødernes ... Talmot:** See '*The Confession of the Jews*: Content' in ch. 2 for information about the Talmud.

21: 23–26   **Effther ... me*n*nisckæ:** Once again according to Pfefferkorn, Jewish activities are directed against Christians. Not only do they use curses, but they also make use of fancy arguments to mock Christianity. Behind this accusation lies the notion of Jews as a schooled literate group; they are well-informed and often highly educated rejecters of Christians and Christianity. Victor von Carben (1508) also asserted that it was unwise to enter into religious debate with Jews as they were taught from childhood how to defend their faith. See *JE*, III: 570, *s.v.* 'Carben, Victor of'.

22: 3   **end ... gøre:** Pfefferkorn names the two arch-opponents of Christianity, and explicitly names the Jews as being worse than the Devil. The Jews are thus made inhuman and at this popular level at least were transformed into monsters. This sort of negative dehumanising imagery did massive harm. See Trachtenberg 1993; Bonfil 1988, and Strickland 2003. In *Augenspiegel*, Reuchlin turns the accusation that Jews are like the Devil back onto Pfefferkorn himself (Reuchlin 1961: 41):

> Die xxix. vnwarhait. Sagt Pfefferkorn der iud sei genaturtt wie der tüwfel. das verantwurch ich also/ wir lerne*n* anders inn der waren philosophi/ solt aber das war sein/ so müßt mich nit verwu*n*dern das Pfefferkorn so vil vnwarhait gedar sagen/ die wyler von tüwfelscher natur empfangen vnd geboren were/ vnd tüwfelsche millch gesogen hett.

The 29th untruth: Pfefferkorn says that the Jew is by nature like the Devil. To this I answer thus: we learn otherwise from the true philosophy. However, if it were true, then I would not be surprised that Pfefferkorn says so much untruth because he would have been conceived and born from the Devil's nature and have suckled the Devil's milk.

22: 19 **at ... cristnæ:** On Jewish-Christian disputations, see Rankin 1956; Cohen 1964; Talmage 1975; Berger 1979; Cohen 1982; Maccoby 1982; Chazan 1989; Lasker 2007.

23: 1 **The ... dieffuelen:** Cf. note to p. 22: 3.

23: 25 **Gymach ... sichroe:** 'May his name and memory be obliterated'; see 'Hebrew words in *Secreta Iudeorum*' in ch. 3.

24: 1 **en ... lort:** Pfefferkorn is not repeating the usual accusation against the Jews of Host desecration, in which Jews were accused of endeavouring to torture Jesus once again by boiling, piercing or mutilating the holy communion wafer into which he was transubstantiated. However, he is claiming that Jews have nothing but insults and contempt for the Eucharist and Jesus.

24: 4–5 **See ... besckit:** Cf. note for p. 24: 1. Ræff's Danish translation of the original text is wrong here. The original has 'men hat mettamme gewest. off men hat den zeueltamme gegeuen. id est ille defedatus est [*They have been 'defiling', or they have given the 'defiled crap'. That is, it is defiled*]'. See 'Omissions and simplifications' in ch. 3.

24: 7–10 **Findhæ ... søndher**: On Jews and the Cross, see Horowitz 2008: 149–85, and on desecrating the Cross, see Yuval 2006: 166 n. 66. Cf. also Victor von Carben's words in *Judenbüchlein* (1508: fol. e5^v):

> Die Juden hasszen als ich vor gesagt hab das creütz gar sehr/ vnd legen zwey hälmlein oder höltzlein in jhren heüßeren creützweiß in dem weg/ so ist keyn kindt das so vermüglich wer/ es brech oder stieß sye mit den füssen von einander/ vnd nit mit den händen/ dann es ist jrs bedunckens nit wirdig gnůg/ das man es mit den händen anrůren soll/ kriegen sye aber einen gůten gulden/ vnd ob der x. creütz hette/ sye stiessen ihn nit mit den füssen von jhn/ sunder sye raffelten den mit beyden händen zů jnen

> As I have said before, the Jews hate the Cross very much, and if in their houses, two pieces of straw or sticks lie in the way on top of one other in the shape of a cross, then whatever child is so capable, breaks or kicks it apart with his feet, and not with his hands, because in their opinion it is not worthy enough that it should be touch by one's hands. However, if they get a solid guilder coin and even if there is a Roman numeral x [10] on it, they do not kick it away with their feet but rather grab it towards themselves with both hands.

24: 15–16 **tholoi:** 'The hanged one'; see 'Hebrew words in *Secreta Iudeorum*' in ch. 3.

24: 17 **iesche nozore:** 'Jesus of Nazareth'; see 'Hebrew words in *Secreta Iudeorum*' in ch. 3.

24: 19 **thlue:** 'The hanged one'; see 'Hebrew words in *Secreta Iudeorum*' in ch. 3.

24: 20 **kendeschim:** 'Sodomites' or 'whoremongers'; see 'Hebrew words in *Secreta Iudeorum*' in ch. 3.

24: 21 **tifflos:** 'Absurdity'; see 'Hebrew words in *Secreta Iudeorum*' in ch. 3.

24: 22 **toifos:** 'Hell' or 'imprisoned'; see 'Hebrew words in *Secreta Iudeorum*' in ch. 3.

24: 23–24 **Nar ... maria*m*:** The validity of the testimony of Jews given under oath was frequently drawn into doubt during the Middle Ages. A special form of oath, the *more iudaico* or 'Jewry oath', was created and, together with certain ceremonial actions (such as standing bare-footed on a three-legged stool or a bloodied lamb or sow's hide), was required to be taken by Jews in courts of law. See *EJ*, xv: 362, *s.v.* 'oath'; Kisch 1949: 275–87.

The question of the reliability of a Jew's oath is connected with the *Kol Nidrey* prayer from the service at the start of Yom Kippur which calls for an annulment of all vows, obligations, oaths and anathemas. Although Judaism teaches that this prayer concerns the individual's vows with his or her own conscience and God (that is, not vows between people), Jews have been obliged to defend the *Kol Nidrey* prayer since the thirteenth century against charges that it allowed them a means of getting out of obligations that they had made in regard to other people. Pfefferkorn points out another way in which Jews escape the promises they make, *viz.* by swearing their oaths on Christian figures such as Jesus and Mary to whom they do not feel bound.

25: 1–3 **Uij ... oss:** According to Pfefferkorn, the Jewish community felt more secure when their Christian neighbours were preoccupied with other matters. This can be compared with p. 9: 10–18 (with note).

25: 9–12 **Swo ... gømæ:** The image of Jews living in Christian lands being like a 'fire in one's lap' or 'a snake in one's arms' is far from unique to Pfefferkorn. Long before Pfefferkorn, in a letter dated 1205, Pope Innocent III (1198–1216) wrote to the archbishop of Sens and the bishop of Paris (quoted in Chazan 1997: 104):

> Because of their perfidy, even the Saracens who persecute the Catholic faith and do not believe in the Christ whom the Jews crucified cannot tolerate the Jews and have even expelled them from their territory, vehemently rebuking us for tolerating those by whom, as we openly acknowledge, our redeemer was condemned to the suffering on the cross. Thus, the Jews ought not to be ungrateful to us and ought not requite Christian favour with contumely and intimacy with contempt. Yet, while they are mercifully admitted into our intimacy, they threaten us with that retribution which they are accustomed to accord to their hosts, in accordance with the common proverb: 'Like a mouse in a pocket, like the snake around one's loins, like a fire in one's bosom.'

After Pfefferkorn, the snake simile is repeated, for example, by Georgius Nigrinus (1570; fol. L2ᵛ): Allowing Jews to live among Christians 'heisset Schlangen im Büsem wermen / vnd Wölffe im Hause auffzeihen / was die für Lohn geben / weis man wol [*means warming snakes in one's bosom and raising wolves in one's house. What payment they give in return is well known*]', and in a Jewish convert to Lutheranism, Samuel Friedrich Brenz's book of 1614, *Judischer Abgestreiffter Schlangenbalg* ['Jewish brood of snakes revealed']. The comparison with a fire or a snake is meant to exemplify how the Jews harbour deadly and secret animosity towards the very Christendom that has taken them in and shown them hospitality.

25: 14 **Købstædher:** At the beginning of the sixteenth century, there were some eighty or so 'købstæder' (market towns, but translated as cities to avoid repetition) in Denmark. Most of them were rather small with fewer than a thousand inhabitants. The largest city was by far Copenhagen with between ten and fifteen thousand inhabitants. References to market towns are not found in the Latin original and have presumably been included by Poul Ræff as it is particularly here that he sees a relevance for his publication. See 'Additions' in ch. 3.

26: 11–12 **I... troen:** Pfefferkorn criticises the authorities' protection of the Jews and their corrupt business.

26: 15 **sle*m*me hwndhæ:** Uncivilised people (particularly of the east) were usually equated with dogs (Strickland 2003: 204). They cannot communicate the word of God, as their mouths do not speak words — they merely bark. For example, in Marvede Church on Sjælland, there is a wall-painting (*c*. 1500) that includes a diminutive man with a dog-like head mocking Christ during the Passion. The use of the dog as an image for the Jews is probably based on biblical antecedents. For example, Revelation 22: 15: 'For without are dogs, and sorcerers, and whoremongers, and murderers, and idolaters, and whosoever loveth and maketh a lie.' Cf. also Isaiah 56:10; Psalms 22: 16, 20; Psalms 59: 6, 14. See also p. 3: 12, where Jews are called 'fwlæ honde [*vile dogs*]'. The major study on the association between Jews and dogs is Stow 2006.

26: 16 **aagher:** On usury see Baron 1952–83, 11: 139–46; Shatzmiller 1990: 43–70; Lipton 1999: 30–53.

27: 7–8 **Twingher ... fødhæ:** The notion of forced labour for Jews was developed further in 1543 by Martin Luther in his *On the Jews and Their Lies* (*WA* LIII: 525–26).

27: 10–11 **Twingher ... predicken:** Forced attendance at conversionary sermons was mandated in parts of Europe from the mid-thirteenth century. The insistance upon attendance at sermons is a sign of the Dominicans' hand in writing the booklet (Spanier 1936: 219). See Carlebach 2001: 59–62 on sixteenth-century conversionary preaching aimed at the Jews.

27: 19–21 **theris ... fæææ:** See note for p. 26: 16.

28: 17–18 **aff Frankæ righæ:** The Jews were expelled several times from France in the fourteenth century, culminating in the exile of 1394. See Roth 2003: 245–48, *s.v.* 'Expulsion, France'.

28: 18 **aff Hispanien:** The Jews were expelled from Spain in 1492. See Roth 2003: 248–49, *s.v.* 'Expulsion, Spain'.

28: 18 **aff Nørrenbergh:** The Jews were expelled from Nuremberg (Nürnberg), in Bavaria, Germany, in 1498–99. The Jewish population in Germany was not subject to wholesale expulsion, due to the country's political fragmentation. Instead, Jews were expelled from individual territories and cities, often as part of a broader strategy to serve local political interests by reducing the emperor's influence (Rummel 2002: 6). For example, Trier (1418), Cologne (1424), Saxony (1432), Augsburg (1440), Bavaria (1442/50), Würzburg (1453), Mainz (1479), Bamberg (1475), Passau (1478), Mecklenburg (1492), Württemberg (1498), Brandenburg (1510), Ansbach-Bayreuth (1515), and finally Regensburg (1519). On the Jews in Germany until the time Pfefferkorn was writing, see Herzig 1993.

28: 18 **aff Ulmæ:** The Jews were expelled from Ulm in Baden-Württemberg, Germany, in 1499.

29: 13–16 **Nar ... ku*n*ne:** During the sixteenth century there was an increasing number of cases of fraudulent conversion, whereby baptism was undertaken solely for the material benefits it offered. That converts received a baptismal gift only encouraged the practice of travelling from place to place and being converted many times. The phenomenon affirmed Christians' suspicions that Jewish converts were not sincere. See Carlebach 2001: 44–45.

29: 16–17 **Sidhen ... igen:** As it was a crime for converts to renounce their new religion and revert back to their former religion, it is difficult to ascertain the number of reversions. However, there were converts who renounced their baptism and rejoined Jewish communities. These relapses tended to strengthen the belief in Jewish stubbornness and obstinacy, and furthermore undermined the idea that Jews would convert *en masse* in the final days. See Carlebach 2001: 42–45.

30: 17–19 **then ... figuræ:** The literal (and less important) meaning of the text compared with the spiritual, higher meaning of the text. The word *figuræ* almost certainly refers to the prefigurations and proof-texts in the Old Testament that foreshadow events and persons in the New Testament.

APPENDIX I

Pfefferkorn's publications

An overview of his works in German, Latin, Hebrew and Danish with summaries of each

The following overview of Johannes Pfefferkorn's publications includes works in German (G), Latin (L), Hebrew (H) and Danish (D).[1] Each entry includes a short description of the works' contents as well as references to modern editions of the text. The locations of the extant original publications by Pfefferkorn are provided by Kirn 1989: 201–04 and Schmitz 1990: 97–115. The earliest bibliographic mention of Pfefferkorn's works is in Johann Christoph Wolf's *Bibliotheca Hebræa* from the beginning of the eighteenth century. In his list of 'Scriptores anti Judaici ex Judæi' (Wolf 1715–21, II: 1011), we read:

> *Pfefferkornii* (Iohan.) Speculum Manuale contra Iudæos & libros Talmudicos: Celeusma contra infideles Iudæos: Speculum Adhortationis Iudaicæ ad Christum: Hostis Iudæorum. […]

> *By Pfefferkorn, Johannes. Hand Mirror against the Jews and the Books of the Talmud; A Call against the Jewish Infidels; Mirror of Exhortation to Turn Jews to Christ; The Enemy of the Jews. […]*

Most of the Latin translations of Pfefferkorn's German works are thought to have been undertaken by Ortwin Gratius. Pfefferkorn claimed that he oversaw and checked these translations (see 'Johannes Pfefferkorn: Early Life' in ch. 2).

A **The Mirror of the Jews (Mirror of Exhortation to Turn Jews to Christ)**
  1507 (G) *Der Joeden spiegel* (Cologne: Johannes Landen)
  1507 (G) *Der Juden Spiegel* (Nuremberg: Wolfgang Huber)

---

1. Many of the German and Latin editions are available online from *Münchener Digitalisierungs-Zentrum: Digitale Bibliothek* at http://www.digitale-sammlungen.de.

1507 (G) *Der Juden Spiegel* (Cologne: Martin von Werden)

1507 (L) *Speculum adhortationis iudaice ad Christum* (Cologne: Martin von Werden)

1507 (L) *Speculum adhortationis iudaice ad Christum* (Speyer: Conrad Hist)

1508 (L) *Speculum adhortationis Judaice ad Christum* (Cologne: Martin von Werden)

1508 (L) *Speculum adhortationis iudaice ad Christum* (Cologne: Johannes Landen)

In this pamphlet, Pfefferkorn demands that the Jews stop practising usury, that they find 'normal' work, that they be forced to hear Christian preaching, and that they stop using the Talmud (the source of their enmity towards the Christians). However, he condemns the persecution of the Jews, as this would hinder their conversion and he furthermore defends the Jews against the accusation of ritual infanticide.[2] The use of the term *spiegel* ('looking-glass') in this and other of Pfefferkorn's titles is a common metaphor in book titles of the period and promises an accurate mirroring of matters usually distorted or hidden.

Edition: Kirn 1989: 205–30; Cape and Diemling 2011. See also Frey 1990.

B **The Confession of the Jews**

1508 (G) *Ich heyß eyn buchlijn der iuden beicht...* (Cologne: Johannes Landen, 14 Aug. 1508)

1508 (G) *Ich heyss ain büchlein der iuden peicht...* (Augsburg: Jörg Nadler)

1508 (G) *Ich heyss ein büchlein...* (Augsburg: Hans Froschauer)

1508 (G) *Ich heyß ein buchlein der iuden peicht...* (Nuremberg: Johannes Weissenburger)

1508 (G) *Ich heysch eyn boichelgyn der ioeden Bicht* (Cologne: ?)

1508 (L) *Libellus de Judaica confessione* (Cologne: Johannes Landen)

1508 (L) *Libellus de Judaica confessione* (Nuremberg: Johannes Weissenburger)

1516 (D) *Nouiter in lucem data: iudeorum secreta* (Copenhagen: Poul Ræff)

A pamphlet that ridicules Jewish customs and rituals leading up to and during Rosh Hashanah and Yom Kippur. In addition, it describes the dangers of contact with Jews and presents a number of solutions to the Jewish threat.

---

2. In the beginning of the sixteenth century, the Jews were still being accused of ritual infanticide in Germany (for example, in Freiburg 1503; see Oberman 1983: 46; Rowan 1975: 7).

Edition: Rummel 2002: 69–81 (an English translation of excerpts from the German). See also Deutsch 2012: 177–21.

C **<No title>**
    1508 (H) - - - (Cologne: Johannes Landen)

A single folio containing Hebrew translations of *Pater Noster*, *Ave Maria* and *Credo*. It is unlikely that Pfefferkorn was able to translate these prayers; more likely, they are the work of the Dominicans.

D ***How the Blind Jews Keep Easter***
    1509 (G) *In diesem buchlein vindet yr ein entlichen furtrag wie die blinden Juden yr Ostern halten...* (Cologne: Johannes Landen, 3 Jan. 1509)
    1509 (G) *In diesem buchlein vindet Jez ain entlichenn fürtrag wie die blinden Juden yr Ostern halten* (Augsburg: Erhard Öglein)
    1509 (L) *In hoc libello comparatur absoluta explicatio quomodo ceci illi iudei suum pascha servent...* (Cologne: Heinrich von Neuß, Feb. 1509)

The book is in many ways a continuation of the *Confession of the Jews*. It describes Jewish customs during Passover and shows that they reflect Christian practices and spirit, thereby proving the truth of Christianity. For a discussion, see Martin 1994: 100.

E ***The Enemy of the Jews***
    1509 (G) *Ich bin ein buchlein Der Juden veindt ist mein namen...* (Cologne: Johannes Landen, 31 Jan. 1509)
    1509 (G) *Ich bin ain Buchlinn der Juden veindt ist mein namen...* (Augsburg: Erhard Öglein)
    1509 (L) *Hostis Iudeorum* (Cologne: Heinrich von Neuß, Mar. 1509)

In this pamphlet Pfefferkorn reveals the Jews' hatred towards Christians and the danger they pose Christians through usury and medicine. Again, Jewish books are seen as the source of the Jews' hatred.

Edition: Rummel 2002: 53–67 (an English translation of excerpts from the German).

F ***A Letter from Johannes Pfefferkorn***
    1510 (G) *Allen vnd ieglichen geistlich oder weltlich in was stat...* (1510)

This public letter (now in the Wolfenbütteler Library, with a copy in the flyleaf of a manuscript in the Staatsbibliothek in Berlin) calls for the confiscation of the Jews' books from their synagogues and libraries and for the punishment of the Jews who are a danger to Christians.

Editions: Böcking 1864–69, II: 73–74; Spanier 1934.

G   ***In Praise and Honour of the Most Glorious and Powerful Duke and Lord Maximilian***

    1510 (G) *In lob und eer dem Allerdurchleuchtigsten Großmechtigsten Fursten und heren hern Maximilian...* (Cologne: Heinrich von Neuß)

    1510 (G) *Zu lob vnd Ere des aller durchleichtigisten vnd großmechtigisten Fürsten vnd herren. Her Maximilian...* (Augsburg: Erhard Öglein)

    1510 (L) *In laudem et honorem Illustrissimi maximque principi...* (Cologne: Heinrich von Neuß; translated on the behest of Andreas Kanter[3])

A description of the events leading up the removal of the Jews' books and a plea to the emperor to uphold the confiscations.

H   ***Hand Mirror***

    1511 (G) *HAndt Spiegel...* (Mainz: Johann Schöffer)

This is Pfefferkorn's very public response to Reuchlin's recommendation whether or not to confiscate the Jews' books. He had felt insulted by Reuchlin who had drawn the reason for his conversion to Christianity into doubt. *Handt Spiegel* derides Reuchlin, suggests dishonourable motives for his decision and claims he does not understand the Talmud.

I   ***Fire Mirror***

    1512 (G) *ABzotraiben und aus zuleschen eines vngegrunten laster buechleyn mit namen Augenspiegell... Brantspiegell* (Cologne: Herman Gutschaiff)

This, Pfefferkorn's response to Reuchlin's *Augenspiegel*, blames him for the failure of his plan to confiscate Jewish books. He underlines the importance of the persecu-

---

3. Fol. E6ʳ: 'Andreas Kanter Frisius lectori. ostendit libellum hunc teutonicum mihi Iohannes pfefferkorn voluitque vt latinum facerem [*Andreas Kanter, from Frisia, teacher, showed me, Johannes Pfefferkorn, this booklet in German and he wanted me to translate it into Latin*]'.

tion of the Jews as the Christians' enemies and calls for the forced baptism of Jewish children.

J **Storm Bell / Alarm Bell**
    1514 (G) *Sturm Johansen Pfefferkorn vber vnd wider die drulosen Juden… Sturm Glock* (Cologne: Quentelsöhne)

Another attack on the Jews and Reuchlin's *Augenspiegel* in which he makes public the judgement of the University of Paris from 28 August 1514 which had condemned Reuchlin's book as heretical.

K **Defence of Johannes Pfefferkorn**
    1516 (G) *Beschyrmung…* (Cologne)
    1516 (L) *Defensio Ioannis Pepericorni Contra Famosas et Criminales Obscurorum Virorum Epistolas…* (Cologne: Heinrich von Neuß)

Pfefferkorn presents himself as the victim of the Devil's work.

Edition: Böcking 1864–69, I: 81–176;

L **Defence of Johannes Pfefferkorn against the Dark Men**
    1516 (G) *Streydtpuechlyn vor dy Warheit vnd eyner warhafftiger Historie…* (Cologne)

Pfefferkorn attempts to counter some of the degrading remarks about his character and includes supportive documents.

M **A Compassionate Plaint**
    1521 (G) *Aın mitleydliche Claeg vber alle claeg…* (Cologne: Servas Kruffter, 21 Mar. 1521)

This is Pfefferkorn's final triumphant publication in which he greatly insults Reuchlin.

APPENDIX II

The broadsheet against Pfefferkorn

An introduction to and edition of the broadsheet belonging to Hebrew Union College, CIN Special Collections

Among the special collections of Hebrew Union College Library in Cincinnati, USA, can be found a broadsheet that lampoons Johannes Pfefferkorn.[1] It reads as a sort of warrant that enumerates the numerous crimes of which he was guilty before his conversion to Christianity. Although this is the only extant libellous broadsheet concerning Pfefferkorn, we find references to its contents in other writings. For example, *Epistolae obscurorum virorum* I, 23:[2]

> Sed dicitur hic quod Ioannes Pfefferkorn, quem etiam defenditis vos, est malus nequam, et non est factus christianus amore fidei, sed propterea quod Iudęi voluerunt eum suspendere propter suas nequitias, quia dicunt quod est fur et proditor, et sic fuit baptizatus;

> *But it is said here that Johannes Pfefferkorn, whom is defended by you, is a bad man, and did not become a Christian for love of the Faith, but rather because the Jews wished to have him hanged for his wrong doings, for they say that he is a thief and a traitor, and that is why he had himself baptised.*

And in *Epistolae obscurorum virorum* II, 3:[3]

> Iudęi faciunt iniuriam Iohanni Pfefferkorn, quia nunquam furavit aliquid, neque malefecit etiam quando fuit Iudęus, sicut est pie credendum.

---

1. Hebrew Union College, CIN Special Collections (A-85 1196, A-85 1197). In all, the library has about forty tracts penned by eleven or twelve participants in the struggle between Pfefferkorn and Reuchlin.
2. Böcking 1864–69, I: 36, ll. 11–15.
3. Böcking 1864–69, I: 190, ll. 20–22.

> *The Jews do Johannes Pfefferkorn an injury, as he never stole anything, nor did he do any wrongdoing when he was a Jew, as it is piously to be believed.*

Its contents appear to have been common knowledge among Pfefferkorn's opponents. Indeed, in his *Streydtpuechlyn* from 1516, he found it necessary to include an attestation from the mayor and councillors of Dachau that he had never been convicted there of theft (fols e4^v–f1^r):

> Wyr Burgemeister vnd Radt. der Stadt Dachaw Bekennen offentlich mit diesem Brieffe [… || …] Soe haben wyr von gedachten Johannes Pfefferkorn. dieweil vnd er bey vnd neben vnz zů Dachaw eyn jůd gewest Nachuolgend eyn crist worden von diesen obenangetzeygten artikel vnd puncten bey jm nie erfonden. auch kaynerley diepstal vnd begreyffung

> *We, the mayor and councillors of the city Dachau attest publicly with this letter […] As far as the aforementioned Johannes Pfefferkorn (who was once a Jew in Dachau and who subsequently became a Christian) is concerned, we have never found him involved in any of the aforementioned articles and points, and in no way involved in theft or arrest.*

Note, however, that in the *Acta judiciorum inter F. Iacobum Hochstraten & Iohannem Reuchlin* (1518), we read:[4]

> Hac non obstante inhibitione interea multi famosi libelli aduersus Iohannem Reuchlin lite pendente profecto ut patet modeste quiescentem & omnia molesta sine repercussione tollerantem a Iacobitis inordinati sunt quibus tamen libellis nullam fidem adhibent probi uiri. Scientes illos authore iudæo quodam tincto editos esse, qui crucifer ante aliquot annos a duabus crucibus patibularibus[5] data pecunia ut publica fama fert & notorium extat liberatus est.

> *In the meantime, without letting themselves be hindered by this prohibition, the Jacobites [i.e. the supporters of Jakob Hoogstraten] published many libellous texts against Johann Reuchlin, who — while the case was ongoing — held himself humbly back and put up with all these unpleasant things without answering back. But no decent people would place their trust in these publications. They are known by the*

---

4. Reuchlin and Hoogstraten 1518: fol. i5^v, ll. 2–9.
5. On this word for gallows, see Böcking 1864–69, II: 605 n. 16, *s.v.* 'patibulum'.

> *Jewish author, in whose ink they are published; he was to be executed on two fork-shaped gallows, [but] money was paid so that public opinion was swayed and the news released that he was to be set free.*

That it is notorious that he was bought off the gallows twice is precisely what it says in this broadsheet.

The broadsheet, which has been reproduced before, was acquired by the Hebrew Union Library in 1929.[6] It is written in a form of southern German (note, for example, the spellings with ⟨ai⟩ — *ain, stain, aigen, arbait*). The catalogue dates it to 1515 and names Tübingen, in central Baden-Württemberg, as its place of origin. Given the date of Pfefferkorn's defensive counterattack in *Streydtpuechlyn* (1516) *op. cit.* and the dialect of the text, I see no reason to contest the dating or place of publication. Hans Kirn, however, views the use of a hare as a symbol for Reuchlin as evidence that the broadsheet must have appeared after Pfefferkorn's last publication in 1521, in which he uses the image of a hare on the title page and elsewhere to refer to Reuchlin.[7]

Transcription

Des Pfefferkorns Leben
¶ Der Pfefferkorn / ist zů liegen vnd triegen gebornn / falsch spilen vnd stelen hat in ernert / des galgen sich noch nit erwert

¶ Item Zů Dachaw am Behemer Wald bei der Schwartzenburg ist er als ain dieb der gestolen hat gefangenn gelegen / in gewalt her Heinrichs vonn Gůtten stain / da richt man im einen sonderenn aigen galgenn vff / new gebauen / der stat noch / aber durch fleissig arbait sines schwehers den man nennet Lemlinn ward er von dem selben galgen erlöst. Vnd nam Herr Hainrich vonn Gůtenstain obgemelt von seinem schweher Lemlin hundert vngerisch gülden vnd ließ in ledig

¶ Item Pfefferkorn hat von Bani Tsubin von Derüiß vff ettlich müntz dar vnder vil blei vnd falscher zeug gewesen entlehnet hundert guldin / vnnd da mit hinweg gezogen gen Prag zů / da rait im Tsubins schwager nach / den mann genent hat Schönman / vnd ylet im ab bei den lxxx gülden / die vberigen het er verthon

---

6. See the facsimile in Zafren 1961: 142. Kirn has published a transcription (Kirn 1989: 179–81), but there are a few errors and one of the place-names has also been misidentified (Weissenburg), which he places in Alsace rather than Middle Franconia; cf. Kracauer 1887: 248.
7. Kirn 1989: 180–81.

¶ Item zů Werd wer der Pfefferkorn vmb diepstal auch gefangen worden het in der Richter von Wyssenburg nit mit gelt erlediget das sine fründ fur in geben haben Vnd da ist im der diepstal vnnd das gelt so er gestolenn noch bei im het / wider genomen wordenn

¶ Item Er hat dem Reichenn Isack da malß Zů Wyssenburg im Norkow zwey guldin fingerlin oder ring vß der teschen gestolen

¶ Item Er hat ain Wirtin zům Nüenmarck vmb ainen silberin becher betrogen vnd den selben an anderen orten versetzt / vnnd als er des hart gelegnet hat / da ist die sach luter an den tag gebracht / darumb er ist gewichen vnd alßo entrunnen

¶ Item Zů Brin in Merhern hat er ainen gulden rinck entlehnet geschetzt bei hundert gulden wert vnd hat darnach das verlögnet / vnd behend sich vß dem land gethon

Vil andere Ertzbüberei als das er sinen fründenn da er ain metzger oder flaisch-hacker was schelmig todte vich für lebendig vnd frisch vßgehawen hat / vnnd vil falscher spil geüppt / darumb er ist ain schelmen schinder genant / beleipt ietzt vber / aber laßent euch nit verlangen es wurdt bald mer kummen

Das alles gehört zů dem Schmachbüchlin so Pfefferkorn schrybt
wider den christlichen doctor Johan Reüchlin
Des Pfefferkorns galg zů Dachaw

> Mich wundert das man du Schelm dich hat gdult
> So du den galgenn wo hast bschuldt
> Vnd dir nit thůt noch dynem recht
> So dan alle sachen wurden schlecht
>
> Du Hundt / du Schelm merck eben das
> Hie steet der galg in grienem graß
> Der Haß lygt nit / ich sag dir war
> Frembd hendt wirst haben in dym har
> Hab acht Sesse das dir
> der Haß nit entlauff

Translation

The Life of Pfefferkorn
Pfefferkorn was born to lie and deceive. Cheating and stealing have sustained him. He has not yet managed to avoid the gallows.

- He was caught in Dachau in the Bohemian Forest close to Schwarzenburg as a thief who had been stealing, and was imprisoned by Heinrich von Gutenstein. He was built his very own set of gallows. Newly constructed, it is still standing. However, due to the hard work of his brother-in-law, called Lemlin, he was released from these very gallows. And the aforementioned Heinrich von Gutenstein received one hundred Hungarian guilders [*florins*] from Pfefferkorn's brother-in-law Lemlin and released him.

- Furthermore, Pfefferkorn borrowed a hundred guilders from Pán Tsubin of Třebíč [*in Moravia, or, rather less likely, Derwitz in Brandenburg*] in return for some coins, including much lead and fake scrap, and with that money he went off to Prague. Then Tsubin's brother-in-law, a man called Schönmann, rode after him and got nearly eighty guilders out of him. Pfefferkorn had spent the rest.

- Pfefferkorn was also arrested for theft in Donauwörth. The judge in Weissenburg [*Middle Franconia, Bavaria*] did not release him despite the money that his relatives had paid for him. And in this way, the stolen goods and money that he had stolen and still had in his possession were returned.

- From the wealthy man Isaac at that time in Weissenburg im Nordgau [*Bavaria*] he stole two gold rings or a bracelet out of his bag.

- He tricked a landlady in Neumarkt out of a silver cup and pawned it in another town, and he vigorously denied it, when the matter came to light, which is why he has run away and disappeared.

- In Brno in [*southern*] Moravia, he borrowed a gold ring, valued to be worth a hundred guilders, and afterwards he denied it and quickly made his way abroad.

There is still much more villainy to tell of, such as when he was a meat-seller or butcher and made cuts from the carcasses of perished cattle for his relatives pretending they were from living and fresh (animals). And he has engaged in much cheating, which is why he is now called a villainous knacker[i]. But do not allow yourselves to hanker for more, there will soon come more!

This can all be found in the libellous booklet that Pfefferkorn writes against the Christian doctor Johannes Reuchlin.

Pfefferkorn's gallows in Dachau:

> I am amazed that they could stand you,
> As you deserve nothing less than the gallows.
> And they have not done to you what would be right,
> So that all affairs become resolved in a just manner.
> You dog! You scoundrel! Take note!
> The gallows are standing here in the green grass
> The hare[ii] doesn't lie, I'm telling you the truth,
> You will have the hands of strangers in your hair.
> Watch out! Mind[iii] that the hare doesn't run from you!

Notes on the text:
i. The German *schinder* means 'knacker', that is someone who renders animals that are unfit for human consumption. It was considered a dishonest trade for unworthy characters. As in English, the term is also used pejoratively to mean an anti-social person, a good-for-nothing. The compound *schelmen schinder* can furthermore be interpreted as a rather unpleasant term for a 'washer of corpses', probably intended to refer to Pfefferkorn's passing off the meat of carcasses as clean, fresh cuts. The writer of the broadsheet clearly intended some sort of a pun here.
ii. The hare is a symbol for Johann Reuchlin here. See Kirn 1989: 181.
iii. *Sesse* is the call used to alert dogs and start them running during a hunt. Rather like the English use of 'tally-ho!' in fox-hunting.

Des Pfefferkorns Leben

¶ Der Pfefferkorn/ist zů liegen vnd triegen gebornn/falsch spilen vnd stelen hat in ernert/des galgen sich noch nit erwert

¶ Item zů Dachaw am Behemer Wald bei der Schwartzenburg ist er als ain dieb der gestolen hat gefangenn gelegen/in gewalt her Heinrichs vonn Güttenstain/da richt man im einen sonderenn aigen galgenn vff/new gebawen/der stat noch/aber durch fleissig arbait sines schwehers den man nennet Lemlinn ward er von dem selben galgen erlöst. Vnd nam Herr Hainrich vonn Gütenstain obgemelt von seinem schweher Lemlin hundert vngerisch gülden vnd ließ in ledig

¶ Item Pfefferkorn hat von Bani Tsubin von Derüiß vff ettlich müntz darvnder vil blei vnd falscher zeug gewesen entlehnet hundert guldin/vnnd da mit hinweg gezogen gen Prag zů/da rait im Tsubins schwager nach/den mann genent hat Schönman/vnd ylet im ab bei den lxxx gülden/die vberigen het er verthon

¶ Item zů Werd wer der Pfefferkorn vmb diepstal auch gefangē worden het in 8 Richter von Wyssenburg nit mit gelt erlediget das sine fründ fur in geben haben Vnd da ist im der diepstal vnnd das gelt so er gestolen noch bei im het/wider genomen worden

¶ Item Er hat dem Reichenn Isack da malß zů Wyssenburg im Norkow zwey guldin fingerlin oder ring vß der teschen gestolen

¶ Item Er hat ain Wirtin zům Nüenmarck vmb ainē silberin becher betrogē vnd den selben an anderen orten versetzt/vnnd als er des hart gelegnet hat/da ist die sach luter an den tag gebracht/darumb er ist gewichen vnd also entrunnen

¶ Item zů Brin in Merhern hat er ainen gulden rinck entlehnet geschetzt bei hundert gulden wert vnd hat darnach das verlögnet/vnd behend sich vß dē land gethon

Vil andere Ertzbüberei als das er sinen fründenn da er ain metzger oder flaischhacker was schelmig todte vich für lebendig vnd frisch vsgehawen hat/vnnd vil falscher spil geüppt/darumb er ist ain schelmen schinder genant/beleipt ietzt vber/aber lassent euch nit verlangen es wurde bald mer kummen

Das alles gehört zů dem Schmachbüchlin so Pfefferkorn schrybt wider den christlichen doctor Johan Reüchlin

Des Pfefferkorns galg zů Dachaw

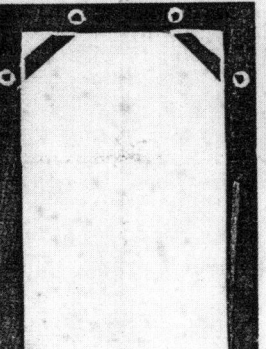

Mich wundert das man dich hat gdult
So du den galgenn wol hast bschuldt
Vnd dir nit thůt noch dy nem recht
So dan alle sachen wur den schlecht

Hab acht Sesse das dir

Du Hůdr/du Schelm merck eben das
Hie steet d̄ galg in grienem graß
Der Haß lygt nit/ich sag dir war
Frembd hendt wirst haben in dym har

der Haß nit entlauff

Figure 13
Facsimile of the broadsheet against Pfefferkorn. With permission of Hebrew Union College, Cincinnati.

Bibliography

ABULAFIA, Anna Sapir. 1985. 'Invectives against Christianity in the Hebrew Chronicles of the First Crusade', in Edbury, pp. 66–72.

ADAMS, Jonathan. 2000. 'An Introduction to the Danish Translations of St Birgitta's *Revelations*', in Morris and O'Mara, pp. 87–105.

———. 2010. 'Hebraiske ord i *Jødernes hemmeligheder* (1516)', in *Danske Studier* 105, pp. 31–50.

———. 2012. 'Grumme løver og menstruerende mænd: Forestillinger om jøder i middelalderens Danmark', in *Rambam* 21, pp. 78–93.

———, and Katherine HOLMAN, eds. 2004. *Scandinavia and Europe 800–1350: Contact, Conflict and Coexistence*. Medieval Texts and Cultures of Northern Europe 4. Turnhout: Brepols.

ADLER, Marcus Nathan, ed. and trans. 1907. *The Itinerary of Benjamin of Tudela*. London: Oxford University Press.

AGNON, Shmuel Yosef. 1965. *Days of Awe, Being a Treasury of Traditions, Legends and Learned Commentaries Concerning Rosh Ha-Shanah, Yom Kippur and the Days Between*. Introduction by Judah Goldin. New York: Schocken Books.

AILI, Hans, ed. 1992. *Sancta Birgitta: Revelaciones. Book IV*. SFSS Ser. 2, 7: 4. Stockholm: Almqvist & Wiksell.

ALLEN, Percy Stafford, ed. 1906–58. *Opus Epistolarum Des: Erasmi Roterodami*. 12 vols. Oxford: Clarendon Press.

ALMOG, Shmuel, ed. 1988. *Antisemitism through the Ages*. Oxford: Pergamon Press.

ANDERSEN, Poul, *et al.*, eds. 1974. *Festskrift til Kristian Hald, 9. september 1974*. Navnestudier udgivet af Institut for Navneforskning 13. Copenhagen: Akademisk Forlag.

ANDERSON, Andrew Runni. 1932. *Alexander's Gate: Gog and Magog and the Inclosed Nations*. Monographs of the Medieval Academy of America 5. Cambridge (MA): The Medieval Academy of America.

ANDERSSON, Aksel. 1890. *Variarum rerum vocabula cum sueca interpretatione: Stockholm 1538. Glosor till Terentii Andria med inledning, anmärkningar och alfabetisk index över de svenska orden. I: Täkst*. Uppsala: Almqvist & Wiksell.

ANDERSSON, Roger. 2003. 'Om de femton platser Maria besökte efter Jesu död: Den fornsvenska texten', in Härdelin *et al.*, pp. 107–35.

ARING, Paul Gerhard. 1998. 'Pfefferkorn, Johannes', in Bautz *et al.* 1975–, XIV, cols. 1359–60.

ARIOSTO, Ludovico. 1611. *Ariostos seven Planets Gouerning Italie. Or his satyrs in seven Famous discourses ... Newly Corrected and Augmented, with many excellent and worthy notes, together with a new Addition of three most excellent Elegies, written by the same Lodovico Ariosto, the effect whereof is contained in the Argument. Qui te sui te sui.* Trans. and ed. by Robert Tofte. London: William Standsby.

ARNOLD, Elliott. 1967. *Night of Watching.* New York: Charles Scribner.

BAK, Sofie Lene. 2010. *Ikke noget at tale om: Danske jøders krigsoplevelser 1943–1945.* Afterword by Bjarke Fjølner. Copenhagen: Dansk Jødisk Museum.

———. 2012. *Da krigen var forbi: De danske jøders hjemkomst efter Besættelsen.* Copenhagen: Gyldendal.

BALE, Anthony. 2006. *The Jew in the Medieval Book: English Antisemitisms, 1350–1500.* Cambridge Studies in Medieval Literature. Cambridge: Cambridge University Press.

BARON, Salo Wittmayer. 1952–83. *A Social and Religious History of the Jews.* 2nd edn. 18 vols. New York: Columbia University Press.

BAR-ZOHAR, Michael. 1998. *Beyond Hitler's Grasp: The Heroic Rescue of Bulgaria's Jews.* Holbrook (MA): Adams Media Corp.

BÄUMER, Remigius, and Leo SCHEFFCZYK, eds. 1988–94. *Marienlexikon.* 6 vols. St Ottilien: EOS Verlag.

BAUTZ, Friedrich Wilhelm, *et al.*, eds. 1975–. *Biographisch-Bibliographisches Kirchenlexikon.* 14 vols, 20 supplements and 1 index [as of 2012]. Herzberg: Verlag Traugott Bautz.

BECH, Sven Cedergreen, ed. 1982. *Dansk biografisk Leksikon XII: Rasmusen–Scavenius.* Copenhagen: Gyldendal.

BECKER, Reinhard Paul. 1981. *A War of Fools: The Letters of the Obscure Men: A Study of the Satire and the Satirized.* New York University Ottendorfer Series. Neue Folge 12. Bern: Peter Lang.

BELL, Dean Phillip, and Stephen G. BURNETT, eds. 2006. *Jews, Judaism and the Reformation in Sixteenth-Century Germany.* Studies in Central European Histories 37. Leiden: Brill.

BENDZ, Gerhard. 1965. *Ordpar.* Svenska Humanistiska Förbundet 74. Stockholm: Norstedt & Söner.

BENGTSON, Arne. 1947. *Nils Ragvaldi: Domareboken och Linköpingslegendariet. En filologisk författerbestämning och ett bidrag till kännedomen om det senmedeltida vadstenaspråket.* Lundastudier i nordisk språkvetenskap 4. Lund: Berlingska boktryckeriet.

BERGEN, Fanny D. 1890. 'Some Saliva Charms', in *The Journal of American Folklore* 3: 8, pp. 51–58.

BERGER, David. 1975. 'Christian Heresy and Jewish Polemic in the Twelfth and Thirteenth Centuries', in *Harvard Theological Review* 68, pp. 287–303.

———. 1998. 'On the Uses of History in Medieval Jewish Polemic against Christianity: The Search for the Historical Jesus', in Carlebach, Efron and Myers, pp. 25–39.

———, ed. 1979. *The Jewish-Christian Debate in the High Middle Ages. A Critical Edition of the* Niẓẓahon Vetus *with an Introduction, Translation and Commentary*. Judaica I: 4. [Philadelphia:] The Jewish Publication Society of America.

BERGH, Birger, ed. 1967. *Den heliga Birgittas Revelaciones Bok VII*. SFSS Ser. 2, 7: 7. Stockholm: Almqvist & Wiksell.

———, ed. 1991. *Sancta Birgitta: Revelaciones. Book VI*. SFSS Ser. 2, 7: 6. Stockholm: Almqvist & Wiksell.

BERULFSEN, Bjarne. 1958. 'Antisemittisme som litterær importvare', in *Edda: Nordisk tidsskrift for litteraturforskning* 58, pp. 123–44.

BESTUL, Thomas H. 1996. *Texts of the Passion*. Philadelphia: University of Pennsylvania Press.

BETTAN, Israel. 1939. *Studies in Jewish Preaching. I: Middle Ages*. Cincinnati: Hebrew Union College Press.

BIALE, David. 1999. 'Counter-History and Jewish Polemics against Christianity: The "Sefer toldot yeshu" and the "Sefer zerubavel"', in *Jewish Social Studies*, New Series 6: 1, pp. 130–45.

BIENERT, Walther. 1982. *Martin Luther und die Juden*. Frankfurt am Main: Evangelisches Verlagswerk.

BILDHAUER, Bettina. 2003. 'Blood, Jews, and Monsters in Medieval Culture', in Bildhauer and Mills, pp. 75–96.

———, and Robert MILLS, eds. 2003. *The Monstrous Middle Ages*. Toronto: University of Toronto Press.

BIRKELUND, Palle, *et al.*, eds. 1949. *Dansk Boghaandværk gennem Tiderne 1482–1948*. Copenhagen: Fischers Forlag.

BLÆDEL, Nicolaj Gottlieb. 1884. *Udvidet Confirmations-Undervisning efter evangelisk-luthersk Kirkelære*. 2nd edn [first published in 1876]. Copenhagen: Gyldendalske Boghandels Forlag.

BLÜDNIKOW, Bent. 1983. 'Synagogen i København — 150 år', in *Dansk Jødisk Historie* 12, pp. 22–31.

BLUMENKRANZ, Bernhard. 1966. 'Jüdische und christliche Konvertiten im jüdisch-christlichen Religionsgespräch des Mittelalters', in Wilpert, pp. 264–88.

BÖCKING, Eduard, ed. 1864–69. *Ulrichi Hutteni equitis Operum supplementum: Epistolæ Obscurorum Virorum cum inlustrantibus adversariisque scriptis.* 2 vols. Leipzig: B. G. Tevbnerus.

BOLVIG, Axel. 2003. *Den ny billedbibel.* Copenhagen: Politikens Forlag.

———, and Phillip LINDLEY, eds. 2003. *History and Images: Towards a New Iconology.* Medieval Texts and Cultures of Northern Europe 5. Turnhout: Brepols.

BONFIL, Robert. 1988. 'The Devil and the Jews in the Christian Consciousness of the Middle Ages', in Almog, pp. 91–98.

BOSWELL, John. 1981. *Christianity, Social Tolerance, and Homosexuality.* Chicago: The University of Chicago Press.

BRADLEY, Sid A. J. 1969. 'The Translator of *Mandevilles Rejse*: A New Name in Fifteenth-Century Danish Prose?', in Pearsall and Waldron, pp. 146–54.

———. 1976. '*Mandevilles Rejse*: Some Aspects of its Changing Rôle in the Later Danish Middle Ages', in *Mediaeval Scandinavia* 9, pp. 146–63.

———. 1993. 'Mandevilles Rejse', in Pulsiano *et al.*, p. 404.

———, ed. 1999. *The Danish Version of 'Mandeville's Travels' in Sixteenth-Century Epitome.* Scandinavian Studies 4. Lewiston (NY): The Edwin Mellen Press.

BRANDT, Carl Joakim. 1857. *Gammeldansk Læsebog: En Håndbog i vor ældre Literatur på Modersmålet.* Copenhagen: Iversens Forlag.

———. 1859. *De hellige kvinder: En Legende-Samling.* Copenhagen: G. E. C. Gad.

———. 1882. *Om Lunde-Kanniken Christiern Pedersen og hans Skrifter.* Copenhagen: G. E. C. Gad.

———, and Th. FENGER, eds. 1850–56. *Christiern Pedersens danske Skrifter.* 5 vols. Copenhagen: Gyldendal.

BRAUDE, Benjamin. 1996. '*Mandeville's* Jews among Others', in LeBeau and Mor, pp. 133–58.

BRENZ, Samuel Friedrich. 1614. *Judischer Abgestreiffter Schlangenbalg. Daß ist: Gründtliche entdeckung unnd verwerffung aller Lästerung und Lügen, derer sich das gifftige Judische Schlangenzifer und Otterngezicht, wider den Frömbsten, unschuldigen Juden Christum Jesum ... theils in den verfluchten synagogen, theils in Häusern und heimlichen zusammenkunfften pflegt zugebrauchen.* Nuremberg: B. Scherff.

BREUER, Mordechai, ed. 1978. *Sefer Niẓaḥon Yašan.* Jerusalem: Bar-Ilan University.

BROD, Max. 1965. *Johannes Reuchlin und sein Kampf: Eine historische Monographie.* Stuttgart: W. Kohlhammer.

BRØNDUM-NIELSEN, Johannes. 1914. *Sproglig Forfatterbestemmelse: Studier over dansk sprog i det 16. århundrede.* Copenhagen: Gyldendalske Boghandel.

——————. 1928–74. *Gammeldansk Grammatik i sproghistorisk Fremstilling.* 8 vols. Copenhagen: J. H. Schultz Forlag.

——————. 1934. 'Om Fragmenterne af den gammeldanske Siæla Trøst', in *Acta Philologica Scandinavica* 9, pp. 187–92.

——————, ed. 1955. *Et gammeldansk digt om Christi opstandelse efter Fragment Stockh. *A 115 (c. 1325).* Det Kongelige Danske Videnskabernes Selskab. Historisk-filologiske Meddelelser 35: 1. Copenhagen: Munksgaard.

——————, and Aage ROHMANN, eds. 1929. *Mariaklagen efter et runeskrevet Haandskrift-Fragment i Stockholms kgl. Bibliotek.* Copenhagen: J. H. Schultz.

BRONNER, Simon J., ed. 2008. *Jewishness: Expression, Identity, and Representation.* Jewish Cultural Studies 1. Portland (OR): Oxford.

BRUUN, Christian. 1870–98. *Aarsberetningen og Meddelelsen fra det store kgl. Bibliothek.* 4 vols. Copenhagen: G. E. C. Gad.

——————, ed. 1866. *Modus confitendi. De passione Domini: Et tabt dansk Skrift fra c. 1500.* Copenhagen: G. E. C. Gad.

BUCKL, Walter, and Silke EGBERS. 1994. 'Speculum humanae salvationis', in Bäumer and Scheffczyk 1988–94, VI, pp. 227–31.

BURNETT, Stephen G. 1994. 'Distorted Mirrors: Anthonius Margaritha, Johann Buxtorf and Christian Ethnographies of the Jews', in *Sixteenth Century Journal* 25: 2, pp. 275–87.

BUXTORF, Johannes. 1989 [1680]. *Synagoga judaica.* Reprod. Hildesheim, Zürich & New York: Georg Olms Verlag.

CAMPBELL, Mary B. 1988. *The Witness and the Other World: Exotic European Writing, 400–1600.* Ithaca: Cornell University Press.

CAPE, Ruth I., and Maria DIEMLING, eds. 2011. *The Jews' Mirror (Der Juden Spiegel) by Johannes Pfefferkorn.* Medieval and Renaissance Texts and Studies 390. Tempe (AZ): Arizona Center for Medieval and Renaissance Studies.

CARBEN, Victor von. 1508. *Judenbüchlein: Hyerinne wuert gelesen, wie Her Victor von Carben, welcher ein Rabi der Juden gewesst ist, zu christlichem glauben kommen.* Cologne: [s.i.].

CARLEBACH, Elisheva. 1996. 'Attribution of Secrecy and Perceptions of Jewry', in *Jewish Social Studies* 2, pp. 115–36.

——————. 2001. *Divided Souls: Converts from Judaism in Germany, 1500–1750.* New Haven: Yale University Press.

———, John M. EFRON and David N. MYERS, eds. 1998. *Jewish History and Jewish Memory: Essays in Honor of Yosef Hayim Yerushalmi*. Hanover (NH): Brandeis University Press.

CARPI, Daniel, ed. 1993. *Shlomo Simonsohn Jubilee Volume. Studies on the History of the Jews in the Middle Ages and Renaissance Period*. Tel Aviv: Tel Aviv University.

Catechism of the Catholic Church. 1994. London: Geoffrey Chapman.

CHAZAN, Robert. 1989. *Daggers of Faith: Thirteenth-Century Christian Missionizing and the Jewish Response*. Berkeley: University of California Press.

———. 1997. *Medieval Stereotypes and Modern Antisemitism*. Berkeley: University of California Press.

———. 2004. *Fashioning Jewish Identity in Medieval Western Christendom*. Cambridge: Cambridge University Press.

———. 2006. *The Jews of Medieval Western Christendom, 1000–1500*. Cambridge Medieval Textbooks. Cambridge: Cambridge University Press.

CHRISTENSEN, Karsten. 1987. 'Jochim Jøde i Helsingør i 1592', in *Dansk Jødisk Historie* 24, pp. 11–16.

COHEN, Jeremy. 1982. *The Friars and the Jews: The Evolution of Medieval Anti-Judaism*. Ithaca: Cornell University Press.

———. 1992. 'Towards a Functional Classification of Jewish Anti-Christian Polemic in the High Middle Ages', in Lewis and Niewöhner, pp. 93–114.

———. 1993. 'Profiat Duran's "The Reproach of the Gentiles" and the Development of Jewish Anti-Christian Polemic', in Carpi, pp. 71–84.

———. 1999. *Living Letters of the Law: Ideas of the Jew in Medieval Christendom*. Berkeley: University of California Press.

———. 2007. *Christ Killers: The Jews and the Passion from the Bible to the Big Screen*. Oxford: Oxford University Press.

COHEN, Martin A. 1964. 'Reflections on the Text and Context of the Disputation of Barcelona', in *Hebrew Union College Annual* 35, pp. 157–92.

COHEN, Richard I. 1998. *Jewish Icons: Art and Society in Modern Europe*. Berkeley: University of California Press.

COLDING, Poul Jensen. 1626. *Dictionarium Herlovianum*. Copenhagen: Salomon Sartor.

COLLIJN, Isak. 1913. 'Nyfunna fragment af fornsvenska handskrifter bland räkenskapsomslagen i Kammararkivet', in *Samlaren* 34, pp. 275–93.

COOPERMAN, Bernard Dov, ed. 1983. *Jewish Thought in the Sixteenth Century*. Cambridge (MA): Harvard University Press.

COUDERT, Alison, and Jeffrey S. SHOULSON, eds. 2004. *Hebraica Veritas? Christian Hebraists and the Study of Judaism in Early Modern Europe*. Philadelphia: University of Pennsylvania.

CROMPTON, Louis. 2006. *Homosexuality and Civilisation*. Cambridge (MA): Harvard University Press.

CROSSAN, John Dominic. 1996. *Who Killed Jesus? Exposing the Roots of Antisemitism in the Gospel Story of the Death of Jesus*. San Francisco: Harper.

CUTLER, Allan. 1965. 'The Ninth-Century Spanish Martyrs Movement and the Origins of Western Christian Missions to the Muslims', in *Muslim World* 55, pp. 321–39.

DAHAN, Gilbert. 1990. *Les intellectuels chrétiens et les juifs au moyen âge*. Paris: Le Cerf.

DAHLERUP, Pil. 1998. *Dansk litteratur: Middelalder*. 2 vols. Copenhagen: Gyldendal.

──────. 2010. *Sanselig middelalder: Litterære perspektiver på danske tekster 1482–1523*. Århus: Aarhus Universitetsforlag.

DAL, Erik. 1982. '50 trykte bøger 1482–1522. Teknik, udstyr, funktion', in *Bogvennen: Skrift, Bog og Billede i Senmiddelalderens Danmark*, pp. 67–86.

──────, and Rafael EDELMANN. 1965. 'Ahasverus, den evige jøde', in *Fund og Forskning* 12, pp. 31–46.

DALMAN, Gustaf Hermann. 1893. *Jesus Christ in the Talmud, Midrash, Zohar, and the Liturgy of the Synagoge: Texts and Translations*. Introduction by Heinrich Laible. Translated and expanded from the German [*Jesus Christus im Thalmud*] by A. W. Streane. Cambridge: Deighton, Bell, and Co.

DASYPODIUS, Petrus. 1995. *Dictionarium latinogermanicum*. Introduction by Gilbert de Smet. Documenta Linguistica. Quellen zur Geschichte der deutschen Sprache des 15. bis 20. Jahrhunderts 1. Facsimile reproduction of the 1536 Strassburg edition. Hildesheim: Georg Olms Verlag.

DAVID, Abraham, ed. 1984. *Kroniqah 'ivrit miPrag merešit hame'ah ha-yudzayin: A Hebrew Chronicle from Prague (c. 1616)*. Kuntresim Texts and Studies 65. Jerusalem: The Dinur Center, The Hebrew University.

DAVIS, Natalie Zemon. 1973. 'The Rites of Violence: Religious Riot in Sixteenth-Century France', in *Past & Present* 58, pp. 51–91.

DELUZ, Christiane, ed. 1988. *Livre de Jehan de Mandeville, une 'géographie' au xive siècle*. Publications de l'Institut d'Études Médiévales: Textes, Études, Congrès 8. Louvain-la-Neuve: Université Catholique de Louvain.

DEUTSCH, Yaacov. 2004. 'Polemical Ethnographies: Descriptions of Yom Kippur in the Writings of Christian Hebraists and Jewish Converts to Christianity in Early Modern Europe', in Coudert and Shoulson, pp. 202–33.

———. 2006. '*Von den Juden Ceremonien*: Representations of Jews in Sixteenth-Century Germany', in Bell and Burnett, pp. 335–56.

———. 2010. 'Jewish Anti-Christian Invectives and Christian Awareness: An Unstudied Form of Interaction in the Early Modern Period', in *Leo Baeck Institute Year Book* 55, pp. 41–61.

———. 2012. *Judaism in Christian Eyes: Ethnographic Descriptions of Jews and Judaism in Early Modern Europe*. Translated from the Hebrew [*Yahadut be'enayim nozriot*] by Avi Aronsky. New York: Oxford University Press.

DIDERICHSEN, Paul. 1935–36. 'Texthistoriske Bemærkninger til *Reuelaciones Sancte Birgitte*', in *Acta Philologica Scandinavica* 10, pp. 232–49.

———, ed. 1931–37. *Fragmenter af de gammeldanske Haandskrifter*. Universitets-Jubilæets Danske Samfund. Copenhagen: J. H. Schultz.

DIEMLING, Maria. 1999. '"Christliche Ethnographien" über Juden und Judentum in der Frühen Neuzeit: Die Konvertiten Victor von Carben und Anthonius Margaritha und ihre Darstellung jüdischen Lebens und jüdischer Religion'. Unpublished PhD thesis. University of Vienna.

———. 2005. '"As the Jews Like to Eat Garlick": Garlic in Christian-Jewish Polemical Discourse in Early Modern Germany', in Greenspoon, Simkins and Shapiro, pp. 215–34.

———. 2006. 'Anthonius Margaritha and His "Der Gantz Jüdisch Glaub"', in Bell and Burnett, pp. 303–33.

DINZELBACHER, Peter, and Dieter R. BAUER, eds. 1990. *Volksreligion im hohen und späten Mittelalter*. Quellen und Forschungen aus dem Gebiet der Geschichte 13. Paderborn: Schöningh.

DISSEN, Yonah Y., ed. 1978. *Sefer minhagim lerabeinu 'Avraham Kloyzner* ['Minhagim (Customs) of Rabbi Abraham Klausner']. Jerusalem: Mifal Torath Chachmey Ashkenaz.

DOUGLAS, Mary. 2002. *Purity and Danger: An Analysis of Concepts of Polution and Taboo*. Routledge Classics Edition [same as 1966 edition, but with a new preface by the author]. London: Routledge.

DRUMONT, Édouard. 1886. *La France Juive: Essai d'histoire contemporaine*. Revised edition. 2 vols. Paris: Ernest Flammarion.

DUNDES, Alan. 1991. *The Blood Libel Legend: A Casebook in Anti-Semitic Folklore*. Madison: University of Wisconsin Press.

EDBURY, Peter W., ed. 1983. *Crusade and Settlement*. Cardiff: University College Cardiff Press.

EDELMANN, Rafael. 1948. 'Dansk Bog om Antisemitisme', in *Jødisk Samfund* 22 (September), pp. 10–11.

EDWARDS, John. 1988. *The Jews in Christian Europe 1400–1700*. Christianity and Society in the Modern World. London: Routledge.

EISENBERG, Ronald L. 2004. *JPS Guide: Jewish Traditions*. Philadelphia: The Jewish Publication Society.

EKLUND, Sten, ed. 1991. *Sancta Birgitta: Opera Minora III. Quattuor Oraciones*. SFSS Ser. 2, 8: 3. Stockholm: Almqvist & Wiksell.

ELBOGEN, Ismar. 1931. *Der jüdische Gottesdienst in seiner geschichtlichen Entwicklung*. 3rd edn. Schriften herausgegeben von der Gesellschaft zur Förderung der Wissenschaft des Judentums. Grundriß der Gesamtwissenschaft des Judentums. Frankfurt am Main: J. Kauffmann.

———. 1993. *Jewish Liturgy: A Comprehensive History*. Translated from the German [*Der jüdische Gottesdienst in seiner geschichtlichen Entwicklung*] by Raymond P. Scheindlin. Ed. by Joseph Heinemann *et al*. Philadelphia: The Jewish Publication Society.

ELIAV-FELDON, Miriam, Benjamin ISAAC, and Joseph ZIEGLER, eds. 2009. *The Origins of Racism in the West*. Cambridge: Cambridge University Press.

ENGELSTOFT, Christian Thorning. 1848. 'Paulus Eliæ, en biografisk-historisk Skildring fra den danske Reformationstid (Anden Afdeling)', in *Nyt Historisk Tidsskrift* 2, pp. 415–554.

EPSTEIN, Marc Michael. 2002. 'Review Essay. Re-Presentations of the Jewish Image: Three New Contributions', [review article] in *AJS Review* 26: 2, pp. 327–40.

ERASMUS, Desiderius. 1974–93. *Collected Works of Erasmus*. 86 vols. Translated by R. A. B. Mynor *et al*. Annotated by Peter G. Bietenholz *et al*. Toronto: University of Toronto Press.

FOA, Anna. 2000. *The Jews of Europe after the Black Death*. S. Mark Taper Foundation Imprint in Jewish Studies. Berkeley: University of California Press.

FREDERIKSEN, Britta Olrik. 2001. 'Review of Pil Dahlerup. 1998. *Dansk litteratur: Middelalder*. 2 vols. Copenhagen: Gyldendal', [review article] in *Alvíssmál: Forschungen zur mittelalterlichen Kultur Skandinaviens* 10, p. 88–106.

FREUNDENTHAL, Max. 1931. 'Dokumente zur Schriftenverfolgung durch Pfefferkorn', in *Zeitschrift für die Geschichte der Juden in Deutschland* 3, pp. 272–32.

FREY, Winfried. 1990. '"Der Juden Spiegel": Johannes Pfefferkorn und die Volksfrömmigkeit', in Dinzelbacher and Bauer, pp. 177–93.

FRIEDMAN, John Block. 1981. *The Monstrous Races in Medieval Art and Thought*. Cambridge (MA): Harvard University Press.

FRIEDMAN, Yvonne, ed. 1985. *Petri Venerabilis: Adversus Iudeorum inveteratam duritiem*. CCCM 58. Turnhout: Brepols.

FROJMOVIC, Eva, ed. 2002. *Imagining the Self, Imagining the Other: Visual Representations and Jewish-Christian Dynamics in the Middle Ages and Early Modern Period.* Cultures, Beliefs and Traditions 15. Leiden: Brill.

FUNKENSTEIN, Amos. 1968. 'Hatemurot bewikuaḥ hadat šebein yehudim lenoẓrim beme'ah ha-yud-beit [*Changes in the debate between Christian anti-Jewish in the twelfth century*]', in *Ẓiyon* [*Zion*] 33: 3–4, pp. 125–44.

—————. 1971. 'Basic Types of Christian Anti-Jewish Polemics in the Later Middle Ages', in *Viator* 2, pp. 373–82.

—————. 1993. *Perceptions of Jewish History.* A Centennial Book. Berkeley: University of California Press.

GAD, Tue. 1963. 'Jøder', in *KLNM* VIII: col. 74–76.

—————. 1964. 'Kristus', in *KLNM* IX: cols 365–77.

GEETE, Robert, ed. 1907–09. *Svenska böner från medeltiden.* SFSS 38. Stockholm: Norstedt.

GEIGER, Ludwig. 1910. *Die Deutsche Literatur und die Juden.* Berlin: Georg Heimer.

GEJROT, Claes. 2000. 'The *Fifteen Oes*: Latin and Vernacular Versions: With an Edition of the Latin Text', in Morris and O'Mara, pp. 213–38.

GELFER-JØRGENSEN, Mirjam, ed. 1999. *Danish Jewish Art: Jews in Danish Art.* Copenhagen: The Society for the Publication of Danish Cultural Monuments.

GHEMEN, Gotfred of. 1915. *Jesu passionsvandring: Opbyggelsesskrift trykt i København af Gotfred af Ghemen.* Facsimile edition with introduction by H. O. Lange. Århus: Aarhus Stiftsbogtrykkeri.

GILMAN, Sander L. 1986. *Jewish Self-Hatred: Anti-Semitism and the Hidden Language of the Jews.* Baltimore: The John Hopkins University Press.

—————, and Steven T. KATZ. 1991. *Antisemitism in Times of Crisis.* New York: New York University Press.

GLASSMAN, Bernard. 1975. *Anti-Semitic Stereotypes without Jews: Images of the Jews in England 1290–1700.* Detroit: Wayne State University.

GOLDSCHMIDT, Daniel. 1956. 'Hašlamah lamaḥzor leyom hakipurim [*Restoration of the missing piyuṭim to the maḥzor for the Day of Atonement (with one facsimile)*]', in *Qiryat Sefer* 31 (1956), pp. 146–51.

GOLDSTEIN, Morris. 1950. *Jesus in the Jewish Tradition.* New York: The Macmillan Company.

GOW, Andrew Colin. 1995. *The Red Jews: Antisemitism in an Apocalyptic Age 1200–1600.* Studies in Medieval and Reformation Thought 55. Leiden: E. J. Brill.

GRAESSE, Jean George Théodore. 1859–69. *Trésor de livres rares et précieux, ou nouveau dictionnaire bibliographique.* 7 vols [bound as 8]. Dresden: Rudolf Kuntze.

GRAETZ, Heinrich. 1866. *Geschichte der Juden* IX: *Von der Verbannung der Juden aus Spanien und Portugal (1494) bis zur dauernden Aussiedelung der Marranen in Holland (1618)*. Leipzig: Oskar Leiner.

———. 1875. 'Aktenstücke zur Confiscation der jüdischen Schriften in Frankfurt a. M. unter Kaiser Maximilian durch Pfefferkorns Angeberei', in *Monatsschrift für Geschichte und Wissenschaft des Judentums* 24, pp. 289–300, 337–43, 385–402.

GREENBLATT, Stephen. 1991. *Miraculous Possessions: The Wonder of the New World*. Chicago: The University of Chicago Press.

GREENSPOON, Leonard J., Ronald A. SIMKINS and Gerald SHAPIRO, eds. 2005. *Food and Judaism*. Studies in Jewish Civilization 15. Omaha (NE): Creighton University Press.

GUGGENHEIM, Yakov. 1995. 'Meeting on the Road. Encounters between German Jews and Christians on the Margins of Society', in Hsia and Lehmann, pp. 125–36.

HAASTRUP, Niels. 1974. 'The Minim-Confusion: Et kritisk analyse fra pælografisk [*sic!*] hold på mulighederne for at dokumentere lydhistorien udfra middelalderlige mss', in Andersen *et al.*, pp. 379–89.

HAASTRUP, Ulla. 1999. 'Jødefremstillinger i dansk middelalderkunst', in Gelfer-Jørgensen, pp. 111–67.

———. 2003. 'Representations of Jews in Medieval Danish Art — Can Images Be Used as Source Material on Their Own?', in Bolvig and Lindley, pp. 341–56.

———, and Robert EGEVANG, eds. 1985–92. *Danske kalkmalerier*. 8 vols. Copenhagen: Nationalmuseet.

HAMPTON FROSELL, Preben. 1987. *Københavnske synagoger gennem tre hundrede år*. Copenhagen: C. A. Reitzel.

HANSEN, Aage. 1934–35. 'Om "ja" og "nej"', in *Acta Philologica Scandinavica* 9, pp. 225–45.

———. 1962–71. *Den lydlige udvikling i dansk fra ca. 1300 til nutiden*. 2 vols. Copenhagen: Gad.

HANSEN, Anne Mette. 2004. 'Den danske bønnebogstradition i materialfilologisk belysning'. Unpublished PhD thesis. University of Copenhagen.

HÄRDELIN, Alf, and Mereth LINDGREN, eds. 1993. *Heliga Birgitta — budskapet och förebilden: Föredrag vid jubileumssymposiet i Vadstena 3–7 oktober 1991*. KVHAA Konferenser 28. Stockholm: Almqvist & Wiksell International.

HÄRDELIN, Alf, *et al.* 2003. *I Kristi och hans moders spår: Om stationsandakter i Sverige*. Sällskapet Runica et Mediævalia Script Minora 8. Stockholm: Sällskapet Runica et Mediævalia.

HARRISON, Dick. 2000. *Stora döden: Den värsta katastrof som drabbat Europa*. Stockholm: Ordfront.

HEDSTRÖM, Ingela. 2009. *Medeltidens svenska bönböcker: Kvinnligt skriftbruk i Vadstena kloster*. Acta Humaniora 405. Oslo: Universitetet i Oslo.

HEIL, Johannes, and Rainer KAMPLING, eds. 2001. *Maria Tochter Sion?* Paderborn: Schöningh.

HEIMANN, Siegfried. 1982. 'Den første jøde i Danmark', in *Dansk Jødisk Historie* 8, pp. 4–10.

HELLER, Marvin J. 1992. *The Printing of the Talmud: A History of the Earliest Printed Editions of the Talmud*. Brooklyn (NY): Im Sefer.

HENRIX, Hans Hermann, ed. 1979. *Jüdische Liturgie. Geschichte — Struktur — Wesen*. Quaestiones disputatae 86. Freiburg: Herder.

HERBERMANN, Franz von, *et al.*, eds. 1913–14. *The Catholic Encyclopedia: An International Work of Reference on the Constitution, Doctrines, Discipline, and History of the Catholic Church*. 16 vols. New York: The Knights of Columbus Catholic Truth Committee.

HERGEMÖLLER, Bernd-Ulrich. 2001. *Randgruppen der spätmittelalterlichen Gesellschaft*. 2nd edn. Warendorf: Fahlbusch.

HERTZ, Joseph. H. 1972. *Hebrew-English Edition of the Babylonian Talmud: Shabbath, Vol. I*. Trans. by H. Freedman under the editorship of Isidore Epstein. London: The Soncino Press.

HERZIG, Arno. 1993. 'Die Juden in Deutschland zur Zeit Reuchlins', in Herzig and Schoeps, pp. 11–20.

———, and Julius H. SCHOEPS, eds. 1993. *Reuchlin und die Juden*. Pforzheimer Reuchlinschriften 3. Sigmaringen: Jan Thorbecke.

HINDMAN, Sandra. 1991. *Printing the Written Word. The Social History of Books circa 1450–1520*. Ithaca & London: Cornell University Press.

———, and James Douglas FARQUHAR. 1977. *Pen to Press: Illustrated Manuscripts and Printed Books in the First Century of Printing*. College Park: Art Department, University of Maryland.

HINGELBERG, Poul Nielsen. 1995. *Vocabulorum variorum expositio*. Ed. by Jørgen Larsen. Facsimile edition of 1576. Det 16. århundredes danske vokabularier 5. Copenhagen: Universitets-Jubilæets danske Samfund.

HODGEN, Margaret T. 1964. *Early Anthropology in the Sixteenth and Seventeenth Centuries*. Philadelphia: University of Philadelphia Press.

HOLBERG, Ludvig. 1933. *Ludvig Holbergs samlede Skrifter. XIII: Den jødiske Historie*. Ed. by Carl S. Petersen. Copenhagen: Gyldendalske Boghandel.

HOLLMAN, Lennart. 1956. *Den heliga Birgittas reuelaciones extrauagantes*. SFSS Ser. 2, 5. Uppsala: Almqvist & Wiksell.

HOROWITZ, Elliott. 1986–87. 'Al ketav-yad mazuyar šel sefer Mišneh Torah [*On an illuminated manuscript of* Mishneh Torah]', in *Qiryat Sefer* 61, pp. 358–86.

―――――――. 2008. *Reckless Rites: Purim and the Legacy of Jewish Violence. Jews, Christians, and Muslims from the Ancient to the Modern World*. Princeton: Princeton University Press.

HORSTBØLL, Henrik. 1999. *Menigmands medie: Det folkelige bogtryk i Danmark 1500–1840*. Danish Humanist Texts and Studies 19. Copenhagen: Det Kongelige Bibliotek.

HSIA, Ronnie Po-Chia. 1988. *The Myth of Ritual Murder: Jews and Magic in Reformation Germany*. New Haven: Yale University Press.

―――――――. 1992. *Trent 1475: Stories of a Ritual Murder Trial*. New Haven: Yale University Press.

―――――――. 1994. 'Christian Ethnographies of Jews in Early Modern Germany', in Waddington and Williamson, pp. 223–36.

―――――――. 1995. 'The Usurious Jew: Economic Structure and Religious Representations in an Anti-Semitic Discourse', in Hsia and Lehmann, pp. 161–76.

―――――――. 1997. 'Christian Ethnographies of Jews in Early Modern Germany', in Hsia and Scribner, pp. 35–47.

―――――――. 2009. 'Religion and Race: Protestant and Catholic Discourses on Jewish Conversions in the Sixteenth and Seventeenth Centuries', in Eliav-Feldon, Isaac and Ziegler, pp. 265–75.

―――――――, and Hartmut LEHMANN, eds. 1995. *In and Out of the Ghetto: Jewish-Gentile Relations in Late Medieval and Early Modern Germany*. Publications of the German Historical Institute (Washington D. C.). Cambridge: Cambridge University Press.

―――――――, and Robert W. SCRIBNER, eds. 1997. *Problems in the Historical Anthropology of Early Modern Europe*. Wolfenbütteler Forschungen 78. Wiesbaden: Harrassowitz.

IZYDORCZYK, Zbigniew, ed. 1997. *The Medieval Gospel of Nicodemus: Texts, Intertexts, and Contexts in Western Europe*. Medieval & Renaissance Texts & Studies 158. Tempe (AZ): Medieval & Renaissance Texts & Studies.

JACOBS, Neil G. 2005. *Yiddish: A Linguistic Introduction*. Cambridge: Cambridge University Press.

JAMES, Montague Rhodes. 1924. *The Apocryphal New Testament*. Oxford: Clarendon Press.

JANSEN, Katherine L., and Miri RUBIN, eds. 2010. *Charisma and Religious Authority: Jewish, Christian, and Muslim Preaching 1200–1500*. Europa sacra 4. Turnhout: Brepols.

JOHANSEN, Holger Friis. 1959. 'Et nyt stykke af den gammeldanske Birgitta-oversættelse', in *Danske Studier* 54, pp. 48–52.

JOHNSON, Willis. 1998. 'The Myth of Jewish Male Menses', in *Journal of Medieval History* 24, pp. 273–95.

JOHNSTON, Philip S. 2002. *Shades of Sheol: Death and Afterlife in the Old Testament*. Illinois: InterVarsity Press.

JORDAN, William Chester. 1987. 'The Last Tormentor of Christ: An Image of the Jew in Ancient and Medieval Exegesis, Art and Drama', in *Jewish Quarterly Review* 78, pp. 21–47.

JØRGENSEN, C., ed. 1879. *Det philologisk-historiske Samfunds Mindeskrift*. Copenhagen: Rudolph Klein.

JØRGENSEN, Harald. 1981. 'Københavnske synagoger i 1700-tallet', in *Dansk jødisk Historie* 5, pp. 4–11.

———, ed. 1984. *Indenfor murene: Jødisk liv i Danmark 1684–1984*. Copenhagen: C. A. Reitzel.

JØRGENSEN, Jens Anker. 2007. *Humanisten Christiern Pedersen: En præsentation*. Copenhagen: C. A. Reitzel.

KALKAR, Otto. 1881–1918. *Ordbog over det ældre danske Sprog*. 5 vols. Copenhagen: Universitets-Jubilæets danske Samfund.

KARKER, Allan, *et al.*, eds. 1956–78. *Kulturhistorisk leksikon for nordisk middelalder fra vikingetid til reformationstid*. 22 vols. Copenhagen: Rosenkilde og Bagger.

KAUFMANN, Thomas. 2006. 'Luther and the Jews', in Bell and Burnett, pp. 69–104.

KEDAR, Benjamin Z. 1971. 'Letoldot hayišuv hayehudi biYrušalayim beme'ah ha-yud-gimel [*The Jewish community of Jerusalem in the thirteenth century*]', in *Tarbiẓ* 41: 1, pp. 82–94.

———. 1973. 'Letoldot hayišuv hayehudi b'Ereẓ Yiśra'el beymei-beinayim [*Notes on the history of the Jews in Palestine in the Middle Ages*]', in *Tarbiẓ* 42: 3–4, pp. 401–18.

———. 1979. 'Canon Law and the Burning of the Talmud', in *Bulletin of Medieval Canon Law* 9, pp. 79–82.

KENDALL SOULEN, Richard. 1996. *The God of Israel and Christian Theology*. Minneapolis: Fortress.

KESSLER, Edward. 2010. *An Introduction to Jewish-Christian Relations*. Cambridge: Cambridge University Press.

KIRN, Hans-Martin. 1989. *Das Bild vom Juden im Deutschland des frühen 16. Jahrhunderts: Dargestellt an den Schriften Johannes Pfefferkorns*. Texts and Studies in Medieval and Early Modern Judaism 3. Tübingen: J. C. B. Mohr (Paul Siebeck).

KISCH, Guido. 1949. *The Jews in Medieval Germany: A Study of Their Legal and Social Status*. Chicago: The University of Chicago Press.

KLEMMING, Gustaf E., ed. 1848–55. *Svenska medeltidens Bibel-arbeten*. SFSS Ser. 1: 7. Stockholm: Norstedt & söner.

——————, ed. 1860: *Bonaventuras betraktelser*. SFSS Ser. 1: 15. Stockholm: Norstedt & söner.

——————, ed. 1862. *Konung Alexander: En medeltids dikt från latinet vänd i svenska rim omkring år 1380 på föranstaltande af riksdrotset Bo Jonsson Grip. Efter den enda kända handskriften*. SFSS Ser. 1: 12. Stockholm: Norstedt.

——————, ed. 1893. *Svenska medeltidspostillor efter gamla handskrifter: Tredje delen*. SFSS Ser. 1: 23. Stockholm: Norstedt.

KNUDSEN, Gunnar, Marius KRISTENSEN and Rikard HORNBY. 1949–64. *Danmarks gamle Personnavne. II: Tilnavne*. Copenhagen: Gad.

KOCH-OLSEN, Ib. 1968. *Danmarks kulturhistorie*. Copenhagen: Dansk Arbejdsmands- og Specialarbejderforbund.

KÖHLER, Hans-Joachim, ed. 1981. *Flugschriften als Massenmedium der Reformationszeit: Beiträge zum Tübinger Symposion 1980*. Spätmittelalter und frühe Neuzeit 13. Stuttgart: Klett-Cotta.

KOK, Johannes. 1878. *Det hellige Land og dets Nabolande i Fortid og Nutid: Til Vejledning og Opbyggelse for Bibellæsere*. Copenhagen: P. G. Philipsen.

KRACAUER, Isidor. 1887. 'Die Konfiskation der hebräischen Schriften in Frankfurt a. Main in den Jahren 1509 und 1510', in *Zeitschrift für die Geschichte der Juden in Deutschland* 1, pp. 160–76, 230–48.

——————. 1900a. 'Actenstücke zur Geschichte der Confiscation der hebräischen Schriften in Frankfurt a. M.', in *Monatsschrift für die Geschichte der Wissenschaft des Judentums* 44, pp. 114–26, 167–77, 220–34.

——————. 1900b. 'Verzeichniss der von Pfefferkorn 1510 in Frankfurt a. M. confiscierten jüdischen Bücher', in *Monatsschrift für die Geschichte der Wissenschaft des Judentums* 44, pp. 320–32, 423–30, 455–60.

KRAUSS, Samuel. 1977. *Das Leben Jesu nach jüdischen Quellen*. Reprint of 1902 edition. Hildesheim & New York: Georg Olm.

KREMERS, Heinz, *et al.*, eds. 1985. *Die Juden und Martin Luther — Martin Luther und die Juden: Geschichte, Wirkungsgeschichte, Herausforderung*. Neukirchen-Vluyn: Neukirchener.

KRISTENSEN, Marius, *et al.*, eds. 1932–48. *Skrifter af Paulus Helie*. 7 vols. Copenhagen: Det Danske Sprog- og Litteraturselskab.

KÜHNEL, Bianca, Galit NOGA-BANAI and Hanna VORHOLT, eds. Forthcoming. *Visual Constructs of Jerusalem*. Cultural Encounters in Late Antiquity and the Middle Ages. Turnhout: Brepols.

LAALE, Peder. 1506. *Jncipit iustissimus legifer et diuinarum virtutum optimus preceptor Petrus laale Danorum lux Et doctorum virorum euidens exemplum atque specimen*. Copenhagen: Gotred of Ghemen.

LANGEBEK, Jacob. 1764–65. *Fortegnelse paa de ældste og rareste Bøger, som ere trykt før og i Reformations-Tiden*. 2 vols. Copenhagen: Det kgl. Videnskabernes Societet.

LASCH, Agathe. 1914. *Mittelniederdeutsche Grammatik*. Sammlung kurzer Grammatiken germanischer Dialekte 9. Halle a. S.: Max Niemeyer.

LASKER, Daniel J. 2007. *Jewish Philosophical Polemics against Christianity in the Middle Ages*. 2nd edn. Portland (OR): The Littman Library of Jewish Civilization.

LAUERBACH, Jacob Z. 1936. 'Tashlik: A Study in Jewish ceremonies', in *Hebrew Union College Annual* 11, pp. 207–340. [Reprinted in 1951 as 'Tashlik (1936)', in *Rabbinic Essays*. Cincinnati: Hebrew Union College, pp. 299–433].

LAUSTEN, Martin Schwarz. 1991–92. 'Jødernes hemmeligheder', in *Rambam* 31, pp. 67–81.

—————. 1992. *Kirke og synagoge: Holdninger i den danske kirke til jødedom og jøder i middelalderen, reformationstiden og den lutherske ortodoksi (ca. 1100–ca. 1700)*. Kirkehistoriske studier 3: 1. Copenhagen: Akademisk Forlag. [Reprinted in 2002].

—————. 2000. *De fromme og jøderne: Holdninger til jødedom og jøder i Danmark i pietismen (1700–1760)*. Kirkehistoriske studier 3: 7. Copenhagen: Akademisk Forlag.

—————. 2002. *Oplysning i kirke og synagoge: Forholdet mellem kristne og jøder i den danske oplysningstid (1760–1814)*. Kirkehistoriske studier 3: 8. Copenhagen: Akademisk Forlag.

—————. 2005. *Frie jøder? Forholdet mellem kristne og jøder i Danmark fra Frihedsbrevet 1814 til Grundloven 1849*. Kirkehistoriske studier 3: 10. Copenhagen: Forlaget Anis.

—————. 2007a. *Folkekirken og jøderne: Forholdet mellem kristne og jøder i Danmark fra Frihedsbrevet 1849 til begyndelsen af det 20. århundrede*. Kirkehistoriske studier 3: 12. Copenhagen: Forlaget Anis.

—————. 2007b. *Jødesympati og jødehad i Folkekirken: Forholdet mellem kristne og jøder i Danmark fra begyndelsen af det 20. århundrede til 1948*. Kirkehistoriske studier 3: 13. Copenhagen: Forlaget Anis.

—————. 2012. *Jøder og kristne i Danmark: Fra middelalderen til nyere tid*. Kirkehistoriske studier 3: 17. Copenhagen: Forlaget Anis.

LAZAR, Moshe. 1991. 'The Dehumanization of the Jews in Medieval Propaganda Imagery', in Gilman and Katz, pp. 38–80.

LeBEAU, Bryan, and Menachem MOR, eds. 1996. *Pilgrims and Travelers to the Holy Land*. Studies in Jewish Civilization 7. Omaha (NE): Creighton University Press.

LEVY, Richard S., ed. 2005. *Antisemitism: A Historical Encyclopedia of Prejudice and Persecution*. 2 vols. Santa Barbara: ABC-CLIO.

LEWIS, Bernard, and Friedrich NIEWÖHNER, eds. 1992. *Religionsgespräche im Mittelalter*. Wolfenbütteler Mittelalter-Studien 4. Wiesbaden: Otto Harrassowitz.

LIMOR, Ora. 1996. 'The Epistle of Rabbi Samuel of Morocco: A Best-Seller in the World of Polemics', in Limor and Stroumsa, pp. 177–94.

———— (*forthcoming*). 'Mary in Jerusalem: An Imaginary Map', in Kühnel, Noga-Banai and Vorholt.

————, and Guy G. STROUMSA, eds. 1996. *Contra Iudaeos: Ancient and Medieval Polemics between Christians and Jews*. Texts and Studies in Medieval and Early Modern Judaism 10. Tübingen: J. C. B. Mohr (Paul Siebeck).

————, and Israel YUVAL. 2004. 'Skepticism and Conversion: Jews, Christians and Doubters in Sefer ha-Nizzahon', in Coudert and Shoulson, pp. 159–80.

LINDGREN, Mereth. 1993. 'Birgitta och bilderna', in Härdelin and Lindgren, pp. 231–51.

LINVALD, Steffen. 1982. 'Københavnske synagoger', in *Dansk Jødisk Historie* 10, pp. 34–45.

LIPTON, Sara. 1999. *Images of Intolerance: The Representation of Jews and Judaism in the Bible moralisée*. Berkeley: University of California Press.

LORENZEN, Marius, ed. 1882. *Mandevilles Rejse i gammeldansk Oversættelse tillige med En Vejviser for Pilgrimme efter Håndskrifter udgiven*. STUAGNL 5. Copenhagen: S. L. Møller.

LÖTZSCH, Ronald. 1992. *Jiddisches Wörterbuch mit Hinweisen zur Schreibung, Grammatik und Aussprache*. 2nd edn. Duden-Taschenbücher 24. Mannheim: Duden Verlag.

LOWRY, Lois. 1989. *Number the Stars*. New York: Houghton.

LUTHER, Martin. 1883–2009. *D. Martin Luthers Werke: Kritische Gesammtausgabe*. 120 vols. Weimar: Hermann Böhlau & H. Böhlaus Nachfolger.

LYTLE, Guy Fitch. 1981a. 'Universities and Religious Authorities in the Later Middle Ages and Reformation', in Lytle, pp. 69–97.

————, ed. 1981b. *Reform and Authority in the Medieval and Reformation Church*. Washington D. C.: The Catholic University of America Press.

MACCOBY, Hyam, ed. and trans. 1982. *Judaism on Trial: Jewish-Christian Disputations in the Middle Ages*. East Brunswick (NJ): Associated University Presses.

MAIER, Johann. 1981. 'Hapiyuṭ "Ha'omrim lechilay šo'a" wehapolmus ha'anṭinoẓri [*The piyyut 'Ha'omrim lekhilay shoa' and anti-Christian polemics*]', in Petuchowski and Fleischer, pp. 100–10.

MANUEL, Frank E. 1992. *The Broken Staff. Judaism through Christian Eyes*. Cambridge (MA): Harvard University Press.

MARCUS, Jacob Rader, ed. 1999. *The Jew in the Medieval World: A Source Book 315–1791*. Revised edition by Marc Saperstein. Cincinnati: Hebrew Union College Press.

MARGARITHA, Antonius. 1530. *Der gantz Jüdische glaub*. Augsburg: Heinrich Steiner.

MARTIN, Ellen. 1994. *Die deutschen Schriften des Johannes Pfefferkorn: Zum Problem des Judenhasses und der Intoleranz in der Zeit der Vorreformation*. Göppinger Arbeiten zur Germanistik 604. Göppingen: Kümmerle.

———. 2005. 'Pfefferkorn, Johannes (1468/69–1522)', in Levy, pp. 543–44.

MARX, Alexander. 1944. *Studies in Jewish History and Booklore*. New York: The Jewish Theological Seminary of America.

MARX, Carl, and Jeanne DRENNAN. 1987. *The Middle English Prose Complaint of Our Lady and Gospel of Nicodemus*. Heidelberg: Carl Winter.

McCULLOH, John M. 1997. 'Jewish Ritual Murder: William of Norwich, Thomas of Monmouth, and the Early Dissemination of the Myth', in *Speculum* 72: 3, pp. 698–740.

McMICHAEL, Steven J., and Susan MYERS. 2004. *Friars and Jews in the Middle Ages and Renaissance*. The Medieval Franciscans 2. Leiden: Brill.

McNAMER, Sarah. 2009. 'The Origins of the *Meditationes vitae Christi*', in *Speculum* 84, pp. 905–55.

MELLINKOFF, Ruth. 1993. *Outcasts: Signs of Otherness in Northern European Art of the Later Middle Ages*. 2 vols. Berkeley: University of California Press.

MENTGEN, Gerd. 2001. 'Juden: Zwischen Koexistenz und Pogrom', in Hergemöller, pp. 335–87.

MERḤAVIA, Ḥen. 1972. 'Ha"šamta" besifrut-hapolmus hanoẓrit beymei-habeinayim [*The caustic poetic rebuke (*šamta*) in medieval Christian polemic literature*]', in *Tarbiẓ* 41, pp. 95–115.

MICHEL, Francisque, ed. 1834. *Hugues de Lincoln*. Paris: Silvestre / London: Pickering.

MIESES, Josef. 1916. *Die älteste gedruckte deutsche Uebersetzung des jüdischen Gebetbuches a. d. Jahre 1530 und ihr Autor Anthonius Margaritha. Eine literarische Untersuchung*. Vienna: R. Löwit.

MIGNE, Jacques-Paul, *et al.*, eds. *Patrologiae cursus completus, seu Bibliotheca universalis ... omnium SS. patrum, doctorum scriptorumque ecclesiasticorum sive Latinorum, sive Graecorum, qui ab aevo apostolico ad tempora Innocentii III (anno 1216) pro Latinis et ad concilii Florentini tempora (anno 1439) pro*

Graecis floruerunt, Recusio chronologica, Series Latin. 221 vols. Paris: Garnier, 1844–1905.

MOGENSEN, Michael, ed. 2002. *Antisemitisme i Danmark?* Arbejdsrapporter fra DCHF 5. Copenhagen: Dansk Center for Holocaust- og Folkedrabsstudier.

MOLBECH, Christian. 1836. *Præsten i Odense Herr Michaels tre danske Riimværker fra A. 1496: Om Jomfru Mariæ Rosenkrands, Om Skabelsen, Og om det menneskelige Levnet. Efter den kiøbenhavnske Udgave af 1516 paa ny udgivne, med Oplysninger og Ordforklaringer.* Copenhagen: Samfundet for den danske Literaturs Fremme.

MORRIS, Bridget. 1999. *St Birgitta of Sweden.* Studies in Medieval Mysticism 1. Woodbridge: Boydell & Brewer.

——————, and Veronica O'MARA, eds. 2000. *The Vernacular Translations of St Birgitta of Sweden.* Turnhout: Brepols.

MOSHE, Gil. 1992. *A History of Palestine, 634–1099.* Translated from the Hebrew [*'Ereẓ Yiśra'el batequfah haMuslemit harišonah (634–1099)*] by Ethel Broido. Cambridge: Cambridge University Press.

MURDOCH, Brian. 2003. *The Medieval Popular Bible: Expansions of Genesis in the Middle Ages.* Cambridge: D. S. Brewer.

NICHOLLS, William. 1993. *Christian Antisemitism: A History of Hate.* Northvale (NJ): Jason Aronson.

NIELSEN, Karl Martin, ed. 1945–82. *Middelalderens danske Bønnebøger.* 5 vols. Copenhagen: Det Danske Sprog- og Litteraturselskab.

NIELSEN, Lauritz. 1934. *Dansk typografisk atlas 1482–1600.* Copenhagen: Gyldendalske Boghandel.

——————. 1982. 'Ræff, Poul', in Bech, pp. 507–08.

——————. 1996. *Dansk bibliografi 1482–1600.* 5 vols. 2nd edn. Copenhagen: C. A. Reitzel.

NIELSEN, Niels, ed. 1937–52. *Sjælens Trøst („Siæla Trøst") (Cod. Ups. C 529 og Cod. Holm A 109).* 2 vols. Copenhagen: Universitets-Jubilæets danske Samfund.

NIGRINUS, Georgius [Georg Schwartz]. 1570. *Jüden Feind/ von der Edelen Früchten der Thalmudischen Iüden/ so jetziger Zeit in Teutschlande wonen/ ein ernste/ wolgegründe Schrifft/ darin kurtzlich angezeiget wirdt/ Das sie die gröste Lesterer vnd Verechter unders Herrn Jesu Christi/ Darzu abgesagte vnd unuersündliche Feinde der Christen sind.* Oberursel: Nicolaus Henricus.

NORDSTRÖM, Folke. 1956. *Virtues and Vices on the 14th Century Corbels in the Choir of Uppsala Cathedral.* Figura Studies Edited by the Institute of Art History University of Uppsala 7. Stockholm: Almqvist & Wiksell.

OBERMAN, Heiko A. 1981a. *Wurzeln des Antisemitismus: Christenangst und Judenplage im Zeitalter von Humanismus und Reformation*. Berlin: Severin und Siedler.

———. 1981b. 'Zwischen Agitation und Reformation: Die Flugschriften als "Judenspiegel"', in Köhler, pp. 269–89.

———. 1983. 'Three Sixteenth-Century Attitudes to Judaism: Reuchlin, Erasmus and Luther', in Cooperman, pp. 326–64.

———. 1993. 'Johannes Reuchlin. Von Judenknechten zu Judenrechten', in Herzig and Schoeps, pp. 39–64.

OLDEN-JØRGENSEN, Sebastian. 1994. *Femten bønner til den korsfæstede frelser*. Lejre: Bjarne Balleby.

OVERFIELD, James H. 1971. 'A New Look at the Reuchlin Affair', in *Studies in Medieval and Renaissance History* 8, pp. 167–207.

———. 1984. *Humanism and Scholasticism in Late Medieval Germany*. Princeton: Princeton University Press.

PARKES, James. 1938. *The Jew in the Medieval Community: A Study of His Political and Economic Situation*. London: The Soncino Press.

PEARSALL, Derek. A., and Ronald. A. WALDRON. 1969. *Medieval Literature and Civilization: Studies in Memory of G. N. Garmonsway*. London: The Athlone Press.

PEDERSEN, Christiern. 1973. *Vocabularium ad usum dacorum*. Ed. by Inger Bom and Niels Haastrup. Facsimile edition of 1510. Det 16. århundredes danske vokabularier 1. Copenhagen: Universitets-Jubilæets danske Samfund.

PETERSE, Hans. 1995. *Jacobus Hoogstraeten gegen Johannes Reuchlin: Ein Beitrag zur Geschichte des Antijudaismus im 16. Jahrhundert*. Veröffentlichungen des Instituts für europäische Geschichte Mainz. Abteilung für abendländische Religionsgeschichte 165. Mainz: Philipp von Zabern.

PETERSEN, Erik. 1991. 'Om den hellige ægteskabs stat, om frugtsommelige kvinder og om det rige der kaldes Utopia: Peder Palladius' *Tuende merckelige Tractater* og deres forlæg', in *Danske Studier* 86, pp. 29–56.

PETUCHOWSKI, Jakob J., and Ezra FLEISCHER, eds. 1981. *Studies in Aggadah, Targum and Jewish Liturgy in Memory of Joseph Heinemann*. Jerusalem: The Magnes Press.

PICKTHALL, Marmaduke, trans. 1992. *The Koran*. Intro. by William Montgomery Watt. London: Everyman's Library.

POPPER, William. 1899. *The Censorship of Hebrew Books*. New York: The Knickerbocker Press.

PULSIANO, Phillip, *et al*., eds. 1993. *Medieval Scandinavia: An Encyclopedia*. New York: Garland.

PUNDIK, Herbert. 1999. *In Denmark It Could Not Happen: Flight of the Jews to Sweden in 1943 in Pictures and Documents*. Jerusalem: Gefen.

RANKIN, Oliver S., ed. 1956. *Jewish Religious Polemic*. Edinburgh: University Press.

RAVID, Benjamin. 2008. 'All Ghettos Were Jewish Quarters, but Not All Jewish Quarters Were Ghettos', in *Jewish Culture and History* 10: 2–3, pp. 5–24.

RAZ-KRAKOTZKIN, Amnon. 2004. 'Censorship, Editing and the Reshaping of Jewish Identity: The Catholic Church and Hebrew Literature in the Sixteenth Century', in Coudert and Shoulson, pp. 125–55.

———. 2007. *The Censor, The Editor, and The Text: The Catholic Church and the Shaping of the Hebrew Canon*. Translated from the Hebrew [*Haẓensor, ha'orech wehaṭeksṭ: Haknesiyah haqatolit wehasifrut ha'ivrit bame'ah hašeš'ešreh*] by Jackie Feldman. Philadelphia: University of Pennsylvania.

REIF, Stefan C. 1993. *Judaism and Hebrew Prayer. New Perspectives on Jewish Liturgical History*. Cambridge: Cambridge University Press.

REINACH, Salomon. 1929. 'Joseph Scaliger et les Juifs', in *Revue des Études Juives* 88, pp. 171–76.

REITER, Paul. 2005. 'Self-Hatred, Jewish', in Levy, pp. 647–49.

REMAUD, Michel. 2003. *Israel, Servant of God*. Translated from the French [*Israël — Serviteur de Dieu*] by Margaret Ginzburg and Nicole François. London & New York: Continuum T & T Clark.

RESNICK, Irven. 2000. 'Medieval Roots of the Myth of Jewish Male Menses', in *Harvard Theological Review* 93, pp. 241–63.

REUCHLIN, Johannes. 1961. *Doctor Johansen Reuchlins Warhafftige Entschuldigung gegen und wider ains getaufften Iuden genant Pfefferkorn vormals getruckt ussgangen unwarhaftigs schmach Büchlin Augenspiegel (Tübingen, Thomas Andshelm, 1511)*. Afterword by Josef Benzing. Quellen zur Geschichte des Humanismus und der Reformation in Faksimile-Ausgaben 5. Munich: Johan Froben.

———. 1965. *Gutachten über das jüdische Schrifttum*. Ed. and trans. by Antonie Leinz-v. Dessauer. Pforzheimer Reuchlinschriften 2. Stuttgart: Jan Thorbecke.

———. 2000. *Recommendation Whether to Confiscate, Destroy and Burn All Jewish Books: A Classic Treatise against Anti-Semitism*. Translated from the German [*Gutachten über das jüdische Schrifttum*] and edited by Peter Wortsman and Elisheva Carlebach. New York: Paulist Press.

———, and Jakob van HOOGSTRATEN. 1518. *Acta Judiciorum inter F. Iacobum Hochstraten Inquisito rem Coloniensiem & Iohannem Reuchlin. LL. Doc. ex Registro publico, autentico & sigillis*. Hagenau: Thomas Anselm.

RIDDER, Klaus. 1991. *Jean de Mandevilles 'Reisen': Studien zur Überlieferungsgeschichte der deutschen Übersetzung des Otto von Diemeringen*. Münchener Texte und Untersuchungen zur deutschen Literatur des Mittelalters 99. Munich: Artemis.

RIISING, Anne. 1969. *Danmarks middelalderlige Prædiken*. Copenhagen: Gad.

ROBERTS, Alexander, and James DONALDSON, trans. 1866–72. *Ante-Nicene Library: Translations of the Writings of the Fathers Down to A.D. 325*. 24 vols. Edinburgh: T&T Clark.

ROHRBACHER, Stefan. 2005. 'Hep-Hep Riots (1819)', in Levy, I, pp. 297–99.

ROSENHOUSE, Judith, and Rotem KOWNER, eds. 2008. *Globally Speaking: Motives for Adopting English Vocabulary in Other Languages*. Clevedon: Multilingual Matters.

ROTH, Cecil. 1972. *Studies in Books and Booklore. Essays in Jewish Bibliography and Allied Subjects* [*Meḥqere sefer wesofrim*]. Westmead: Gregg International.

ROTH, Norman, ed. 2003. *Medieval Jewish Civilization: An Encyclopedia*. New York: Routledge.

ROWAN, Steven W. 1975. 'Ulrich Zasius and the Baptism of Jewish Children', in *Sixteenth Century Journal* 6: 2, pp. 3–25.

RUBIÉS, Jean-Paul. 2000. 'Travel Writing as Genre: Facts, Fictions and the Invention of Scientific Discourse in Early Modern Europe', in *Journeys* 1, pp. 5–33.

RUBIN, Miri. 1995. 'Imagining the Jew: The Late Medieval Eucharistic Discourse', in Hsia and Lehmann, pp. 177–208.

——————. 2004. *Gentile Tales: The Narrative Assault on Late Medieval Jews*. Philadelphia: University of Pennsylvania Press.

——————. 2009. *Emotion and Devotion: The Meaning of Mary in Religious Medieval Cultures*. Natalie Zemon Davis Annual Lecture Series at Central European University. Budapest: Central European University Press.

——————. 2010. *Mother of God*. London: Penguin.

RUMMEL, Erika. 2002. *The Case against Johann Reuchlin: Religious and Social Controversy in Sixteenth-Century Germany*. Toronto: University of Toronto Press.

SAPERSTEIN, Marc. 1989. *Jewish Preaching 1200–1800: An Anthology*. Yale Judaica Series 26. New Haven: Yale University Press.

——————. 1996. *'Your Voice is Like a Ram's Horn': Themes and Texts in Traditional Jewish Preaching*. Monographs of the Hebrew Union College 18. Cincinnatti: Hebrew Union College Press.

——————. 2005. *Exile in Amsterdam: Saul Levi Morteira's Sermons to a Congregation of 'New Jews'*. Monographs of the Hebrew Union College 32. Cincinnatti: Hebrew Union College Press.

———. 2010. 'Attempts to Control the Pulpit: Medieval Judaism and Beyond', in Jansen and Rubin, pp. 93–103.

SAPIR, Yair, and Ghil'ad ZUCKERMANN. 2008. 'Icelandic: Phonosemantic Matching', in Rosenhouse and Kowner, pp. 19–43, 296–325.

SARTRE, Jean-Paul. 1946. *Réflexions sur la question juive*. Paris : P. Morihien.

SCALIGER, Joseph Justus. 1669. *Scaligeriana sive excerpta ex ore Iosephi Scaligeri*. 2nd edn. Ed. by Fratres Puteanos [Jacques and Pierre Dupuy]. Basle: Adrianus Ulacq.

SCHEEL, Fredrik. 1923. *Lagmann og Skriver, rettsliv i Norge i det 16de og 17de Århundrede*. Kristiania [Oslo]: Gyldendal.

SCHILLER, Gertrud. 1971–72. *Iconography of Christian Art*. 2 vols. London: Lund Humphries.

SCHLICHTING, Günter. 1982. *Ein jüdisches Leben Jesu*. Tübingen: Mohr [Siebeck].

SCHMITZ, Wolfgang. 1990. 'Die Überlieferung deutscher Texte im Kölner Buchdruck des 15. und 16. Jahrhunderts'. Unpublished higher doctoral thesis (Habilitationsschrift zur Erlangung der venia legendi in Bibliothekswissenschaft). University of Cologne.

SCHOEPS, Julius H. 1993. 'Der Reuchlin-Pfefferkorn-Streit in der jüdischen Historiographie des 19. und 20. Jahrhunderts', in Herzig and Schoeps, pp. 203–12.

SCHONFIELD, Hugh Joseph, ed. 1937. *According to the Hebrews: A New Translation of the Jewish Life of Jesus (the Toldoth Jeshu), with an Inquiry into the Nature of Its Sources and Special Relationship to the Lost Gospel According to the Hebrews*. London: Duckworth.

SCHRECKENBERG, Heinz. 1994. *Die christlichen Adversus-Judaeos-Texts und ihr literarisches und historisches Umfeld (13.–20. Jh.)*. Europäische Hochschulschriften 23: 497. Frankfurt am Main: Peter Lang.

SCHUDER, Rosemarie, and Rudolf HIRSCH. 1989. *Der gelbe Fleck: Wurzeln und Wirkungen des Judenhasses in der deutschen Geschichte. Essays*. Berlin: Rütten & Loening.

SCHUDT, Johann Jacob. 1714–18. *Jüdische Merckwürdigkeiten*. 4 vols. Frankfurt: Samuel Tobias Hocker.

SEARBY, Denis, and Bridget MORRIS, eds and trans. 2006. *The Revelations of St. Birgitta of Sweden. Volume I: Liber Caelestis, Books I–III*. New York: Oxford University Press.

———, eds and trans. 2008. *The Revelations of St. Birgitta of Sweden. Volume 2: Liber Caelestis, Books IV–V*. New York: Oxford University Press.

SEIP, Didrik Arup. 1934. *Studier i norsk språkhistorie*. Olso: Aschehoug.

SEYMOUR, Michael C. 1967. *Mandeville's Travels*. Oxford: Clarendon Press.
―――――――. 1993. *Sir John Mandeville*. Authors of the Middle Ages 1. Aldershot: Variorum.
―――――――, and Ronald A. WALDRON. 1963. 'The Danish Version of "Mandeville's Travels"', in *Notes and Queries* 208, pp. 406–08.
SHACHAR, Isaiah. 1974. *The Judensau: A Medieval Anti-Jewish Motif and Its History*. Warburg Institute Surveys 5. London: The Warburg Institute.
―――――――. 1981. *Jewish Tradition in Art: The Feuchtwanger Collection of Judaica*. Translated from the Hebrew [*'Osef Fukhtonger: Masoret we'omanut yehudit*] by Rafi Grafman. Jerusalem: The Israel Museum.
SHAMIR, Avner. 2011. *Christian Conceptions of Jewish Books: The Pfefferkorn Affair*. Copenhagen: Museum Tusculanum Press.
SHAPIRO, Marc B. 2003. 'Of Books and Bans', in *The Edah Journal* 3: 2, pp. 2–16.
SHATZMILLER, Joseph. 1990. *Shylock Reconsidered: Jews, Moneylending, and Medieval Society*. Berkeley: University of California Press.
SHERESHEVSKY, Esra. 1969. 'Hebrew Traditions in Peter Comestor's "Historia Scholastica": I. Genesis', in *The Jewish Quarterly Review*. New Series. 59: 4, pp. 268–89.
SIMON, Marcel. 1986. *Verus Israel: A Study on Relations between Christians and Jews in the Roman Empire (135–425)*. Translated from the French [*Israël: Etude sur les relations entre chrétiens et juifs dans l'empire romain (135–425)*] by Henry McKeating. New York: Oxford University Press.
SIMON, Maurice, ed. and trans. 1948. *Berakoth: Translated into English with Notes, Glossary and Indices*. London: The Soncino Press.
SINGER, Isidore, Cyrus ADLER *et al.*, eds. 1901–06. *Jewish Encyclopedia*. New York: Funk and Wagnalls.
SKAUTRUP, Peter. 1968. *Det danske sprogs historie*. 4 vols. Copenhagen: Gyldendal.
SKEMER, Don C. 2006. *Binding Words: Textual Amulets in the Middle Ages*. Magic in History. University Park (PA): Pennsylvania State University Press.
SKOLNIK, Fred, *et al.*, eds. 2007. *Encyclopaedia Judaica*. 2nd edn. 22 vols. Detroit: Macmillan Reference (in association with Jerusalem: Keter Publishing House).
SKOVGAARD, Simon. 2005. 'Filologiske studier i hr. Michaels Rosenkransdigt'. Unpublished Master's dissertation. Department of Scandinavian Studies and Linguistics. University of Copenhagen.
SMALLEY, Beryl. 1964. *The Study of the Bible in the Middle Ages*. Notre Dame (IN): University of Notre Dame Press.

SMITH, Henrik. 1974. *Libellus vocum Latinarum*. Ed. by Jørgen Larsen. Facsimile edition of 1563. Det 16. århundredes danske vokabularier 4. Copenhagen: Universitets-Jubilæets danske Samfund.

SNÆDAL, Thorgunn. 2002. *Medan världen vakar: Studier i gotländska runinskrifternas språk och kronologi*. Runrön 16. Uppsala (Uppland): Uppsala universitet.

SOULEN, Kendall R. 1996. *The God of Israel and Christian Theology*. Minneapolis: Fortress Press.

SPANIER, Meier. 1934. 'Pfefferkorns Sendschreiben von 1510', in *Monatsschrift für Geschichte und Wissenschaft des Judentums* 78 (Neue Folge 42), pp. 581–87.

——————. 1936. 'Zur Charakteristik Johannes Pfefferkorns', in *Zeitschrift für die Geschichte der Juden in Deutschland* 6: 4, pp. 209–29.

SPITZER, Shlomoh J., ed. 1989. *Sefer Maharil: Minhagim šel rabeinu Ya'akov Mulin zaẓal* ['The Book of Maharil: Customs by Rabbi Yaacov Mulin']. Jerusalem: Mifal Torath Chachmey Ashkenaz.

SPURKLAND, Terje. 2004. 'Literacy and "Runacy" in Medieval Scandinavia', in Adams and Holman, pp. 333–44.

STEINSALTZ, Adin. 2006. *The Essential Talmud*. Translated from the Hebrew [*Talmud lakol*] by Chaya Galai. 30th anniversary edition. New York: Basic Books.

STEMBERGER, Günter. 1996. *Introduction to the Talmud and Midrash*. 2nd edn. Translated from the German [*Einleitung in Talmud und Midrasch*] by Markus Bockmuehl. Edinburgh: T&T Clark.

STEPHENS, George, ed. 1847–74. *Ett forn-svenskt Legendarium: Efter gamla Handskrifter*. 3 vols. SFSS Ser. 1: 7. Stockholm: Norstedt & söner.

STERN, Moritz. 1932. 'Zu den Wormser Dokumenten', in *Zeitschrift für die Geschichte der Juden in Deutschland* 4, p. 64.

——————, ed. 1894–96. *Die israelitische Bevölkerung der deutschen Städte. Ein Beitrag zur deutschen Städtegeschichte mit Benutzung archivalischer Quellen. III: Nürnberg im Mittelalter*. Kiel: H. Fiencke.

STOKES, Francis Griffin. 1909. *Epistolæ Obscurorum Virorum: The Latin Text with an English Rendering, Notes and an Historical Introduction*. London: Chatto & Windus.

STOW, Kenneth R. 1992. *Alienated Minority: The Jews of Medieval Latin Europe*. Cambridge (MA): Harvard University Press.

——————. 2006. *Jewish Dogs: An Image and Its Interpreters*. Stanford Studies in Jewish History and Culture. Stanford: Stanford University Press.

STRÆDE, Therkel. 2009. *Jødehad i danske medier*. Odense: Danmarks Mediemuseum.

STRICKLAND, Debra Higgs. 2003. *Saracens, Demons & Jews: Making Monsters in Medieval Art*. Princeton & Oxford: Princeton University Press.
STRUMPF, David. 1920. *Die Juden in der mittelalterlichen Mysterien-, Mirakel- und Moralitäten-Dichtung Frankreichs*. Ladenburg a. N.: Ludwig Nerlinger.
TALMAGE, Frank E., ed. 1975. *Disputation and Dialogue: Readings in the Jewish-Christian Encounter*. New York: Ktav.
TELUSHKIN, Joseph. 2001. *Jewish Literacy*. 2nd edn. New York: HarperCollins.
TEMAN, Elly. 2008. 'The Red String: The Cultural History of a Jewish Folk Symbol', in Bronner, pp. 29–57.
THOMAS of Monmouth. 1896. *The Life and Miracles of St William of Norwich*. Ed. by Augustus Jessop and Montague Rhodes James. Cambridge: Cambridge University Press.
THORÉN, Ivar. 1942. *Studier över Själens tröst: Bidrag till kännedom om den litterära verksamheten i 1400-talets Vadstena*. Nordiska texter och undersökningar 14. Uppsala (Uppland): Hugo Geber.
TOLDBERG, Helge. 1961. 'Lidt om Hr. Michaels og Per Ræff Lilles kilder', in *Danske Studier* 56, pp. 17–39.
TORM, Axel. 1984. *Er du Kristus? Jødisk syn over for kristen tro*. Copenhagen: G. E. C. Gad.
TRACHTENBERG, Joshua. 1993. *The Devil and the Jews: The Medieval Conception of the Jew and Its Relation to Modern Anti-Semitism*. [The same as the 1943 edition, but with a foreword by Marc Saperstein]. Philadelphia: The Jewish Publication Society.
TRAUTNER-KROMANN, Hanne. 1993. *Shield and Sword: Jewish Polemics against Christianity and the Christians in France and Spain from 1100–1500*. Texts and Studies in Medieval and Early Modern Judaism 8. Tübingen: J. C. B. Mohr (Paul Siebeck).
TURSEN, Jon. 1975. *Vocabularius rerum*. Ed. by Jørgen Larsen. Facsimile edition of 1561. Det 16. århundredes danske vokabularier 3. Copenhagen: Universitets-Jubilæets danske Samfund, 1975.
TZANAKI, Rosemary. 2003. *Mandeville's Medieval Audiences: A Study on the Reception of the Book of Sir John Mandeville (1371–1550)*. Aldershot: Ashgate.
UNDHAGEN, Carl-Gustaf, ed. 1978. *Sancta Birgitta: Revelaciones. Book I*, with *Master Mathias' Prologue*. SFSS Ser. 2, 7: 1. Stockholm: Almqvist & Wiksell.
———, and Birger BERGH, eds. 2001. *Sancta Birgitta: Revelaciones. Book II*. SFSS Ser. 2, 7: 2. Stockholm: Almqvist & Wiksell.
UNTERMAN, Alan. 1991. *Dictionary of Jewish Lore and Legend*. London: Thames and Hudson.

VILHJÁLMSSON, Vilhjálmur Örn. 2005. *Medaljens bagside: Jødiske flygtningeskæbner i Danmark 1933–1945*. Copenhagen: Vandkunsten.

VILLUMSEN, Jakob. 1569. *Elementale Ebraicvm ea praecipve complectens, qvæ ad facultatem & rationem rectè legendi Ebraica faciunt: conscriptum A Iacobo VVilhelmio Nestuædensi Dano*. Wittenberg: Clem. Schleich & Ant. Schöne.

WADDINGTON, Raymond B., and Arthur H. WILLIAMSON, eds. 1994. *The Expulsion of the Jews, 1492 and After*. Garland Studies in the Renaissance 2. New York: Garland Publishers.

WALLMANN, Johannes. 1987. 'The Reception of Luther's Writings on the Jews from the Reformation to the End of the 19th Century', in *Lutheran Quarterly* 1: 1, pp. 72–97.

WATERS BENNET, Josephine. 1954. *The Rediscovery of Sir John Mandeville*. The Modern Language Association of America Monograph Series 19. New York: The Modern Languages Association.

WEBER, Jens Jacob. 1782–85. *Hielmstiernes Bogsamling, tienende til Oplysning af de under den danske Regiering liggende Staters Litteratur*. Copenhagen: Nicolaus Möller.

WEBSTER, John. 1964. *The Dutchess of Malfi*. Ed. by John Russel Brown. London: Methuen.

WEINHOLT, Karin. 2003. 'Martin Schwarz Lausten: Kirke og Synagoge: De fromme og jøderne. Oplysning i kirke og synagoge', [review article] in *Rambam* 12, pp. 133–37.

———. 2008. 'Om mastodontserien Kirke og Synagoge', [review article] in *Rambam* 17, pp. 66–78.

WEINREICH, Uriel. 1968. *Modern English-Yiddish Yiddish-English Dictionary*. New York: YIVO Institute for Jewish Research.

WENNINGER, Markus J. 1981. *Man bedarf keiner Juden mehr: Ursachen und Hintergründe ihrer Vertreibung aus den deutschen Reichsstädten im 15. Jahrhundert*. Beihefte zum Archiv für Kulturgeschichte 14. Vienna: Hermann Böhlaus Nachf.

WERBLOWSKY, R. J. Zwi, and Geoffrey WIGODER, eds. 1997. *The Oxford Dictionary of Jewish Religion*. New York / Oxford: Oxford University Press.

WEST, Jonathan. 1989. *Lexical Innovation in Dasypodius' Dictionary: A Contribution to the Study of the Development of the Early Modern German Lexicon based in Petrus Dasypodius' Dictionarium Latinogermanicum, Straßburg 1536*. Studia Linguistica Germanica 24. Berlin: Walter de Gruyter.

WEX, Michael. 2006. *Born to Kvetch*. New York: Harper Perennial.

WEYLLE, Christen Ostersen. 1652. *Tractat offver alle de Faldsmaal oc Bøder som findis udi alle voris (her udi Glossario allegerede) Lower oc Statuter: som begyndis paa 1. Skillings Bod oc følger siden ordentlig effter hver andre op ad indtil den høyeste Bod som er et Tusinde Dalers Bøder*. Copenhagen: Melchior Martzan.

WIGODER, Geoffrey. 1986. *The Story of the Synagogue*. London: Weidenfeld and Nicolson.

WILPERT, Paul, ed. 1966. *Judentum im Mittelalter: Beiträge zum christlich-jüdischen Gespräch*. Miscellanea Mediaevalia 4. Berlin: De Gruyter.

WIMMER, Ludvig F. A. 1879. 'Småbidrag til nordisk sproghistorie: *IV*. Et gammelt gullandsk sprogmindesmærke i Danmark', in Jørgensen, pp. 193–96.

——————. 1887. *Døbefonten i Åkirkeby Kirke*. Copenhagen: Gyldendalske Boghandel.

WITTENDORFF, Alex. 2003. *Gyldendal og Politikens Danmarkshistorie VII: På Guds og Herskabs nåde 1500–1600*. Copenhagen: Gyldendal.

WOLF, Johann Christoph. 1715–27. *Bibliotheca Hebræa*. 3 vols. Hamburg: Chr. Liebezeit.

WOLF, Kirsten. 1997. 'The Influence of the *Evangelium Nicodemi* on Norse Literature: A Survey', in Izydorczyk, pp. 261–86.

WOLFF, Abraham Alexander. 1878. *Talmudfjender: Et Genmæle mod de seneste Angreb paa Jøderne og Jødedommen*. Copenhagen: C. A. Reitzel.

WOLFTHAL, Diane. 2002. 'Imagining the Self: Representations of Jewish Ritual in Yiddish Books of Customs', in Frojmovic, pp. 189–211.

WOLLIN, Lars. 1981–83. *Svensk latinöversättning*. 2 vols. SFSS Ser. 1, 74. Lund: Bloms Boktryckeri.

WYSCHOGROD, Michael. 1989. *The Body of Faith: God in the People Israel*. San Francisco: Harper and Row.

YERUSHALMI, Yosef Hayim. 1970. 'The Inquisition of the Jews of France in the Time of Bernhard Gui', in *Harvard Theological Review* 63, pp. 317–76.

——————. 1975. *Haggadah and History. A Panorama in Facsimile of Five Centuries of the Printed Haggadah from the Collections of Harvard University and the Jewish Theological Seminary of America*. Philadelphia: The Jewish Publications Society.

YUVAL, Israel Jacob. 1993. 'Haneqem wehaqlalah, hadam wehaʿalilah (meʿalilot qedošim leʿalilot dam) [*Vengeance and damnation, blood and defamation: From Jewish martyrdom to blood libel accusations*]', in *Ẓiyon* [*Zion*] 58, pp. 33–90.

——————. 2006. *Two Nations in Your Womb: Perceptions of Jews and Christians in Late Antiquity and the Middle Ages*. Translated from the Hebrew [*Šenei goyim beviṭnech*] by Barbara Harshav and Jonathan Chipman. Berkeley: University of California Press.

ZAFRAN, Eric. 1979. 'Saturn and the Jews', in *Journal of the Warburg and Courtauld Institute* 42, pp. 16–27.

ZAFREN, Herbert C. 1961. 'Printed Rarities in the Hebrew Union College Library', in *Studies in Bibliography and Booklore* 5, pp. 137–56.

ZEITLIN, Solomon. 1963. 'Mumar and Meshumad', in *The Jewish Quarterly Review*. New Series 54: 1, pp. 84–86.

ZETTERHOLM, Delmar O. 1947. 'Den springande punkten', in *Nysvenska studier* 27, pp. 83–91.

ZUNZ, Leopold. 1855. *Die synagogale Poesie des Mittelalters*. Berlin: Julius Springer.

————. 1932. *Die gottesdienstlichen Vorträge der Juden, historisch entwickelt*. 2nd edn. Berlin: A. Asher.

————. 1954. *Hadrašot beYiśra'el wehištalšelutan hahisṭorit*. Translated from the German [*Die gottesdienstlichen Vorträge der Juden, historisch entwickelt*] by M. A. Jacques [Zhernensky]. Introduction by Chanokh Albeck. Jerusalem: Mosad Bialik.

Index

A

A Beautiful Exposition on the Rosary of the Blessed Virgin Mary (Rev. Michael, 1515) *80, 82–84, 123, 125, 141, 189*
A Compassionate Plaint (Pfefferkorn, 1521) *99, 108–09, 301*
Aakirkeby Church (Bornholm) *8–11*
Aaron (Biblical figure) *232–35, 286*
'Aba 'Arika (rabbi) *285*
Abraham (patriarch) *36, 210–12, 214–15, 269, 277*
Absalom (David's son) *33*
Acre (Holy Land) *79*
Acta judiciorum inter F. Iacobum Hochstraten & Iohannem Reuchlin (1518) *304*
Acts of Pilate *13*
Acts of the Apostles *13, 59*
Adrian, Johann (convert) *100*
Ærø (Danish island) *21*
Aff konung Alexander. See On King Alexander
Against Celsus (Origen) *61*
Agnus Dei (Jesus) *21*
Ain clare Verstentnus (Reuchlin, 1512) *96, 105*
Ain mitleydliche Claeg vber alle claeg. See A Compassionate Plaint
Akiva (rabbi). See 'Aqiva ben Yosef
'Aleinu lešabeaḥ (prayer) *170, 172, 232–33, 285–86*
Alexander the Great (king) *36, 76*
Alfonso Buenhombre (friar) *82*
Allen vnd ieglichen geistlich oder weltlich in was stat (Pfefferkorn, 1510) *299*
Amazons *75–77, 86*
'Amidah (prayer) *38, 268*
Anna (Johannes Pfefferkorn's wife) *93, 107*
Annas (high priest/Jewish leader in New Testament) *12–13, 18, 53, 55, 66–67, 83, 85*
Ansbach-Bayreuth (German principality) *295*
Antichrist *75*
Apostolic Creed *266*
'Aqiva ben Yosef (rabbi) *276*
Aramaic *26, 102*
'Arbaʿah Ṭurim (Rabbi Yaʿakov ben 'Ašer) *273*
Århus (Jutland) *123–24*
Ariosto, Ludovico (poet) *20*
Arnold, Elliot (author) *2*
Ascensius, Josse Badius (printer) *61*
Auerbacher, Philip (convert) *100*
Augenspiegel (Reuchlin, 1511) *104–05, 107, 290, 300–01*
Augsburg (Bavaria) *100, 190, 295, 298–300*
Augustine, St. *14, 34, 62, 163*
'Avinu malkeinu (prayer) *218–21, 276*
'Awen gilayon (derogatory term for the gospels) *113, 174*

B

Baden-Württemberg (German state) *295, 305*
Bamberg (Upper Franconia) *90, 100, 295*
Barth, Hans (printer) *124*
Basle (Switzerland) *284*

Bavaria (German state) *295, 307*
Benjamin of Tudela (rabbi) *79*
Berachot (Talmud) *287*
Berg, Claus (artist) *21*
Berlitz (town) *117*
Beschyrmung. See *Defence of Johannes Pfefferkorn*
Bible; Hebrew (Tanach) *xv, 13, 35–38, 62, 71–73, 101–03, 113–14, 175–77, 223, 247*; New Testament *xv, 14, 18, 21, 25, 34, 44, 51, 57, 68, 79, 86, 104, 114, 116, 118, 261, 272, 296*; Old Testament *xv, 7, 40–41, 44, 68, 82, 85, 89, 101, 112, 114, 118, 120, 165, 176–77, 210–11, 214–15, 222–23, 234–35, 244–45, 260–61, 296*; The Septuagint *36–37, 176–77*
Bibliotheca Hebræa (Wolf, 1715–33) *297*
Bielke, Carl Gustaf (nobleman) *192*
Bielke, Nils (nobleman) *192*
Bielke Library (Skokloster Castle, Uppland) *127, 181–87, 192*
Bingen (Baden-Württemberg) *101*
Birgitta of Sweden, St. *18–19, 26, 29–36, 41–42, 44, 53, 68*
Black Death *117*
Blood curse *24–25, 49, 76*
Blood laws *116*
Bohemia *286, 307*
Bomberg, Daniel (printer) *107*
Book of Hours (Pedersen, 1514) *21, 34, 44–45, 53, 61–69, 77*
Book of Miracle Sermons (Pedersen, 1515) *21, 26, 40–42, 44–49, 53*
Bornholm (Danish island) *10*
Brahe, Nils Claes (nobleman) *183*
Brahe, Nils Frederik (nobleman) *183*
Brahe, Nils Magnus (nobleman) *183*
Brandenburg (German principality) *295, 307*
Brandis, Matthæus (printer) *123, 190*

Brantspiegell. See *Fire Mirror*
Bregninge Church (Ærø) *21*
Brenz, Samuel Friedrich (convert) *293*
Breslau (Wrocław, Silesia) *117*
Brno (Moravia) *307*
Brod, Max (scholar) *94, 99*
Brussels (Brabant) *117*
Bruun, Christian (scholar) *14, 16, 20, 23, 38*
Bugenhagen, Johannes (reformer) *123*
Bulgaria *1–2*
Buxtorf, Johannes (Christian ethnographer) *95, 174–75, 284*

C

Caiaphas (high priest/Jewish leader in New Testament) *12–13, 18–19, 47, 52, 55, 66–67, 79, 83, 85*
Canon secundum vsum ecclesie Roschildensis (Ræff, *c.* 1522) *123, 190*
Carben, Victor von (convert) *100, 102, 112, 118, 290–91*
Carinthia (Kärnten/Koroška, duchy) *100–01*
Carniola (Krain/Kranjska, duchy) *101*
Caspian Mountains *75–76*
Christian II (king of Denmark) *44, 127*
Christian IV (king of Denmark) *125*
Circumcision *96, 98, 115, 157, 160, 185, 206–07, 212–13, 220–21, 267, 276*
Cologne (Rhineland) *3, 90–93, 95, 97, 99–100, 102–03, 105, 107–08, 125, 157, 172, 198, 206–07, 266–67, 295, 297–301*; The University *97, 102–03*
Consolation of the Soul (anon., fifteenth century) *36–41, 86*
Constantine I (emperor) *79*
Copenhagen *6, 14, 41, 70, 78, 122–23, 181, 183, 185, 197, 199, 263, 288, 294, 298*; Israels Plads *1*; The Arnamagnæan Collection (Den arnamagnæanske

Samling) *16, 29, 41, 51–52, 58–60, 78–79, 82*; The Danish Jewish Museum (Dansk jødisk Museum) *1*; The Danish National Museum (Nationalmuseet) *10*; The Danish Resistance Museum (Frihedsmuseet) *1*; The National Archives (Rigsarkivet) *29*; The Royal Library (Det kongelige Bibliotek) *14, 16, 20, 23, 33, 38, 41–42, 47, 52–53, 70, 181–82, 185–87, 190, 201*; The University *122*
Cracow (Kraków, Galicia) *117*
Córdoba (Spain) *116*
Corinthians, Epistle to the *34*
Crucifixion *11–14, 16–26, 32, 34, 36–37, 46, 48–49, 51, 53, 64–66, 73–75, 79, 84–85*
Cyprus (Mediterranean island) *34*

D

Dachau (Bavaria) *91, 95, 304, 306–08*
Daniel, Book of *37–38*
Danzig (Gdańsk, Prussia) *100*
Dat schakspel to dude (Jacobus de Cessolis, c. 1490) *190*
David (king, biblical figure) *26, 33, 43*
David, Israel (court jeweller) *6*
Dawid 'Abudirham (rabbi) *287*
Dawid Qimḥi (David Kimhi, rabbi) *97*
De arte cabbalistica (Reuchlin, 1517) *103*
De creatione rerum. See On the Creation of Things
De latina constructione xxv præcepta ad puerorum institutionem (Murmellius/ Ræff, 1519) *123*
De rudimentis hebraicis (Reuchlin, 1506) *97*
De verbo mirifico (Reuchlin, 1494) *103*
De vita hominis. See On the Life of Man
Defence of Johannes Pfefferkorn *93, 109, 125, 301*

Defence of Johannes Pfefferkorn against the Dark Men 95–96, 98, 109, 301, 304–05
Defensio Joannis Reuchlin contra calumniatores suos Colonienses (Reuchlin, 1513) *97, 108*
Deggendorf (Bavaria) *117*
Den danske Krønike. See The Danish Chronicle
Den Jødiske Historie (Holberg, 1742) *5–6*
Der gantz Jüdische glaub (Margaritha, 1530) *190*
Der Juden Spiegel. See The Mirror of the Jews
Der Juden veindt. See The Enemy of the Jews
Der Stürmer (Nazi antisemitic newspaper) *109*
Derwitz (Brandenburg) *307*
Det Mosaiske Troessamfund (Jewish congregation in Copenhagen) *6*
Deuteronomy, Book of *38, 40, 62, 72, 176, 178, 217, 269–70, 274–75, 283*
Deutsch, Yaacov (scholar) *68, 119–21, 169, 174, 276, 278, 283, 288, 299*
Deutz (Cologne) *101*
Devil *34–35, 42–44, 51, 67–69, 81, 85–87, 95, 111, 115–17, 121, 160, 191, 212–13, 244, 246–49, 277, 290–91, 301*
Diemling, Maria (scholar) *20, 89, 93, 100, 112, 298*
Divine Institutes (Lactantius, fourth century) *61*
Dominicans *82, 88, 93, 95, 97, 99, 101, 105, 127, 171–72, 266–67, 286, 295, 299*
Donauwörth (Bavaria) *306–07*
Douglas, Mary (anthropologist) *21, 128*

E

Ecclesia and *Synagoga 116*
Ecclesiasticus (Wisdom of Sirach) *290*
Edelmann, Rafael (scholar) *2, 16, 96, 182*

Een kort vnderwiisning paa then hellige Messe (Helgesen, 1531) *123*

Een kortt oc Christelig vnderwiisning paa thet hemelige stocke ij messen som kaldis Canon (Helgesen, 1531) *123*

Elizabeth (sister of Jesus' mother Mary) *10–11*

Else Holgersdatter (noblewoman) *47, 53*

'Elul (Jewish month, August–September) *110, 267–68*

Emden (Saxony/East Frisia) *100*

Emil, Paul (convert) *100*

Ems (Rhineland) *117*

En sandfærdig Beretning om Jerusalems Skoemager, Hasverus (anon.) *5*

England *85, 117*

Enoch, Book of *72*

Epistle of Rabbi Samuel of Morocco (Buenhombre, fourteenth century) *82*

Epistolae obscurorum virorum (Hutten and Jäger, 1515–19) *89–90, 93–94, 99, 107, 127, 303*

Erasmus, Desiderius (humanist and theologian) *87, 96*

Erfurt (Thuringia): The University *102*

Exodus, Book of *38, 62, 77, 234, 269–70, 273, 287*

Expositio pulcherrima super rosario beate marie virginis. See *A Beautiful Exposition on the Rosary of the Blessed Virgin Mary* (Rev. Michael, 1515)

Ezra, Book of *269*

F

Fire Mirror (Pfefferkorn, 1512) *105, 300*

Fourth Satire (Ariosto, sixteenth century) *20*

France *117, 256–57, 295*

Franciscans *18–19, 95*

Franconia *89, 117, 307*

Frankfurt am Main (Hesse) *92, 100–02, 284*; Institut für Stadtgeschichte *102*

Fredericia (Jutland) *6*

Frederik I (king of Denmark) *44, 127*

Frederik III (king of Denmark) *1*

Freiburg (Baden-Württemberg) *298*

Froschauer, Hans (printer) *298*

Fyn *80, 124*; Dialects *138, 140*

G

Gabriel (angel) *10–11*

Gammeldansk Ordbog ('The Dictionary of Old Danish') *132–39, 141, 143–50, 153, 167*

Gaza (Holy Land) *79*

Gemmingen, Uriel von (archbishop) *101*

Genesis, Book of *77, 80–82, 198, 210–11, 214–15, 267, 269–70, 274*

Georgius Nigrinus. See Schwartz, Georg (cleric)

Germany *88, 94–97, 115–18, 124–27, 179, 267, 295, 298*

Gethsemane (Holy Land) *18–19, 47*

Glogau (Głogów, Silesia) *117*

Glückstadt (Schleswig-Holstein) *125*

Golden Calf *77–78*

Goldschmidt, Meyer (court jeweller) *6, 117*

Golgotha (Holy Land) *5, 18, 48, 52, 57, 79*

Gospel of Nicodemus *12–13, 123*

Gospels. See Matthew, Mark, Luke or John

Gotfred of Ghemen (printer) *14, 16*

Gotland (Baltic island) *10*; Language *10*; Well-poisoning accusation *85, 117*

Gratius, Ortwin (author) *97, 99, 107, 297*

Greifswald (northeastern Germany) *44*

Grundtvig, Nikolaj Frederik Severin (pastor and author) *163*

Gui, Bernhard (inquisitor) *271, 286*

Guide for Pilgrims (anon., end of fifteenth century) *78–80*

Güstrow (northeastern Germany) *117*
Gutenstein, Heinrich von (baron) *93, 305, 307*
Gutschaif, Herman (printer) *300*

H

Haastrup, Ulla (scholar) *7, 27*
Hadrian (emperor) *79*
Hær begynnes the fœmthen stæder som wor herre tolde syn pyne paa. See *The Fifteen Places*
Ḥagigah (Talmud) *287*
Haifa (Holy Land) *79*
Hand Mirror (Pfefferkorn, 1511) *90, 92, 105, 297, 300*
Handt Spiegel. See *Hand Mirror*
Hans (king of Denmark) *127*
Hebrew; Alphabet *xv*; Language *xv–xvi, 36, 72, 75, 90, 96–98, 101–02, 105, 108, 113, 118, 131–32, 159, 169–79, 232–33*
Hebrew Union College Library (Cincinnati, USA) *93, 303–09*
Hebron (Holy Land) *79*
Heidelberg (Baden-Württemberg); The University *102*
Heine, Henrich (poet) *265*
Helgesen, Poul (humanist) *123–24*
Helsingør (Sjælland) *6, 44, 85*
Herod Antipas (ruler) *18, 53, 55, 83–84*
Herodotus (historian) *119*
Hertug Frederik af Normandi (anon., fourteenth century) *167*
Hess, Ernst Friedrich (Christian ethnographer) *95*
Hist, Conrad (printer) *298*
Historia scholastica (Petrus Comestor) *82, 273*
Hitler, Adolf (Nazi leader) *109*
Holberg, Ludvig (author) *6*

Holocaust (burnt offering) *164, 213, 215, 271*
Holocaust (Shoah) *1, 11*
Holsten-Slesvig. See Schleswig-Holstein
Holy Land *34, 36, 46, 77–80*
Hoogstraten, Jacob van (prior) *95, 102, 105, 304*
Hostis Iudeorum. See *The Enemy of the Jews* (Pfefferkorn, 1509)
How the Blind Jews Keep Easter (Pfefferkorn, 1509) *127, 299*
Huber, Wolfgang (printer) *297*
Hutten, Ulrich von (author) *107*

I

Ich heyß eyn buchlijn der iuden beicht. See *The Confession of the Jews*
Idol worship *45, 61, 63, 77, 156, 161, 175, 230–31, 285–86, 294*
In Praise and Honour of the Most Glorious and Powerful Duke and Lord Maximilian (Pfefferkorn, 1510) *102, 300*
Incipit iustissimus legifer et diuinarum virtutum optimus preceptor Petrus laale Danorum lux et doctorum virorum euidens exemplum atque specimen (Peder Laale, 1506) *115*
Innocent III (pope) *293*
Innocent IV (pope) *112*
Inquisition *88, 95, 116, 267*
Isaac (patriarch) *36, 210–11, 269, 277*
Isaiah, Book of *20, 175, 178, 214–15, 220–21, 234–35, 274, 277, 285, 289, 294*
Islam *23, 46, 71–75, 78–79, 269*
Israel *1, 14, 37, 61–62, 69, 76–77, 79, 116, 126, 163, 217, 269, 275*
Italy *34, 107, 272*
Ivan Løveridder (anon., fourteenth century) *167*

J

Jacobus de Cessolis (author) *190*
Jaffa (Holy Land) *79*
Jäger, Johannes (author) *107*
Japheth (Noah's son) *77*
Jeremiah, Book of *23, 175*
Jerome, St. *36*
Jerusalem (Holy Land) *2, 18–19, 23, 36, 52, 58–59, 63–65, 67, 69, 76–79, 82, 86, 158, 175, 189, 208–09, 230–31, 268, 270*; The Israel Museum *284*
Jesus (of Nazareth) *10–14, 18–23, 25–28, 30–37, 42–49, 51–61, 63–69, 72–76, 79, 82–83, 85–86, 101–05, 108, 111, 113–14, 118, 120, 126, 157–60, 163, 170, 173, 177–78, 189, 216–17, 232, 246–49, 278, 285, 290–93*
Jetsmark Church (Jutland) *17, 27*
Jews; Clothing; Jew hat *27*; Prayer shawl (tallit) *121, 269*; Stereotypes; Animals; Dogs *77, 121, 206–07, 252–53, 294*; Lions *21*; Mice *293*; Snakes *250–51, 293*; Wolves *21, 49, 86, 293*; Blindness *7, 34, 85, 100, 118, 127, 157–58, 161, 261, 272, 299*; Blood libel *85, 109, 117*; Christ killers *11, 12, 14, 18, 24–25, 34–37, 42–43, 53, 60, 64–65, 69, 75–76, 84–85, 116, 118, 129, 293*; Collaborators with Satan *34–35, 42, 44, 51, 60, 67–69, 85–86, 117, 121*; Cruelty *12, 18–19, 21–23, 31–33, 44–49, 51, 64–66, 69, 80, 85–86, 116, 158*; Dispossessed *77, 212–13*; Effeminate *76*; Enemies of Christendom *46, 60, 85–86, 122, 277, 301*; Enemies of God *21, 32, 42, 60, 63–64, 67, 86, 158, 252–53*; Enemies of the Church *253*; Host desecration *23, 35, 85, 109, 117, 291*; *Judensau 84–85*; Male menstruation *76, 86*; Manipulating Jewish leaders. *See* Annas and Caiaphas; Mockery *18–24, 32, 45, 51, 64–65, 74, 79, 86, 104, 111, 161, 230–31, 254–57, 290*; Persecutors of the disciples and Mary *16, 65, 79*; Plague contagion *85, 117*; Poisoning *35, 70, 85, 117–18*; Poking tongues *21*; Red *76, 89*; Ritual infanticide *35, 85, 109, 118, 298*; Secrecy *67–68, 75, 110, 112, 120, 125–26, 157, 168, 179, 267, 285, 294*; Spitting *19–21, 25, 32, 49, 53, 55, 64–65*; Stubborness *7, 13, 34, 45, 85, 116, 146, 168, 238–39, 296*; Supplanted servant of God *45, 61–63, 86, 116*; Talmud Jew *85, 100–01, 110, 112–14*; Uncleanliness *49, 58, 76, 86, 125, 129, 253*; Usury *35, 39–40, 45, 86, 92, 100, 117, 119, 121, 236–37, 246–47, 252–55, 294, 298–99*; Violence *47–48, 51, 60, 86*; Witnesses; of the Crucifixion *85*; of the Incarnation *13, 85*; of the Resurrection *12–13, 85*
Job, Book of *278*
Jochim the Jew (Jochim Jøde) *6*
Johannes Despauterius (humanist) *123*
John (Gospel) *13, 18, 20, 25, 32–33, 42, 44, 46–47, 59, 79*
John (the Evangelist) *22*
John Mandeville (fictitious knight and author) *63, 69–78, 178*
Joseph (Mary's husband) *28*
Joseph of Arimathea (New Testament figure) *13, 47*
Judas (Jesus' disciple) *18, 52, 67, 74–75, 82–83, 93*
Jüden Feind (Schwartz, 1570) *95, 115*
Judenbüchlein (Victor von Carben, 1508) *291*

Judischer Abgestreiffter Schlangenbalg (Brenz, 1614) *293*
Jutland *27, 29, 124*

K

Kabbalah *103*
Kaparot *111, 190, 278*
Keldby Church (Sjælland) *27*
Kings (Bible) *175–77, 269*
Klausner, Abraham (rabbi) *283*
Knittel verse *12*
Knoblauch (Havelland) *117*
Kol Nidrey (prayer) *292–93*
Koran. See Qur'ān (Koran)
Korneuburg (Austria) *117*
Kristi opstandelse. See *The Resurrection of Christ*
Krufter, Servas (printer) *301*
Krystalgade (Copenhagen) *6*
Kuzari (Yehuda Halewi, *c.* 1140) *273*

L

Laa (Austria) *117*
Laale, Peder (author) *115*
Lactantius (author) *61*
Ladino *266*
Lahnstein (Rhineland) *101*
Lamentations, Book of *23*
Landen, Johannes (printer) *198–99, 297–99*
Landskrona (Skåne) *6*
Lauchert, Friedrich (scholar) *99*
Laurentius (Johannes Pfefferkorn's son) *93*
Laurentsen, Peder (reformer) *124, 183–85*
Lausten, Martin Schwarz (scholar) *2, 7, 23*
Lazarus (New Testament figure) *33*
Legenda aurea (Jacobus de Voragine, 1263–73) *18*
Lent *42, 68, 121, 209*
Leo X (pope) *107, 125*

Letter against the Marriage of Priests (Helgesen, 1530) *123*
Levita, Elias (scholar and poet) *97*
Leviticus, Book of *38, 189, 210–11, 240–41, 267–70, 290*
Libellus de Judaica confessione. See *The Confession of the Jews*
Libellus Vocum Latinarum (Henrik Smith, 1563) *167, 288*
Lincoln (England) *117*
Lindgren, Mereth (scholar) *26*
Little Hugh of Lincoln ('child martyr') *117*
Lolland (Danish island) *29, 50*
Longinus (soldier) *17–18, 26–27, 49*
Lorch (Hesse) *101*
Lost Ten Tribes. See Ten Tribes
Lowry, Lois (author) *2*
Lübeck (Schleswig-Holstein) *127, 190*
Luke (Gospel) *13, 32–33, 65, 113, 285, 290*
Lund (Skåne) *6*
Luxdorph, Bolle Willum (nobleman) *14, 16*
Luxdorph Library *14*

M

Ma'asey Taluy. See *Toledot Yešu HaNoẓri*
Ma'asey Yešu. See *Toledot Yešu HaNoẓri*
Maccabees, Book of *72*
Machsike Hadas (Jewish congregation in Copenhagen) *6*
Magen 'Avraham (Rabbi Avraham Gombiner) *273*
Maharil (poseq) *277–78, 288*
Maimonides. See Rambam
Mainz (Rhineland) *101–02, 295, 300*
Malchus (Caiaphas' servant) *83*
Malmö (Skåne) *44, 124*
Malqot 111, 190, 283–84
Manderström, Christofer Rutger Ludvig (nobleman) *183, 185–86*

Mandeville's Travels (anon., medieval) *63, 69–78, 179*
Manuale Curatorum secundum vsum ecclesie Rosckildensis (Ræff, 1513) *123, 190*
Margaritha, Anthonius (convert) *95, 100, 190*
Mariager (Birgittine monastery in Jutland) *29*
Maribo (Birgittine monastery on Lolland) *29, 50*
Marine Issdatter (noblewoman) *33*
Marine Lauridsdatter (noblewoman) *59*
Mark (Gospel) *21, 32, 113*
Marlowe, Christopher (author) *85*
Martha (Mary's sister) *35*
Mary (Martha's sister) *35*
Mary (mother of Jesus) *10–11, 16, 18–20, 22–23, 25, 27–28, 30, 49–51, 57, 60–61, 65, 74, 80, 86, 103, 111, 113, 155, 157–58, 173, 232–33, 246–49, 255–57, 293*
Mary's Lament (anon., c. 1325) *12*
Master Sigreifr (rune-carver) *10–11*
Matador (Danish television series) *2*
Matthew (Gospel) *13, 20–21, 24–26, 28, 32–33, 45, 76, 79, 82, 108, 116, 177, 290*
Maximilian I (emperor) *100, 101*
Mecklenburg (Germany) *295*
Meditationes vitae Christi (Pseudo-Bonaventure, c. 1300) *16, 18, 82*
Menige Danmarkis Rigis Biscoppers och Prelaters christelige oc retsindige geenswar. till the Lwtherianscke artickle (Helgesen, 1533) *123*
Micah, Book of *277*
Michael Nielsen/Clausen (reverend) *80, 82, 123, 125, 141*
Middle Low German *133–34, 136, 138, 140, 143, 145, 150, 167–69*

Mikvah *226–27, 268*
Miracle at Midnight (film) *2*
Mišnah Berurah (commentary on *Oraḥ Ḥaim*) *273*
Missale Nidrosiense (Ræff, 1519) *123*
Mittelberg (Austria) *117*
Modus confitendi (anon., early sixteenth century) *14, 38*
Moravia *90, 307*
Mordechai ben Hillel (rabbi) *97*
Mortensen, Jón (scholar) *14*
Moses (Biblical figure) *58–59, 63, 71, 82, 103, 153, 210–12, 214–19, 234, 240–41, 269–70, 275, 286*
Mount of Olives (Holy Land) *47, 52, 59*
Muḥammad (prophet) *23, 74*

N

Nadler, Jörg (printer) *298*
Nebuchadnezzar (king) *37*
Nehemiah, Book of *19, 277*
Netherlands *117*
Neumarkt (Úterý[?], Plzeň) *306–07*
Neuß, Heinrich von (printer) *299–301*
Nicholas of Lyra (exegete) *82*
Nicodemus, Gospel of *12–13, 123*
Night of Watching (novel) *2*
Nikolsborg (Mikulov, Moravia) *100*
Noah (in Genesis) *77*
Normandy *125*
Norway *34, 123*
Norwich (England) *117*
Nostra Aetate *11*
Number the Stars (novel) *2*
Numbers, Book of *232–33, 270, 286*
Nuremberg (Bavaria) *3, 90, 95, 100, 198, 256–57, 295, 297–98*
Nyborg (Fyn) *123–24*
Nyerup, Rasmus (librarian) *16*

O

Odense (Fyn) *2, 70, 80*; Karen Brahe Library *70*
Öglein, Erhard (printer) *299–300*
On King Alexander (anon. medieval) *76*
On the Creation of Things (Rev. Michael, 1514) *80, 86, 123*
On the Jews and their Lies (Luther, 1543) *62, 119, 294*
On the Life of Man (Rev. Michael, 1514) *80, 123*
Opus Aureum (von Carben, 1504–08) *112*
Oraḥ Ḥaim (portion of *Šulḥan Aruch*) *273, 288*
Origen (theologian) *61*
Oslo (Norway) *122*; The National Archives (*Riksarkivet*) *29*

P

Palestine Post (newspaper) *109*
Paris (France) *44, 61, 117, 293, 301*
Passau (Bavaria) *117, 295*
Passion *12, 14, 18–21, 27, 30, 32, 36, 44, 46, 51, 53, 57, 79, 82–84, 86*
Paul IV (pope) *107*
Paul of Burgos (convert) *103*
Paul of Prague (convert) *100*
Pavia (Lombardy) *100*
Pedersen, Christiern *21, 26, 34, 40–42, 44–49, 53, 61–69, 76–77, 166–68*
Peki'in (Holy Land) *79*
Peter the Venerable (abbot) *112*
Petrus Comestor (theologian) *273*
Pfefferkorn, Johannes (convert): *Confession of the Jews 3, 87–89, 95, 110–22*; Life *88–109*
Pfefferkorn, Johannes (Pfaff Rapp) *88–89*
Pfefferkorn, Meir (Johannes Pfefferkorn's uncle) *90–91*
Pfefferkorn, Minneman (resident of Bamberg) *90*
Pforzheim (Baden-Württemberg) *95*
Pilate. *See* Pontius Pilate
Pirckheimer, Willibald (humanist and author) *87*
Pontius Pilate (prefect) *13, 18–19, 24–25, 33, 36–37, 46, 49, 55–56, 64–65, 76, 83–84, 118, 189, 256–57*
Portugal *116–17*
Posen (Poznań, Prussia) *117*
Prague (Bohemia) *90–91, 100, 117, 305, 307*
Prayer of Azariah *37*
Prayers *20, 25, 27, 30, 32–33, 37–38, 47, 50–69, 92, 97, 102–03, 110–11, 119–20, 122, 158, 160–62, 170, 172, 174–75, 208, 210–17, 220–21, 228–35, 240–42, 248–51, 261, 266, 268–73, 276–77, 283, 285–89, 292–93, 299*
Psalms, Book of *283*
Pseudo-Bonaventure (*Meditationes vitae Christi*) *16, 18, 82*
Pulkau (Austria) *117*

Q

Qidron (river near Jerusalem) *47*
Quattuor Oraciones 32
Quindecim Oraciones. See The Fifteen Oes
Quomodo ceci illi iudei suum pascha servent. See How the Blind Jews Keep Easter
Qur'ān (Koran) *73–75*

R

Ræff, Hans (Poul's brother, bishop of Oslo) *122*
Ræff, Poul (printer) *2–3, 7, 16, 80, 82, 88, 122–24*; *Iudeorum Secreta 2–3, 16, 68, 77, 80, 86, 88, 97, 113, 115, 118, 121,*

349

123–29, 181–96, 265; Language and translation *131–79*; Orthography *132–50*; Style *150–69*; Vocabulary *166–69*; Vocabulary (Hebrew) *169–79*; Life *122–24*

Rambam (Maimonides) *275*

Rashi (Rabbi Šelomo Yiẓḥaqi, Bible commentator) *271, 287*

Rebecca (matriarch) *36*

Réflexions sur la question juive (Sartre, 1945) *5*

Reformation *6, 41, 44, 108, 122, 124, 126–28, 182*

Regensburg (Bavaria) *117*

Regulæ grammaticales (Bugenhagen/Ræff, 1519) *123*

Reuchlin, Johann (humanist and scholar) *88–89, 95–99, 102–09, 113–15, 127, 290, 300–01, 303–08*

Reuchlin-Pfefferkorn Controversy *105, 107–09, 115, 127*

Revelation, Book of *42, 75, 82, 294*

Revelationes Sanctae Birgittae (fourteenth century) *19, 29–36, 41, 44, 53, 68*

Ricius, Paul (convert) *100*

Riising, Anne (scholar) *44*

Romans *11, 19–21, 25–27, 48, 51, 53, 57, 61, 86, 268, 271*

Romans, Epistle to the *45, 100*

Rome *46, 100, 107*

Rosh Hashanah (Jewish New Year) *XV, 3, 110, 121, 190, 267, 269, 288, 298*

Rosh Hashanah (Talmud) *268*

Roskilde (Sjælland) *44, 124*

Rotterdam (Holland) *87, 96*

Röttingen (Bavaria) *117*

Royal Swedish Academy of Sciences (Kungl. Vitterhets Akademien) *183*

Rubin, Miri (scholar) *28, 128*

Rudimenta (Johannes Despauterius/Ræff, 1519) *123*

Runes and runic inscriptions *3, 10, 12*

S

Safed (Ẓefat, Holy Land) *79*

Salsta Castle (Västra Götaland) *192*

Sanhedrin (Talmud) *177*

Sarah (matriarch) *36*

Sartre, Jean-Paul (philosopher) *5, 114*

Satan. *See* Devil

Saturn (planet and god) *163*

Saxony *295*

Scaliger, Joseph (scholar) *87, 131*

Schleswig-Holstein *125*

Schöffer, Johann (printer) *300*

Schwartz, Georg (cleric) *95, 115, 293*

Schwarzenburg (Bohemia) *307*

Scrutinium scripturarum (Paul of Burgos, fifteenth century) *104*

Second Vatican Council (1965) *11*

Sefer HaMordechai (Rabbi Mordechai ben Hillel, thirteenth century) *96*

Sefer Maharil (fifteenth century) *277–78, 288*

Sefer Minhagim (Rabbi Abraham Klausner, fifteenth century) *283*

Sefer Niẓaḥon Yašan (anon., thirteenth/ fourteenth century) *94, 103–04, 114, 174, 178*

Sefer Ṭe'iyot (derogatory term for the gospels) *113*

Segovia (Spain) *117*

Sermons and preaching *20–21, 26, 28, 30, 40–49, 53, 59, 68, 79, 100, 103, 111, 114, 128, 212, 238–43, 261, 270, 294*

Shabbat (Talmud) *277, 289*

Shakespeare, William (author) *85*

Shechem (Holy Land) *79*

Shefar'am (Holy Land) *79*
Shema (prayer) *38*
Shir Hatzafon (Jewish congregation in Copenhagen) *6*
Shofar *111, 267, 275*
Shokling *272–73*
Shylock (*The Merchant of Venice*) *85*
Siæla trøst. See Consolation of the Soul
Šim'on bar Yoḥai (rabbi) *273*
Simon (Jesus' disciple) *75*
Simon of Trent ('child martyr') *117*
Sjælland *6, 27*; Dialects *133–34, 137, 140, 142*
Skåne *10, 42, 44, 124*; Dialects *141*
Skibby Church (Sjælland) *27*
Skokloster Castle (Uppland) *181–83, 186, 192*
Småland (Sweden); Dialects *12*
Smith, Henrik (lexicographer) *167, 288*
Solomon (king, biblical figure) *36, 43, 179, 208–09, 230–31, 238–39*
Song of Songs *287*
Song of the Three Young Men (Daniel) *38*
Spain *34, 95, 116–17, 256–57, 273, 295*
Speculum adhortationis iudaice ad Christum. See *The Mirror of the Jews* (Pfefferkorn, 1507)
Speculum humanae salvationis (anon., early fourteenth century) *18, 82*
Speyer (Rhineland) *298*
St Alban's Church (Odense) *80*
St Pölten (Austria) *117*
Staffelstein, Paul (convert) *100*
Stations of the Cross *18–19, 30*
Statuta synodalia Reuerendi Patris Domini Laghonis Dei gratia Episcopi Roschildensis (Ræff, *c.* 1517) *123*
Steiner, Heinrich (printer) *190*
Stephaton (soldier) *26*

Stephen, St *58–59*
Sternberg (Šternberk, Moravia) *117*
Stockholm (Sweden) *70*; The National Archives (Riksarkivet) *30*; The Royal Library (Kungliga biblioteket) *11–12, 16, 20, 36, 39, 68, 70, 82, 167*
Stockholm Bloodbath (1520) *127*
Stokes, Francis G. (scholar) *99*
Storm Bell (Pfefferkorn, 1514) *107, 301*
Strasbourg (Alsace) *69*
Streicher, Julius (Nazi publisher) *109*
Streydtpuechlyn. See *Defence of Johannes Pfefferkorn against the Dark Men*
Sturm Glock. See *Storm Bell* (Pfefferkorn, 1514)
Styria (Austria) *101*
Sukkah (Talmud) *270*
Sukkot (Festival of Tabernacles) *92, 101*
Sweden *1, 34, 42, 117, 127, 181*
Swedish Academy (Svenska Akademien) *183*
Switzerland *117*
Synagoga iudaica (Buxtorf, 1603) *174, 284*

T

Ta'anit (Talmud) *276*
Talmud *89–91, 101–02, 107, 110, 112–14, 118–19, 126, 222–23, 242, 270, 276, 278, 283, 287–88, 290, 297–98, 300*
Tashlich *111, 190, 277*
Telushkin, Joseph (rabbi) *1*
Temple *37, 86, 165, 231, 268, 270, 272, 283*
Temurah (Talmud) *283*
Ten Tribes *75–76*
The Confession of the Jews (Pfefferkorn) *3, 87–89, 95, 110–22*
The Danish Chronicle (Pedersen, 1515–) *45–46*
The Dictionary of Old Danish. See *Gammeldansk Ordbog*

351

The Duchess of Malfi (Webster, 1614) *20*
The Enemy of the Jews (Pfefferkorn, 1509) *98, 178, 299*
The Fifteen Oes (St Birgitta, fourteenth century) *30*
The Fifteen Places (Gotfred of Ghemen, 1509) *14–31, 33, 36, 53*
The Jew of Malta (Marlowe, 1589/90) *85*
The Merchant of Venice (Shakespeare) *85*
The Mirror of the Jews (Pfefferkorn, 1507) *297*
The Resurrection of Christ (anon., c. 1325) *11–14*
The Women Saints *39*
Thomas of Monmouth (monk and author) *117*
Tiberias (Holy Land) *26, 79*
Tišrei (Jewish month, September–October) *269*
Titus (Roman army leader) *79*
Tobit, Book of *290*
Tofte, Robert (translator and poet) *20*
Toledot Yešu HaNoẓri (anon., medieval) *23, 26, 103–04, 114, 177–78*
Toulouse (France) *271, 286*
Tower of Babel *36*
Tractatus adversus Iudaeorum inveteratam duritiem. See *Treatise against the Longstanding Insensibility of the Jews*
Tranekær (Langeland) *6*
Transitus Mariae *18*
Treatise against the Longstanding Insensibility of the Jews (Peter the Venerable, twelfth century) *112*
Třebíč (Moravia) *307*
Trent (Italy) *117, 120*
Trier (Treves, western Germany) *295*
Trondheim (Norway) *123*
Tübingen (Baden-Württemberg); The University *108*

U

Ulm (Baden-Württemberg) *257, 295*
Uppsala (Uppland); Cathedral *85*; The University Library (Universitetsbiblioteket) *36, 41–42, 68*
Urne, Lave (bishop of Roskilde) *124*

V

Vær velkommen, Herrens år, og velkommen herhid (Grundtvig, 1849) *163*
Valkendorf, Erik (archbishop of Trondheim) *123*
Venice (Veneto) *97, 100, 107*
Via Dolorosa (Jerusalem) *19*
Vickephius, Ioannes (in *Epistolae obscurorum virorum*) *89*
Vienna (Austria); The Austrian National Library (Österreichische Nationalbibliothek) *41*
Vikings *10*
Vita Adae et Evae (anon., early medieval) *82*
Vivar, Manuel Santiago (converso) *116*
Voer hundred (Jutland) *6*
Von den Jüden und iren Lügen. See *On the Jews and Their Lies*
Vor froe Tider. See *Book of Hours*
Vormordsen, Frands (bishop) *124*

W

Wall paintings *17, 27*
Wasserburg (Bavaria) *100*
Webster, John (dramatist) *20*
Weidner, Paul (convert) *100*
Weissenburg (Middle Franconia) *307*
Weissenburg im Nordgau (Bavaria) *307*
Weissenburger, Johannes (printer) *198, 279–82, 298*
Werden, Martin von (printer) *298*
Westin-Berg, Elisabeth (Skokloster Castle) *183*

Wie die blinden Juden yr Ostern halten. See How the Blind Jews Keep Easter (Pfefferkorn, 1509)
William of Norwich ('child martyr') *117*
Willibald Pirckheimer (humanist and author) *87*
Wolf, Johann Christoph (scholar) *297*
Wolfenbütteler Library (Saxony) *300*
Wolff, Philipp (convert) *100*
World War II *1–2*
Worms (Rhineland) *101*
Württemberg (region in Germany) *295, 305*
Würzburg (Bavaria) *23, 295*

Y

Yaʿakov ben 'Ašer (rabbi) *273, 287–88*
Yaʿakov ben Mošeh Halewi Mulin. *See* Maharil
Yad Vashem (Holocaust History Museum, Jerusalem) *2*
Yehudah Halewi (philosopher and poet) *273*
Yiddish *97, 113, 172–75, 266, 272, 287, 289*
Yom Kippur (Day of Atonement) *xv, 3, 38, 92, 110, 112, 120–21, 126, 153, 228–29, 267, 272, 278, 283–84, 288–89, 292, 298*
Younger Futhark (runic alphabet) *10*
Yuval, Israel (scholar) *79, 117, 120, 178, 276, 286, 291*

Z

Zalman (rabbi) *277*
Ẓiẓit 269
Zohar (kabbalistic text) *273*